OUR HUNTING FAT

OUR HUNTING FATHERS

Field sports in England after 1850

edited by R. W. Hoyle

Carnegie Publishing Ltd

Also from Carnegie

A History of Yorkshire: 'County of the Broad Acres' (2005)
David Hey   ISBN: 978-1-85936-122-1   hardback   480 pages, 500 illustrations   £24.00

Rivers and the British Landscape (2005)
Colin Pooley (ed.)   ISBN: 978-1-85936-120-7   hardback   256 pages, 165 illustrations   £18.00

'Iron Harvests of the Field': The making of farm machinery in Britain since 1800 (2007)
Peter Dewey   ISBN: 978-1-85936-160-3   softback   336 pages, 75 illustrations   £18.99

www.carnegiepublishing.com

Our Hunting Fathers: field sports in England after 1850

First published in 2007 by Carnegie Publishing Ltd
Carnegie House, Chatsworth Road, Lancaster LA1 4SL
www.carnegiepublishing.com

Copyright © respective authors, 2007

ISBN 10: 1-85936-157-9
ISBN 13: 1-85936-157-3

British Library Cataloguing-in-Publication data
A catalogue record for this book is available from the British Library

Designed, typeset in Baskerville, and originated by Carnegie Book Production
www.carnegiebookproduction.com
Printed and bound in the UK by Cromwell Press, Trowbridge, Wilts

Contents

Figures

Tables

Preface

FIELD SPORTS have been one of the most divisive and contested areas of recent political debate. For their practitioners and advocates, they represent all that is best of English culture and customs. For many who have secured even modest financial success, taking up hunting and shooting – and the lifestyle associated with them – are aspirations achieved. For the opponents of field sports, the killing of animals – often deliberately bred animals – for sport is repugnant. For a small minority amongst them, their perception of the morally reprehensible nature of hunting and shooting fully justifies acts of sabotage, intimidation and even violence. Campaigning against field sports is also a way of getting back at the rich, the landed and the loaded, the active edge of class warfare. Hence there are those who willingly commit their time and money to the furtherance of sports and those who equally willingly commit their time and money to bringing about their downfall. Over the last half century and perhaps longer, the anti-field sports lobbies have had the best of the argument. Some would see the declining standing of country sports at large as reflecting an ignorance amongst townspeople for country ways akin to their disinterest in – but occasional surprise at – the where and how of modern agricultural practice. But opinion polls have persistently shown small majorities in favour of legislative bans and after a long line of legislative false starts, hunting with hounds and hare coursing were respectively curtailed and banned in England by legislation in 2004. Fox hunting continues in an attenuated form: and yet it has been reported that the numbers wishing to join hunts have increased since 2004. It has far from died, but coursing and stag hunting join the list of sports forbidden by statute. As we show in this book, this is merely a further stage in the incorporation of animals within the law. It is possible that in time, the fears of some sportsmen that shooting game birds, stags and even fishing may also be proscribed will be proved correct. So we have a paradox: for some field sports are one of the great glories of England, past and present, and recreations beyond compare: for others they are the distasteful, if not intolerable, recreations of the monied.

The contributors to this volume have no collective stance on the rights or wrongs of field sports. Each, doubtless, has a view: indeed, some may be practitioners, while others might be active opponents. Contemporary attitudes are very polarised, so much so that when writing about these subjects, one is often asked whether one is for or against sports (indeed to be even interested is sometimes seen as doubtful); but it is up to the individual reader to guess where each author's sympathies lie. What the contributors share is the conviction that historians have not served field sports well. Of course it can be argued that given a choice between studying a historical cul-de-sac, activities which have progressively lost moral esteem and which might even in the future disappear, and the rise of modern mass spectator sports, the historical community's efforts are better directed to that which seems relevant, attractive and morally wholesome. And yet it is precisely because of the continuing debate about field sports that there needs to be a historical perspective on them. This perspective was certainly lacking in the debates which attended the successive private members bills after 1997. Questions which might have been asked – how had the sports survived so long, how had they changed over time, whether they might in time disappear without legislation – were never posed.

As this book amply shows, hunting in its various forms, shooting game birds and wildfowl, fishing and coursing have been preoccupations of wealthy and not so wealthy devotees throughout the last two centuries. A minority were full-time sportsmen: a much larger number bought into the sports when they could or enjoyed them as the guests of wealthier friends. For yet larger numbers, their connection with the sport was as followers or even spectators. Unpalatable though some may find it, our recent ancestors were our hunting mothers and fathers. Even if they took no interest in the sports themselves, field sports remained part of a common language until relatively recently. In the post-war years, newspapers continued to carry reports of hunts and coursing meetings. Prime ministers were seen taking to the hills on the Glorious Twelfth. Hunting scenes remained a central part of the representation of the English countryside. Admittedly much of this disappeared quickly from the mid-1960s, but it is pertinent to be reminded just how recently hunting, shooting and fishing remained culturally central to 'Englishness'. In order to understand our hunting mothers and fathers, we need to have some purchase on the activities to which they devoted their energy and directed their enthusiasm. And we need to appreciate what many have left behind and others maintain in order to understand our own preferences and prejudices.

Field sports are worthy of our attention for other reasons, too. The taste for field sports has helped shape the countryside, its appearance and ecology. Field sports have provided employment as well as conditioning relations between landlord and tenant, hunter and farmer, huntsman and follower. At some moments they have been a drag on agriculture: at others sports have almost been a form of agriculture, with the enjoyment of sport a product of the countryside. Historians need to recognise that there were more than farmers and labourers in the countryside: then as now it was a playground for the rich, who found themselves competing, often reluctantly, with poachers and wildfowlers for game and coming face to face with farmers who saw game as vermin and might have ambivalent attitudes towards the hunt and huntsmen. Moreover, field sports have not been unchanging. All have changed with technology: the saddle, the gun, the rod and perhaps most of all the car and the ease of transport it brought with it. Fox hunting has increasingly incorporated women. And all have been moulded by the temper of the times, by public opinion and legislation and by the ability of practitioners to fund sport of the quality they desired.

This book is hardly a final word on any aspect of field sports, but if it serves to encourage other historians to take sporting recreations in the countryside seriously, whilst informing opponents, practitioners and uncommitted readers what field sports were, who financed them and who carried the cost, how they changed, survived, or in some cases disappeared, who followed and who opposed them, it will have fulfilled our ambition to describe and explain.

Finally, this is the occasion to offer my thanks to my fellow contributors, to Alistair Hodge and Anna Goddard and their staff at Carnegie Publishing, especially George Wright, and to note that much of the work on this book was undertaken whilst I held a Research Readership from the British Academy, to whom I am enormously grateful.

RWH
November 2006

CHAPTER ONE

Introduction:
field sports as history

by R. W. Hoyle

AFTER ILLNESS in 1908 brought to an end his years of riding to hounds, Reginald B. (Reggie) Loder of Maidwell Hall, Northamptonshire began to gather materials for a history of the Pytchley Hunt. As with many antiquarians, the enthusiasm for collecting was not transmuted into writing, and when he died, at the age of 67 in 1931, he left his notes for other hands to bring together in a history of the Pytchley.

The completed volume opened with his memoir. Loder was the son of Sir Robert Loder, JP, DL, Conservative MP for Shoreham from 1880 to 1885. Sir Robert, it was reported on his death, 'was well known in the agricultural world as a scientific farmer'. The younger Loder was educated at Eton and Trinity College Cambridge. He was a noted athlete as a young man. In 1881 whilst still in his late teens, he joined the Buckinghamshire yeomanry, becoming captain before resigning in 1898. On his father's death in 1888, Reggie Loder inherited Maidwell Hall and from that time, 'the welfare of the Pytchley Hunt was one of the burning interests of his life'. He was a magistrate and in 1899 High Sheriff. Much of his energy went into charitable work for Northampton General Hospital, whose committee he joined in 1897 and its Board of Management in 1903. He became its President in 1923. Amongst the gifts he brought the hospital was his financial astuteness. He warned for many years, to the point of boring people, of the inevitability of the Slump. Amongst his other public duties was his Presidency of the Northamptonshire Chamber of Agriculture (although it was recalled that he was a disinterested landlord: it was pointedly said that 'To see an estate grow shabby and out of repair, to see fine grazing land going back in quality, did not offend him').

'Deerstalking and gardening were to him matters of first class importance and not, as in the lives of most people, mere relaxations. Into this category of enthusiasms came his devotion to the Pytchley Hunt.' On the hunt's behalf he took 'endless trouble' over the three fox coverts on the Maidwell estate and took it as a personal blow if they were drawn without a fox being found. He took 'personal pains' to ensure that all the earths were stopped if the hounds were to be nearby. He was a deadly shot when stalking in Scotland, but overcautious lest he should miss. 'No man was keener, worked harder, or shot straighter than he, and yet he was curiously unlucky over a period of many years in killing any very good heads.' In later life, as his wife came to dislike the cold of the English winter, the Loders would winter abroad. 'These times were spent chiefly on big game hunting expeditions, and his enthusiasm, energy and concentration on detail made him highly successful. His skill with a rifle also helped tremendously in collecting a wonderful lot of trophies, which now hang in the Abington Museum in Northampton.' On these expeditions, the Loders visited Egypt, Abyssinia, the Sahara, East and South Africa and further afield, Siam (Thailand), Malaya and New Zealand. He was a proficient gardener at Maidwell. 'He rode his hobby horse almost to death, perhaps, but his keenness earned him full forgiveness.'[1] Oddly, he seemed outshone by his brothers – at athletics, at shooting at Bisley, on the Scottish moors and at gardening. One died with a knighthood; another a peerage.

Loder exhibited the interests of an English gentleman. Public service as a magistrate; charitable work; and field sports at home and abroad. It goes without saying that he was a Anglican. A proportion of his life was devoted to his public and charitable work: but an equal or greater part of his life was dedicated to his sport: fox hunting in the winter, deer stalking in the autumn; and when the attractions of winter heat in the tropics grew on him and his wife, their travels were arranged around their big game shooting. (According to *The Times'* obituary, Lady Margaret 'shared her husband's skill with the gun'.) He was not, according to his memoir, the complete all-rounder: if he shot pheasant or partridge at home (Northamptonshire, along with the other Midland shires, was not a shooting county), or went angling, we are not told.

The omissions in his life are perfectly filled by Charles H. Akroyd (1848–1929).[2] In 1926 Akroyd published an artless account of his sporting life, pleading in the preface that he did so with the greatest reluctance, 'the "ars scribendi" not being one of my strong points'. Of course, Akroyd's book is not an autobiography as such: it is a desiccated and statistical account of his life as a sportsman. Born in 1848, Akroyd went to Eton, spent a term or two at Christ Church ('According to my diary, the first account of any reading done by me was after I had been two months at Oxford, but this does not seem to have lasted very long'). His father took him away and sent him on a continental tour, which reached as far as Turkey. Whatever cultural experiences he had on this trip, he only describes the shooting. His formal education completed, Akroyd seems to have spent the remainder of his life fishing and shooting his way round the British Isles, Iceland,

Norway and Canada. He made two trips to the Rockies for the sport, adding such exotica as grizzly bear and beaver to the tally of species killed by him. He was sufficiently cold-blooded to gain satisfaction from shooting seals: but he drew the limit at otter-hunting after a single blank day. In his early years he also rode to hounds and recounts beating Lord de Grey (later Marquis of Ripon and one of the Victorian 'Big Shots') at pigeon-shooting at Hurlingham in 1874. Later in life he was enthusiastic about his golf. He had a yacht for some years. For most of his life he seems to have been entirely itinerant, with no family ties or fixed residence. When he was elected a fellow of the Royal Geographical Society in 1898, he gave his address as the Windham Club, St James's Square.[3] In 1912 he decided that he ought to settle down and had a house built at Brora in Sutherland where he had leased the shooting for many years. Because he seems to have been of no fixed abode, the possibility of public duty did not arise even if Akroyd had had the aptitude or inclination.[4] *The Times*, noting his death in 1929, described him as 'a veteran sportsman, one of the last of the old school … a fine type of an Englishman with a great love for the Highlands'. It comes as a surprise to find that Akroyd died a widower. His wife is never mentioned in his memoir unless concealed behind the occasional 'we', and his son is only mentioned when they shot together.[5] The twin pivots of Akroyd's life, if his memoir is to be taken at face value, were his constant travel in search of game and the repetitious taking of animals.

Akroyd's diary, rather like the memoir of Loder, gives no clue as to how he financed his lifestyle. One can infer no more than they were of independent means, the beneficiaries of inherited wealth. From Akroyd's occasional references to his father, it would seem that he too was an itinerant sportsman, living in a succession of rented country houses.[6] This is not to say that all those who hunted, shot and fished for salmon were of private means. Quite the contrary: many of them were salaried or the owners of businesses. They bought into the sporting lifestyle for days or weeks as they wished. As one writer said in 1908:

> What does the shooter mean today? Generally he means a man in business in London, who has hired an expensive shooting in the country, a shooting which the country gentleman – in these evil days for agriculture – has been only too grateful to lease at such a rent.[7]

Another had written in 1893:

> Shooting is eagerly sought and handsomely paid for by all sorts and conditions of self-made and hard-worked men. It is no longer the exclusive privilege of aristocratic landowners of ancient families and their friends and connections. The successful lawyer, doctor, stock-broker or 'business-man' of whatever shade of politics, seeks nowadays the relaxation and distraction which the hard-worked brain requires in

shooting. He comes into the market with his store of hard-won guineas, hires the land from the family of long descent and looks upon the whole thing as a luxury he had fairly earnt.[8]

In 1881 57,983 game licences were issued in Great Britain: in 1904–05 72,996 – enough for about 1 per cent of adult males to hold a licence for some or all of the year.[9] The contrast was between the occasional and the professional shooters, for whom shooting was a lifestyle rather than a day's holiday:

The great shots probably shoot on average five days a week throughout the shooting season. To the shooters of this type, shooting means a succession of county-house visits, varied by occasional entertainments at his own house and shooting places. The season is passed in going from one place to another – continually shooting – a vast change from the stationary habits of the top-hatted man and his pointer.[10]

One doubts whether there were ever more than a few dozen men who could afford this lifestyle: the shooting parties which Mark Rothery describes later in this book are far more typical of leisured, gentry shooting. In fox hunting as well, many of the field hunted for occasional days, coming from neighbouring towns or even London, often not subscribing but until the introduction of the cap (a day fee) freeloading on the hunt as guests. The range of people hunting also appears to have widened: so towards the end of the century, a Midlands journalist could observe how thirty years before 'the Warwickshire, Staffordshire and Worcestershire hunts received little support from city men: today, hundreds of Birmingham magnates and businessmen devote a large amount of their leisure to the prince of sports'.[11] The number of people for whom sport was a lifestyle, some of whom moved from sport to sport throughout the year, was very small, and for most, if they had any aspiration to the lifestyle of a Loder or an Akroyd (or a Prince of Wales), the best they could achieve was occasional days in the field as a guest or member of a syndicate. Professional or commercial success allowed them to buy into elements of the gentry lifestyle. This is seen in a backhanded sort of way by a comment of the Lincoln agricultural engineer, Joseph Ruston, who explained his success by explaining how as a young man he '... had no hobbies. I had no shooting, no hunting, no racing, and none of the amusements which many people take to divert themselves from their business.'[12]

For all the popularity of field sports and the culture of hunting, we should not assume that the killing of mammals and birds and sport was universally approved of even in the last quarter of the nineteenth century.[13] Some sports were thought repellent and disappeared in the face of public disapproval and legislation. The battue, in which birds were driven towards the guns, was thought unsporting and even un-English by some commentators: the name was French and the practice a shade Teutonic. Hunting with hounds, shooting and angling were, however, mainstream pursuits, and those who condemned them were as likely to do so out of antipathy to the idle rich as on grounds of perceived cruelty to animals. People could devote much of their lives to field sports and not be thought in anyway strange. That said, field sports could be markedly ideological as may be seen by their rejection by some schools, following Dr Arnold's Rugby, in favour of athletics and their maintenance by others.[14] The practice of field sports was seen by its practitioners to be quintessentially English: they associated its survival with the maintenance of English mores. In the posthumous account of Edward VII as sportsman, the Marquis of Ripon expressed his fear that

> Maybe a generation will spring up to whom all these things will be a closed book; but when that day comes England will lose her most attractive and distinctive feature, and one of her most cherished traditions. For the England of whom the poets have sung for centuries will have ceased to exist.[15]

Fifteen years later, Lord Willoughby de Broke offered the opinion that

> If there be any one who is temperamentally opposed to sport [foxhunting] and would injure it if he could, he is hardly worth considering. His whole outlook would probably be anti-social and un-English in what ever rank of life he is to be found.[16]

Or there is the address made at the address made by Dr Norman Lang, Archdeacon of Northampton, at a memorial service for W. N. (Willie) Wroughton, late master of the Pytchley in 1929 or 1930, as reported by the local paper

> Referring to fox-hunting, he observed that it was a priceless heritage of English life and one felt always that if in the course of economic change there was any threat of the extinction of that life and service it would be a bad thing for England and the Empire. It was no mere pastime, but something that went much deeper into English life and brought out and expressed that which was best in the life, heart and soul of the English people – something that was clean, straight, energetic and unselfish.[17]

The same association of hunting and the hunting landscape of the Shires with Englishness may be seen in the work of the painter A.J. (Sir Alfred) Munnings (1878–1959). Munnings was an artist of a decidedly conservative hue (he caused scandal by denouncing modern art in an after dinner speech whilst President of the Royal Academy in 1949), but fashionable in hunting and horse-racing circles in the 1920s and 1930s.[18] His portrait on the Prince of Wales on Forest Witch (Fig. 2.6 below) was amongst the earliest of many commissioned portraits but his subjects were normally masters of hounds. He also painted fox-hunting scenes which, whilst topographically precise,

FIGURE 1.1
Sir Alfred
Munnings,
'A November
Morning'.
Courtesy
of Felix
Rosenstiel's
Widow & Son
Ltd.

had an elegiac air and carried cloying titles of which 'A November Morning' (Fig. 1.1) is an example. These were also circulated as limited-edition prints and were plainly designed to be attractive to a wider audience. In another, 'A little piece of England' (*c.*1932), we have the huntsman in scarlet riding through a meadow, probably with a stream behind the hedge and a willow to the left of the picture, the hounds streaming behind him. In the middle distance is a church. The scene is plainly Leicestershire. The picture is pleasant enough if sentimental, but ultimately pedestrian. Its significance lies in its title and the claim it makes through the title, a claim that this scene – the Shires, the huntsmen, the hounds – is 'England', as opposed some other England.

Of course, this identification of a sport and a particular landscape within England with Englishness was contested and would hardly be accepted today. Indeed, the way we see it articulated suggests that sportsmen knew that they no longer had the purchase on public opinion that they might once had claimed. But it was well ingrained within the upper- (and middle-class)

English psyche: where ever they went, the English took their hunting and shooting with them, importing packs of hounds into improbable places and taking advantage of new and exotic creatures to devise new sports (for instance pig-sticking in India). Killing animals was integral to contemporary ideas of exploration and travelling. Angling and big game hunting were both forms of tourism.[19] Their penchant for killing – which often started in early adolescence – might seem very alien to us.[20] It is one of a number of factors that separates us from them, along with their commitment to religion and their frequently distasteful attitudes to foreigners in general, Jews and non-European ethnic groups in particular, and the domestic working classes. To understand them, we have to meet them on their own terms.

I

The premise underlying this book is that historians – whether rural historians or sports historians – have generally ignored field sports and have been wrong to do so. Rural historians have concentrated on the productivity of the land and the relationship of landlord and tenants and farmer and labourer. This approach, which achieved its apotheosis in the neglect of sports in the otherwise comprehensive *Agrarian History of England and Wales, 1850–1914* is blinkered, for, as this introduction will show, one of the uses of the land, which often compromised the more obvious agricultural uses, was as the venue for sport. Sports historians have, quite reasonably, concentrated on the emerging mass-audience sports. It must be remarked that the contemporary definition of sport was rather broader than that in use today. For Stonehenge's *Rural Sports*, the term 'usually comprehends all those out-door amusements in which man either pursues wild animals for sport, or competes with an antagonist in racing … or indulges in manly games of skill or in artificial modes of locomotion'. It therefore includes 'field sports' (as they have come to be known) but also the equestrian sports, athletics, boating and yachting. Only when it arrives at ball games (cricket, football, bowls and so on) does it describe the major sports of today, treating football, including rugby, in six pages where grouse shooting secures sixteen.[21] Likewise the comprehensive four-volume *Encyclopaedia of Sport and Games* edited by the Earl of Suffolk and Berkshire (1911) includes angling but also alligator and antelope shooting, baseball, billiards and bowls but also bear shooting, big game, bison and buffalo, and bush pig. Late nineteenth-century sporting magazines such as *Baily's* also covered the traditional field sports as well as the emerging spectator sports.

The disinterest of historians in what were once mainstream but are now minority pursuits is all the more surprising given the enormous literature on field sports, admittedly much of it written by practitioners for other participants. There is an abundance of 'how-to' manuals, of memoirs, of weekly, monthly and annual literature for sportsmen and women. There is a profusion of histories of individual hunts. This all remains to be explored.

II

Any account of field sports reveals the extent to which the ownership of land was about much more than simply the receipt of rent. As Edward Bujak reminds us, the Earl of Derby placed rent fourth in the five advantages that the ownership of land brought landowners. What made land valuable to them was also the social importance it conferred and the 'residential enjoyment, including what is called sport'. As Bujak shows – and the careers of the Akroyds father and son may be seen as a confirmation of this – one did not have to buy to secure 'residential enjoyment'. One could rent, possibly to keep assets in higher yielding forms of investment, possibly so that the shooting tenant could shift between different rural lifestyles without becoming financially committed to any one.

Sport and agriculture though were not immediately compatible. Land needed to be set aside as cover in which fox or pheasant might breed and shelter, from which they might be flushed on days of sport. A writer of 1902 suggested that gorse would be extinct in the East Riding but for the interest of the fox hunter in creating and preserving coverts, a clear sign of the non-agricultural utility of land.[22] Woodland and scrub cover was therefore integral to sporting districts. Foxes were vermin but vulpicide was a crime in the eyes of hunts as it diminished their sport (and after all, what was a hunt but a local monopoly to kill foxes?), so hunts found themselves paying compensation for farmers' losses of poultry. The artificially high density of birds, the preservation of hares and the restrictions on farmers shooting rabbits before 1880 must also have served to depress agricultural prosperity. No one reading Mrs Louisa Cresswell's account of trying to farm on the Sandringham estate can doubt the difficulties which the estate's orientation towards shooting placed in the way of the estate's tenants.[23] John Bright gathered evidence in 1845 of the burden that the preservation of game placed on tenants. Moving a bill to repeal the Game Laws in 1848, he offered evidence of the difficulties they brought farmers.[24] Bright quoted Lord Hatherton at length about the impossibility of being an improving landlord and a game preserver: the hares completely undermined any aspiration to improve his land. Once he started destroying the hares, 'I perceive there is an infinitely greater degree of confidence on the part of the tenants in their expenditure'. In addition, since he had acquired a reputation as a destroyer of hares, he found that a better class of tenants applied to take his farms. Bright himself held that

> On a farm where the game was strictly preserved the loss sustained by
> the tenant was greater than the whole amount he had to pay for income

tax, for assessed taxes, for poor rate, for highway rate, for church rate …
The fact was that there were two interests upon the same land, utterly
incompatible and irreconcilable. The tenants took the farm, he stocked
it, he improved it, and he had to pay his rent; but the landlord not only
exacted his rent, but he reserved the power of maintaining upon the
land another description of stock which he [Bright] though if it was
called by its proper name, might be called vermin.

This remained a grievance amongst farmers through to the statutory
abolition of the landlord's right to vermin by the Ground Game Act of 1880
when, as Ian Roberts shows, the abolition of the landlord's exclusive right to
game had unexpected consequences for hare coursing.[25] Radical hyperbole
apart, farmers must have received some credit for their losses to game through
reduced rents (which makes the point that the cost of game to the landlord
was more than the rent of land withheld from cultivation and the wages
of gamekeepers). The secondary, non-productive use of the countryside
for game preservation must have reduced national totals of productivity. It
might be added that one of the most exemplary and advanced nineteenth-
century estates, Holkham in Norfolk, was also a prominent shooting estate.
It would be interesting to know how a compromise was struck here (and
elsewhere) between the demands of capital-intensive agriculture and sport.

By the 1880s and 1890s, however, this was no longer a matter of great
importance as agriculture went into recession and there was, particularly
in arable south-eastern England, neither the imperative nor the incentive
to maximise production. In the worst years, tillage might be maintained
to support the shooting: the total abandonment of root crops would have
deprived partridge of the cover they needed. In this situation, rather than
the sport act as a drag on agriculture, sport became the justification for
continuing arable cultivation. For established landowners, as Bujak shows,
the income from shooting leases might be their salvation, or if not quite
that, a useful way of developing a second income stream. One suspects
that many of the new landowners of the later nineteenth century knew that
there was no money to be made out of agricultural land *per se* and bought
it less for the investment than for the lifestyle it conferred. Stan Terrett, in
an unpublished dissertation, has illustrated this for a largish estate in north
Hampshire. This was bought by a London solicitor in 1890 primarily for its
sport and the farm was left in the hands of a bailiff. It was only in the late
1930s that the purchaser's son gave up his career and moved to the farm to
manage it personally, and started to make a substantial investment so that
the estate moved from ticking over with a small annual loss to being run on
commercially productive lines.[26] That said, after three or four years in which
government exhorted agricultural production, the National Farm Survey of
1941–43 found that nationally 2.5 per cent of farms (comprising 1.3 per cent
of the cultivated area) were held as hobby farms.[27]

In other respects the use of the countryside for game coloured the management of the landscape. Hunting certainly inhibited the adoption of barbed wire which, whilst cheap and efficient for stock, was potentially destructive for horses. There is a deal of comment on the way in which estates resisted wire, but as they dissolved before and after the First World War, the new farmers had neither the obligation placed on them to eschew wire nor the labour at their disposal to maintain hedges. It was said of part of the Wednesday and Friday country of the Pytchley in 1937 that 'this part of the country has deteriorated sadly since the days of Wroughton and Brooksby. From here to Crick via Lilbourne used to be one of the best lines in the whole hunt; but owing to the land being sold to small farmers, and the hedges being rather worn-out, there is a lot more wire than there used to be.'[28] The pressure that individual farmers were under is revealed by this letter to the Master of the Craven hunt in 1931:

> For many years I have allowed the hunt to draw my covers and some one hundred and fifty acres in all, to ride over my land, and place jumps and gates, and I have sent no claim for damages (although one year the whole of my turkeys were taken by foxes) and have always insisted on my shooting tenants preserving my foxes. Recently I was fined by Lambourne 2 sovereigns regarding gates and required to erect four miles extra fencing to keep stock from trespassing. Therefore, I must ask the hunt to pay £20 per annum or refrain from using lands and remove gates and jumps.[29]

Of course, the competition was not merely between agriculture and sport, but between the incompatible needs of shooting, for whom the fox was vermin, and the need of the hunt, for whom the fox was their *raison d'être*. This certainly produced conflict, but opinion seems to be that when each party approached the other in the spirit of compromise, accommodations were possible.[30]

Highland Scotland had its own issues of land use and game preservation. The cult of the Grouse, coupled with a decline in wool and mutton prices, encouraged a reversal of landscape changes in which heather moor had been converted to poor grassland for sheep. In a parallel of the East Anglian situation

> Proprietors … are now becoming every year more alive to the importance of everything conducing to the breeding of a good crop of grouse, on which the incomes of so many of them largely depend. Twenty years ago [*c*.1875] sheep were the main consideration with them. Grazing rents bulked more largely in their eyes than the amounts paid by their shooting tenants, who were expected to be content with second place. But while grazing returns have been steadily decreasing, or disappearing altogether, through causes patent to all [New Zealand

refrigerated mutton for one], grouse rents have been steadily rising until they now hold by far the more important position on northern rent-rolls.[31]

In the same way the area of deer forest for stalking increased, from 1.9 million acres in 1883, to 2.4 million in 1892 and 3.5 million in 1906. This reflects the progressive abandonment of marginal agriculture for sport.[32]

III

If field sports had an impact on both the landscape and the farming which went on within it, they are never far from the issue of power in the countryside. We have already hinted that sports were only possible in the landscape because of the controlling influence of landowners. Dorchester, in 1935, reflected how

> Gone too are the days of the despotic landlord whose word was law over all his huge property. Such a man could, and usually did, insert clauses in his tenant's leases, whereby the latter agreed to allow the hounds over their land at all times, engaged themselves to walk a hound puppy, and furthermore undertook to keep up their fences without resort to wire – all this without any promise of compensation. Almost feudal were the relations between such a man and his tenants, and which were emphasized if he happened to be MFH as well.[33]

One can suggest that without landlord preferences for game, foxes and hares would have been destroyed and pheasants exterminated: but in the counterfactual that is England after 1925, following the great early twentieth-century dissolution of estates, the hunt continued much as before even if, as we saw, the farmers' ability to accommodate their needs might have worn thin.

The preservation of game birds produced different problems to the preservation of foxes. Birds had to be bred to produce an artificially high population in order to secure a satisfactory shooting experience. Landowners with shooting estates therefore had a big investment in semi-wild birds on their land.[34] These were, inevitably, a temptation to the poacher, whether the local man who took a few birds for his own consumption or local sale, or the armed gangs that occasionally appeared. It must be recalled that the nineteenth-century countryside was lightly policed so it was for landowners to make their own arrangements to deter and catch poachers. In the rural districts of England before the First World War, there were twice as many gamekeepers as policemen. The number of gamekeepers in England and Wales doubled over Victoria's reign and, according to census figures, peaked at about 17,000 in 1911. By 1921 the figure had reduced to 9,000 but bounced back a little to 11,000 in 1931 after which the number of men identified as gamekeepers progressively fell. In Scotland, the peak in 1891 was about 5,500 men: thereafter the same pattern is displayed as in England. The distribution of gamekeepers is a fairly reliable measure of the distribution of shooting estates. In 1911, the most densely keepered county was Suffolk, with ten keepers per 10,000 acres of land against only five per 10,000 acres for Cornwall, the most lightly keepered. On this measure, the most densely keepered counties after Suffolk were Norfolk, Hampshire, Hertford, Surrey, Sussex, Berkshire, Dorset, Kent and Shropshire, all, save the last, eastern or south-eastern counties. The counties where keepers were thin on the ground were the hunting counties of Northamptonshire, Huntingdonshire and Leicestershire together with the East Riding, Devon and Cornwall, Cumberland and Westmorland, Cambridgeshire and Lincolnshire. Most of Wales was thinly keepered with the exception of Flint, Denbigh and Anglesey. Thompson, on whose work these comments are based, also suggests that the Victorian growth in the number of keepers was concentrated in a few sporting counties.

The night conflicts between poachers and gamekeepers have sometimes been romanticised by those who have seen poaching as the legitimate answer to repressive landlordism in the countryside. The poacher is heroic; the gamekeeper has attracted less sympathy from liberal opinion, sometimes being regarded as no more than a hired thug. This robs him of his standing. As Walsingham and Payne-Gallwey said in their chapter on keepers, 'The principal tasks a keeper has to perform consist in rearing game, destroying vermin, and protecting the birds from poachers; and he must also have a knowledge of the habits and haunts of game and the best methods of obtaining it.'[35] This was skilled – if poorly paid – work. *The Encyclopaedia of Sports and Games* observed in 1911 that

> Great changes have taken place in the duties of the gamekeeper during the last twenty years. Formerly the protection of game and the showing of a fair head on shooting days were practically all that was required. Any keeper, however ignorant, if sober and honest, was then, at least to this extent, competent to establish this. Now, however, when the rearing of and management of shooting are reduced to a science, intelligence is indispensable to success.[36]

Head keepers had highly responsible posts, overseeing a dimension of the estate which cost their employers a great deal of money and on which their prestige depended (Fig. 1.2). Moreover, as the breeding and preservation of pheasant became more sophisticated, so the responsibility increased. Head keepers also needed to have strong organisational skills to direct their beat keepers and the personality to act as master of ceremonies at shoots. For this reason, good keepers were always in demand and could move between estates.[37]

FIGURE 1.2
The Head
Keeper
at Warter
Castle with
his beaters
(standing) and
the fruits of
his work (on
the ground).
From J.
Ruffer, *The
Big Shots* (1989
edn), p. 118.

The countryside was where agriculture was practised but overlying it was the pursuit of game. This was its attraction for the rich and the middle-class sportsman. Hunting and shooting were networks of sociability: an extension of school and Oxbridge, the London Club and (increasingly) the professional association. The shooting party could have something of the air of a political soiree. At a less exalted level it was another chance to people acquainted from the magistrate's bench and later the County Council chamber to meet. Mark Rothery gives us our best insight to date of the composition of the parties who were invited to a second rank shooting estate, showing how the shooting party might serve to achieve a degree of social mixing. Nick Mansfield's essay later in this collection examines the overlap between the hunt and the yeomanry. The latter, he suggests, must be seen as an alternative political network in the counties and one which was inherently conservative in its character.

This has interesting implications for any future analysis of rural society in terms of its networks and allegiances. It also, like all the essays in this volume, leaches over into unexplored subjects, in this case the whole question of the relationship between the army and rural society. Contemporaries were well aware of the connections between the regular army and hunting. Captain Hayes, in his *Riding and Hunting*, commented that '... the greater number of varieties of riding a man knows, the better horseman he is. This fact has been recognised by all our great generals from Wellington to Roberts, all of whom have done everything to encourage hunting among their officers.' A Major King, who contributed to the same book, held that 'Most of the officers who join the army have ridden from childhood … they are encouraged to hunt and play polo from the time they join a regiment, which makes them first-class horsemen'.[38] Officers garrisoned near a hunt were invariably welcomed in the field as were officers recuperating in England during the First World War.[39] Provocatively Mansfield also identifies a cavalry cast of mind. Here future research into the background of MFH's may be reveal more of the connections between the Yeomanry, cavalry and hunting: but for the moment we might note the figure of Major C. A. Pelham, of the family of the Brocklesby Hunt, author of *Questions and Answers for the Imperial Yeomanry* (1904) and *Questions and Answers for Cavalry, Yeomanry and Mounted Infantry* (various editions after 1905); MFH of the Isle of Wight Hounds, 1916–20; secretary of the Pytchley and honorary secretary of the Masters of Foxhounds Association.

The hunt (and the hunt ball), the shooting party and the yeomanry and its social occasions were all pivotal moments when county society met. They must be read as cultural as well as social occasions. One of the questions which is raised more or less explicitly in this book is how far they acted to integrate new men of wealth into county society. Certainly, there is much social comment about the integrationist character of hunting in particular, but also unguarded comment about its infiltration by tradesmen and others who lacked the social graces. Hunts were voluntary bodies within rural society, run by enthusiasts and which attracted a broad penumbra of less-committed sportsmen and women, many of whom shifted allegiance from hunt to hunt. One of the advantages of taking a house at Melton Mowbray was that it gave ready access to a number of hunts: it was placed centrally for the 'Shires'.[40] Lady Diana Shedden and Lady Diana Apsley, in their manual for the aspirant female hunter of 1932, offered advice as to how to *choose* a hunt: they also urged that women hunting should secure some experience of the classic shire hunts.[41] Local loyalties had no part in their calculations, and fashionable hunts in particular may well have suffered from a floating population of footloose sportsmen and women who took the place and times of meets from *The Times* and the sporting press. Dorchester, writing in the mid-1930s, regretted the disappearance of the 'hunting yeoman farmer, the man who farmed his three hundred to six hundred acres, and was as much a pillar of the hunt as any of the big landlords' which at least confirms that there had been such a person. He also deplored the practice of hunters motoring to distant hunts and wondered how long the 'farmers and existing members and subscribers' could be expected to 'welcome an influx of strangers'.[42] The penetration of hunts by strangers notwithstanding, it is not wholly silly to view hunts alongside county antiquarian and naturalist societies with whom they shared, if not members, then aristocratic patronage and an enduring resilience borne of their circles of committed members drawn from a local clientele of landowners and enthusiasts.

If hunts were committed to being hospitable to strangers, they were equally vulnerable through their need for masters of fox hounds with deep pockets: as the account of the Oakley shows, these men might have little loyalty to their hunt and accept more prestigious masterships elsewhere. (Hunts might also be quick to dispose of an unpopular or unsuccessful MFH.) This may help explain why there was a perceived decline in the standing of the Master of Foxhounds.[43] There are also hints in my account of the Oakley that new entrants into county society – in this case Bedfordshire – could quickly acquire a portfolio of public and charitable offices, of which a mastership or hunt committee membership might be one. The incorporation of new wealth was necessary as the old families ran down their capital and left the county scene.

This is a pattern which is marked in all field sports. There were, it is true, families whose commitment to a sport or even a pack of hounds could justly be called hereditary. One might note, for instance, the Earls of Sefton and hare coursing. It is not too hard to find instances where families served for three or even four generations as masters: given that packs tended to emerge as private possessions, this is perhaps not surprising.[44] But this book is also peppered with instances of men of relatively new wealth who developed sporting interests on the back of earnings from industry and commerce. Edward Bujak, in his chapter, shows the migration of plutocrats into Suffolk. The Arkwrights left commerce for hunting. Two generations of Arkwrights were Masters of Foxhounds for the Oakley. So far as can be told though, they were not significant landowners. The Oakley also saw new money in the form of Lord Melchett, son of Ludwig Mond, the founder of ICI, and the Lawson Johnston family, whose wealth came from the Argentinian meat trade, Bovril and a number of other household brands. C. H. Akroyd's money came from the family textile firm in Halifax. Lord Burnham, on whose Hall Barn estate near Beaconsfield took place the largest recorded pheasant shoot in England, was a self-made man and proprietor of the *Daily Telegraph*. Ian Roberts mentions the miller J. V. Rank (1881–1952) as a notable patron of coursing: he was also a notable bloodstock owner who won the St Leger in 1938 and bred Great Danes as well as greyhounds. His younger brother, the much better known J. Arthur Rank (cr. Lord Rank, 1957), miller and film-maker, was also noted as a shooter who rented Tichborne Park near Alresford (1929–34) for partridge shooting, and then acquired the Sutton Scotney estate in Hampshire in 1934, revealingly enough from a scion of the Courage brewing family. He increased the estate from 3,000 to 14,000 acres (much of which was sold to meet his death duties) and developed it a shooting estate.[45] Roberts also introduces us to another patron of hare coursing, Major G. A. Renwick (1883–1956), whose money, made in haulage, was used to establish an estate in Northumberland. Amongst more recent figures, Lord King (1919–2005), latterly of British Airways, but another self-made man, was master of the Badsworth, 1949–58 and the Belvoir 1954–72. He bought an estate of 2,000 acres in Leicestershire.[46] Examples could be multiplied and it would appear that the attraction for the newly rich of the shooting estate or a mastership of hounds has by no means diminished. This leads us into other controversies – over the character of the English gentleman, over the claim that English industrialists and entrepreneurs established themselves as squires, over the acquisition of land by industrialists – which it is not our concern to follow here. But there is plenty of evidence in this book for the subscription of men of new wealth to field sports: it is one of the ways in which they flaunted their money and 'rested their brains'.

The old aristocracy were doubtless grateful in a way to their shooting tenants and Bujak's men of new wealth who bought their estates from them. Cartoons lampooning new entrants to the hunting field who could master neither the rituals of the field nor their horse were a staple of *Punch*. But perhaps the finest instance of a man of new wealth who tried to adopt the veneer but completely lacked the substance comes from the pen of Lord Dorchester and, as it defies ready summary, it is given here in full except for a short excision at the end.

My host was an extremely able politician, immensely rich, very kind, passionately devoted to the pleasures of the table, but no sportsman, and quite ignorant of the very rudiments of shooting. Need I say he was entirely in the hands of his keepers, of whom he kept six on a two-thousand-acre estate![47] Incidentally the shoot was held to celebrate the bestowal of a recent peerage – by a grateful political party.

I arrived by train and directly I stepped out on to the platform I noticed that it was covered with pheasant feathers. The porter, when questioned on the subject, informed me that many hundreds of live pheasants had arrived in hampers that morning for — Park, where there was to be a great shoot the following day.

Actually the *battue* was regarded by our host and hostess as merely incidental to a large Saturday-to-Monday party, and that eating and contract bridge were the really important features of the entertainment.

We had an immense dinner, followed by a snack at about Midnight: and so to bed. 'No late hours' said our host; 'we must keep our eyes clear for to-morrow'.

The guns, nine in all, were called early – at 8.30, breakfast having been advanced to 9.30 for those hardy enough to partake of it downstairs. I was young in those days, and quite equal to the most sumptuous repast I had ever encountered at that hour of the morning. By 10.30 the 'sportsmen' and their loaders paraded in front of the mansion for a special photograph, in which was included our host's new motor-car – a Dennis, I remember, for this was 1901 and motor cars were few and far between.

Immediately in front of the house stretched a very flat park, edged in the distance by plantations of rhododendrons, azaleas and many kinds of flowering shrubs such as berberis and the like. There were two great masses of laurels still *in situ*, although many had been grubbed to make way for more aristocratic shrubs.

About three hundred yards from the house, and about two hundred from the shrubberies, was a line of nine-hurdle butts newly thatched with green whin branches.

The head keeper, resplendent in green velvet, allotted us to our positions – I imagine in accordance with his calculations as to our tipping resources. As a mere subaltern, I was an outside gun that beat, and during all the others. There were fifty beaters, in white smocks with blue collars, under the supervision of the remaining five keepers, and every gun had a keeper and dog to pick up behind him. These latter had been invited by the head keeper to help.

The beat started – that is, the beaters entered the far end of the shrubberies and began to advance and tap. Nothing happened for a long time, except that a few startled pheasants appeared at the edge of the rhododendrons, ran along them and dodged back in again.

As the beaters approached, so more and more bewildered pheasants could be seen, and now a few ran out into the rough grass and squatted. By the time the first beater became visible in the distance, there must have been hundreds of pheasants squatting in the open, but never a bird attempted to rise.

I saw the head keeper forsake his *poste-de-commandement* in the inner flank and rush into the centre of the beat, accompanied by his dog. The beaters redoubled their efforts – they had been pretty noisy as it was – and their shouts now made the welkin ring.

Out came a rabbit, which bolting through the squatting birds, was apparently making for the line. I think all nine of us made ready for him, but he most unfortunately popped into a hole under a tree.

The pheasants, however, began to show signs of restiveness and soon, running and fluttering, they streamed towards the butts in hundreds. I think we all wondered what to do, but not so our host. He just banged off at everything, as far as I could see. Personally, I did not shoot at the actual runners, many of whom lacked tail feathers, but I certainly shot at nothing more than twenty feet above the ground.

The whole thing was a disgusting farce. Two such beats we had, and then adjourned to a group of tables, where liveried attendants restored our exhausted frames with every kind of liqueur, besides the appropriate sandwiches, *pâté de fois*, caviare, etc.

It sounds unbelievable, but it is a fact. At three o'clock we stopped shooting – this fashion was copied from Sandringham I was told – and we all proceeded to a marquee pitched within a quarter of a mile of the house, where, as the local papers would say, 'a hearty meal was the enjoyed'.

…

This day gave me such a sickener that it was years before I could regard the pheasant as a really wild bird …[48]

In fact we will encounter what is probably an even more mortifying story about bought-in pheasants, but this story does point up some of the features of the preceding discussion. The *nouveau riche* who wished to flaunt his wealth (not only in the shoot, but the strategically placed car and the 'sumptuous' food), who brought his friends from London and doubtless elsewhere to shoot at his estate, without really understanding the mores of shooting; and his reliance on gamekeepers for the successful management of the shoot. All this happened *in* the countryside even if it was not *of* the countryside. Just as twenty-first century farmers have to come to terms with a countryside in which productivity is no longer at a premium, so rural historians have to acknowledge the uneasy relationship between production and play in the historic countryside.

IV

Whilst a developed knowledge of the history of field sports has the capacity to elaborate and deepen our knowledge of the countryside, the essays in this book also show how it may modify our understanding of other branches of history. A theme of several of the essays is the interconnections between hunting in its various forms and environmental history.[49] Fox hunting certainly necessitated maintaining the population of foxes at a higher level than might naturally have been the case, including making good the year-by-year loss of foxes to the hunt. If it is too much to say that foxes were bred, earths were certainly provided give them space to breed. Masters might also buy in foxes if short – the trade in French foxes through Leadenhall market was notorious – and as late as the 1950s Churchyard alleged that bagged foxes might be transferred between hunts when one had a sufficiency and the other was suffering from 'blank' days.[50] This, of course, went on without the connivance of the masters (or at least with a blind eye turned). The fox population was certainly managed.

The situation with game birds was more complicated. There are indications that pheasants were deliberately introduced into some parts of England. In the 1848 debate on the Game Act, Bright quoted Sir J. Graham's view that 'he had observed that since the introduction of pheasants into that part of the country where formerly they were unknown, a great increase had taken place in poaching'.[51] The population of pheasants and partridges was further manipulated by the introduction of foreign species. Rothschild, writing in 1911, thought that the common pheasant (*Phasianus colchicus*) had originated in south Russia, Transcaucasia and Asia Minor but was now distributed all over western Europe. He thought that in many parts, including Great Britain, it was impossible 'to find a pure-bred true "Common Pheasant" as, through the introduction of other pheasants, the true race has been swamped, and we only find hybrids showing traces of tree or four different species, which might almost be called mongrel'. He identified thirty species or sub-species, including the ring-necked pheasant which he thought had been introduced from the New World in the early sixteenth century: it had widely cross-bred with the common pheasant in England to produce a hybrid which was better for both the table and for sport. The Japanese pheasant had been, introduced into Britain by the Earl of Derby in 1840 ('they fly ... splendidly and give great sport'). In 1898 Rothschild had recommended the introduction of the Mongolian Pheasant and the Prince of Wales' Pheasant: in 1911 he commented that since he had first written, both had been introduced on a large scale. The pure-bred Mongolian pheasants tended to get too fat and heavy to fly: the Prince of Wales' pheasant, in both its pure and cross-bred forms, had proved to be an excellent sporting bird.[52] The nineteenth-century domestic partridge population contained both the native Grey Partridge (*Perdix perdix*) and the Redlegged Partridge (*Alectoris rufa*) which, tradition holds, was introduced into Suffolk by the Marquis of Hertford and Lord Rendlesham in 1770. Later in the century Hungarian birds were introduced through an import trade in eggs. Charles C. Tudway, writing on the Partridge in the *Encyclopaedia of Sport and Games* (1911) recommended the purchase of Hungarian Partridge eggs (at 9*s.* a brace!).[53] Again, Rothschild recommended the introduction of other partridge species to supplement the native and naturalised species.

The adulteration of the native species with imported birds went hand in hand with a considerable increase of the density of birds on shooting estates. It was Payne-Gallwey's view that 'till about 1820, pheasants were somewhat scarce on large shooting estates' and without a combination of artificial rearing and feeding, and the deliberate development of ground cover for them, they would have remained so. Figures from an unnamed Norfolk estate published by Lord Walsingham (perhaps from Walsingham's own estate) gave the numbers killed in 1821 and 1825 as fewer than 100; in 1830 and 1835 at fewer than 300; in 1845–54 at between one and two thousand;

in 1860–69 between two and three thousand; but over five thousand in 1875 and 1881.[54]

Whilst larger estates reared their own birds, an estate with a shortfall could always buy in mature birds (although not always with reliable results) from the nascent game farming industry. Efficient keepering and the development of new technologies of rearing produced unsustainably high populations of birds for the season, relatively few of which would survive to the next season when their numbers would again be reinforced by fresh drafts of reared birds. The carry forwards of birds was helped by the end of season practice of not shooting hen birds; it was also the practice on some estates to hold back a proportion of the hen birds as the basis of a breeding stock. The levels of birds were also maintained by the vigorous culling of vermin: predatory birds, crowns, magpies, hawks and small mammals, stoats, rats, even domestic cats, by keepers. These labour-intensive methods were the background to the enormous bags which characterised the half-century before the First World War. The peak, if so it was, came at a shoot at Hall Barn near Beaconsfield the property of Lord Burnham, proprietor of the *Daily Telegraph*, in 1913, which was attended by both George V and the Prince of Wales. On this occasion, a few short of 4,000 pheasants were killed by seven guns in a single day. Even George V thought that this was excessive, saying to his son that 'Perhaps we went a little too far today, David'.[55] On one contemporary estimate, the numbers of game shot increased 15-fold between 1860 and 1912.[56]

FIGURE 1.3 Long-term trend in the national bag of pheasants from 72 estates (line), compared to the numbers reared on 11 lowland estates where complete rearing records were kept (bar chart). Courtesy of Steve Tapper and the Games Conservancy Trust.

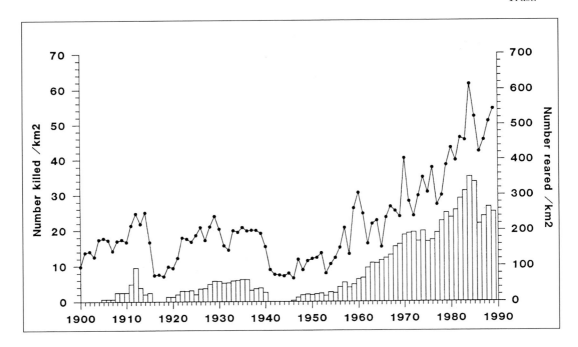

1912 marks a peak in another respect. Tapper has published a graph of the 'national bag' of pheasants shot on 72 estates between 1900 and 1990 (Fig. 1.3). This, expressed in the number of pheasants per square kilometre, was at about 18 in the first decade of the century, but reached 25 in 1912 and 1914. There was then a substantial fall over the war years and pre-war levels were only achieved again in about 1926. The Slump produced a further fall in numbers, but they then returned to around 20 per square kilometre in the later 1930s. Numbers fell precipitately in war time and remained very low until the late 1950s, but from this point the new technologies of rearing (which were influenced by commercial poultry farming and innovations in foodstuffs) produced a density of birds far in excess of anything achieved before the First World War. By comparison, the numbers of the native Grey Partridge collapsed after the Second World War. They were the victims of habitat change: herbicides removed the flora they fed off; they suffered from the removal of hedgerows and the decline in the number of keepers made them vulnerable to uncontrolled predators. Partridge shooting has become much more reliant on reared Redlegged Partridges.[57]

Grouse have proved to be much less tractable than either pheasant or partridge to artificial rearing. Moreover, attempts to introduce them into lowland England have generally failed. It was discovered around 1860 that numbers could be improved by the rotational burning of moorland heather to increase the amount of young heather available (the tips of young heather being their staple food). The careful management of moors could therefore substantially increase the density of the birds they carried. However, grouse numbers were also prone to fluctuate widely over time, and this prompted investigations from the late nineteenth century onwards into 'grouse disease', including an enquiry established in 1905 under the auspices of (but not at the expense of) the Board of Agriculture. This may be seen as an early instance of the use of biology to help understand the population dynamics of a game animal, half a century before the Nature Conservancy became involved in the study of the otter.[58] The research effort on grouse was later emulated for the partridge and with similar conclusions: that much of the mortality could be attributed to intestinal threadworms.[59]

Geese and wildfowl though are considered to be wild creatures, being migratory and therefore beyond the ability of keepers to breed, but there is some evidence for the introduction of geese into England for sport. It was the case though that the sportsman could attract ducks to his land by the provision of ponds and doubtless some feeding. Some duck were bred for sport: the pioneer in this unexplored area may have been Sir Richard Graham at Netherby (Cumberland) who was rearing up to 10,000 duck (mostly mallard) a season at the beginning of the twentieth century.[60] Nonetheless, geese and other wild remained much more wild than partridges and pheasants and this may explain some of the attraction they held for shooters. In these various ways, we can see how the bird populations carried by shooting estates in the late nineteenth-century were decidedly artificial.

Human agency therefore went a great way towards enhancing the population of selected animals whilst diminishing the numbers of others. Less could be done for those animals whose biology remained mysterious to the Victorians. Harvey Osborne, in his essay, shows how early Victorian sportsmen were largely ignorant of the breeding cycle and biology of the salmon. Roberts refers to the popular misconceptions about the breeding of hares whilst Watkins shows how it was only in the 1950s that a deliberate effort was made to elucidate the biology of the otter. It was not out of ignorance but in a spirit of scientific debate that Akroyd fell to arguing at a dinner in Edinburgh in 1899 with Sir Thomas Clouston (the psychiatrist) and Sir John Murray (the oceanographer) over whether 'salmon fed in fresh water'. 'As is usual on the matter, there was plenty of argument, but no conclusion so far as I was concerned.' (The question, in part, was whether salmon rose to the fisherman's fly because they were feeding, or because they were attracted by its motion on the water.)[61] Osborne shows how a perception of the declining numbers of salmon forced measures to protect them and, in particular, the stamping out of the traditional, 'unsporting' ways of taking the fish. Scarcity made them into a luxury item: but it may be argued that scarcity was brought about as much by man-made environmental changes and pollution as overfishing. It was these changes which made figures like Akroyd and Dr Rothery's Sibthorps look to Iceland, Norway and Canada for pristine rivers. Pollution was also the reason for the reduction in otter numbers which Watkins and his colleagues discuss. Confidence that the otter really was in decline came, oddly enough, from a tabulation of the records of otter hunts. The foxes and smaller game birds therefore lived within artificial ecologies. Man-made environmental change operated to devastate the salmon and the otter, and a realisation of their diminishing numbers forced a keener appreciation of the consequences of human actions (and even remedial steps). In these and other ways, the study of field sports has a contribution to make to the study of environmental history.

The essays presented here also point to the overlap between natural history and the shooting fraternity. Whilst one would not wish to speak for all of them, it is clear enough that some had significant intellectual interests outside the covert. Whilst Lord Walsingham's reputation as a shooter rests on the staggering tally of birds he shot, he was also, with Ralph Payne-Gallwey, the author of some of the classic texts on shooting. Walsingham's recent biography in the *Oxford Dictionary of National Biography* is almost of another man, concentrating on Walsingham the entomologist whose collections and library were purchased by the British Museum in 1910. The degree to which the shooters overlapped with membership of the early ornithological societies remains to be determined, but at least one of

Martin's wildfowlers made a significant contribution to scientific literature. This was J. G. Millais (1865–1931), son of the painter Sir John Millais. Millais started to collect birds in his teens: 'at the age of 13 he started to wander along the east and north-east coasts of Scotland in search of birds for his collection'. He was the author of a number of works on the biology of birds as well as works of travel writing (*Far Away up the Nile*). He travelled (and of course shot) in Africa as well as Iceland, the west of America, Canada, Newfoundland, Norway, Alaska and the Arctic regions, and, for variety, the Carpathians. He was also known for his landscape gardening and book illustrations. *The Times'* obituary, written at a time when his activities could be viewed more sceptically, tells us that 'Millais did not kill for the sake of killing; his collection of some 3,000 birds that regularly visit these islands set up in his museum … is of obvious scientific value'.[62] This takes us to a point made by Martin in his contribution. In an age before field glasses, the shooting of a bird was the only way to verify its identity (or prove the observation): equally the collection of type specimens in age before photography had a didactic purpose.[63] It was doubtless for this reason that Loder's gifts of stuffed animals to the Northampton museum were of greater significance to the people who saw them than as mere momentos of his big-game holidays. This was made redundant by the development of photography. Where one Prince of Wales (later Edward VII) travelled with a taxidermist in his entourage, his grandson, David Prince of Wales, later Edward VIII, was a convert to cine photography as a substitute for shooting.[64]

On the other hand, it cannot be disputed that much field sport was the shooting of alpha-male animals by alpha-male humans. The competitive objective in deer stalking was to take the most magisterial stag judged by the number of points on its antlers. To shoot a smaller, younger animal, even by mistake, could lead to ribbing and mockery.[65] The preservation of stag's heads, tiger skins, alligators and crocodiles cannot be disassociated from male boastfulness and achievement: the equivalent in the shooting field was the biggest bag and in fox hunting the longest run. Whilst sportsmen doubtless had their personal bests and maintained sporting diaries, the very best from the sporting press and elsewhere were gathered together by Sir Hugh S. Gladstone of Capenoch, Dumfriesshire (d. 1949) in his *Record Bags and Shooting Records*, the *Guinness Book of Records* of its day. This first appeared in 1922 and in a revised and expanded edition in 1930. George VI was once heard to express hopes of a further edition to include the sporting achievements of his generation.[66] And yet Gladstone brings us full circle. He was also the author of *Birds of Dumfriesshire* (1910, with later supplements) and the *Catalogue of the Vertebrate Fauna of Dumfriesshire* (1912). For all that he plainly relished the achievements of the big shots and set out to chronicle them at a time when shooting had passed its apogee, he was a well-respected ornithologist.[67]

The pivotal figure in the overlap between shooting and conservation may yet turn out to be Sir Peter Scott (1909–89). Martin quickly considers his contribution to knowledge and understanding of wildfowl but a little more can be said. Scott started punt-shooting and wildfowling whilst an undergraduate in Cambridge. Doubts set in early. After shooting 80 pinkfoot geese with a companion on a single night in 1932, his circle agreed to limit their bags to a dozen each. He continued shooting until 1951–52 after which he only shot reluctantly and to secure taxonomic specimens.[68] He was in the vanguard of the movement to create reserves for migrant wildfowl, but many of his associates in the movement – and here one might note the Duke of Edinburgh – were themselves shooters. Elsewhere, Matless, Merchant and Watkins have noticed the untidy relationship of wildfowling and the early conservation movement in Norfolk, with the suppression of ungentlemanly shooting and the reluctant toleration of regulated shooting, a halfway house which can be paralleled at Scott's reserve at Slimbridge (Gloucestershire).[69]

V

The essays in this book also draw attention to the underexplored history of the politics of field sports and the way in which declining public support for the more overtly cruel sports was transformed into legislation to prohibit them. This is by no means only a twentieth-century phenomenon: the movement for the welfare of animals has nineteenth-century origins. There was an appreciation in the third quarter of the century that public opinion could be hostile to sports. The hunting, shooting and fishing Tory MP William Bromley Davenport (1821–84), who appears later in this book as the officer commanding the Staffordshire Yeomanry who died of a heart attack when they ran amuck in Lichfield, expressed his fears as early as 1853:

> Brother sportsman, staunch protectionists! rejecting all that's new,
> Oh! the future that's impending is a queerish one for you;
> For I look'd into its pages and I read the book of fate
> and saw Fox hunting abolished by an order of the State.

The year he died the National Sports Defence Association was founded. This enlarged its aims to include the encouragement, as well as the defence, of hunting, racing, shooting, fishing and coursing the following year and renamed itself the Field Sports Protection and Encouragement Association. After a further change of name in 1908, it was folded into the British Field Sports Society on the latter's establishment in 1930. The BFSS was a response to the League against Cruel Sports' campaign against Kentish and Somerset stag hunting.[70] A recent paper by Anthony Taylor shows the degree of hostility to royal and aristocratic hunting and shooting in the late nineteenth-century radical press.[71] Elite activities they may have been, but they were never above criticism, even when practised by royalty.

Opposition to field sports has always been based on two main lines of argument, the first that sports were cruel to animals, a position which led logically to the espousal of vegetarianism, and the second that sports – including the preservation of game – were a display of power by landed elites which needed to be curbed. Over time, the second position has probably diminished in its force as the heat has gone out of debates over the ownership of land or the role of the aristocracy in society. The truth was, however, that the adherents of field sports, especially hunting, were drawn from a wider social spread than the anti-sports lobby liked to admit. There were miners' hunts. Hare coursing, despite its patrician overtones, was a working-class sport; and there were those sports which were distinctively plebeian, such as rabbit ferreting. Poaching could be viewed as a working-class recreation. Rough shooting, as opposed to battue shooting, was also widely practised. The anti-field sports lobby has always tended to be weary of criticising fishing for which there is indisputably a very wide working-class constituency. The attempt to adopt the abolition of hare coursing and fox hunting as a Labour Party manifesto commitment drew complaints from within the party in 1978 (when it was proposed) and 1983 (when it was finally achieved). Even in the years before the suppression of hunting with hounds, there were a few Labour MPs and lords who were prepared to speak in its support just as there were a few Conservatives who were anti-hunting. The majority of Labour MPs in the commons of 1945 were instinctively hostile to hunting: but the Labour Party at large was not, and field sports proved to be an issue over which the party was capable of tying itself in knots.

Field sports was one of the issues adopted by the Humanitarian League when it was founded in 1891.[72] (The League's remit was wide: besides various animal rights issues including vivisection and the trade in feathers, the League was also concerned with prison conditions, the amendment of the criminal law and women's work – at home and abroad.) The leading figures in the League, Henry S. Salt, a former master at Eton, the Socialist thinker Edward Carpenter and the playwright George Bernard Shaw all leaned to vegetarianism. The League tended to fight shy of any direct attack on fox hunting which, it acknowledged, had something of the status of a national sport, concentrating its efforts on the more obviously barbaric sports or ones which hunted tame animals. Its campaigning contributed to the demise of the royal buckhounds in 1901: in 1910 it brought a prosecution against some Cambridge students for hunting carted deer. It was hostile to the Game laws which it saw as a form of class-based property right: but the author of its pamphlet on the Game Laws, the Irishman Jim Connell, also defended the coursing of hares by dogs as a legitimate sport not least because the animals could outwit their hunter and escape. There was some overlap in membership between the Humanitarian League and the early Independent Labour Party. Connell was branch secretary of the ILP in Clapham, London. Keir Hardie chaired the League's conference in 1895 when he attacked deer stalking. Other prominent party members supported the League but the early Labour Party kept the 'old cranks, humanitarians and vegetarians' at arm's length.

The League collapsed in 1919 by which time shooting in particular was coming under criticism on novel grounds, for its extravagance and the drag it placed on agricultural productivity.[73] It was replaced by the League against Cruel Sports, founded in 1924 and avowedly a single-issue pressure group without any position on vegetarianism or vivisection. The League quickly captured Labour Party policy on hunting, the motion to make its abolition party policy being moved at the 1928 party conference by Tom Williams. Yet, despite occasional private members bills in the 1930s, there was no real move against field sports until the election of the Labour government in 1945.

And yet that government, with a commanding majority, went out of power in 1951 with nothing more achieved than the establishment of a committee to look at the issues involved in hunting. The reasons why no legislation was achieved have been explored in a recent paper by Michael Tichelar.[74] The reintroduction of the private members bill ballot in early 1949 after its suspension in wartime produced two successful bills, one sponsored by Seymour Cocks for the prohibition of the hunting of deer, otters and badgers and hare coursing, the other, sponsored by Frank Fairhurst, for the abolition of fox hunting. In part the introduction of two bills reflected the views of the RSPCA and wider opinion: the RSPCA supported the first bill but not the fox hunting bill.[75] The success of the sponsors of the bills in the private members' ballot produced its own counter-lobbying by not only the field sports societies but also the farmers. Farmers, it must be remembered, had something of a heroic status in 1949 having successfully supplied the domestic market during the war. They had been rewarded with the 1947 Agriculture Act which maintained agriculture on its wartime footing. The success of state management of agriculture during the war had also encouraged the Labour Party to revise its views on land nationalisation. In short, the farmer had ceased to be the class enemy but had become the tool through which party policy could achieved.[76] It was therefore important not to alienate the farming community. In the second reading debate, it was alleged that nine of the County Agricultural Executive Committee chairman had told Tom Williams, now Minister of Agriculture, 'that he could forget about cropping targets if the bill were passed'. Moreover, there were electoral considerations. Labour had polled well in rural districts in 1945 and did not want to jeopardise its chances of repeating this in the forthcoming election. In any

FIGURE 1.4
'A-Hunting we will go!' *Punch*, 3 March 1949. Courtesy of the Punch Cartoon Library.

case, its core rural vote, the agricultural labourers, was lukewarm about the bills and the unions as a whole unenthusiastic. As *The Times* reported on 18 February,

There is a chill wind of opposition to these bills blowing from constituencies in the rural areas. It is in these areas that the Labour party is

weak and the Opposition strong, and the prospect of loosing votes for the sake of bills which do not embody any cardinal party principle is leading ministers to depreciate support of the bills … mainly on the ground that the time is not opportune.[77]

When the Cabinet came to consider its attitude it recognised that public opinion was not behind the bills. A cartoon in *Punch* (Fig. 1.4), published after the failure of the Cocks' bill, showed bucolic policemen on bicycles and motorbikes arresting fox-hunters in the field and loading them into a Black Maria. Whilst poking gentle fun at the idea that fox hunting might be suppressed, it also made a more serious point about enforcement.

The private members bills promised to be a mire in which the government was eager to avoid treading. It therefore maintained the principle of the free vote on the bills whilst making its opposition known. When Cocks' bill went to the Commons on 17 February, its rejection was moved by the chairman of the Parliamentary Labour Party. Another Labour member said 'that he was amazed when he heard the speech of the chairman of the Labour Party: it did not represent the feeling and views of the movement, either in the house or the country', a sentiment which was cheered. Tom Williams had the uncomfortable experience of speaking against the bill on behalf of the government. *The Times* reports that he was greeted with 'hoots of derision' from his own backbenchers. Ten of the fifteen cabinet ministers who sat in the Commons attended to vote for the bill's rejection.[78] It was lost handsomely (214 votes to 101) and subsequently the Fairhurst bill was withdrawn. Later in the month the government accepted a motion that it should establish a committee to consider the issue of cruelty in field sports. This enquiry, under John Scott Henderson KC, was packed with sporting sympathisers and its report, published in June 1951, gave little solace to the opponents of field sports, being largely permissive of the status quo. As the Conservatives were then in power, it prompted no legislation. The pro-field sport lobbies cited it as an authoritative statement and circulated a reduced version: its impartiality was questioned by the abolitionists.[79] And until the inclusion of abolition as a manifesto commitment in 1983, successive Labour governments was happy to leave legislation against field sports to private member's initiatives.

It is always possible to argue that in 1949 the Labour government lost its nerve and caved into the farmers' and aristocratic lobbyists. But one has to say that abolition in 1949 was not practical politics, not least because the Parliament Act would have needed to have been invoked to secure the passage of the bill. In turn, that implies that the government would have needed to adopt it as its own measure. The Lords could all too easily have argued that public opinion was not in favour of the statute and employed their delaying powers. In any case the time scale involved implied that the government could have changed (or would have needed to fight an election on hunting) before passage under the Parliament Act could have been secured.

If it seems as though little was done in the years between the publication of the Scott Henderson report and the emergence of the Hunt Saboteurs in 1963–64, time was on the abolitionist's side and public opinion slowly came round to their point of view. Just how far this had gone may be seen in the hostile reaction to the Queen and Duke of Edinburgh's big game shooting on their Indian tour in 1961.[80] The slow slippage of sports from public esteem was appreciated amongst the more forward looking members of the hunting and shooting communities. In 1946 the Duke of Beaufort wrote to all Masters of Foxhounds:

> Apart from actual adherence to the written laws of foxhunting, I feel that in the future much will depend upon the way in which individual hunts are conducted. In these days of intensive press reporting, the eyes of the world are upon us, and the vast majority of the world knows nothing of foxhunting except what it reads in the general press, with the result that the mistakes of one hunt become the criterion by which all are judged.[81]

There were also many who felt that hunts ought to be above cultivating the press and that they should rely on an innate deference to their activities which could no longer be ensured. Dorian Williams described a meeting with masters of foxhounds in 1958 in which his platform for modernising hunting – including its relations with the press – was received in silence. Williams remarked that the 'so-called upper classes' despised publicity. Clayton has suggested that the strong military element amongst the post-war MFHs deterred debate in the ranks.[82] On might add that hunting probably seemed out of tune with the general austerity of the 1950s.

For these reasons, hunting in the 1950s was probably ill-equipped to deal with its fleeter-footed opponents. It was not only the press, but hunting also had to cope with some notable apostates, especially Robert Churchyard who, as a former Master of Foxhounds, was able to give chapter and verse on the less reputable practices of hunts. Before his Damascene conversion he 'hunted, shot and fished in the British Isles from 1913 to 1953, and travelled extensively in pursuit of big game in south America, the USA, Canada and Africa'. Or, as Caroline Blackwood said, 'He arranged his life so that there was not a month in the year when he was deprived of the opportunity to kill some animal'. In about 1953 he underwent a damascene conversion and published a series of articles in *The People* exposing the practices of the hunts. He was, for instance, willing to admit that as MFH he had supplied foxes in sacks to neighbouring hunts and that foxes were bred in artificial earths to maintain their numbers. He detailed other unpalatable practices (including cutting the pads of bagged foxes) although he was careful to blame these on the hunt servants and not the more patrician (and unseeing) masters. Churchward's articles were later issued as a pamphlet (*A Master of Hounds speaks*) by the League against Cruel Sports. Churchward became a vice-president of the League: he later contributed a chapter to Patrick Moore's *Against Hunting* (1965). Not surprisingly Churchward was ostracised by his former fellows. Some held that the practices that he described were specific to the South Shropshire hunt: Churchward himself won a libel action against *Horse and Hound*.[83] Another was the journalist L. G. Pine, better known today for his writings on heraldry, who was editor of the *Shooting Times* from 1960 to 1964. Pine, who was not drawn from within the sporting community, resigned his editorship to write a survey of field sports under the title of *After their Blood*, much of it based on his experiences as a guest at sporting events.

Field sports, and especially foxhunting, were plainly on the backfoot after 1945. There was, throughout the 1950s, an active lobby against them in the National Society for the Abolition of Cruel Sports and the League against Cruel Sports. The LACS ran an efficient rebuttal service, employing a press cutting service to collect stories about fox hunting from the provincial press and using its members to write anti-hunting letters in response, some of which were published.[84] There were intermittent hostilities over stag hunting in the West County. In 1957 a NSACS- and RSPCA-sponsored petition calling for the prohibition of deer and stag hunting, containing 800,000 signatures, was presented to the commons. A private member's bill for the protection of deer made no progress in the Commons in February 1958 (although it provoked a lively protest meeting in Dulverton) and the government later refused to allocate it any time.[85] The RSPCA declared itself against stag hunting, but this was a mere prelude to a protracted struggle by the anti-fox hunting lobbies to swing the policy of the Society behind their objectives. It was a characteristic of the war against stag hunting and fox hunting in the 1960s and after that much of the action took place in bodies for whom hunting was a peripheral concern: the RSPCA, the National Trust, in attempts to persuade local authorities to bar hunts from their land (a particular campaign of the early 1980s).[86] From 1964 hunts also had to cope with a new militant wing of the movement, the Hunt Saboteurs, who based their direct action tactics on the Committee of 100.[87] If nothing else, this put the hunts under a new level of scrutiny by people who were only too anxious to find evidence of wrong-doing.

There was an awareness amongst the field sports fraternity that they were engaged in a war and that they needed to maintain and even build public support. One development designed to meet this need was the Game Fair. The idea for this originated with Nigel Gray of the ICI Game Advisory Service in 1956 and it seems clear that the original idea was to tap into the interest in shooting. The County Landowners Association agreed to act as sponsor and the first Game Fair was held at Stetchworth in July 1958. Gray expected a maximum of 2,000 people, but 8,000 came over two days. The decision was quickly taken to hold a second game fair and include fishing in its remit. Royal patronage was also sought and found in the Duke of Gloucester. This second Fair, at Hackwood Park in Hampshire, attracted 12,000 people; the third, at Castle Howard, in 1960, 20,000 visitors. The CLA fairs at Chatsworth and Glanusk Park in 1975 and 1976 attracted in excess of 75,000 visitors.[88] The idea seems to have been widely emulated (the Oakley had a share in one from 1964).

Yet there is little sign that any of the field sports were in real danger of disappearance for want of supporters in the years after 1945. Of course, there were thin years. Martin's *The Great Shoots* shows just how far many of the familiar Edwardian shoots had declined by the 1980s, with the cessation of large-scale breeding and an acceptance of much smaller bags. But then, the appetite for battue shooting on a grand scale had mostly gone by the time of George V's death in 1935. Some writers of that decade looked back on that style of shooting with embarrassment rather than nostalgia. Within a few years of George V's death, his biographer Gore wrote that

> The present age is not in tune with solemn discussions of the records and achievements of Lords Ripon, Walsingham, Forester and Huntingfield, of Mr Rimington Wilson and the rest of the Victorian and Edwardian cracks. The heyday of the 'crack shot' virtually closed with the war which ended, except on a few favoured estates, the days of enormous bags and the era of keen rivalry in statistical records.[89]

Or the Duke of Portland, 'When I look back at the game book I am quite ashamed of the enormous number of pheasants we sometimes killed. This is a form of shooting I have no desire to repeat.'[90]

VI

Advances in technology allowed the evolution of all the sports under consideration. In angling, Harvey Osborne shows how the sport was transformed by developments in the rod and the fly which allowed salmon to be caught in ways previously impossible. The older, cruder, but no less effective ways of taking salmon with a spear were condemned as ungentlemanly and banned. Fishing was further revolutionised by the introduction of the fixed-spool reel, invented by a Bradford textile manufacturer, Alfred H. Illingworth, in 1905. This was based on a technology with which Illingworth was familiar, the spinning bobbin. Previous reels, notably the Nottingham centre pin reel had lacked ease in use. Illingworth's innovation served to increase the audience for the sport.[91] John Martin draws attention to the introduction of field glasses as an aid to identifying a bird without

FIGURE 1.5
Changing
guns. From
Earl of
Suffolk and
Berkshire
(ed.), *The
Encyclopaedia
of Sport* (4
vols, 1911), II,
pp. 374–5.

CHANGING GUNS. THE LOADER HAS CARTRIDGES READY FOR THE EMPTY GUN IN HIS RIGHT HAND.

LOADING.

FIGURE 1.6
Old style
shooting.
'Partridge
shooting'
by Samuel
Alken,
1784–1825.
Courtesy
of National
Museums
Liverpool
(The Walker).

shooting it. Payne-Gallwey and Walsingham recommended that keepers be supplied with them so they could see poachers at a distance. Field glasses gave the deer stalker an additional advantage over his quarry.[92] Shooting saw a whole range of innovations: the appearance of the double-barrelled, breach-loading shotgun, the appearance of factory-produced cartridges and technical changes in the formulation of the explosive charge they contained, not only in their power but also the introduction of smokeless charges, all allowed the appearance of the large scale shooting of the late Victorian and Edwardian Big Shots. Technology was then taken a stage further by choreography. Each shooter would be supported by one or more loaders who would take the discharged gun from the shooter, reload it and then pass it back in return for a discharged gun. (Figure 1.5 shows how it was done.) Two loaders a piece were usual at Sandringham. The passing of the gun from shooter to loader, the recharging and exchange back required practised dexterity: one account has Lord de Grey (the Marquis of Ripon) being caught at a country house party practising with his loaders after the house had turned in for bed. The result was that a shooting party or six or eight guns might actually have the firepower of twenty or more guns, with its members able to fire more or less continuously. Hence Ripon's claim to have shot 28 pheasants in a minute is made explicable.[93]

These technical changes transformed game shooting. Early nineteenth-century shooting took the form of 'walking up' birds. In the innumerable illustrations of shooting sport of this time, of which Fig. 1.6 is an example, the shooters are seen out with their dogs: as the dogs flushed birds out of the undergrowth, the shooters fired at them as they flew away. After each shot, the gun had to be recharged with powder and shot: the speed at which the

gun could be fired was therefore limited. The development of the gun and increased firepower made possible a new style of shooting, the battue, in which the guns were stationary and concealed behind hedges or trimmed firs (as in Fig. 1.7) or butts in grouse shooting (Fig. 1.8). The game was driven towards them by beaters.[94] The emergence of the battue is a matter which requires additional research. The first use of the word in *The Times* comes in 1828 when it reported a battue at the Duke of Norfolk's at Fornham near Bury St Edmunds. The following year the paper reprinted a piece from *Blackwood's Magazine* in which the author was critical of contemporary gentry mores, complaining that landowners spent too much time in London and found sport, including foxhunting, a bore 'unless in a regular *battue*, when a dozen lordlings murder pheasants by the thousand'.[95] It is not clear that these early references indicate more than shooting on a prodigious scale, but the possibilities presented by the new firearm technology, which in turn allowed for the game to be driven at and over the shooters, prompted innovations in the breeding of partridges and pheasants and the appearance of specialist bird suppliers so that practitioners of the battue had more sport available to them than could be obtained from essentially wild populations of birds.

This not to say that the old style continued in less formal rough shoots: some regarded this as the superior test of the sportsman, and debates about the merits of battue shooting rumbled on into at least the last years of the nineteenth century. Payne-Gallwey and Walsingham, for instance, disliked the word and were extremely defensive about it: they stressed the skill in shooting pheasants flying high and fast.[96] Mrs Cresswell, spoke for many when she recalled with nostalgia the old style of shooting. She admired the new style for its 'marksmanship' only, holding that 'for involving neither danger nor fatigue it can hardly be called "sport"'.[97] In 1895 MacKenzie held that driving birds had become acceptable because of its adoption by royalty. Historically, this is rather a questionable premise, but he pointed out that the older Prince of Wales was establishing a new fashion by having his deer driven at Balmoral.

> Driving, accordingly, enjoys royal patronage almost exclusively, and, despite the animadversions of the old school of gunners, who are still pleased to denounce it as an indolent form of so-called sport, it is seen flourishing exceedingly and [is] increasingly fashionable with all shooters from north to south.[98]

There were similar innovations in wildfowling: the wildfowler changed over time from moving towards the birds whether on foot or in a punt, to taking the birds as they flew towards ponds designed to attract them. Punt mounted guns and the punt itself also changed over time.

The other major technological change which altered the practice of field sports (as every other aspect of society) were the new forms of transport, first in the train and then in the motor car. The railway was regarded with horror by fox hunters who saw it cutting through their traditional hunting areas. They learnt to cope with it. Indeed, Trollope in the 1860s thought that railways had been the salvation of hunting.

> ... railroads have done so much towards hunting, that they may almost be said to have created the sport anew on a wider and much more thoroughly organised footing that it ever held before. They have brought men, and with the men their money, from the towns into the country; and the men and the money together have overcome all those difficulties which the railroads themselves have produced ... Hunting as it is practised today could not exist without railroads ...[99]

A more serious problem was that the new ease of transport left hunts open to members and strangers who could take an early train from London and return to the capital at the end of a day in the shires.

The railway also served to open the Highlands to English shooters. In 1894 A.J. Stuart-Wortley published an account of travelling north from Euston on the night Scotch mail and claimed that one could start from Bloomsbury and have taken one's first Perthshire grouse in the space of 16 hours.[100] Reaching the very far north of Scotland took longer of course. The general increased ease of travel made trips to Norway, Iceland or even Canada a practicality for sportsmen who wished to encounter exotic creatures or landscapes with had not yet been hunted or fished out. Akroyd's criss-crossing of the British Isles in search of game and his forays to North America would have been impossible without the new forms of transport. By the 1920s sportsmen who wanted to holiday and shoot in Africa could do so. Finally, we might note that the railway made possible the dispatch of live birds to shoots, a trade we have already encountered. Not only might these not fly, but Hartopp claimed to have been at a shoot for which the birds had missed their train. The shoot had had to be delayed until they arrived and the mystified shooting party entertained with a visit to the home farm. This mishap – or another one like it – was turned into a cartoon in which His Royal Highness is kept waiting for the pheasants to be turned into the coverts (Fig. 1.9).[101] Oddly, buying in birds seems to have been accepted where buying in foxes was deemed unsporting.

Daniel Allen has a few wise words on the impact of the car on otter hunts. The car freed them from meeting at stations to connect with trains. It allowed both the hunter and the hounds to travel further to the meet and to return to home and kennels at night. But not all could see the advantages of motor transport. The historian of the Pytchley describes how

> Another novelty, which [Lord] Annaly was called on to face, was the automobile. Some few misguided people were actually beginning to drive to the meet in these noisy, stinking contraptions, one of which

broke the leg of a much-loved hunter of Mrs Renton's. Someone said that the Duke of Westminster, who was then Master of the Cheshire, had, or was going to have, one of the things made for his hounds, and perhaps his horses. No one believed it; it was impossible; no horse would go into such 'a disgraceful thing'. The hounds could not possibly hunt. They would be frightened to death, choked by the smell, and would not get to the meet more than one day a week, as the 'thing' would break down. Annaly dealt with the nuisance summarily, by issuing an edict that no motor car was to come within half a mile of the meet; and woe betide anyone who disobeyed.[102]

FIGURE 1.9
'Waiting for
the train'.
From Brian
P. Martin, *The
Great Shoots*
(1987), p. 234.

Motorised hound vans (for which there were horse-drawn precedents) allowed the pack to arrive fresh. The car-borne hunter could set out later and return sooner if he or she had a groom to hack to and fro with the horse. The full advantage of the motor car did not arrive until the affordable horse box came on the market: Dorchester though that they were having a pernicious effect on hunting in the mid-'30s. He identified the practice of hunters driving to a second hunt a couple of days a week taking their horses with them. Strangers from outside the district proliferated at meets. Hayes also reports the reduction of trade in the hunting towns as hunt members preferred to drive back to Town rather than take lodgings. The

THE SINEWS OF SPORT.—*The Marquis (to head keeper).* " Now, Grandison, His Royal Highness will be tired of waiting ; why don't you send in the beaters ? " *Head keeper (sotto voce).* " Beg pardon, my lord, the London train's late this morning with the pheasants—we must have half an hour to get 'em into the coverts ! "

additional problem arose of the car follower, a figure towards which hunts had decidedly mixed feelings. There were other unpredicted consequences. Tarmac roads held the scent of the fox badly: but they were a deal easier to ride on than the old roads surfaced with loose stones and ruts.[103] Other than getting too and from the shoot, cars probably had less impact on shooting than hunting: but John Scott-Montague of Beaulieu was keen to advocate their use on shoots as early as 1903.[104]

VII

There is a final matter which await a more detailed exploration than this book can offer. This is the whole question of field sports as gendered activities and not merely the role of women in sports which, *ipso facto*, we might think were heavily dominated by men. This is not only a simple matter of social conformity and preference, nor apparently does it arise from any male view that women should not kill or be party to the killing of animals. There are questions about dress and decorum: women's conventional dress was not suitable for outdoor pursuits (or conversely that outdoor dress, especially trousers, was not suitable for them).[105] In hunting there is the whole question of riding side-saddle. The side-saddle did undergo development in the later nineteenth century but was progressively abandoned as women took to sitting astride the horse after the fashion of men. Some opinion saw medical (and sexual) dangers arising from women riding with an orthodox saddle. The appearance of women in numbers in the hunting field is dated by Carr to the 1850s.[106] Over the following seventy years the field probably achieved a degree of parity, but women remained excluded from Masterships of Foxhounds. Their opportunity came with the call-up of men into the forces after 1914.[107] Women were forced to turn out in numbers to keep hunts turning over. Dorchester thought that

> The pre-War hunting men went to the War in a body, and such of their hunters as were not requisitioned for the War were at the disposal of their wives and daughters, who hunted them as a matter of duty, to keep the horses fit and keep hunting alive against the return of their lords … these ladies thus acquired an intimate knowledge of and interest in hunting, and whereas in former years, they had ridden only well-mannered horses and had looked to a pilot, they now had to think and act for themselves.

Dorchester also suggested that changes after the war left a void for women to fill.

> Since the War the former fox-hunting classes have become so impoverished that most of the men have had to devote themselves almost entirely to their businesses, and can only manage one day a

week at the most, so that the family horse or stud is at the disposal of the wives and daughters most of the time.

He elaborates on this further, suggesting that in his own country (by which he probably meant the Garth, south-west of London) in the mid-'30s, women would form 65 per cent of the field on a fashionable day but 70–80 per cent on the other three days of the week. He thought too that the quality of women's riding had improved with the adoption of riding astride, but he was disapproving of women riding in point-to-point races.[108] The end of the war probably also marks the moment at which increasing numbers of women came to serve as Masters. Seen in this light, Clayton's sociological observations of 1984 seem well pre-empted: he identified

> a professional man's wife [who] puts her husband on the London train at Northampton, Bicester or Oxford, then drives the family car to play school to drop her infant before hastily changing into hunting kit, hitching up the trailer to the same car and arriving at the meet for a day with the Pytchley, Grafton … or any other of the Midland packs … apart from farmers and others with close rural links, the male section of the mounted field in mid-week in Midland packs is either young or fairly senior where the 'young wives club' is out in considerable strength.[109]

One of the untold stories of foxhunting is therefore its progressive feminisation.

Shooting remained much less accessible to women and its practitioners overwhelmingly male. For all Dorchester discusses the place of women in fox hunting, he makes no comment on their role in shooting. There were always a small minority of women who insisted on shooting. Queen Victoria (inevitably) disapproved, seeing them as fast women: the same slur had been made of women pioneers in the hunting field. For the old guard, women's place at a shoot was back at the house. When they were allowed to join the guns, it was as passive spectators (as in Fig. 1.5). For Mackenzie, writing in 1895, the greater involvement of women in shooting was inevitable. He acknowledged the feminisation of first hunting and then fishing, and suggested that with the emergence of lighter guns, all that was stopping greater female involvement was the failure of their tailors to evolve satisfactory dress.[110] Whether women did come to command the shooting field may be doubted. It is possible to point to twentieth-century women who shot, for instance, Deborah Countess of Devonshire.[111] Such single examples do nothing to dispel the conclusion that shooting remained a strongly male activity throughout the century.

It is perhaps with the men and their idea of maleness that we should end. There are questions to be explored about the sexuality of the male participants in sports, and especially hunting. Akroyd, in a rare reflective moment, complained about women on shoots and in shooting parties. 'Men seem to be much more effeminate than they used to be: it's the women that seem to wear the "breeks".' Shooting and fishing were no longer arduous: there were cars to take the sportsman out and bring him back and much of the hardship and physicality had been lost. 'After dinner, of course, comes bridge, which to my mind has spoilt a great deal of country-house life. There is hardly such a thing nowadays as the men sitting round the smoking room fire swapping stories and going to bed in decent time.'[112] In the 1949 debate on Seymour Cocks' bill, Cocks made a jovial aside about a report that the fox-hunters were to ride down Piccadilly in protest. 'He thought it would have amused Oscar Wilde to see the unspeakable pursuing the uneatable in the vicinity of Leicester Square.' The Commons – some of them at least – laughed. Later in the debate, the Earl Winterton, an Irish peer, then in his late sixties and a pre-first world Diehard, who had held cabinet posts under Chamberlain, addressed the house. Winterton rose to the reference to Oscar Wilde. In the words of *The Times'* reporter:

> Hundreds of people outside the house supported the bill, but there were others behind it of a much less desirable kind. They were the Bloomsbury boys who invented the satirical phrase 'Huntin', shootin' and fishin'' (Laughter.) He would not have thought that Mr. Cocks would have regarded Oscar Wilde as a desirable supporter. (Laughter.) None of the Bloomsbury boys, or their patron saint Oscar Wilde, indulged in hunting, shooting and fishing because those were outdoor sports, requiring courage, endurance and physical fitness, every one of which was anathema to them. (Loud Opposition laughter and cheers.)[113]

If, for Ackroyd, the muscularity had gone out of shooting by the 1920s, courage, endurance and physical fitness were still the true marks of the sportsman and identified his sexuality for the older post-war generation.

VIII

This book is intended to be a work of advocacy, not for field sports, but for the history of field sports. The history of field sports has to be reclaimed by historians. It has the possibility of illuminating many other areas of interest, from the nature of Englishness, the social behaviour of the middle classes and the standing of women to the environmental history of the landscape. At a time when the countryside is valued less and less for its productive capacity and more for its landscape and recreational potential, there may well be much to be learnt from the non-productive uses of the historic countryside that can illuminate and inform our understanding of present and future conditions.

CHAPTER TWO

Royalty and the diversity of field sports, c.1840–c.1981*

by R. W. Hoyle

ANY DISCUSSION of field sports in England has to confront the role of monarchy as practitioners, patrons and exponents whose tastes have been widely emulated. Over the past century and a half, members of the royal family have practised virtually the whole range of sports available to landed and moneyed individuals. The future George VI played in the men's doubles at Wimbledon in its centenary year, 1926: one should not be surprised that for most of the last century there was a royal racing pigeon loft.[1] Throughout, they have shown a marked preference for competitive out-of-doors sports, whether equestrian (hunting, steeplechasing, polo, racing, where successive monarchs have maintained prominent stables, eventing, latterly carriage-driving), or shooting, fishing, tennis, yachting, flying and, most recently skiing. The family have been exponents of muscular Christianity, setting out to excel at physical and sometimes dangerous sports. Edward Prince of Wales was a daredevil steeple chaser in the mid-1920s, suffering concussion in a fall at Arborfield in 1924 following which he was confined to bed for a month. Both his father and the prime minister urged him to desist, but it was only after his father's near-fatal illness in 1929 that his mother persuaded him to give up hunting and steeplechasing. 'And so I reluctantly abandoned the one pursuit which gave outlet to my competitive spirit.' Instead he turned to golf ('Golf is regarded as too slow a game by many present-day members of the royal family', according to one writer in 1980).[2] The present Prince of Wales rode competitively for a short period before his marriage. When it came to shooting, successive monarchs were

---

*   This is a first attempt at such an essay, based largely on published sources and newspaper reports. It does not claim to be a definitive or final account. In this paper, Edward VII is called Albert Edward, Prince of Wales before his accession: his son George V was Duke of York before his accession; his elder son, Edward VIII was known as Edward Prince of Wales before his accession (but as David to family members) and the Duke of Windsor after his abdication. George V's second son, who took the title of George VI on his brother's abdication, was previously the Duke of York.

invariably claimed to be amongst the best shots of their day – at least whilst they lived![3] Whilst the competitive spirit is plainly strong, sport, together with a successful naval command, has perhaps been seen as a way of demonstrating fitness for leadership as well as their quintessential Englishness. Field sports have also soaked up some of the energies of the heir to the throne as he waited to enter into his inheritance and adult duties.

The British monarchy remains markedly equestrian. This is perhaps a necessity when much of the public ritual of monarchy is conducted on horseback. George V expressed himself dissatisfied by the quality of his elder son's horsemanship: 'If you can't ride you know, I'm afraid people will call you a duffer.' As the Duke of Windsor recalled, 'he even tried to put me to shame by telling me he had heard how impressed the British cavalry officers in India had been by the horsemanship of the Crown Prince of Germany' and as a result, the Prince was tutored in riding whilst an undergraduate. (This gave him a taste for hunting.)[4] The ability to ride, and ride well, remains a necessary skill for the job (if redundant in society generally), but the post-war generations of the royal family have gone well beyond this, the Queen with her racing stables, the Duke of Edinburgh with his polo and carriage-driving, Prince Charles with his hunting and steeplechasing, Princess Anne with her distinguished career in eventing (with her first husband, Captain Mark Phillips). In these ways the royal family has remained rooted in the land, in the preferences of inter-war landowners (to which, admittedly, many amongst the self-made rich also aspire) and in minority sports and recreations. This pattern has been perpetuated amongst the rising generation of royals.

As we shall see, the family has been surprisingly sensitive to comment on its sporting activities. Field sports have never been uncritically accepted and there has been a long vein of comment from those concerned about animal welfare, criticising the royal family for setting a poor example. The problem for royalty, particularly over the last quarter century, has been how to square their taste for field sports with their concept of service to a nation which had largely ceased to admire their sporting choices, indeed, had come to have little knowledge or understanding of either agricultural practice or rural society and whose enthusiasm has been directed towards mass, non-participant, professionalised sports. One aspect of this is that the royal family and their biographers have increasingly withdrawn from discussing the royal family's involvement in field sports. Much more is found on Edward VII's shooting in the first generation of biographers than in the most recent studies. A quarter of a century ago, it was still possible to publish books with such cloying titles as *Prince Charles, Horseman* or *Sporting Royals, Past and Present*, but one strongly suspects that books describing the royal family's hunting, shooting and fishing would not receive the co-operation of the royal household today. Indeed, recent studies of the Queen and Prince Philip say remarkably little about their sporting interests although shooting has plainly been a major recreation for both of them over the years. There was contrived outrage in 2000 when the Queen was photographed twisting the neck of a winged bird on a Sandringham shoot.[5] In the same way, modern accounts of Sandringham, including those on the estate's own website, glide over the sporting aspects of the estate.

This essay follows royal sport as far as the early 1980s: sufficiently far in the past for people to be reasonably relaxed about royal activities but also the moment of the marriage of Charles, Prince of Wales and Lady Diana Spencer, after which nothing royal was quite the same.

I

In two important respects, the modern fortunes of the royal family have differed from British landholders as a whole. Because of its advantageous tax arrangements, it has not found itself compelled to sell its broad acres to meet death duties. On the contrary, it has come through the hostile tax climate of the twentieth century largely unscathed and it is probably correct to suppose that collectively, it owns more land now than it did in 1900. In addition, the Civil List has freed it from dependency on its landed income and allowed it to engage in sports on a much greater scale than any equivalent landowner might have been able to afford.

From the early 1860s to the present day, the royal family have had three sporting estates at their disposal. The first, Windsor, was the least important of the three. It also differs from the other two, Sandringham in Norfolk and Balmoral on Deeside in Scotland in that it was deemed to belong to the State. Windsor has always been used for shooting. The Prince Consort shot there and developed it as a shooting estate. Prince Christian improved the shooting, but it was said to be in a poor state at the time of the Queen Victoria's death in 1901. Edward VII put its management on a new footing and whilst monarch, held annual shooting parties at Windsor to entertain his brother monarchs. A new pheasantry was started and, under his direction, the few hundred head killed annually was turned into a little under 9,000 in 1909–10, mostly pheasant.[6] George V used the shooting to entertain government ministers and others who could not be absent from the capital for two or three days at a time. The Duke of Windsor recalled that he was shooting in Windsor Great Park when he was called to Sandringham to his father's last illness.[7] In more recent years shooting has continued there under the direction of the Duke of Edinburgh.[8]

Balmoral and Sandringham were – and remain – the private possession of the monarch. A lease on the Balmoral estate was first acquired by Queen Victoria and the Prince Consort in 1848 and the freehold in 1852. The royal couple had been considering acquiring a Scottish property from their first visit to the Highlands in 1842 but were deterred by climate. In 1847–48 it was suggested that Deeside would be a better location for them as the climate was drier and the air bracing, and the lease of Balmoral was acquired without the royal couple having visited the house. When they did so, both were enthusiastic about their acquisition, the Prince saying that it reminded him of Thuringia. A neighbouring estate, Birkhall, was also acquired and the Abergeldie estate leased. The house at Balmoral was rebuilt between 1852 and 1855, the gardens laid out and a model farm constructed by the Prince Consort (although it was completed posthumously). The estate came to encompass 42,770 acres, to which the present Queen added a further 6700 detached acres when she bought a grouse moor at Delnadamph in 1977. The possibilities for farming at Balmoral are decidedly limited: in 1980 it was stated that only 380 acres were farmed with the remainder being mountain, moorland or forest. There were, though, around 2,500 deer.[9]

Sandringham was bought by Edward VII when Prince of Wales in 1862. What he acquired was the house, described as a shooting box, five farms, a number of other houses and cottages and 7,000 acres: a smallish estate with a reputation for its shooting.[10] The estate then became a royal plaything. Not only was the house rebuilt on much grander lines, but the estate was reshaped, and a model farm and village (at West Newton) established. It was also enlarged over the years by the purchase of additional land and the drainage of coastal marshes so that by the third quarter of the last century it extended over 21,100 acres.[11] The estate though was not, at some periods at least, co-terminus with the shooting. Certainly at the end of the nineteenth century, George Duke of York (George V) rented additional shooting in his own name so that he had, at his disposal, including Sandringham, some 30,000 acres of shooting.[12] Exactly how much of this additional shooting was still in hand at the time of his death is unreported.

Both Balmoral and Sandringham passed by inheritance to Edward VIII. His biographer comments that the king associated Sandringham with some of the most boring and unhappy periods of his life and suggests that he might have been inclined to dispose of both estates. Certainly they reminded him of the Victorian attitudes and cultural preferences of his father.[13] Edward was out of salts with field sports after the fashion of his father and was not prepared to carry the cost of running the two estates from his own pocket. 'No expense had been spared to maintain Sandringham as a model property: but that praise-worthy reputation had been preserved only by dipping into the privy purse with a prodigality that was the wonder of my father's neighbours' was his considered comment.[14] He horrified his mother by referring to Sandringham as his father's 'hobby'. He asked his brother, the Duke of York (George VI), to undertake with Lord Radnor a review of the Sandringham estate and recommend savings: as a result the estate workforce was severely trimmed (from 400 to 300) but the King went beyond this by offering for sale farms acquired by his father in 1915.[15] He made only one fleeting visit to Sandringham during his reign and then showed himself largely indifferent to the house and its staff. At Balmoral he oversaw reductions in the estate establishment without conferring with his brother who was distressed to discover what had been done without his knowledge. At least some of Edward VIII's changes were reversed after his abdication: as the estates were his private property, George VI had to purchase both from his brother. He quietly withdrew the Sandringham farms from sale, having already acquired for himself some of the shooting shed from Balmoral.[16] Of course, Edward VIII acknowledged that of the two, the Duke of York was most like his father: and it may be supposed that the abdication, by maintaining the essential cultural continuity of the monarchy, ensured that the Windsors maintained their place at the head of aristocratic landowning society.

Edward VIII apart, there is general agreement that Sandringham had a special place in the affections of the royal family. It was not only that Sandringham was the source of great pride and affection. For George V, it was 'Dear old Sandringham, the place I love better than anywhere else in the world'. George VI said, 'I have always been so happy here.'[17] Their control over the estate was close and personal with regular reports on estate business being sent to Windsor or Buckingham Palace in the months when they were not resident. It was a refuge from other business: they also became a part of Norfolk society with the pretensions of landowners rather than monarchs, entertaining their gentry neighbours and mounting tenants' dinners. When a practical joker sent out invitations round north Norfolk to join the Prince and Mr Gladstone for lunch on April Fools Day 1883, no one suspected that anything was amiss until those invited arrived and found they were not expected.[18] George V's house guests were expected to join him in his inspection of the estate on a Sunday afternoon. It was reported that he knew his tenants and employees by name: he also had long friendships with Mr Jones, the village schoolmaster and an amateur naturalist, and George Brereton, a farmer and his shooting companion.[19] George VI died after a 'Keepers Day' shoot: an end of season shoot in which he was joined by a number of his own tenants, the local police, keepers from adjacent estates and friends. The late Colin Matthew wrote that Edward VII 'started the Sandringham style amongst the royals, but balanced it with Paris and the continent: George V made the country habits and dress of the Norfolk gentry central to the royal style ...'[20]

At Balmoral the sport was deer stalking and grouse shooting. At Sandringham, it was shooting pheasant, partridge and increasingly wildfowl (an attempt to establish grouse having failed). That the family had these estates, each of which specialised in different types of sport, allowed for the possibility of moving from estate to estate over the annual cycle of the year. Edward VII, both as Prince of Wales and as monarch, developed a regular cycle of seasonal movements which his son, George V, maintained and which his son, Edward VIII, described in his autobiography as being like the seasonal migration of a flock of birds. '... My father, a man of fixed habits, settled into an annual routine that became as regular, as unchanging, as permanent, it seemed, as the revolution of a planet in its orbit.'[21] Edward VII might spend Christmas and the New Year at Sandringham. A week or more in January would be spent shooting on the estates of one of his friends, be it the Duke of Devonshire at Chatsworth or Lord Iveagh at Elveden. February was spent in London, March and April in Paris or the Mediterranean. The summer was dedicated to racing: Ascot in June, Goodwood in July, then to sailing at Cowes in August followed by a rest cure at a German spa. September and October was Scotland for grouse shooting and deer stalking with a return to Sandringham for the king's birthday (9 November) which marked the beginning of the Sandringham season.[22] As Duke of York, George V normally went to either Studley or Bolton in Yorkshire for the opening of the grouse season before going to his house at Abergeldie. He normally made a succession of visits to shooting estates in the Autumn. Inevitably war interrupted this pattern and it was 1921 before the king felt able to return to settled ways.[23] This pattern survives in the present royal family: the summer at Balmoral, the winter at Sandringham: one observer suggested in 1977 that the Queen spent four months of the year in the country, most of January at Sandringham, August and September at Balmoral and April at Windsor.[24]

However, the royal family were never self-sufficient in sport. In some respects their resources were fairly small: Albert Edward Prince of Wales, for instance, had Sandringham, but his income did not match that of the larger landowning aristocrats of his age. Rumours circulated about his finances and a select committee considered his income in 1889.[25] Both he and George V were regular visitors at the houses of fellow aristocrats and joined shooting parties arranged in their honour. This was a considerable expense for the hosts and, to ensure that their guest had the cream of the game, no shooting was done before he arrived.[26] They might also go abroad for sport. Novel creatures, not available in England, were shot on tour, a practice which survived into the 1970s (at least). What the royal family lacked was hounds. Albert Edward Prince of Wales sold the pack at Windsor in 1869 for £2,000 as an economy.[27] Until 1901 there were buckhounds at Windsor, but they seem to have had little patronage from the royal family. Fox hunting was secured by partaking in other people's hunts, sometimes by staying with landowners (such as the Dukes of Beaufort) who still maintained their own packs of hounds. A variation on this was the country house hunting party. It was fashionable in the 1920s to take a house – especially one in or near Melton Mowbray – for the season and it was at a weekend house party arranged by Lady Furness, the Prince of Wales's current mistress, that he first met Mrs Simpson (who did not herself hunt) whose husband was ingratiating himself with English landed society.[28]

It is perhaps a reflection of the attractions of Sandringham that both George V and George VI lived on the estate in small and undistinguished houses throughout their respective father's lives. The acquisition of Highgrove by the present Prince of Wales in 1980 therefore marked something of a break with previous practice. Highgrove is not a sporting estate: but it will be suggested that the Prince's preference for living in Gloucestershire is not without significance in any account of the royal family and field sports.

II

Of the range of sports and recreations pursued by modern royalty, five are the subject of particular discussion in this paper: shooting birds, shooting deer at home and big game abroad, and hunting foxes and carted deer with hounds. (The latter were deer which were taken to the meet in a cart or wagon, and then released for the hounds to follow.) Fishing is largely omitted, not because the royal family were disinterested in scaled animals – some certainly were – but because the principle of fishing has never been a major source of controversy. Fishing was part and parcel of the Balmoral experience. The most prominent royal fisherman of the last century was Queen Elizabeth, the Queen Mother, who learned to fish as a child and in turn passed her enthusiasm on to the present Prince of Wales.[29]

One feature of all these sports is that they were gender specific, albeit to different degrees. Women did not, for the most part, have a role in shooting. Nor were they encouraged to take part in deer stalking. In general women were not taught how to handle guns. Queen Elizabeth II has stalked deer but does not shoot birds. It is an interesting speculation to wonder whether she was taught to shoot because the times had changed or because as heir-apparent to the throne, facility with a shotgun and rifle was expected of her.

Shooting made successive generations of royal wives into grass widows. Queen Victoria was anxious about the Prince Consort's hunting and for that reason welcomed his discovery of stalking: but she also disliked guns. In fact the Queen probably came to resent his stalking as well, for once at Balmoral, Albert was completely obsessed with stalking, going out everyday and leaving the Queen to her own amusements. In 1853, in six weeks at Balmoral, he shot 26 stags.[30] Occasionally she went with him. But she did not shoot, holding in 1882 that whilst it was acceptable for women to be spectators, 'only fast women shot'.[31] That said, her experience with the Prince Consort may have encouraged her to sympathise with her daughter in law who was left to amuse the ladies at the Prince of Wales's shooting parties. The women joined the men for luncheon and were then permitted to stay with them for the afternoon as the shoot made its way back to Sandringham.[32] The house party then came together for afternoon tea. Dinner was a mixed occasion, but after dinner the men withdrew. After they returned, the princess would lead the women to their beds whilst the men would stay up drinking and playing billiards or cards.[33]

This was the pattern of the county house shooting party through to the Second World War: it plainly allowed the women plenty of opportunities for intercourse amongst themselves whilst keeping them largely at a distance from the shooting and male conversation. In the first decade of the century the Duchess of York declined to follow her husband on his summer sporting programme, preferring Frogmore to racing, yachting and itinerant shooting. She would take their children to Abergeldie for the end of August where the Duke would join them for grouse shooting and, when the grouse were mostly shot, deer-stalking. Whilst the Duke was 'banging away with shotgun and rifle', the Duchess would take the children 'carriage riding for picnics'.[34] Women were much more integrated into fox hunting. There were those who continued to disapprove, but after the 1850s women were frequently to be seen in the hunting field and on more equal terms with men. That the men and women hunted side-by-side may have appealed to bachelor princes, but fox hunting also seems to have been conducted on more of a day-to-day basis with many of those participating going home at the end of the day's chase. The development of the Melton house party changed much of that, but the gender dynamics of the sports remained subtly different.

They also differed in one other important respect. Shooting, for the most part, took place on the secluded private property of the landowner hosting the shoot with an invited shooting party. Large crowds would, in any case, have disturbed the birds and made it hard, if not impossible, for the beaters to direct them towards the guns. There were exceptions to this: for instance a story of Edward VII shooting at Chatsworth in front of a crowd of 200 or 300 people watching from a public road who cheered when the King took a particularly high flying pheasant. When the King was a guest at Lord Stamford's house at Bradgate, some of the Leicester manufacturers declared a half-holiday. As a result several thousand men came to Bradgate to watch the shooting, impeding the shooting party and even sitting in trees in the line of fire to get a better view.[35] Deer stalking also took place away from crowds, on private moorlands (Fig. 2.1.)

Fox hunting was different. Word that a celebrity was hunting brought out the crowds and made a satisfying chase impossible. Albert Edward Prince of Wales attended a number of meets in the mid-1860s, all of which were marred (from the sporting point of view) by large fields and crowds of onlookers. At Snettisham in Norfolk in January 1863, a special train delivered 250 county and civic dignitaries. Many others made their own way

FIGURE 2.1
'The Prince
of Wales
stalking at
Balmoral
with two
sidars from
his regiment,
11th Bengal
Lancers,
1876'. From
Courtney,
Sporting Royals,
p. 109.

and the crowd was estimated at 1,500–2,000 persons and 500–600 horsemen. The sport, as described by the *London Illustrated News*, was pretty indifferent. Two years later, at Merton Hall in Norfolk, it was reported that 'upwards of 200 carriages of various descriptions and from 400–500 horsemen [were] at the meet. Persons on foot were not allowed into the park around the house and consequently the roads around the park were so thickly lined with people that they gave little chance for a fox getting away.' The crush of spectators at this meeting can just be seen in Fig. 2.2. At Sandringham in early 1866, about 500 horsemen, 200 carriages and numerous spectators on foot appeared, 'seriously hampering sport'. In short, these meets became county occasions to which a goodly number of sightseers, perhaps displaying popular royalism or merely curiosity, came to gawp. Nor was this simply a Norfolk phenomenon associated with the novelty of a royal houshold in the county. When the Prince of Wales hunted with the Quorn in 1873, 400 horsemen took the field with him. At a meet attended by him in Dorset in 1878, between 2,000 and 3,000 horsemen were said to have attended. 'The number of pedestrians was incalculable. Carriages were drawn up in long rows, the horses being taken out to economise space.' Likewise the Prince

FIGURE 2.2
'Visit of
the Prince
of Wales to
Merton Hall,
Norfolk' 14
January 1865
(*Illustrated
London News*,
21 Jan. 1865,
p.72).

and Princess attended a meet of the Essex hounds in 1889, 'the meet was the occasion of an immense gathering, people of all classes being attracted ... one of the grandest meets that has ever taken place in Essex ended in a blank day ...' In similar circumstances, when George Duke of York paid a visit to Bristol in 1902 and stopped off at Badminton for a day with the Beaufort, a field of 600 appeared and 10,000 spectators. The sport was spoiled. The answer in part was to arrange for the Prince to hunt on a by-day, advertised to a select few. This had been done when Albert Edward Prince of Wales hunted with the Quorn in 1871. Charles, Prince of Wales, adopted similar strategies, keeping his intention to hunt a secret from all except the master (although by the 1980s word of his plans might encourage big fields of hunt saboteurs as well as huntsmen.) His first hunting was done on a specially arranged by-day with the Beaufort.[36]

Queen Victoria had an view on this too, but not the one that one might expect. She disliked the exclusive character of shooting and compared it unfavourably to hunting (which, she admitted, she disliked) whose openness was the source of its popularity, and she urged her son to hunt more and shoot less.[37]

As a social activity amongst men, shooting had its international dimension.[38] Successive monarchs went abroad to shoot. Big game hunting we consider

FIGURE 2.3
The inevitable
photograph:
the extended
royal
family at
Sandringham,
1902. The
party also
included the
Kaiser and
members of
the Danish
royal family.
© V&A
Images/
Victoria
and Albert
Museum

later, but shooting was part and parcel of the pre-First World War European tour. Edward VII shot boar in Russia, elk in Sweden, and bear in Germany.[39] In 1890 he was the guest of Baron Maurice de Hirsch (1831–96) at his shooting estate at St Johann in Hungary. Hirsch, by origin an Hungarian Jew, had made a fabulous fortune out of railway development in the Ottoman Empire and whilst *persona non grata* at the Imperial court, he was made welcome in England by the Prince of Wales and maintained a house in London and racing stables at Newmarket. He also rented shooting in England. Hirsch's fortune allowed him to offer shooting on a prodigious scale. 'The bag of partridges was often something like 3,000 a day. No fewer than 200 beaters were employed. They started in a circle of about seven miles in circumference, driving the birds to the guns, who stood about sixty yards apart in a circle, which perhaps extended over three acres.' The Prince told the Duke of York that the sheer opulence of Hirsch's sport would spoil things for him at home. That said, Hirsch's game methods were not uninfluential at Sandringham.[40] The Duke of York shot Capercaillie on a state visit to Austria in 1903 and went salmon fishing in Sweden when attending the coronation of King Haakan and Queen Maud in 1906.[41]

In turn, European royalty came to England for the sport. Tsar Nicholas II sailed to Scotland in 1896 and spent time as a guest at Balmoral where he was taken stalking – which he did not enjoy – by his cousin.[42] Edward VII entertained his fellow monarchs at Windsor during his reign. The Kaiser came to England in 1902 (Fig. 2.3) and 1907 and shot at Windsor and Sandringham, going on in 1907 to shoot grouse with Lord Lonsdale at Lowther near Penrith. The Archduke Franz Ferdinand, assassinated in 1914, came over in 1913 and was nearly killed when one of the loaders fell and discharged his gun towards him while shooting at Welbeck. Whilst shooting was a social lubricant between heads of state, it was easy to be tripped up by cultural differences. The Kaiser, who was disabled from birth in one arm, impressed with his one-armed shooting, but the English were aghast at some of the activities of his entourage, including one who was found to be trying to shoot pheasant with a small bore rifle.[43]

The First World War brought an end to this sociability between heads of states. It had not completely gone though: we find Prince Philip flying to France in 1952 to shoot with the French President and Prince Bernhardt of the Netherlands and shooting with Bernhardt in Germany a few years later. Prince Charles shot wild boar, pheasant and hare whilst on a tour of Austria in 1978 and was criticised for it.[44]

III

Shooting is a catch-all term for a whole range of activities. Few types of animals have not been shot at some point by the royal family either at home or abroad. Big game shooting we consider in the next section, but the range of animals shot in England and Scotland ranges from small mammals such as rabbits and hares through to large game such as deer (and even, on one occasion, cattle[45]) and a whole variety of birds, from pigeons through pheasant, partridge and woodcock to grouse and other upland game birds.

Rabbits were part of the game provided by any shooting estate: as vermin, they could be shot without hesitation and had no closed season. The game cards for Windsor Great Park show large numbers of rabbits being shot in the reign of Edward VII, but this was after the King had stumbled over a rabbit hole and injured himself, and a decision taken to reduce their numbers. When hare shooting ceased to be practised is a bit of mystery. We find the Prince Consort stocking Windsor with hares in the early 1840s and, at about the same time, shooting them whilst visiting Stowe. The Prince of Wales certainly shot them at Sandringham, having them beaten towards the guns battue-style; and his disenchanted tenant, Mrs Cresswell, suffered from them terribly, maintaining that they were bought in to stock the estate.[46]

The royal family is, however, known for its deer stalking at Balmoral.[47] The skill is to approach the deer without being seen, heard or smelt by crawling through the heather and then dispatching a stag with a single rifle shot. The sport was introduced to the royal family by the Prince Consort and it became his major preoccupation whilst at Balmoral. After his death the Queen continued to take an obsessive interest in her guests' stalking and maintained the Stag Books herself. Since her time, every successive generation of the family has practised stalking, with shooting of the first stag being, it would seem, a royal rite of passage to be achieved by teenage princes (and, in the case of the present Queen at least), princesses. Prince

Philip, an enthusiastic stalker when younger, was initiated into the sport by his father-in-law. Princess Diana, who had shot her first stag before she married, caused an outcry by shooting another on her honeymoon. It was reported in 2001 that Prince Charles spent a fortnight stalking each October and that the royal family and their guests shot 350 deer a year.[48] Whilst the Highland deer herds were plainly managed by shooting and culling (the older stags being the prized animals in stalking), and, for long periods, maintained at artificially high levels, stalking, like big game hunting generally, came to be justified by the needs of conservation. 'Prince Philip's personal reply to the anti-blood sports people has, over the years, been streamlined into two sentences: "I don't hunt – I shoot. If you don't shoot stags in Scotland, you get overpopulation".'[49]

Whilst Balmoral is also a grouse-shooting estate, the shooting seems to have little developed over the old Queen's reign and to have always played second fiddle to the stalking. Fifty brace in a day was considered to be a good bag in the 1890s, but after the Duke of York took charge, bags increased to 500 a day and, on a day in 1922, 589 brace. He continued to develop the shooting there after he became monarch.[50] This increase in numbers was also associated with a shift towards driven grouse, forced partly by the increasing age and portliness of the Prince of Wales but also the fact that his racing commitments kept him from Balmoral at the opening of the season, after which the birds were too wild to be successfully walked-up. The adoption of driving at Balmoral gave this form of grouse shooting the royal imprimatur and it was widely followed elsewhere.[51]

Sandringham was acquired for the shooting and it remained primarily a sporting estate, with the subordination of agriculture to sport, into the twentieth century. One of the tenants on the estate when the Prince purchased it, Mrs Louisa Cresswell, finally gave up her tenancy and emigrated to the United States, but not before she published a memoir of her *Eighteen Years on the Sandringham Estate* which described her attempts to farm under the Prince's heavy-handed regime. Where, under the Prince's predecessor

> One man and a few helpers had sufficed for Mr Cowper, but now a newly-imported head keeper, with an organised staff of officials, took possession of the place in military style, and parcelled out my farm, like policeman's beats, some of the battalion being told off in charge, and a cottage built for them at either end ...[52]

The bird population was enormously increased by a number of devices. Rearing and feeding was common enough, and it was a criticism of the reared birds that they were close to tame. As Mrs Cresswell recalled, 'Any fine autumn evening at Sandringham you may see them [pheasants] perched on the park wall and not greatly disconcerted at your approach.'

(A much later visitor to Sandringham observed that 'One sees pheasants everywhere in the parks and gardens, the place is literally crawling with them'.[53]) It was sporting opinion though that after a few weeks in the wild, reared birds flew as well as wild ones.[54] That said, some observers in the reign of George V though the sport excessively easy ('They call it sport!!! Shooting tame pheasants. It does puzzle me').[55] Artificially high populations of birds were also maintained by ecological changes. Mrs Cresswell had to put up with game shelters being planted on her land as the Prince improved the sport. Later he adopted the remise method having seen it practised on Baron Hirsch's estate in Hungary. There were four remises on the estate by c.1910, each of from 12 to 20 acres in extent, planted with buckwheat, mustard and gorse: they gave additional cover for partridge to nest and feed in.[56] The result was a great increase in the supply of birds. At Sandringham (for which no systematic figures for the numbers of birds shot have ever been released), the numbers of *game* (not birds) apparently quadrupled from about 7,000 in the early 1870s to nearer 30,000 in the first decade of the next century. The insider who wrote *The Private Life of King Edward VII* said that between 1870 and 1880, the season's head of game varied from 6,800 to 8,700, but since 1880 the bags had grown from 10,000 to the 16,000 achieved in 1885–86, but it is not clear whether

FIGURE 2.4 The Prince of Wales's shooting companions: 'A big shoot at Sandringham' by T. Jones Barker (1867). The Royal Collection © 2005, Her Majesty Queen Elizabeth II.

these are figures for the birds alone. Dutt, describing the estate in 1903 or 1904, agreed that 10–12,000 pheasants were reared annually. The best season had been that of 1896–97 when 13,958 pheasants, 3,965 partridges, 836 hares, 6,185 rabbits and 453 other birds of various sorts, in all 25,397 birds and mammals, had been shot. The record bag came that season: 3,114 pheasants on 14 November 1896.[57] The increase in numbers may well reflect the extension of the area shot as well as the increased sophistication of the keeping. A letter of the Duke of York's refers to two days shooting at Sandringham with bags of over 2,000 each.[58]

After his purchase, the Prince of Wales adopted the methods pioneered at Holkham where he was a frequent guest in the 1860s.[59] He adopted 'Holkham time' (putting the clock forwards by half an hour): he was envious of the Holkham game larder and had one of his own constructed.[60] Sandringham came to be run to produce the maximum sport for the Prince and his guests (Fig. 2.4). As Mrs Cresswell described, on shooting days agricultural work was stopped and a silence settled over the estate. The day's shooting began with the Prince appearing at half past ten and the guests being conveyed by charabanc or waggonette to the site of the first drive. They would shoot until two in the afternoon and then take luncheon either in a marquee erected for the purpose or indoors if the weather was especially inclement. The prince had inherited from his father a distaste for cold luncheon so lunch was cooked on portable stoves. At luncheon the shooting party would be joined by their wives before shooting started again in the afternoon before retiring back to the house as the light failed. 'The Sandringham corps of beaters' was described as being forty strong, each member wearing 'a Norfolk smockfrock of brown fustian, with a number of a red badge' in 1877 but about 60 beaters were deployed at the turn of the century.[61] This was all done with little or no regard for the interests of the Prince's farming tenants: Mrs Cresswell complained of the damage that the beaters, shooting party and their followers did to fences, gates and crops as well as well as that caused by his hares and kangaroos.[62]

Sandringham was an estate configured around a notion of hospitality. How long did this continue after the death of Edward VII? As we saw, it is generally held that the extravagant shooting of the Edwardian age had disappeared by 1939. Whilst post-war shooting may have been coloured by the experience of wartime stalemate in Flanders, low rentals and high taxation must have prompted all but the very rich to cut their estate costs. As an illustration of one possible endgame, no less a figure than Lord Walsingham, practitioner and advocate of the mass slaughter of birds, was forced to sell up in 1912 and died abroad.[63] There was therefore a reversion to simpler, arguably more skilful types of shooting. Wentworth Day would have us believe that George V was in tune with these developments. In the King's Silver Jubilee year, he portrayed the King as a fully up-to-date figure:

The King is no lover of big bags. The artificial standard of the last generation which judged the day's sport by the numbers killed had no appeal for him. He is purely and simply a sportsman of the old order, liking to see his birds properly worked for, properly brought to the gun, cleanly shot.

He then goes on to eulogise the king's taste for wild fowling, 'one of the last forms of exercise left to the man whose heart and soul are so essentially masculine that he must by necessity escape from the shams, conventions and orthodoxies of modern life'.[64]

Against this we have to weigh the Duke of Windsor's recollection of his father's conservatism, his satisfaction with all things Sandringham and the excessive expenditure on the estate which the Duke inherited (although the estate was also known for its poor wages) before the First World War. The Duke recalled that the disregard of the tenants' interests continued into his father's time. All of this makes it unlikely that George V wholly abandoned the shoot conducted on Edwardian lines: indeed bags of 1,000 in a day are reported from Sandringham in the 1920s.[65] Windsor recalled that his father obtained more satisfaction from the 'small days' shooting and his wild fowling. He continued to peregrinate between the large houses for his shooting, expecting big bags to be laid on for him.

It may therefore be reasonable to suggest that the Edwardian age at Sandringham was ended by Edward VIII. He could, and did, shoot, but he seems to have become less interested in it with age. His disillusionment may be seen through his foreign trips. When in India in 1921–22, Lord Cromer reported, 'One of the tragic things about this tour is that HRH is not really keen on big-game shooting or shooting of any kind', preferring polo, and this caused puzzlement and hurt amongst his Indian hosts. In East Africa in 1928, his equerry noted that he was 'definitely bored by shooting and fishing', and when he returned there in 1930, he took a cine camera in place of a rifle.[66] He was therefore well out of salts with the Sandringham style before his accession. As we saw, he looked for savings in the Sandringham establishment and barely went there in the part-year he reigned. His younger brother, the Duke of York, who so unwillingly ascended the throne after the abdication as George VI, was more committed to shooting, but there is no sign that he sought to restore the glories of Edwardian Sandringham.[67] Like his Father, George VI was acknowledged to be an exceptional shot. He had taken part in the grand Edwardian battues, having joined his first shooting party at Sandringham in January 1910 (when the bag was 312 pheasants, 352 in all) and took part in such set-piece occasions as at Sandringham the following year (427 in total) or at Castle Rising with his Father and other family members in December 1925 (871 pheasants, 1,029 in all). The chronicler of the king's shooting, Buxton, suggests that he rethought his approach to shooting in and after 1921, the reason for this 'awakening' being his acquaintance with his future wife's estate at Glamis, and he evolved a style more akin to rough shooting, with a taste for wild fowling on the coastal marshes round Sandringham. After he came into Sandringham, he seems to have focused much more on the shooting of flighting duck. Duck, many of them reared, had been shot on game shoots in the late king's time, but this now became the exception and, of 567 duck recorded at Sandringham in 1937, 526 were shot on flight. The King was therefore out in the early morning and at the end of the day in his waders to catch the duck as they followed their own daily cycle. This is not to say that he eschewed grouse at Balmoral or pheasant and partridge at Sandringham. It is noticeable though, from the extracts from his game book published by Buxton, that his party on these occasions was family, including his brothers in law, and a small circle of friends.[68] Nor were the bags especially large. The Sandringham days noticed by Buxton in 1951 produced an average of 235 birds: the three days in the King's last weeks in 1952 – admittedly at the end of the season – an average of 102. The post-war days shooting at Holkham, St Pauls Walden and elsewhere, where he was guest, largely of pheasant, made an average of 469.[69]

Little is available on the conduct of shooting on the Sandringham estate over the past half century. Neither the Queen nor Princess Margaret took to the shotgun. The management of the Queen's estates therefore passed to the Duke of Edinburgh who had been tutored in shooting by his father in law. 'Mrs Helen Cathcart' reported in 1961 that 'The Duke of Edinburgh, throughout his first critical decade as a Norfolk squire, has evinced the same discriminating trend towards simplicity. The partridge drives are fewer, the birds wilder ... the Duke is better pleased with smaller occasions, enriched by a diversity of experience, in the company of close friends.'[70] The estate continued to be capable of making big bags: reportedly 9,000 in 1973–74 and 6,500 in 1979–80, but a quarter or a third of the 1890s peak.[71]

Sandringham was one of a small elite of estates – Payne-Gallway noted twelve 'successful pheasant preservers' – which were orientated towards the production of massive bags of game.[72] Agriculture was subordinated to this aim at least until 1914 and probably until 1936 when the estate establishment was severely curtailed. At the same time Sandringham seems to have lost its role as the place where a heir to the throne or monarch entertained society, and became more a retreat for the royal family, where they could go and entertain their friends and neighbours. How far the estate remained geared towards game production, and such essential facts as the numbers of gamekeepers, the numbers of birds reared, the extent of the area shot and the overall cost of the sport at all periods must remain open questions.

Stalking at Balmoral has already been mentioned. But other than deer, the opportunities for shooting big mammals were limited in Britain.[73] Travel into Europe allowed opportunities for shooting wild boar, but it was Africa and Asia which offered a palate of real exotica. 'The ambition of all sportsmen, however, turns to what is known as big game and His Royal Highness's greatest longing from the moment he set foot in India was to hunt elephant and shoot tigers.'[74] The royal highness in question was Albert Edward, Prince of Wales, but this could equally apply to successive generations of royalty.

On his early trips abroad, Albert Edward was promiscuous in what he shot. In the Holy land and Egypt in 1862 and 1869, he is said to have shot everything except chickens and goats and had to be persuaded from shooting on Sundays. The author of *The Private Life* through it entirely admirable that the young prince should have been out at six in the morning to stalk crocodile in the Nile. When they prudently stayed away, he shot flamingos, spoonbill and storks, duck and pelicans. He travelled, incidentally, with a taxidermist in his party whose duty it was to prepare some of the rarer species for a posthumous exhibition in England. On his tour of 1875–76 he shot tiger in India and elephant in Ceylon as well as going pig-sticking.[75] These were the conventional recreations of the English abroad.[76]

Successive generations took the opportunity to engage in these same sports. Prince Eddy, Edward VII's elder son, who died prematurely in 1892, shot tigers whilst in India in 1889–90. His brother, George V, Duke of York, was intending to go tiger-shooting on his Indian tour in 1903 but this stage of the tour had to be cancelled. He made up for his loss on his accession tour of India in 1911. Lord Crewe held that the King's determination to shoot big game during this tour verged on the unhinged: '… it is a misfortune for a public personage to have any taste so strongly developed as the craze for shooting is in our beloved ruler … His perspective of what is proper seems almost destroyed,' but the King took the view that having been thwarted once, this was likely to be his sole opportunity to experience this type of shooting.[77] He secured a bag of 21 tigers, eight rhinoceros and a bear. His son, the Prince of Wales, shot tigers in India in 1921–22 and the Duke and Duchess of York shot a wide range of game, including rhinoceros and elephant, in East Africa in 1924–25. Indeed, they enjoyed it so much they recommended a safari to the Prince of Wales as a tonic (although, as we noticed, his enthusiasm for the slaughter of the safari waned).[78]

It was the 1950s before British royalty ventured so far again. The Duke of Edinburgh continued the tradition of crocodile hunting. He was so taken with it in Australia in 1956 that he had a crocodile shoot arranged when he visited the Gambia river later that year.[79] By the time the Queen and

FIGURE 2.5
The last-but-
one royal
tiger hunt:
the tiger shot
by the Duke
of Edinburgh
at Sawai
Madhopur,
24 January
1961.
*Illustrated
London News*,
4 Feb. 1961,
p. 166.

the Duke visited India in 1961, domestic attitudes to big game hunting had changed. A tiger shoot had been arranged for them as the guests of the Maharaja of Jaipur in the fourth week of January, and after several fruitless days, two tigers were seen and then worked by 200 beaters into a clearing. The first was shot by the Duke, the second by his household treasurer, Admiral Bonham-Carter. *The Times* observed that the Queen would miss her opportunity to shoot a tiger as the party had to return to Delhi (Fig. 2.5). The shoot drew hostile comment in the British and Australian press: the *Melbourne Times* referred to the 'carefully organised shooting of a hearthrug'. A lesson had been learnt. Elaborate arrangements had been made in Nepal for the second sporting interlude at the end of February. There was, *The Times* reported, confidence that at least six tigers would be available. Three hundred and twenty five elephants were on hand to take part in the drive, but the Duke appeared with his hand bandaged, having acquired what one of his biographers has called a 'diplomatic whitlow'. Neither he nor the Queen shot: instead a tiger was shot by Admiral Bonham-Carter whilst the Foreign Secretary, Lord Home, made a fist of shooting a tigress. This episode was filmed, but the BBC declined to show it, and it remained unseen for quarter of a century. When finally aired in 1986, the Queen's distaste for the episode was apparent. In this way royal big game hunting was brought to an abrupt end, killed certainly by press and television coverage and public opinion, less certainly by an infected finger.[80]

V

Hunting foxes with hounds was the quintessential English sport. Odd though it might seem to modern eyes, it was, as Queen Victoria acknowledged, seen as a democratic sport, especially by comparison with shooting. Anyone with a horse could come along and hunt. Even after hunts came to rely on subscriptions, the instinct to offer a day in the field to everyone who sought it remained strong. The Prince Consort hunted both around Windsor (and with the Buckhounds) and with the Belvoir in 1843. It would seem that he cut an impressive figure in the field and this endeared him to gentry society.[81] Albert Edward Prince of Wales did his first hunting while at Oxford and then hunted intermittently through to the early 1880s, going out intermittently with the West Norfolk Hounds from Sandringham. As was shown earlier, these were probably not satisfactory sporting occasions because of the large numbers who came to see the Prince. He appears to have retired from the field in the early 1880s, his increasing stoutness

FIGURE 2.6 Sir Alfred Munnings, 'The Prince of Wales on Forest Witch' (1921). Courtesy of Felix Rosenstiel's Widow & Son Ltd.

doubtless being one reason for this, but one suspects that his heart was in shooting rather than riding to hounds. His old sporting companion, Henry Chaplin, thought that he was a better sportsman at hounds than at shooting, and wrote that 'I have no doubt that, if he had lived in a hunting rather than a shooting country, he would have continued to do so'. This is an interesting piece of geographical determinism: but it overlooks the fact that shooting, when compared to hunting, offered quite different opportunities for entertaining.[82]

The Duke of York, later George V is, like his father, thought of as a shooting rather than hunting man: yet he hunted on occasion. That his sons became enthusiastic hunters perhaps requires some explanation, but none can readily be given (Fig. 2.6). Edward, Prince of Wales had his first taste of hunting whilst a pre-war undergraduate at Oxford. After the war, he began to hunt in earnest, starting with the Pytchley and other Shire packs and moving to the Beaufort in the 1922–23 season.[83] Ziegler holds that the Duke of Beaufort disliked his forward conduct in the field and the Duchess was plotting a marriage for her daughter: after a season the Prince returned to Leicestershire.[84] Throughout the 1920s he kept a flat in Melton Mowbray and hunted regularly with the fashionable Midland packs. As we noticed, this was a sore point with his parents, his steeplechasing more so, and especially after he had a bad fall in 1924. In early 1929 he bowed to renewed requests that he should stop and sold his horses in February. That said, he seems to have continued hunting intermittently over the next few years and both Melton and the Shires continued to see him. He was still a subscriber to the Quorn in 1932.[85] His younger brother, the Duke of York, was also smitten. Starting in 1920, he too quickly established a considerable reputation for his horsemanship and showed his commitment by taking houses in the hunting shires for the season. In 1931 he decided to retire from hunting and put his stable up for auction: this was portrayed as the Duke making his contribution to the alleviation of the economic crisis. From then, the Duke's major recreation seems to have been shooting and it is as a shot that he is best known today.[86] George V's third son, Henry, Duke of Gloucester (1900–72), was known as an 'outstanding horseman and shot', who was attracted to the life of a cavalry officer; the youngest brother, George, Duke of Kent (1902–42), 'was a good shot, relishing stalking in the highlands, rode courageously to hounds and was a zealous golfer'.[87]

In the opinion of Lady Apsley, the involvement of the Prince of Wales in hunting saved the sport at a time when it was at a low ebb. 'Only those who were trying to restart hunting at that time can appreciate what it meant when the "world's most popular young man" bought a stud of the best blood-hunters and began to hunt regularly – the popularity of hunting was assured for another generation.' Hence it may be appreciated why the extension of the Prince's patronage to the Pytchley encouraged them to commission the

FIGURE 2.7 'Three royal brothers with the Quorn. The then Prince of Wales (afterwards Duke of Windsor) with the Duke of Gloucester and the Duke of Kent'. From Ulrica Murray Smith, *Magic of the Quorn* (J. A. Allen & Co., 1980).

rising artist Alfred Munnings (1878–1959) to paint the Prince on 'Forest Witch' in 1921 (Fig. 2.7). The commissioning of portraits of MFHs was not unusual but this was a rare, if not unique, accolade.[88]

After the early 1930s hunting seems to have largely lapsed amongst the royal family. The Queen is known to have gone hunting with the Beaufort in 1943 but she has never hunted as queen.[89] Her equestrian interests are well known, but focused on racing. Nor, so far as I can discover, has the Duke of Edinburgh whose interests focused on polo, and then, after arthritis made that impossible, on carriage driving. It is interesting to speculate why the Queen never took to the hunting field again. Of course, it may be a simple

FIGURE 2.8
'Watched by
the Queen,
Prince
Charles sits
astride the
Master's
hunter when
he attended
a meet of the
West Norfolk
foxhounds
at Harpley
Dams, near
Sandringham,
in January
1955.' This
innocent
photograph
raised the ire
of the League
against
Cruel Sports.
Courtesy of
Popperfoto.
com.

matter of preference: it may also be because it was deemed inappropriate after fox hunting came under parliamentary scrutiny in 1948–49. To hunt with hounds after that time was to make a political statement. It is not unreasonable to suspect that there was a tacit understanding about hunting of the sort which the League Against Cruel Sports accused Princess Anne of breaking in 1973. 'It has long been an accepted convention that the royal family does not take part in politics and other controversial matters: blood sports are even more controversial than politics.'[90]

On the other hand, the royal children were not kept so far removed from fox hunting and hunters. The National Society for the Abolition of Cruel Sports became exercised over pictures of Prince Charles and Princess Anne at a meeting of the West Norfolk foxhounds in 1955 (Fig. 2.8) and positively overheated at the thought they might be blooded (at the prospect of which they wrote to the Queen). In 1959 they wrote a letter of protest at Prince Charles attending a meeting of the West Norfolk on his pony.[91]

This surely showed that to espouse hunting would create a furore amongst the abolitionists. That such calculations played a part in the selection of royal sports is confirmed by a television interview with the Duke of Windsor in early 1970. 'I saw my great-niece, Anne, last year and said to her, I said "I know you ride very well; and I'm so glad that you enjoy riding as much as I did. But", I said, "Why don't you ever go fox-hunting?". And she said two words: "Blood Sports". So I thought to myself "Oh, what a pity!".'[92]

Within two years she had thrown such caution to the wind, going out with the Zetland twice in November 1972. This produced exchanges in the House of Commons, a Labour member saying that, '... some of us are concerned with the company she is keeping. Will she give a little less time to masters of foxhounds and a little more to the lads on the shop floor?' The League against Cruel Sports commissioned a poll which found 65 per cent of those polled disapproved of fox hunting, and 63 per cent approved of a ban on the sport. Forty-eight per cent responded that they did not think it right for the Princess to go fox hunting, 38 per cent thought she should be allowed to hunt and 15 per cent were undecided. The League claimed that it had informants in Windsor Castle who fed it information on the Princess's sporting activities: the RSPCA weighed in with a claim that she had recently been to a pheasant shoot at Sandringham. *The Times* editorialised, defending both her right to privacy and her right to hunt. Princess Anne did not stop hunting.[93] Nor did this fuss deter her elder brother from taking the field. With the encouragement of the Crown Equerry, Sir John Miller, and instruction from his sister and brother-in-law, Captain Mark Phillips, Prince Charles hunted for the first time with the Beaufort at a specially arranged day in February 1975.[94] Again, this drew criticism. The RSPCA inveighed against both the Prince of Wales and Princess Anne in November 1975. In 1978 members of the Hunt Saboteurs Association (who were carrying a banner reading 'Would One please stop hunting foxes') clashed with Princess Anne when she was out near Bicester. She was reported to have asked: 'Who is paying you?' and to have received the retort '*We* are paying *you*'. Princess Anne and Captain Phillips both justified their hunting in an interview in April 1976. So did Prince Charles when asked about it after a lecture in Cambridge in November 1978.

> The fact that I go hunting and shooting is not because I actually enjoy massacring other creatures. I deeply revel in nature. I really do enjoy animals as such. It is part of man's curious instinct over thousands and thousands of years to go hunting but perhaps my breeding is wrong.
>
> Because you kill animals does not mean that you do not appreciate them fully, and want to conserve them. I think if people did not partake in country sports in this country there would not be many animals left. And there would not be the countryside we have now. It would be a basically average desert because most farmers would rather plough up hedges for more productive land.

This did not persuade public opinion. Another poll commissioned by the League Against Cruel Sports in September 1980 found that 66 per cent were opposed to the Prince and Princess's fox hunting and only 17 per cent approved.[95] But public opinion did not alter the Prince's determination.

He made it his aim to hunt with as many packs of hounds as possible (46 by the time Clayton published his book on the Prince in 1987). This was unquestionably a world in which he felt comfortable. Like his great uncle he was said to be the model huntsman, courteous and never over pushy in the field. He told the centenary dinner of the Masters of Foxhounds Association in 1981 'of his pleasure in the opportunity which hunting gives him to meet the "ordinary British bloke"'.[96] And he continued hunting to the end.[97]

The Prince of Wales' commitment to hunting goes a long way towards explaining his decision to live at Highgrove. In the early 1970s he had been offered the use of Chevening in Kent which he first declined and then accepted. By the time Holden wrote his biography of the Prince (1978–79), he had been but an intermittent visitor to the house and was renting out its shooting.[98] In July 1980 it was reported that he was negotiating for the purchase of Highgrove near Tetbury, which the Duchy of Cornwall secured for him the following month. As *The Times'* correspondent noted, it was eight miles from Princess Anne's house at Gatcombe Park, 'and it is in the heart of the Beaufort hunting country, near Badminton, the Duke of Beaufort's home'. It was also well located for polo at Cirencester and racing at Newbury and Chepstow.[99] When the Prince and Lady Diana Spencer announced their engagement in February 1981, *The Times'* correspondent wrote that 'We note with gloom that he has got a country house in Gloucestershire to be near the hunting and the older Hooray Henrys, who seem to the captious to be too numerous amongst his close friends'.[100] *The Times'* royal wedding special issue carried an article on Highgrove which fills out this bald statement. Charles, it believed, had probably been first drawn to Gloucestershire by Captain Mark Phillips whose parents lived in the county. For Charles, the attraction was the Beaufort: 'For Charles is out with the Beaufort far more than the press records. Discreetly, he does not join at the meet, but at the prearranged first cover and duties permitting, he is out with them certainly twice a week, often more.' In Gloucestershire he was amongst friends: the Duke of Beaufort, 'a tremendous patriarchal figure hereabouts and father-figure to the young royals'; his son Edward Somerset; and 'the nearest personal friends of their own age group are Andrew and Camilla Parker Bowles, to whose son the Prince is godfather. They live nearby outside Chippenham and one hopes, will form the nucleus of a circle of like-minded co-evals.' As the same article pointed out, 'Lady Diana, unusually among English aristocratic girlhood, is not renowned as a rider'.[101] We can see the seeds here of an unhappy marriage. One spouse did not enjoy her horses where the other was an enthusiastic rider to hounds and had moved into a district to be close to his hunting mentor, old girl friend and circle of horsy friends. It marked a re-orientation of the royal family from Norfolk to Gloucestershire, from shooting to foxhunting.

FIGURE 2.9
Releasing the
carted stag,
1899. From
J. N. P. Watson,
*Victorian and
Edwardian
Field Sports
from old photo-
graphs* (1978),
p. 44.

VI

If the younger generations of the contemporary royal family clung to fox hunting to the very end, their behaviour forms an interesting counterpoint to the end of the Royal Buckhounds (staghounds) who were much criticised in the 1890s and abolished in 1901.[102] The buckhounds chased carted deer. These were semi-domesticated deer held in paddocks at Swinley near Windsor: they numbered 25 in 1892, all of them named. They were taken out by cart to wherever the hounds and field were gathered, released from the cart and then the field would follow as the deer led them (Fig. 2.9). At the end of the day the deer were carted back to the paddocks at Swinley – or, if that was too far, kept in a loose box rented for this purpose until the cart could sent to collect them (Fig. 2.10). Lord Ribblesdale, who was master from 1892–95, tells of one deer, 'The Miller', which was hunted for eleven successive seasons. They were certainly capable of long runs. Ribblesdale tells of an eight-mile run by a hind called 'Hawthorn' from Ascot Heath towards Wokingham. On another occasion, a deer called 'Lord Clanwilliam' was started at Cobham and managed to keep going until the pack lost him in the dusk, and he then remained at liberty for two or three weeks before he was caught and brought back to Swinley. One of the most famous (or infamous) runs, and one in which Albert Edward, Prince of Wales took part, was in 1868 from Denham Court near Uxbridge: the deer headed to past Pinner and Harrow Hill, then to Wormwood Shrubs and was finally cornered in the goods yard of Paddington Station. This illustrates the problem that the

Queen's buckhounds increasingly faced. The county over which they hunted was becoming progressively suburbanised and the deer had the habit of taking refuge in places – outbuildings, suburban gardens – where they were seen by a hostile public. According to Rev. J. Stratton of Wokingham, the staghounds' implacable opponent, they ran into Wokingham four times in the last months of 1892 and into Reading once, and into Wokingham twice in late 1893.[103] One letter writer to *The Times* defended staghunting, but not in metropolitan Berkshire and Surrey:

> No one can fairly deny that it is a cruel spectacle to see a stag driven through the back gardens of a town, over spiked railings and barbed wire, amongst broken bottles, tin kettles and other dangerous refuse. Clearly, every possible means should be taken to avoid such an *unsportsmanlike* exhibition.[104]

FIGURE 2.10
Recapturing
the stag: 'Stag
hunting in
Surrey: taking
the deer,
Shackleford
Pond'. From
The Graphic,
3 Jan. 1874.

Insiders, such as Lord Ribblesdale, master 1892–95, held that the hunting was not cruel to the deer. They were well looked after and the hounds were called off before they did them any harm. Mr Stratton drew on eyewitness reports to prove the contrary, and it seems well demonstrated that a minority of chases ended with injury to the deer or even its death. In December 1894 a stag was released at Gerrard's Cross. It took refuge in a garden by the canal at Iver and was chased by the hounds into the canal. They leapt into

the canal after it and could not be called off. When the deer was finally pulled from the canal, it was found to be badly bitten round the head and Ribblesdale ordered that it should have its throat cut there and then. Its corpse was then left in an outhouse until a cart could be sent to retrieve it. Or there was the end of 'Guy Fawkes' who was lost when being hunted near Marlow. When the hunt went found him, the stag had been lacerated by barbed wire and partially disembowelled on a fence. It too had to be destroyed.[105]

The buckhounds operated like a late eighteenth-century pack of foxhounds. Its patron provided sport for those who sought it. The Master of the Buckhounds was a salaried court officeholder, but he was, in the nineteenth century, a political nominee who changed with the government, Lord Ribblesdale coming into the mastership as a Liberal appointee in 1892 and Lord Coventry in 1895 with the Conservatives. The mastership was not in the royal gift, nor was it in the royal gift to disband the buckhounds which were supported out of the civil list vote. As Stratton was told in 1895, it was a matter for the government.[106] Nor were the buckhounds particularly patronised by the royal family. The Prince of Wales hunted with them in the 1860s: the Prince Imperial is noted to have been out with them in 1877. In fact the field was mostly local, and seems to have contained many farmers.[107]

Exactly when the agitation against the buckhounds began cannot be discovered. The earlier part of the Home Office file on the Buckhounds has been destroyed and what remains contains nothing before mid-1897. Certainly their continuance was a political issue when the Liberals returned to government in 1892. *The Times*, noting the beginning of the Staghounds season, also noted that this might be their last, for proposals circulated to abolish them, send them to the New Forest to hunt wild deer, or convert them into draghounds. Ribblesdale, the new master, held office as an interim appointment whilst the government decided how to proceed. In fact the government seems to have become deadlocked. Two parliamentary questions inviting it to announce its policy were laid in the Commons in the autumn of 1893 and when the Chancellor answered the second by saying, 'I am sorry this difficult question has not yet been solved', there was laughter in the chamber.[108] The Liberals went out of power in 1895 without any decision having been taken and Ribblesdale was replaced by Lord Coventry.

The reasons for the government's interest may well have arisen, in part, from the buckhounds running into Reading in late 1892 which prompted the Humanitarian League to gather a petition of 8,000 names in the town against stag hunting and Rev. Stratton a further 1,800 names in Reading and Wokingham. The Reading petition was dismissed by the supporters of the staghounds because it was signed by 'hundreds of girls from the celebrated Reading biscuit works'. It drew a counter petition said to have been signed by 15,000 farmers 'and other leading men over whose land the royal pack hunts': 'your petitioners beg to deny most emphatically that cruelty can be justly attributed to hunting with your Majesty's buckhounds'. A meeting in Windsor on 15 November resolved to petition the Queen to tell her of the injury to trade which Windsor and district would suffer the buckhounds were abolished.[109] A correspondence which ran in *The Times* over several days in January 1893 included a letter from a farmer in Wokingham saying how supportive his farming neighbours were of the hounds.[110]

This was a war of attrition. In 1894 the Humanitarian League managed to have a petition laid before the Queen and received an encouraging letter from her private secretary, Henry Ponsonby, saying that she was personally opposed to stag hunting. In the winter of 1894–95 there were moves to enact a bill to ban the hunting, coursing or shooting of semi-domesticated animals: this failed to secure a second reading in February 1895. In 1896 a letter condemning the buckhounds was sent to Lord Salisbury: amongst its signatories was the Archbishop of Canterbury. In April 1897 a meeting at Windsor of the buckhounds's supporters condemned the unfair reporting of their activities and alleged cruelties and established a committee to safeguard their interests. When a question was asked about their future in the Commons in July 1897, the government replied that there were as many who desired the continuance of the hounds as sought their abolition. In 1898 the League managed to have a selection of Stratton's pamphlets and leaflets placed before the Queen. A further parliamentary question in 1899 asked about press reports of a deer being mistreated during a chase. (This was denied by Lord Coventry.) In May the Humanitarian League convened a meeting which proposed putting forwards a 'Spurious sports bill' to suppress 'tame deer hunting, pigeon-shooting, and rabbit coursing'. When Coventry indicated that he wished to retire from the mastership in 1900, Lord Chesham was appointed in his place.[111] This was all in the face of a great deal of adverse press comment which the Humanitarian League was only too happy to gather up and reprint in its pamphlets.[112] Even the sporting press regarded the buckhounds as a 'mere fiction of chase'.[113]

Chesham was in South Africa at the time of his appointment and it is not clear whether he returned to England in time to take up the mastership before the buckhounds were abolished. On Victoria's death, the Humanitarian League moved to have a petition placed before Edward VII asking him to 'bring a prolonged agitation to a close by the discontinuance of the royal buckhounds or their conversion into a drag hunt'. They attached a list of over 200 names of people who had associated themselves with the campaign, including a good number of bishops (from both the established and Roman Catholic churches), MPs and such figures as the agricultural trade unionist Joseph Arch. There was some discussion within government as to how to proceed. It was finally decided that the League should simply be told that its petition had been placed before the King and to say no more.[114] Yet, whilst the Conservative government seems to have been more favourably inclined to the buckhounds than its predecessor, its constant peppering by the grapeshot of the Humanitarian League and unsympathetic MPs, and that the fact that the buckhounds were a lost cause at the bar of public opinion, persuaded it that they were impossible to maintain in the longer term. When the Select Committee on the Civil List convened in mid-March 1901 to examine the arrangements to be made for new reign, it was told of a proposal to abolish the buckhounds and substitute in their place a pack of foxhounds. A meeting to defend the buckhounds was convened in Windsor on 18 March and its supporters mobilised. But events were against it; when the committee reported on 4 April, it recommended both that the buckhounds be discontinued and that no hunt should be substituted its place. Its report was not debated by the House of Commons until 9 May, but to make it plain that there was to be no reprieve for the buckhounds, *The Times* reported on 13 April that the deer at Swinley had been shot. All that remained was a valedictory dinner at Windsor for the followers of the buckhounds, attended by its former masters, and, at a different time and place a presentation to Stratton for his contribution towards their abolition and other services to the humanitarian cause.[115]

Ostensibly, the end of the buckhounds was about economy. Nonetheless, it was claimed that the decision to abolish them had been the king's own, taken before the Select Committee had convened.[116] Of course, he had no need for them, for his days in the field had ended most of a quarter-century earlier. Neither the Duke of York nor any other members of his immediate family were known to be supporters of the hounds and so they could reasonably be claimed to be redundant as royal recreation. But they were the *royal* buckhounds, and based at Windsor, and their unpopularity was a charge on the popularity of monarchy generally.

VII

The importance of field sports to monarchy may now be appreciated and likewise the importance of monarchy to field sports. Activity in the field, whether shooting or hunting, was one of a number of ways in which members of the royal family have proved their fitness to lead. Of course, most royal sports have not involved killing, but almost all have involved a physicality, a muscularity, a degree of danger. Participation in previously masculine sports has been extended to a female monarch. Field sports have also been occasions to network and socialise with elite groups sympathetic to (or perhaps merely craven towards) monarchy, whether Edward VII's shooting parties or Charles Prince of Wales' hunting.

One may also notice a pattern emerging. Let us feed into this two references to sports which we have not previously considered. The first is pigeon-shooting, a fashionable mid-Victorian sport in which specially bred pigeons were released from traps to be shot at close distance by the patrons of gun clubs. The most prestigious ground was at Hurlingham, in Fulham: this is where Albert Edward first encountered Lady Mordaunt in 1868, at a 'pigeon match' between Warwickshire and Norfolk.[117] The Prince was a not infrequent patron of these matches: in 1871 the House of Commons defeated the House of Lords by 71 birds to 60 (with 81 birds missed or mangled) with the Prince of Wales taking the part of the Lords. It was notably cruel. The *Daily News* carried a scathing account of this match: *The Times* held that 'potting at pigeons' ranked below the lowest field sport. In 1872 the RSPCA addressed a memorial to the government asking it to discourage, if not actually prohibit, pigeon-shooting. The government declined to act. The Prince of Wales did, however. In 1873 he announced that he would be no longer be supporting gun clubs.[118] A little under a hundred years later, a supporter of the National Society for the Abolition of Cruel Sports wrote to the Queen about otter hunting. This was, as Charles Watkins and his colleagues show later, the moment at which concern about the declining numbers of otters became a matter of public discussion and pressure for the cessation of otter hunting grew. 'Thank you for your letter to the Queen of 8 June [1967]. Her Majesty used to subscribe to the Eastern Counties hunt up to two years ago but she no longer does so.'[119] The surprise is not that the Queen used to subscribe. Doubtless it was a small subscription, paid in a neighbourly fashion to a society of longstanding and even local prestige: but when it became morally contested, the Queen was out.

If to have been a subscriber was a minus, to have resigned before otter hunting became a matter of public concern was a plus which almost expunged years of subscriptions. Here we can see a pattern emerging. The royal family since the age of the Prince Consort have drunk heavily at the fountain of field sports. But as each individual field sport has come to be contested, the family have quietly dropped it and turned their attention elsewhere. Pigeon shooting, the royal buckhounds, quite probably fox-hunting in the later 1940s, big game hunting and latterly otter hunting, as each as has come to be contested, the royal family have quietly withdrawn their patronage and come to focus on other sports. Deer stalking, whose morality has also been questioned, is fudged and turned into a matter of managing the deer herd by selective culling. In this way, sport becomes justified in terms of conservation, an argument whose evolution deserves examination. The surprise is that fox hunting came to receive so much royal patronage after the early 1970s when the younger royals so willingly, even deliberately, set out to defy public opinion on the matter. And at the end of the twentieth century, the British monarchy still remained a hunting, shooting and fishing monarchy, rooted in the traditions of the landed gentry and their followers.

CHAPTER THREE

Sport and the survival of landed society in late Victorian Suffolk

by Edward Bujak

T HE FIFTEENTH EARL OF DERBY famously listed five reasons to explain the attraction of owning land. Firstly, there was the political influence; secondly, there was the social importance; thirdly, there was the pleasure of improving an estate and the power landowners enjoyed over the tenantry; fourthly there was the rent; and finally, there was the residential enjoyment 'including what is called sport'.[1] By 1907 the Breckland estates of Euston, Culford, Elveden, Barton and Ickworth and the Rendlesham and Sudbourne estates, on the light soils of the Suffolk Sandlings along the coast, were banded together with the Thornham, Orwell, Easton, Benacre, Henham, Downham, Flixton, Heveningham and Sotterley estates, on the heavier lands, as being 'some of the more noteworthy estates where most excellent sport is obtainable'.[2] But who are we looking at here? Who are the Edwardian owners of these noteworthy sporting estates? Elveden was owned by the plutocratic Guinness family; Euston by the Duke of Grafton, who had redeemed government sinecures valued at half-a-million pounds; Culford was owned by Earl Cadogan, who owned property worth millions of pounds in the West End of London; the Crossleys or Lords Somerleyton, with their fortune from Halifax's Crossley Carpets owned Somerleyton; the Pretymans at Orwell Park owned the port of Felixstowe. The Downham estate was owned by the civil engineering contractor Edward Mackenzie, whose neighbour, the bookseller W. H. Smith, also owned a huge sporting estate around Downham Market. By contrast, Thornham was owned by Lord Henniker, Rendlesham by Lord Rendlesham and Ickworth by the Marquis of Bristol who, together, prove the point that after 1879, 'the economic distinction was certainly becoming more marked year by year between landowners who were purely agricultural and landowners who were guaranteed a share in the wealth generated by industry and commerce'.[3]

I

After 1879 maintaining the façade of the sporting/country-house lifestyle proved increasingly difficult for purely agricultural landowners because the perennial problem of aristocratic indebtedness was now coupled to the collapse of their farm rents. The causes of indebtedness were varied. Some arose from the provision landowners were required to make for their daughters and younger sons. Under the will of Sir William Middleton, drawn-up in 1857, a portion of £30,000 was to be paid to his niece Frederica Broke on her twenty-first birthday or on the date of her marriage, whichever occurred first. The payment of such a sum could, of course, have only been met by mortgaging part of the estate. Similarly, under the proposals relating to the marriage settlement of Colonel Joshua Rowley, he was granted the power of raising £20,000, the whole to be paid out as portions to his younger children.[4] The payment of portions, and the accumulation of capital debt, could be obviated by charging annual annuities to an estate. Under the deed of settlement, arranged on the marriage of the second Marquis of Bristol to Lady Katherine Manners in 1830, annual annuities were provided for their younger children.[5] As a result, the income enjoyed by the third Marquis of Bristol from the Ickworth estate was reduced by £2,000 per annum; an additional £400 was owed to each of his two great aunts. On the other hand, whilst 'this method of provision diminished the income at the disposal of the head of the family it did not involve him in the creation of capital debt'.[6]

Alongside these familial charges, however, have to be placed improvement charges. To the second Earl of Stradbroke, President of the Suffolk Agricultural Association from 1831 to 1865, and the 'diehard Tory Protectionist' John Tollemache, the Corn Laws represented a bulwark protecting 'the agriculturalists of this country against foreign competition'.[7] Given the likelihood of the Corn Laws' repeal, agricultural improvements to boost the productivity, efficiency, and overall competitiveness of the pre-existing system of 'high' farming were thought to be the only way for arable farming to move forward. In the opinion of James Caird, 'if the farmers of England are to be exposed to universal competition, the landlords must give them a fair chance [and if] they refuse to part with the control of their property for the endurance of a lease' thanks to the growing popularity of the tenancy-at-will, then 'they must themselves make such permanent improvements as a tenant-at-will is not justified in undertaking,'[8] such as better accommodation for stock. The improvement of field-drainage was another area where landlords were expected to assist the farmer. Fortunately, landowners could spread the cost of these improvements by borrowing the money from one of the new Improvement Companies, and placing a charge on the estate. Unfortunately, the decision, by members of landed society, such as Lord Waveney at Flixton, to continue to invest in the improvement of arable farming into the 1870s was a mistake. For as Lord Ernle was to observe, 'since 1862 the tide of agricultural prosperity had ceased to flow; after 1874 it turned, and rapidly ebbed, a period of depression then began which, with some fluctuations in severity, continued throughout the rest of the reign of Queen Victoria, and beyond.'[9] Here we come to the nub of the matter. During the era of high farming, improved productivity and an expanding industrial working class (and, crucially, the absence of wheat from Russia and the United States on the market) produced rising rents, which meant existing debts could be carried without discomfort. As David Cannadine has asked, 'provided [indebtedness] could be sustained without discomfort, why should the tenant for life bother to reduce it?'.[10]

More importantly, additional mortgage debt could be added to the books 'without discomfort' to pay for building or modernising a country seat, especially with land values approaching 40 to 65 years' purchase in the 1860s. The country house building boom of the mid-nineteenth century reflects the over-confidence of mid-Victorian landowners who mortgaged their estates on the assumption that their expensive agricultural improvements had guaranteed buoyant agricultural revenues and rising land values far into the foreseeable future. Of course, should farm rents decline, as they did after 1879, the continued indebtedness of landed families became decidedly uncomfortable, forcing them, ironically, to let their new homes to help cover the mortgage repayments incurred by building them!

Mortgages were the only way to cover the cost of building or remodelling a country seat. In Suffolk, the Rous, Adair, Thellusson and Tomline families all decided to either remodel or completely rebuild their homes in the mid-nineteenth century. Sir Charles Barry was commissioned by the Earl of Stradbroke to redesign the eighteenth-century exterior of Henham Hall. After a fire had completely destroyed the interior of Flixton in the early 1840s, Sir Robert Adair commissioned Anthony Salvin (who also designed High House, Campsea Ashe for John Sheppard) to completely rebuild the Hall in the new Jacobean style. Rendlesham Hall, which was designed and built by William Burn between 1868 and 1871 for Frederick William Brook Thellusson, Lord Rendlesham (1840–1911), was also built in the Jacobean style. By comparison with Flixton, it was a singularly 'uninspired building' and it was certainly a poor imitation of the original seventeenth-century hall, which burnt down in 1830, and which had been described as a 'princely residence ... surpassed by few in the Kingdom'.[11] By the 1860s, all that remained of the original Rendlesham hall were the ruins of the front doorway. The loss was therefore a considerable one and was compounded by the loss of most of the furnishings. The overall damage was estimated at around £100,000, but, as no part of the property was insured, the cost of rebuilding and refurnishing the Hall in the 1870s fell on Lord Rendlesham. Fortunately, Lord Rendlesham's building programme was funded out of his share of the Thellusson fortune.[12] George Tomline, meanwhile, could cover the cost of William Burn's redesign of Orwell Park (completed between 1851 and 1853) out of his grandfather's clerical fortune. But for those without a family fortune, the large, short-term expenditure associated with country house-building could not have been borne without resort to external assistance in the form of a mortgage.[13] Indeed, Sir Robert Adair raised a mortgage for £51,000 at around the same time as work commenced on rebuilding Flixton Hall in 1844. Clearly, such a large sum could have had only one purpose: to pay for the re-building of the Hall. Heavy borrowing to cover rebuilding the Hall would also explain why Lord Waveney subsequently decided to embark on a programme of improvements to the somewhat neglected farms on the estate.[14]

Moreover, the effects of an earlier round of house-building were still being felt. In the eighteenth century, the Vanneck family commissioned Sir Robert Taylor and James Wyatt to build Heveningham Hall. The Hall was described by the Duc de la Rochefoucauld as 'extremely dignified and magnificent' and, whilst no figures exist regarding the cost of building the Hall, it comes as no surprise to find that, in 1839, the estate was still burdened by a mortgage for £110,000. Following the death of the second Lord Huntingfield in 1844, his Trustees used £29,000 of the £33,239 which was yielded by his life policy to repay part of this huge sum; nonetheless, the family remained deeply in debt.[15] On the other side of the county, the fourth Earl of Bristol began work on Ickworth Park, the central rotunda and the east wing of which had to be completed by the fifth Earl at a cost of nearly £40,000. Ickworth was eventually finished in 1829, but the existence of a mortgage in a set of accounts for 1865, for £7,000, raised in 1827 with Frederic Corrance of Parham Hall, provide us with a clear indication of how the sums needed to finish it were obtained; and, of course, the longevity of these debts.[16]

Landed society was, therefore, burdened by the payment of charges, annuities and the repayment of mortgages when rents began to fall in the 1870s. Despite falling rents, the full implications of what was about to befall landed society were not fully appreciated at the time – how could they be, after two decades of rising prosperity which had allowed for children to be generously provided, farms to be improved, homes to be remodelled and for ever greater quantities of game to be preserved and shot by guests staying in the Hall?

II

Back in the 1850s and 1860s, there was no real need for the landowner to consider how he spent his money after the estate's farms had been improved as the investment was sure to produce higher rents. Consequently, money was lavished on country houses and the sport that was at the heart of the sporting/country-house lifestyle. Owning and maintaining a large country house, employing a large staff and ensuring plenty of sport for one's guests was all part of that residential enjoyment which made owing land such a pleasure. The growing importance of the country house/sporting lifestyle and the shooting house-party is shown by F. M. L. Thompson who points out that during the mid-nineteenth century, the rearing and preservation of game became the most, 'widespread and most rapidly growing country pursuit' of the Victorian aristocracy and gentry, and the one pastime, 'which more than any other made country life and the ownership of estates gratifying'.[17] Similarly, as Archdeacon Grantly observed in Anthony Trollope's, *The Last Chronicle of Barset*, published in 1867, 'land gives so much more than the rent. It gives position and influence and political power, to say nothing about the game'.[18]

The growing addiction to shooting among Victorian landed society was certainly recognised by those businessmen, such as Sir Morton Peto (who built Somerleyton Hall, which was later sold to Francis Crossley) who wished to become members, and whose new homes, consequently, 'reflected the self confidence of a new race of self-made men – manufacturers, merchant princes and nouveaux riches – who had got where they were by hard work and a good head for business in an increasingly commercial world, and wanted everyone to know it'.[19] They also appreciated that 'a grand new mansion, with generous entertainments for the neighbours held within it, was a useful means of accelerating acceptance by the county'.[20] The entertainment was also to be had outside. This is why the brewer Sir William Gilstrap, after having purchased the Fornham Park estate in 1862, also decided the following year to buy an additional 2,400 acres of light land, in and around the parish of Herringswell for its sport.

In so doing, Gilstrap was buying into the key accessory to the country house – the quality of the surrounding sport. Improving the quality of sport was at the forefront of landowners' minds, on a par with improving their homes and their farms. Throughout the period we can see evidence of this in the size of the bags being taken. Frederic Corrance, reputedly one of the most distinguished sportsmen in Suffolk, recalled that,

> with the increase of game a change in guns took place. First, a powerful loading rod superseded the ramrod and materially increased the speed of loading [but this was very dangerous and] Lord Rendlesham and Admiral Rous each lost a finger. It is probable the second barrel had been left on cock ... very shortly after ... sportsmen gave up loading for themselves and employed a servant to carry a second gun. When well served the user of the old weapon could shoot nearly as rapidly as with the breechloader at a hot corner or at driven birds; and when walking up partridges there was no halt after a shot.[21]

The practice of 'walking up partridges' was described by T.W.Turner, a former head-keeper on the Elveden estate during the time it was owned by the Maharajah Duleep Singh, the last native ruler of the Punjab, who spent his latter days shooting pheasants and partridges under the watchful eye of Her Majesty's Government, and at its expense. As to the practicalities of the sport, Turner records that when out partridge shooting with muzzle-loaders 'the Maharajah [who] had three double-barrelled guns, and two loaders with blue and green coats and waistcoats, powder flasks and leather shotbags [would walk] in seed clover, which was ideal for partridges to settle in'.[22] The evidence from Elveden is illustrative of the increase in game being reared on estates in the county, especially pheasants, whose numbers increased greatly thanks to the introduction of a new system of rearing under coops.[23] In 1834, the total for the year was 674 pheasants, 392 partridges, 710 hares, 248; rabbits and 34 woodcock. By 1857, the number of pheasants and partridges shot had risen considerably: pheasants, 1,823; partridges, 3,258; hares, 821; rabbits, 368; woodcock, 33. However, these totals came from two different styles of shooting.

Pheasants were driven toward the guns whilst partridges were shot on the move. According to Corrance,

> Pheasant shooting became more of an art as more trouble was taken in the flushing of the birds. It soon became the custom to put them up so that they rose over high trees before coming to the gun. But the bouquet of birds in a grand rush seldom gave the chance of getting four cocks with four barrels [by contrast, partridges were shot on the walk, over] white turnips [where] even the red-leg would consent to remain long enough for a shot. The lines were kept with mathematical precision, and when a halt was made to load, even if a bird was winged neither dog nor man dared to forestall the advance, [so] there was a second halt to pick up. No doubt there was a certain degree of monotony in the solemn and noiseless tramp, but there was always something in front, and it was at least better than the long wait for the driven bird.[24]

The growing reputation of Elveden as a sporting estate attracted the Maharajah Duleep Singh. In the same year as Gilstrap bought Fornham, the Trustees of the Maharajah purchased the Elveden estate for £105,000 (raised through a loan at 4 per cent interest from the India Office) from the executors of the will of the late William Newton. Subsequently, in 1869, the Maharajah's Trustees also decided to purchase the neighbouring Eriswell estate for £120,000 from the New England Company for Propagating the Gospel in Foreign Parts. By now, however, an average *day's* bag had risen to between 300 and 400 pheasants, while at Heveningham and the other larger estates in the county 600 to 700 was being obtained by big shoots.

The Maharajah set out to match and surpass these figures. By 1883, the Elveden Hall estate comprised 17,210 acres of Breckland. Surprisingly, the rental value of this huge property was under £5,000 per annum. This was because only 5,000 acres were actually under cultivation and this was only undertaken because game would not stay on uncultivated land. The rest was left as uncultivated heathland and rabbit warrens and devoted to the rearing of game. The scale on which the rearing and preservation of game was undertaken on the estate aroused considerable comment. Indeed, in 1879, the Indian Government communicated its concerns to the Secretary of State for India.

> The question is not whether His Highness the Maharajah shall be maintained at [the] expense [of the Indian Treasury] in a manner befitting his historical position and his proper dignity, but whether he shall be enabled to go on enjoying the luxury of preserving game, and rendering a great estate totally unprofitable.[25]

A game card for 1877 (Table 3.1), captures their point. In just four days, the Maharajah and his guests accounted for 6,539 winged and ground game, such was the abundance of game on the estate. The sharp rise in partridges of 5 December and sharp drop in the number of pheasants would suggest a day spent walking up through turnips, but this card refers to just four days. The total for the season, September 1876 to February 1877, was 55,086 winged and ground game, whilst for the season 1885–86 the figure was 81,577 (see Table 3.2).

Table 3.1 *Game shot on the Elveden estate, 4–7 December 1877*

	Pheasant	Partridge	Hares	Rabbits	Woodcock	Gild Duck	Total
4 Dec	2,017	62	207	170	1	55	2,512
5 Dec.	6	165	43	2	1	–	217
6 Dec.	916	3	219	337	4	–	1,479
7 Dec.	1,820	44	201	262	4	–	2,331
Total	**4,759**	**274**	**670**	**771**	**10**	**55**	**6,539**

Source: Game Card, Suffolk RO (Bury), HA513/16/16.

Table 3.2 *Game shot on the Elveden estate, September 1876 to February 1877 and September 1885 to February 1886*

	Pheasant	Partridge	Hare	Woodcock	Duck	Snipe	Various	Rabbits	Total
1876–77	9,803	11,823	1,724	26	–	31	70	31,609	55,086
1885–86	11,921	9,491	1,815	77	8	1	124	58,140	81,577

Source: Nicholas Everitt, 'Shooting', in *VCH Suffolk*, II, p. 365.
Note: for 1885–86, the total for partridge includes 6,500 killed in 16 days' 'driving' by three guns.

Elveden was now in a class of its own, with bags of between 6,000 to 8,000 partridges being considered a good season. It was an extreme example of the growing popularity for rearing and preserving game, producing bags significantly higher than those taken on any of the other estates in the county, such as Euston (see Table 3.3), Thornham, Rendlesham or Heveningham. This was because the Duke of Grafton and Lords Henniker, Rendlesham and Huntingfield were also committed to improving the productivity of their farms as well as their shooting. But here too, four days shooting on these estates in the 1870s still produced bags of between 2,000 to 3,000 head of game for between six to eight guns. This is clear evidence of the sums being expended on both rearing and preserving game on these estates, which, in turn, is indicative of the confidence of the aristocracy in the apparent success of their agricultural improvements. They may also have taken their eye off the ball when it came to their debts. As Cannadine states, there can be little doubt that an important element in the aristocratic anguish felt at the end of the nineteenth century arose out of the continued burden of encumbrances, both in terms of the difficulty of providing adequate security when the capital value of land had to be written down, but also as regards the greater burden of interest charges when current income was reduced.[26]

Table 3.3 **Game shot on the Euston estate, 29 October to**
1 November 1878

	Pheasant	Partridge	Hares	Woodcock	Rabbits	Total
29 Oct.	555	51	165	1	10	782
30 Oct.	45	361	74	–	2	482
31 Oct.	3	407	13	–	6	429
1 Nov.	311	100	29	1	12	543
Total	**914**	**919**	**281**	**2**	**30**	**2,146**

Source: Game Card, Suffolk RO (Bury), HA513/16/1.

III

While spending the summer of 1879 in Southampton, the third Marquis of Bristol was surprised to receive a letter from his agent suggesting that he offer one of his tenants an abatement of rent given that 'the weather is now finer. I think it may be the same at Ickworth'; in fact, 'the crops do not look badly about here – though late.' The final decision was referred back to the agent 'if you think [it is] necessary you can offer an abatement of rent for two years of £30'.[27] The Marquis of Bristol was not alone in being sceptical of the need for wholesale reductions in rent, after the price of wheat began to fall after 1874. Given the widespread assumption that the price had dropped due to a run of poor seasons, Sir Edward Kerrison was equally cautious and did not think it 'right to reduce upon the whole in the first instance', preferring instead to take 'special cases: and all those cases where either fresh property had been brought in or a fresh tenancy had been created', reducing 'each of those as I saw fit'.[28] Of the 58 tenants on the neighbouring Flixton Hall estate (recorded in the mortgage held by the Hand in Hand Insurance Society), 41 were still paying the same rents in 1885 as they had paid in 1882. Of the remainder, 6 were paying between 10 per cent and 20 per cent less in 1885 than in 1882, whilst only 11 were granted reductions in excess of 25 per cent. As a result, Lord Waveney's overall rental income in the years preceding 1885 fell by around 9 per cent. Similarly, by the early 1880s, out of 47 farms on the neighbouring Henham Hall estate, rents had been reduced on 30. Of these, the Earl of Stradbroke granted reductions in excess of 30 per cent to only four tenants. Seven received reductions of between 20 and 30 per cent, 12 of between 10 and 20 per cent, whilst 7 more had had their rents reduced by 10 per cent or under. These adjust-ments meant that, by 1882, the Earl's overall rental income had also fallen by around 10 per cent.[29]

These modest re-adjustments confirmed the widely held belief that high farming had successfully met the challenge of global competition following the removal of tariffs in 1846. In reality, foreign competition had been held in check by the Crimean War and the American Civil War. With the conclusion of these wars, the opening up of the vast hinterlands of the United States and Imperial Russia by railways and the appearance of the Atlantic steamer, high farming was doomed. After 1884–85, as the price of wheat began to collapse, rents had to be hurriedly and drastically reduced to avoid farmers going bankrupt, but what was the impact of this on landed society and the country-house/sporting lifestyle?

By 1895, the Marquis of Bristol's rents from the Ickworth estate had fallen by 54 per cent. Across Suffolk, landlords had, by the mid-1890s, been forced to make similar reductions. The Lords de Saumarez and Henniker, William Lowther, Colonel Barnardiston, Hugh Berners, Ernest Pretyman and W. H. Smith, were all operating on rents rolls 50 per cent below their 1874–75 level. In the early 1900s, Colonel Barnardiston calculated that the loss upon his rentals since the 'good times' amounted to nearly 70 per cent and that around 60 per cent was the general figure. The rent received by the third Earl of Stradbroke from the Henham Hall estate in the early 1890s was 64 per cent lower than that received by his father in the mid-1870s. Unsurprisingly, as rents had to be reduced further and further, the pressure to sell increased. According to Fox, there were 'several landowners who are getting absolutely nothing from their property after paying out-goings and family charges'. Indeed, in the opinion of one agent, given their low incomes and high overheads, many landowners would have been 'considerably better off' if even they had given their estates away.[30]

What is more surprising, given the depressed state of affairs in the countryside in the 1880s and 1890s, is that buyers were still forthcoming. Hengrave, for example, was sold in 1897 to Sir John Wood, a wealthy cotton manufacturer from Glossop in Derbyshire, whilst, the Rougham Hall estate, which had been sold for £80,000 (having been valued at £250,000 in the 1870s) to Edwin Johnston in 1893, was resold to the publisher Sir George Agnew. Other buyers included the actuary Sir Gerald Ryan who purchased the Hintlesham Hall estate in 1909, and the brewer Sir Edward Greene, the MP for Bury St Edmunds, and the stockbroker Sir Cuthbert Quilter, the MP for South Suffolk, who had both set about building up great estates in the county. Meanwhile, the pattern of an estate passing through a rapid succession of hands was repeated by the Sudbourne estate (which neighboured the Rendlesham estate). The 11,200-acre estate was purchased in 1884 by the Liverpool banker Arthur Heywood from Sir Richard Wallace (the millionaire art collector and illegitimate son of the Marquess of Hertford) who presumably sold the estate precisely because it was a vast undeveloped game preserve and his interests lay elsewhere. Heywood, however, resold the Hall in 1898 to A. E. Wood, who, after substantially increasing the number of game on the estate, sold it in 1904 to Kenneth Mackenzie Clark, of a cotton manufacturing family hailing from Paisley. Clark, like Wood, had both the genuine desire and the where-with-all necessary to continue developing Sudbourne as one of the great sporting estates in the county. But what was the continuing attraction of buying land?

Buyers were attracted by the enduring social position and by the sport which came with the ownership of a large landed estate. In reviewing his father's decision to pour the profits of cotton-spinning into Sudbourne, Kenneth Clark recalled,

> My home was Sudbourne Hall. It had belonged to the Marquis of Hertford who bequeathed it to his son Sir William Wallace ... He gave shooting parties, after which guest were given souvenir game-books, recording the week's bag ... exquisitely bound in green morocco, with gold pheasants and partridges tooled on back and front, but the number of birds shot was relatively small. By the time my father came to Sudbourne the bags had increased enormously [under A. E. Wood], and this, of course, was his reason for buying it, he was an excellent shot and he was determined that his guests should have the opportunity of shooting more pheasants than anywhere else in Suffolk.[31]

As Girouard states, buyers 'wanted to be country gentlemen not because it would help them to get a title but because they were in love with the idea of being a country gentleman, strolling with gun under arm round their own acres'.[32] It follows that they wanted to be accepted as part of a landed society that was still wedded to the sporting tradition and studded with recognisably old names. In the 1890s, the *Estates Gazette* highlighted both the sport available on the Brecklands and the social advantages of buying an estate. One would be,

> surrounded by the estates of the Duke of Grafton, Earl Cadogan, the Marquis of Bristol, Lord de Saumarez, Lord Iveagh, Sir Robert Affleck, Sir Charles Bunbury, Sir William Gilstrap, Prince Victor Duleep Singh, Mr. Harry McCalmont, Mr. Spencer Waddington, Mr. William Angerstein, the Rev. J. S. Holden and many others.[33]

But not everyone chose to sell because landowners still had a few cards left to play; in particular, rather than sell, they could let as there were tenants ready to keep their Halls aired.

In these circumstances, landowners such as Lord Henniker, who was encumbered by what the present Lord Henniker has described as 'astronomical debts'[34] could effect a successful retrenchment. The 1880s saw him break-up his household which, in 1851, had included two governesses, a nurse, a nurse maid, a still-room maid, a needlewoman, a ladies' maid, a house-maid, a butler, two footmen, a cook and four kitchen-maids. He then let both Worlingworth Hall and Thornham Hall and applied to Queen Victoria for paid employment. Similar arrangements began to made across the county, because, as Wilson Fox reported,

> I venture to assert that the majority of estates in Suffolk either large or small, cannot be maintained in a state of efficiency out of the present rentals, and at the same time leave a sufficient margin for the landowners to live in any comfort on their property, particularly if they have a family to educate … [in fact] *some cannot [even] afford to live in their residences* … I am not referring to men who have squandered money, but to those who have always done their best … [however] small owners are usually in the worst plight.[35]

It had, of course, always been the practice among landed families to let a secondary residence. Sir William Middleton, of Shrubland Park, also owned Bramford Hall, Bosmere Hall and Livermere Park. As a result, he looked to let Livermere Park: the net annual loss to the estate when it was left unlet in 1856–57 was £600. Similarly, when Sir George Broke Middleton of Broke Hall moved into Shrubland Park on the death in 1860 of his uncle, Sir William Middleton, he too was keen to let his other homes. The difference in the 1880s and 1890s was that families now began to let their principal residences. For example, whilst Lord Henniker let Thornham, John Lloyd-Anstruther let Hintlesham Hall to the stockbroker William Quilter; Marlesford Hall, the seat of Miss Shuldham, was let to Edwin Darvall; Robert Sheriffe let Henstead Hall to Heneage Bagot-Chester; Colonel H. M. Leathes let Herringfleet Hall to Colonel Edward Butler, whilst George Holt Wilson, having successfully managed to let Redgrave Hall, removed his family to the nearby rectory. Pamela Horn has calculated that two out of every three country seats in Suffolk were let, primarily to so-called 'sporting' or 'shooting' tenants.[36]

Across Suffolk, for those aristocratic and gentry families below the emerging *über* rich plutocracy, whose incomes were tied to their farm rents and who formed the bulk of landed society, the sporting tenant was a God-send akin to the arrival of the Scottish and West County dairy and stockmen who were happy to take good mixed arable and livestock farms at knockdown rents. As one landowner revealed in 1882,

> we have five farms on our hands ... we have hired for a trifling rent the Rectory in our parish, which chanced to be vacant. We have broken up our establishment, and shut up our house [and as a result] we have a better balance at our bankers than we have ever had in our lives before.[37]

Finding a tenant, however, was a far better solution to shutting up a Hall but why would a tenant wish to hire a Hall in the midst of the agricultural depression? The answer is the same as that which motivated the buyer – country pursuits – and there were few counties better to pursue them than Suffolk. According to Nicholas Everitt, 'no counties in the Kingdom can compare with Norfolk and Suffolk for pheasant and partridge shooting, which is the better county of the two is difficult to say'.[38] Given that most Halls were not up for sale, but were available for hire, why not hire, until one came up for sale, especially as Halls were being let with the attendant sporting rights to the surrounding estate? When, as Wilson and Mackley have shown, it would have made more sense for landowners to pull their houses down and plough up the park, this is why they did not do so. Preferring to let their homes 'indicates a strong reluctance to sweep away a potent symbol of landed status, and where owners had gone elsewhere to restore their fortunes, faith that the move was just a temporary one'.[39]

It was, however, the sporting tenantry who, having hired the homes of the landed aristocracy and gentry, kept occupied the most potent symbols of landed society in the English countryside and thus perpetuated its visible continuance up to the Great War even if it was, to coin Lawrence Stone, aristocratic window-dressing. There were other tangible benefits for the landowner who still dominated the countryside. When we first see William Quilter (the future squire of Bawdsey Manor) in the county in 1882, hiring Broke Hall from Sir George Broke Middleton, with its attendant shooting-rights, for £530 per annum[40] and then, by 1885, hiring Hintlesham Hall and its shooting, we also see him on the Magistrates' Bench. The occupation, by *pseudo*-gentry, of two-thirds of the seats in the county, itself represents a major reconfiguration of landed society, but it helps to explain why a sporting tenant was accepted onto the Bench. Here, was a ready-made opportunity for an aristocracy to avoid finding themselves socially isolated in both the countryside, surrounded by empty Halls, and isolated on the Bench. The sporting tenantry, like the buyers of sporting estates, were, after all, natural allies of landed society, as they all the shared the same enjoyment of sport, and the sporting/country-house lifestyle and all that it symbolised.

In essence, the cash from sport allowed landed families to continue to live in the countryside and thereby continue to fulfil their traditional administrative functions on local elected bodies by tapping into the deferential voting patterns of the labourers and farmers who lived and worked on their estates. This, in turn, perpetuated the social influence of the great landowners which both hirers and buyers hoped would rub off on them and in the case of buyers rub the shine off their new money or titles. In 1897, for example, the Marquis of Bristol let the shooting rights of the Ickworth estate for just under £1,000 per annum.[41] Granted he did not let Ickworth, but this was a desperately needed injection of cash (eventually his nephew would pump tens of thousands of pounds into the estate to save it from destruction) enabling the Marquis to stay in the county and continue in his duties as Lord Lieutenant. Similarly, in 1889, Lord Henniker became Chairman of East Suffolk County Council. Both were in debt, both had let their shooting and, in so doing both had avoided having to sell their homes and their estates. As Charles Adeane and Edwin Savill observed, 'owing to the late agricultural depression landowners [were] often compelled through stress of circumstances to forgo their pleasures for the sake of income'.[42]

The aristocracy were fortunate to find in the sporting tenantry wealthy individuals who wanted to be country squires, who wanted to live in a draughty Hall and who wanted to shoot – because that's what a country gentleman did, they did not farm, they shot! With agriculture in the doldrums, Rider Haggard's tour of the county in 1901 exposed the total relegation of agriculture to sport. When interviewed by Haggard, the Reverend John Holden, the owner of Lackford Manor estate, disclosed that 'during the last fifteen years, every property within a radius of six miles had changed hands, for the most part fetching good prices, not on account of their agricultural value, but because that was splendid game country'. Holden considered 'local agriculture to be dead and that the land was kept in cultivation merely as a home for game, to bring in sporting rents and generally used for pleasure purposes by its owners or hirers'. Indeed, estates on the Brecklands still fetched a good price 'not on account of their agricultural value [which given the low price of wheat and the heavy inputs required to boost fertility was almost nil] but because it was splendid game country'.[43]

The degree to which farming in the 1890s and early 1900s was being governed by the requirements of sport is open to considerable debate.

Martelli suggests that high farming was necessary to produce the best sport, because otherwise game would go elsewhere. But given the collapse in the value of wheat, only someone as rich as Lord Iveagh could afford to persist with the classical four-course rotation of wheat or rye, roots, barley or oats and then seeds, with a flock of sheep on-hand to tread and manure the soil. The Reverend Holden informed Haggard that only his shooting rents allowed him to keep his light land in tillage: this land 'was not cropped on a four-course shift but was worked as cheaply as possible, the common plan being to lay down a field for three years or so, then break it up and take a root crop'.[44] What is very clear is the importance attached to keeping land in cultivation to support game and thus attract a buyer, or a hirer who would then underwrite the cost of both cultivation as well as the rearing and preservation of the game. Indeed,

> the economic value of shooting is well known ... At the present day [1907] nearly all [the Breckland estates have] been purchased or leased by men of wealth who cultivate the 'Brecks' for game, in order to improve their shooting; game thriving best where cultivation is carried on. Now-a-days ... landowners and labourers profit by the system of letting the land to a shooting tenant instead of allowing it to lie waste.[45]

The essential point was that in places where the land was uncultivated, game, especially partridges, would not stay. So, the priorities for the landowner were firstly, to keep land in cultivation as a home for game, by keeping farm tenants happy with absurdly low rents and avoid the expense of having to do it themselves, and secondly, attract a sporting tenant ready to cover any expenses as might arise. The alternative was sale. As another Suffolk landowner informed the Royal Commission on Agriculture in 1894, 'I would not let the shooting if I could possibly avoid it, but I could not hang on here if I did not'. But then, to quote the Reverand Holden, shooting rents were many landlords 'only hope [and] alone enabled him to keep his light land under the plough'.[46]

IV

Alongside the issue of keeping the land in cultivation, there was the issue of preserving the game from the predations of poachers. As noted above, by being willing to forsake their pleasures, many aristocratic landowners were able to carry on in their roles as local satraps, especially on the Magistrates' Bench. From their position on the rural Bench landowners could advertise their continued hegemony over the countryside by clamping down on poaching. The preservation of game was what often brought the labourer into contact with the judicial authority still vested in the landowner up to the First World War. To many ordinary labourers, pheasants, partridges, woodcocks, snipes, hares and rabbits had no legal owner, no more than 'thrushes or blackbirds do'.[47] Similar sentiments were expressed with regards to the eggs laid by pheasants and partridges. In 1874 a story appeared in *The Times* concerning a gentleman who confronted 40 to 50 men taking eggs from one of Lord Rendlesham's coverts. On pointing out that these belonged to His Lordship, they replied that they had as much right to them as anybody else.[48] This was described in *The Times* as an act of open defiance and is thus illustrative of both how far the preservation of game was the cause of considerable tension in the countryside and the extent to it was deemed to be an integral part of the privileges of landownership.

With regard to the former point, in 1878 Queen Victoria chided Duleep Singh for his excessive preservation of game on the Elveden estate, 'I have for some time wished to mention to you, as it is unpopular in the country … the great extent to which you preserve game – it is very expensive and much disliked for many reasons in the country'.[49] What was particularly disliked was the vigour with which landowners went after poachers. As a pheasant or a rabbit, being a wild animal, could have no legal owner, the actual 'crime' in poaching was in trespassing onto private property. Under the 1862 Prevention of Poaching Act, the 'poor man on foot with bulging pockets' could be stopped and searched by police officers if they suspected an offence had been committed. As Section Two of the Act states, 'it shall be lawful for any Constable or Police Officer … to search any person whom he may have good cause to suspect of coming from any land where he shall have been unlawfully in search or pursuit of Game'.[50] The labourer would then be summoned before Petty Sessions and fined or imprisoned. Of the 319 individuals who came before the Bench in Suffolk, in 1869, 318 were eventually prosecuted; which compares with the situation elsewhere in East Anglia (see Table 3.4). As R. M. Garnier argued, in an attempt to explain away such a vigorous application of the law, 'when a landed proprietor goes to considerable expense to confine, breed, rear and preserve naturally wild animals, it would be decidedly unjust to refuse him rights of property over them'.[51]

The great irony is that game could be reared from eggs which were poached from neighbouring estates. A case heard in Stowmarket County Court in 1864, and reported in *The Times*, centred on the reimbursement demanded by a former gamekeeper for buying eggs from poachers 'but he never bought any of his own eggs if he knew it'. Partridge eggs were 2s. per dozen in the early part of the season and pheasants were 6s. per dozen. Under the law (1 and 2 William IV, sec. 24) the buying of eggs from anyone other than a recognised game dealer was unlawful and consequently the plaintiff was unable to recover the 30s. he had expended. The importance of this case is that it raises the possibility of a gap developing in the 1860s,

Table 3.4 *Convictions under the Game Acts for the year 1869 in the Eastern Counties*

County	Total	Summary convictions				On indictment		
		Trespassing in daytime pursuit of game	*Night poaching and destroying game*	*Illegally selling or buying game*	*Total convictions*	*Overall prosecution rate (%)*	*Poaching Act (1862)*	*Being out armed, taking game and assaulting game keepers*
Suffolk	319	298	13	4	315	99	3	1
Essex	310	298	3	–	301	97	9	–
Herts.	302	259	23	–	282	93	15	5
Norfolk	258	233	–	–	233	90	22	3
Cambs.	110	92	11	–	103	94	6	1
Total	**1,299**	**1,180**	**50**	**4**	**1,234**	–	**55**	**10**

Source: 'Returns of the number of convictions under the Game Laws in separate counties in England and Wales for the year 1869', *British Parliamentary Papers* 1870, LVII, p. 105.

between the growing demand for more game for *battues*, highlighted by Corrance, and actual supply. This would certainly explain the development of programmes for rearing game under coops. The other result was an illicit trade in eggs between keepers and poachers and the emergence of the 'dirty worke, rogs tricks and disgrassful acxions'[52] of netting birds from neighbouring estates. The editor of *The Times* was appalled by the case as 'the worst of it is that, although every voice will undoubtedly be loud against the acts now made public, they only represent, in an exaggerated form, what, in a less avowed manner, is not an uncommon occurrence in game preserving districts [whereby] you create a class of poachers who are actually taken into the service of the game preservers'.[53]

If, on the one hand, the instruction to 'get eggs, honestly if you can, but get eggs' is indicative of demand outstripping supply, we can perhaps begin to understand the determination (and hypocrisy) of landowners who, on the other hand, sought to preserve every reared bird and to prosecute poachers without remorse. Is it any wonder that the labourer was angered and bemused by the attitude of landowners in seeking to preserve birds that may have been reared from eggs obtained from a poacher? Of course, the rewards offered to labourers for any nests found and for any vermin destroyed was an alternative way to preserve game and protect eggs from poachers, and thereby mitigate the impact of sport upon the labourer, but what was the attitude of the tenant-farmers toward the growing taste for shooting among their landlords?

The damage caused by ground game was a major bone of contention between landlords and tenants in Suffolk throughout the nineteenth century. Writing in 1852, Robert Raynbird complained to Sir Thomas Gage of Hengrave Hall of the damage done to his crops by hares and rabbits.

Many farmers also deeply resented having gamekeepers wandering over their farms. As one Suffolk farmer recalled, 'the Rendlesham Hall estate was [always] highly preserved for game'; in consequence, 'there was a small army of keepers all dressed in a livery of blue velvet with buttons bearing their master's coat of arms, parading about the countryside'.[54] The tenant could clearly see the overlap between farming and game preservation when he went into his fields to scare off rabbits, partridges, pheasants and hares. But, to the landlord, the issue of sport or pleasure and the day to day running of the farming side of the estate were separate. We can see this in the compensation agreements offered to tenants. On the Euston Hall estate, the Duke of Grafton granted tenants the right to claim compensation for,

> hay, manure, tillages, seed, and rent and rates of roots, and of fallows. Cost of small seeds and sowing them, farmhouse fixtures [stoves and coppers etc.]. The incoming tenant pays cost of the threshing, dressing, and delivering to market of the last years crop of corn, receiving the straw, chaff and colder arising there from as equivalent.[55]

There were also compensation agreements covering improvements, should the tenant leave a farm before receiving the full value of any improvement he had paid for, be it for draining a field or erecting a building, but there is no mention in these traditional agreements of compensation for the damage done to the crop by game. But then traditional 'custom of the country' agreements pre-dated the large-scale rearing and preservation of game. Moreover, there was the *quid pro quo* option referred to in the *The Times*, in 1864, whereby game-dealers in Leadenhall market would provide landlords with their pheasants in September, which the farmer 'upon condition of being one of the guests will readily let [the landlord] turn out upon his stubbles and shoot them off'.[56]

In addition, as compensation for any improvements was generally agreed informally between the landlord and the farmer, it would seem reasonable to assume that there would have been informal understandings between the two parties regarding compensation for any despoliation caused by game. In 1873, for instance, a prospective tenant looking to rent one of the farms on Lord Waveney's Flixton Hall estate, having assured the agent he had the £10 an acre necessary to properly stock the 300-acre farm, hoped for a clear understanding about the rights of shooting 'which I am rather fond of'.[57] It was in the best interests of both parties to find some form of compromise. Frederic Corrance, believed that on the whole, on the question of game preservation 'relations between the owner and the cultivator were friendly, and the farmers doing pretty well [during the era of high farming] in other respects, with wheat at 65s. could afford to take some interest in the sport'.[58] The involvement of the tenant farmer in shooting is significant, as it illustrates the growing influence of the large farmer because as a rule in the early Victorian era 'no tenant-farmer shot', although on the Barking Hall estate, in 1841, the Earl of Ashburnham divided his shooting-rights between his tenants in return for £100 per annum, each tenant paying a 'fair proportion of the same [for] the privilege'.[59]

It is a moot point as to how extensively this practice was followed across the county given that, from 1842 to 1853, the Earl stayed on his ancestral estates in Sussex. In this regard, the Ashburnham example looks like an arrangement opted for by an absentee landlord. But for those farmers who did not shoot and who were not prepared to tolerate game despoiling their crops, compensation was available, especially with the expansion of game preservation on the back of the growing success of artificially reared game. On estates which were highly preserved, 'tenant farmers are liberally compensated for any damage done to crops; and they are given many days sport amongst themselves'.[60] Given this situation pertained in one of the most highly preserved counties in England, we can perhaps begin to see why the Gladstonian Ground Game Act of 1880 with its allowances for tenants to shoot game without the written permission of the landlord, failed to bring the farmer into the Liberal camp despite the farmer now not doing quite so well. As the preamble to the Act states,

> it is expedient in the interests of good husbandry, and for the better security of the capital and labour invested by the occupiers of the land in the cultivation of the soil, that further provision should be made to enable such occupiers to protect their crops from injury and loss by ground game.[61]

What is important here, however, is that, with the passage of the 1880 Ground Game Act, surely the landlord would also be more at liberty to let his shooting rights to complete strangers as the landlord no longer needed to be personally involved in placating angry tenants? Clearly, this could, in turn, free those landed families in financial difficulty from any worries about the reactions of their tenantry, enabling them to raise a valuable source of extra income that would allow them to hold onto their estates. The irony, then, for the Liberal party after 1886, after the secession of the Old Whigs, is that one could argue that the Ground Game Act provided a line of credit from sporting tenants to the very people whom the Liberals were committed to overthrowing. What should not be forgotten, however, is that, alongside the relatively impoverished members of landed society, and with agriculture relegated to second place, there were now landowners, such as the Earl of Iveagh, and lessees, who were expending enormous sums of money on taking sport to the whole new level with the development of the *grand battue*.

V

In 1894 Elveden was bought by the Guinness brewing magnate Lord Iveagh from the Trustees of the Maharajah Duleep Singh. With the millions of pounds at his disposal the sport to be had on the estate expanded even further. With 70 men employed in the game department, including 24 'liveried' men (presumably, keepers, watchers and rearers), 30 warreners, and 16 horsemen and wire-fence-men, every effort was now made to maximise the number of game being reared. With 20,000 pheasants reared every season it was considered to be a 'poor day' if fewer than a thousand head of game was killed. As the magazine *Mayfair* noted, the whole estate was in effect a 'large game preserve' largely because 'the soil is poor … and does not repay cultivation'.[62] The shooting parties, usually of eight or nine guns, were driven to the first beat in shooting brakes. The beaters, a hundred strong, wore white smocks with red collars and chummy hats with red bands; the keepers, bowler hats, brown suits and leather gaiters. The whole of this array, this *grand battue*, was then marshalled and directed in its operations by the head gamekeeper, riding a pony, signalling his orders by blasts of a German hunting horn. Each drive was said to have the precision of a military manoeuvre and the birds were concentrated for the kill with smooth efficiency. Each of the guns had his own attendant although when Edward VII would come to shoot, he was attended by two loaders, a cartridge boy and a private detective. The pattern of the *grand battue* was mimicked at Sudbourne where,

> The birds were driven over the guns by an army of beaters who wore specially designed smocks with red lapels … They were accompanied by keepers who wore bowler hats. Each district had about five beats and the six or seven guns were so aligned that the birds flew out of the wood high over their heads. No-one, of course, could have been invited who was not a good shot as this was a highly competitive sport, and throughout England, shots were graded, like seeded lawn-tennis players, with Lord Ripon and the Prince of Wales at the summit.[63]

The game books at Elveden record that on the 15 November 1899, the future George V accounted for 368 pheasants, 177 partridges, 28 hares, 51 rabbits and a pig! George V was also present on 5 November 1912, when the biggest recorded bag for one day of 3,247 winged and ground game was achieved. The largest aggregate bag of the century was achieved in 1899, when 103,392 head was taken off the Elveden estate, including 21,053 pheasants. Killing on this scale was achieved thanks to the expansion of the pheasant laying pens, or pheasant 'mews' on the estate. Whole coverts, varying in size between 20 and 100 acres, were now enclosed to create massive laying pens from which pheasant eggs were collected twice a day during the laying season. These eggs were then placed under broody hens or bantams in purpose-built, enclosed hatching pens.[64]

On the Euston estate, meanwhile, a system was developed for rearing more partridges. This was the so-called Euston System and it was widely adopted across the county. Starting in mid-May, the gamekeepers began collecting the eggs from every grey partridge nest they could find on their beat. The position of the nest would be marked on map whilst the wild eggs would be substituted with dummy eggs. The eggs would then be placed under broody hens to incubate for about 10 days. As soon as the eggs were about to hatch, they were returned to the nests whence they were taken. So what had been gained by all this effort? The benefits of this system were that the gamekeeper could amass a considerable quantity of eggs and return 20 or 25 eggs to the nest rather than the approximately 15 eggs that a partridge would hatch in the wild. Moreover, the period of time during which the partridges sat on the eggs was reduced by between 9 and 11 days. Under this system, the gamekeeper could operate multiple cycles of incubation. The net result was more 'wild' young were being hatched. The Euston system was also applied to the rearing of pheasants. In a letter to *The Times*, the Duke of Grafton explained,

> In 1882, I sent for my keeper and told him I meant to have no more rearing and turning out of barn-door pheasants, he was to take all eggs laid in places liable to be taken … and add them to nests of wild birds; but at his request I allowed him to put these eggs under hens until near the time of hatching and then put them into wild birds nests, and so all were hatched wild.[65]

More bizarrely, back in the days of the Maharajah Duleep Singh, efforts had been made to introduce red grouse to the heathlands of Breckland. In 1864 and 1865, red grouse were brought down from the Maharajah's Scottish estate, Grantully in Perthshire, but the experiment failed. The failure of these efforts did not deter Lord Rendlesham from also trying, again unsuccessfully, to introduce red grouse to the Suffolk Sandlings.

These eccentricities aside, what we see with the development of the Euston and Elveden systems in the 1880s is a step change in the artificial rearing of game. Back in the 1860s it was thought in some quarters that the best way to was to 'hatch all your partridges at home, and to take up the old ones the day before you propose to shoot; and as to pheasants, that it is cheaper and surer to have them all down from London and turn them into the coverts the night before the intended *battue*'.[66] The problem with this method was, of course, where to get more eggs to boost supply, hence the emergence of the illicit trade between keeper and poacher. Having said this, growing demand in the 1860s meant 'the production of tame game is become a business; tame birds are kept in thousands in our towns and their eggs are hatched either in the town or in the country'. Given these conditions why breed pheasants at all and have to 'count the cost of keepers and watchers, and barley ricks, and altercations with tenants about rabbits and hostilities with neighbouring towns about poachers and the difficulties of keeping down the vermin and keeping up the game, to say nothing of the suspicions of the Hunt'? The answer appears to be in the desire for 'wild' game and the elimination of barn-door pheasants, but what of the cost? In the opinion of Lord Walsingham, with favourable soil, good coverts, fair neighbours, honest keepers, and good management, the artificial rearing of pheasants was remunerative 'from a pecuniary point of view, leaving out the question of sport'.[67] The key was to boost the number of birds being artificially hatched under coops and then reared, shot and sold indeed

> until the quantity of pheasants annually reared and killed was alike increased, about the year 1860, the cost of preservation was very decidedly large in proportion to the returns than it has been of late years, nor did the value of the game killed in any season cover the expenses, whereas under the existing system it undoubtedly does so.[68]

The issue here is whether, by the 1880s, landowners were 'leaving out the question of sport'. Lord Walsingham calculated that, on average, between 1865 and 1882, a shot pheasant sold at 2s. 6d. Applying these figure to those available for Elveden, the pheasants shot in the 1876–77 season would have sold for £1,225 7s. 6d.; those shot in 1885–86 would have sold for £1,490 2s. 6d.; while the 21,053 killed in 1899 would have generated a return of £2,631 12s. 6d. But these figures need to be balanced against the costs of preservation and rearing. Walsingham calculated that to rear 1,000 pheasants required a staff of one man to feed and look after 40 coops and three men or two men and a boy to assist in preparing the food. 'Their services would be required for about sixteen weeks – say up to 1 September – and if we take their wages at an average of 15s. a week, the cost is £36,' a further sum of £50 would be 'amply sufficient' to provide the necessary food, assuming 1s. for the feeding of each pheasant.[69] Hens, bought in February or March for 2s. or 2s. 4d. each, could also be sold again in August at 1s. 6d. to 1s. 8d. and by allowing 30s. for the wear and tear of coops 'and without calculating anything for the rent of the land occupied, the cost of each pheasant when turned off into the covert will be about 1s. 7d. from the time of hatching'.[70] According to these figures there would be a margin of 11d. between the cost of rearing a pheasant and selling a dead pheasant. This suggests a theoretical profit margin on the Elveden estate of £449 6s. 1d. for 1876–77 (against the cost of rearing pheasants of £776 1s. 5d.); £545 11s. 1d. (against costs of £943 14s. 11d.) for 1885–86 and £964 18s. 7d. (against costs of £1,666 13s 1d.) for 1899.

But 11d. per bird is a remarkably tight margin and as Walsingham himself admits 'it may be found in many places that this estimate is much exceeded'.[71] Moreover, this figure does not take into account the actual cost of preservation. If we take Walsingham's weekly wage of 15s. and multiply this by the 24 permanent staff of 'liveried' keepers, watchers and rearers on the Elveden then their annual salary would be £936. Of course, whilst not all estates employed a staff as large as this, we can infer the existence of a large number of gamekeepers from comments made about them by tenants on the Rendlesham estate. Given the need to preserve ever greater quantities of game, there would obviously be an increased the need for keepers. In addition, given that the cost of rearing could exceed Walsinghams' figures and that the selling cost of game would inevitably plummet as a glut of game poured onto the market, the point is underlined that sport was in fact a rich man's fancy. As a popular saying of the time went, 'Up gets a guinea, bang goes a penny halfpenny, and down comes half-a-crown'.[72] It was also a fancy that could easily escalate out of control as demonstrated by the absurd rivalry over the number of game reared and shot under the Edwardians. Indeed, is it such a surprise to find keen sportsmen, such as Lord Rendlesham and Lord Walsingham, raising money by selling land very heavily before the First World War? Nor then, should it be a surprise to find major landowners, such as the third Marquess of Bristol, choosing to leave the sporting obsessed and *über* rich to their pleasures while following the example of the landed gentry and letting his shooting to the expanding sporting tenantry?

VI

The key point is that under the Victorians, Elveden had been viewed as something of an aberration, something of an extreme case. By contrast, under the Edwardians, the other great estates began to catch up, after all, as at Sudbourne, the shooting house-parties were 'those great events in our lives at Sudbourne, which were in effect the only point of our living there at all'.[73] Under the Edwardians, Elveden re-entered the mainstream and now set the standard of what a great shoot ought to be. Thus we find Nicholas Everitt, in the *Victoria County History of Suffolk*, highlighting the fact that on another of the noteworthy estates, 20,000 pheasants and nearly 100,000 rabbits had been shot in 1905–06. This is because, having entertained the King at Elveden, Iveagh had set the standard for his fellow landowners who wished to also entertain the King. The effort involved can be gauged from a letter sent by Lady Augusta Hervey to her son, the fourth Marquis of Bristol, regarding the prospect of a visit being made by the King to Ickworth. 'There is no doubt that the King will want to shoot some day at Ickworth. The point uppermost with me is the physical exertion for you [what with] the House, the staff [etc.]. Middle-class entertaining won't do nor really bad shooting.'[74] This is why, across the county, despite the near collapse of farm rents, the Edwardian period witnessed an Indian Summer of *grand battues* and shooting parties. Those landowners without the necessary funds had, of course, either let their homes and shooting or sold their estates. But those landowners with funds settled in to enjoy themselves after a real scare and looked to entertain the King. The third Earl of Stradbroke, for example, having seen his agricultural rents fall by over 60 per cent, was still able to entertain the Prince of Wales at Henham Hall in 1906. Given that the household staff required to run the Hall included a housekeeper, a nurse, three ladies'-maids, a cook, four housemaids, four laundry-maids, two still-room maids, a schoolroom maid, a nursery maid, two kitchen maids, a scullery maid, three footmen and a butler, the Earl must have had to make recourse to non-agricultural funds.[75] Subsequently, in 1912, the Earl sold off the 1,316-acre Darsham Hall estate in 19 lots. This sale, which included 12 farms as well as several smallholdings and cottages, raised £25,200. A few years later, in 1918, the Earl's 1,251-acre Bruisyard Hall estate, 'a compact agricultural and sporting estate … capable of holding a considerable head of game' was also put up for sale in 14 lots.[76]

Lord Rendlesham of Rendlesham Hall was in a similar predicament. As farm rents began to fall and funds began to get tighter, a mortgage was raised in 1896 for £17,100 and a further mortgage for £28,000 in 1904. So the last thing Lord Rendlesham needed (with also nearly 3,000 acres in hand) was a visit from the King to one of the best shoots in England. Unfortunately, this occurred in 1907, when 2,250 partridges were killed in four days of shooting, and as middle class entertaining simply would not do, was this the event that tipped the scales which led the sixth Lord Rendlesham to start selling land after 1911?[77] The alternative to having the King descend was to move abroad. The second Lord Cranworth, closed up Grundisburgh Hall and moved to Uganda, drawn by a love of big game shooting and a shortage of cash, to enjoy 'a perfect life – aristocracy on the cheap'.[78]

By contrast, most landowners chose not to follow this example of moving to the Colonies. They preferred to follow the example of the 'big guns' and dig in. Of course, the way most found to stay put was to let their Halls and their shooting to sporting tenants but, by so doing, many of the same faces were seen on shoots, and many more new faces bolstered landed society in the dying days of the Victorian era. But eventually, as the price of agricultural land began to improve in the 1900s, more and more land began to appear on the market. Before the Great War, however, whilst one edge of landed society was looking like threadbare tweed, the other edge was lined with ermine. With *grand battues* and Royal entertainments at Elveden, Sudbourne, Rendlesham, Euston and Henham thunderously echoing across the Brecklands, the Sandlings and High Suffolk, and with aristocrats chairing the County Councils and the Bench of Magistrates, landed society looked in fine fettle. At first glance, it would appear that the

Edwardian aristocracy was enjoying one last hedonistic hurrah before the apocalypse of the Great War. In reality, of course, there had been a massive reconfiguration of landed society before the First World War with nearly two-thirds of the county's seats being occupied by sporting tenants. On the other hand, by letting their homes and their sporting rights, the gentry were still visible in the countryside and able to make their influence felt in the farmhouse and the cottage and on the sporting-field. Indeed, landed society itself seemed to be in rude health with a multiplication of squires – with established squires in the rectory or the home farm enjoying an influx of cash from the sporting tenantry, a pseudo-squirearchy, living in their Halls. What this also means is that those aristocratic families who remained seated in the county, the heavyweights like the Lord Lieutenant, the Marquis of Bristol, were not left socially isolated: the surrounding Halls, therefore, still had smoke coming out of their chimneys, the benches of the County Council Chamber and especially the Quarter Sessions were still liberally filled with squires and the sound of shooting still echoed across the countryside. But it was the financial and moral support of the sporting tenantry, attracted by the lure of the sporting-field, that perpetuated the social influence of landed society at the same time as the plutocracy was giving its membership a thunderous farewell.

CHAPTER FOUR

The shooting party: the associational cultures of rural and urban elites in the late nineteenth and early twentieth centuries*

by Mark Rothery

S HOOTING has always been a popular pastime among the English landed gentry and aristocracy. From the late eighteenth century, the sport changed from open shoots across broad stretches of ground to one that was focused on a more defined area of land, usually centred on a landed estate, in which the game was reared and strictly preserved.[1] Game books, listing those invited to each shooting party and the number of game killed, began to appear in this period and many landowners started to spend larger amounts of money on gamekeepers and game preservation.[2] Growing enthusiasm for the sport led to regular friction and conflict between landlords and tenants in the early nineteenth century under the legal conditions of the game laws and the harsh penalties for poaching they imposed.[3] Between the 1830s and 1850s, the popularity of shooting temporarily waned. But the mid-nineteenth century saw another peak in the granting of game licences, which lasted until the First World War.[4] After the 1831 and 1880 game acts, which relaxed the rules on game and gun licences and helped widen access to non-landowners,[5] the tensions in rural society previously caused by shooting generally subsided.

Shooting was not a public sport in the way of foxhunting. It usually took place on private land away from the crowds of onlookers and supporters

* The author wishes to communicate his thanks and appreciation to Dr Dennis Mills and Joan Mills, who have been very helpful in supplying some of their research and notes on the Sibthorps, Canwick and on Lindum, in Norway. The research presented here was carried out whilst the author was undertaking his doctorate in the Department of History, University of Exeter and he would also like to thank the academic staff there, especially Dr Tim Rees, for their advice and support. Appreciation is also extended to the Arts and Humanities Research Board, who supported the author's researches between 2001 and 2004.

associated with the hunting field. However, the shoot performed a number of important social and political functions for landed society beyond its attractions as a leisure pursuit. The shoot provided an opportunity for gentry and aristocratic landowners to display their propertied wealth and status to their guests. Visitors from beyond the locale were to be impressed by the family's country house, estate and dutiful servants. Similarly, local elites were to be affected by the ability of their local squire to attract high status and wealthy visitors. The shoot helped to underpin the territorial power of the gentry by associating their authority with a specific place. Local tenants were offered the patronage of the landowner in allowing them to shoot at certain times of the year. Furthermore, the shooting party was a significant form of social interaction. It was an opportunity to mix with social peers and a way of defining acceptable society: a form of social closure. Those few elite individuals who were invited to the shoot each year and received the hospitality of the landowner benefited from the social patronage this represented.

In these ways, rural sports such as shooting were an important reflection of the social position of landownership, and of the broader structure of elite 'society'. Over the past forty years various historians of the landed gentry and aristocracy have made brief comments on the significance of rural sports.[6] There are also a large number of collections of contemporary accounts of country-house shooting.[7] However, no historian, to date, has contributed an interpretation based on any significant amount of empirical research.

This chapter will make a modest start to exploring the main issues through a micro-history of one specific example: the shooting parties at Canwick, the seat of the Sibthorp family, in Lincolnshire. Rather than focus on the history of shooting as a sport per se, the analysis will focus on the function and meaning of the shooting party as a form of social interaction and associational culture involving the gentry and other elites. The second section introduces the shooting books, discusses the pattern and frequency of shooting parties up to 1914 and goes on to examine the spatial and social origins and identities of the guests. The third part explores the connections between the Sibthorps and their elite guests that formed the basis for constructing the shooting parties. It reveals the social and familial networks that lay behind the shooting parties, showing how Canwick and the Sibthorps were part of a broadly defined associational culture. In order to examine the significance of shooting further it is necessary to begin firstly, in section one, with a brief description of the family and the locale that form the subject of this discussion.

During the medieval period the Sibthorp family had been yeoman farmers in Nottinghamshire. Robert Sibthorp, who married in 1507, was the first of the family for whom any written record survives. The first major Lincolnshire estates brought into the family were obtained through the marriage of Robert's great-grandson, Gervaise (1584–1625), into the Bellamy family, of Kettlethorpe, Lincolnshire. Later Gervaise's son, also named Gervaise (1624–1704), married a merchant's widow and by the mid-seventeenth century the Sibthorps were a wealthy mercantile family living in St Mark's parish, Lincoln.

From this point onwards the Sibthorps began to accumulate landed property at Canwick through a series of marriages to co-heirs and by purchase. The Canwick estate was started by John's widow, Mary, in 1730, with the purchase of 300 acres and was extended to 600 acres in 1787. The descendants of John and Mary purchased and inherited land in the Lincolnshire marshes, in Nottinghamshire, Hertfordshire, Devon and Oxfordshire and bought property in Hatton, an estate near Canwick. Their main seat during the nineteenth and twentieth centuries, Canwick Hall, was built in 1811 (Fig. 4.1).

By 1875, at the time of the *Parliamentary Return of Owners of Land*, the Sibthorp family were the owners of 6460 acres in Lincolnshire, worth around £10,000 in rental each year. During the later nineteenth century, much of their land outside Lincolnshire was sold to service debts accrued by Charles de Laet Sibthorp, MP (1783–1855). These debts had accumulated through a combination of Charles' lavish personal and political expenditure and some longer-term problems with the purchase and management of the estates.[8] Between the 1870s and the First World War the estate around Canwick was consolidated through the purchase of Sudbrooke Holme, the building of the Dower House at Canwick, the extension of Canwick Hall and the purchase of Canwick House. By 1914, the Sibthorp's Canwick estate had reached its maximum extent.

The Sibthorps used their accumulation of landed wealth and status as a basis to access high status positions in local society and to obtain political office in Westminster. This began with John (1669–1718) who served as MP for Lincoln (1713–14). Later generations served as MP for Lincoln, county sheriff, deputy lieutenant, justices of the peace and as officers in the county militia. For much of the early and mid-nineteenth century, the Sibthorps were the main political influence in Lincoln. Charles De Laet served as the Tory MP for Lincoln almost continuously from 1826 to 1855.[9] His son, Gervaise (1815–61), served as MP for Lincoln between 1856 and 1861, and was a major in the militia.

FIGURE 4.1
Canwick
Hall.
Courtesy of
Dennis Mills.

The generation of Sibthorps that followed Gervaise, the ones who were in control of the estates during the late nineteenth and early twentieth centuries, were far less active or successful in their assumption and monopoly of office. In fact, it could be said that the Sibthorps entered the political wilderness in this period. Gervaise Sibthorp was the last of the line to hold office at Westminster since neither of his two sons, Coningsby (1846–1932) and Montague (1848–1929), stood as candidates for Parliament for the city of Lincoln or for the county.[10] The Sibthorps did continue to serve as magistrates and deputy lieutenants in Lindsey and Kesteven.[11] However, after the establishment of County Councils in 1889, the real power of these offices generally declined and landowners became a minority of magistrates, particularly in Lindsey.[12] Unlike many other Lincolnshire landed families, the Sibthorps did not become members of the County Council, either as councillors or aldermen.[13] The official links of the Sibthorps with the city of Lincoln were also lost as neither Coningsby nor Montague served as city magistrates.[14] However, despite the way the family withdrew from political life and senior positions of authority in the city, the Sibthorps continued to interact closely with the elite of Lincoln, as the shooting books show. Part of the underlying reason for this was undoubtedly the close proximity of Canwick and Lincoln.

The parish of Canwick lay adjacent to the city of Lincoln, situated in the mid-west part of the county, on the northern perimeter of the administrative

FIGURE 4.2
Canwick
and the City
of Lincoln
before
the First
World War.
Reproduced
from 1890
Ordnance
Survey map
with the kind
permission of
the Ordnance
Survey.

area of Kesteven, a mere two miles south-east of the city (Fig. 4.2).[15] Canwick
Hall, the home of the Sibthorps, had good views of the city and the
Cathedral. Although part of the petty administrative division of Grantham,
there were a number of legal and constitutional links between Canwick and
the city of Lincoln. Throughout the period the Corporation of Lincoln were
lords of the manor and, along with the Sibthorps, the main landowners in
the parish. Canwick was also a part of the Lincoln Poor Law Union and
county court district.[16]

The population of Canwick grew slightly during the nineteenth century, from 190 in 1814 to 226 in 1901. Much of this growth occurred in the final third of the century. Population levels were sustained for the remainder of the period, so that by 1931 Canwick's inhabitants numbered 231. Earlier suburban development to the south-east of Lincoln would have produced higher rates of population growth. However, in demographic terms Canwick was hardly experiencing absolute decline in this period, in either the county or national context.

There was also a level of continuity in the socio-economic structure and composition of Canwick. This was, again, largely because the city of Lincoln grew comparatively little during the period covered here, especially when compared to other urban centres in the county such as Scunthorpe. The residential suburbanisation that did take place occurred towards the south-west and the north-west of the city, rather than in the direction of Canwick, which developed later, after the Second World War.[17] This was undoubtedly due to the Sibthorps' ownership of land in the Canwick area, which they did not sell until 1940. It was as a result of later land sales by the new owners, Jesus College, Oxford, that Canwick became part of this process.[18]

The 1881 and 1891 census shows that most residents in the village were agricultural labourers, farmers or servants of the Sibthorp family: the others were involved in trades that serviced agriculture. There had been some industry in the parish, with a working mill dating from the thirteenth century and owned by the Sibthorps for much of the eighteenth and nineteenth centuries.[19] However, by the 1860s the mill had stopped production and the mill house was inhabited by estate workers and craftsmen.[20] Agriculture and related rural industries remained the main employer at Canwick.[21]

In this sense, Canwick fitted into the wider socio-economic structure of Lincolnshire at this time.[22] Lincolnshire's economy was mainly agrarian in nature and was dominated by farming. Likewise, there was a lack of concentrated urban populations and heavy industry on the scale of counties such as Lancashire and West Riding. Industry employed around fifteen per cent of the county's working population in 1881. However, heavy industry accounted for a mere three per cent of employed workers.[23] The city of Lincoln was more of an administrative centre, populated by professionals and those engaged in services, rather than an industrial and commercial one. Much of the industry that developed there did so to service agriculture.

Due to the domination of agriculture in Lincolnshire as a whole, the landowners and farmers of the county suffered relatively badly during the agricultural depression between the mid-1870s and the mid-1890s, as rents and prices declined. The national and localised effects of the depression varied according to the type of farming in each area. The areas in Lincolnshire worst hit by the depression were the lowland arable areas in the marshes, and the clay vales. Canwick was in the Trent Vale in the west of the county, which was mainly a clay area, although it also faced the cliffs to the east leading up to the heaths of mid-Kesteven.[24] In the vales to the east, where there was a concentration of landed estates, land rentals fell by an average of sixteen per cent between 1870 and 1895.[25] In contrast, the owner-occupier farmers of the Holland fens, where there were very few gentry estates, did relatively well during the depression by converting from wheat, oats and barley to the production of meat, vegetables and dairy produce, often for the expanding London market.[26] Thus, the agricultural depression served to undermine the financial basis of the gentry's power and privilege in the county.[27]

There were also changes, subtle though they were, occurring in the urban and industrial economies of the county. Despite the continuing domination of agriculture, there was a growing concentration of industry developing in Lincolnshire from the late nineteenth century onwards. In 1927 the amateur historian, Charles Brears, reflected retrospectively on these developments. He noted that there had been a growth in the manufacture of agricultural machinery at Lincoln, Grantham and Gainsborough, in ironstone mining at Scunthorpe and an expansion of Trent-side shipping in West Lindsey.[28] Clayton and Shuttleworth were amongst the largest manufacturers of agricultural machinery in the country. By 1885 they employed over 2,000 workers at their Stamp-End Works, in the city of Lincoln.[29] Brears also pointed out that Lincoln was famous for the production of tanks during the First World War and that Grimsby had grown into the world's greatest fishing port.[30] This growth of industry was beginning to alter the structure of employment in the county. By 1901 twenty-eight per cent of the working population was employed in industry, compared to one third in agriculture and almost forty per cent in the service sector. The growth of industry and the services became the general pattern of Lincolnshire's development during the twentieth century.[31]

Thus, many of the changes serving to alter the socio-economic structure of English society during this period were having an impact in Lincolnshire. The declining monopoly and remunerative value of agriculture in Lincolnshire's economy led to a rising number of wealthy elites, such as Nathaniel Clayton and Joseph Shuttleworth, whose growing incomes derived from industry and the services rather than the rental of land. Given the close proximity of Canwick to the city of Lincoln, itself a central part of these broader changes, it is not surprising that the society gathered there for shooting reflected such developments.

II

The shoots on the Sibthorp estates in and around Canwick took place between September and December each year. The details of Canwick shoots were recorded in the shooting books for 42 years, from 1884 through to 1926.[32] The numbers of shooting parties, guests and game killed have been sampled for twenty-one of these seasons. Beginning with the first listed season in 1884, samples were taken every fifth year in the long period until 1914. Every season between 1914 and 1927, including those that took place during the First World War, was then included. The guest lists were sampled from five of the seasons covered by the books, in 1884, 1894, 1904, 1913 and 1924.

The books contain lists of signatures for most shoots during each season, between September and December. It appears that all those who shot signed the books, irrespective of their status or relationship with the Sibthorps. As well as the guests, the books also detail the number of shoots in each season and the number of game shot. Although the book continues until 1940, the entries are less diligently filled out in the later period and the numbers of shoots and guests at the estate becomes very small. For this reason, the detailed analysis ends in 1924.

The number and frequency of the shoots varied as the period progressed, as did the amount of game killed during each season. Until the start of the First World War, there were around forty shoots per season. This meant that in each season of three months, the Sibthorps and their guests were shooting every second or third day. This earlier period was, thus, a very active one for Canwick shooting. During the four seasons examined, between 1884 and 1913, a total of 29,337 head of game were killed in 170 shoots. The most 'successful' shooting day was listed as the 12 December 1911, on which almost 1700 head of game were shot. Unquestionably, there was some very effective game preservation and shooting taking place at Canwick. This was achieved partly through the employment of three permanent game-keeping staff: the head gamekeeper and two underkeepers. In the context of the late Victorian and Edwardian periods, the number of game killed was a fairly common one. During the 1909 shooting season, the Duke of Portland later recalled, there had been a record number of 2,500 pheasants shot on each day for three successive days at Lord Ripon's estate in Yorkshire.[33] This reflected the rising popularity of shooting between the 1850s and the First World War that reached a crescendo in the early twentieth century. The number of guests shooting at Canwick each year remained fairly buoyant during the late nineteenth century, at between 30 and 40 per season. In the Edwardian period, however, the number of guests increased substantially to around 50 or 60 per season.

The lists of invitees to the Canwick shoot always began, of course, with the resident members of the Sibthorp family. The owner in 1884, Coningsby Charles Sibthorp, did not sign the books, although he was undoubtedly present at most shoots. In the first three sampled years Coningsby was resident in Canwick Hall with his wife Mary. Later, in 1910, he moved into the Dower House, in Canwick, upon which his brother, Montague, took up residency in the Hall.[34] In 1881 Montague was living with his wife and family at the Dower House in Canwick.[35] Montague regularly signed the book in each of the seasons between 1884 and 1924.

The wider circle of Sibthorp relations resident elsewhere in Lincolnshire were also invited. They made up a significant proportion, around ten per cent, of visitors in each sampled year, including the 1924 and 1926 seasons. These were relations deriving from female marriage as well as from the male line.[36]

The Sutton and Sutton-Nelthorpe families were particularly frequent guests throughout the period. They were resident gentry landowners at Scawby, near Brigg and in Southwell. They owned around ten thousand acres in Lincolnshire.[37] Two of the daughters of Rev. Robert Sutton, Mary and Mabel, had married the two eldest sons of Gervaise Sibthorp, Coningsby and Montague, on the same day in 1876. The two sisters were resident at Canwick for the duration of their married lives. Their four brothers, Robert, Henry, Hugh and Francis, are listed in the book from 1884 through to the First World War.[38] Also, a kin relation of the Sutton family, R. Pryor, appears in the list of names for 1884 and 1913. He was a relation of Edith Pryor, who married Francis Sutton in 1881 and whose father was a landowner at Hylands, in Essex. There were a number of visits by Rev. Charles Ellison, whose family the Sibthorps married into twice during the late eighteenth and early twentieth centuries. Other relations invited from 1904 onwards were Montague Cholmoley, John Fox, the Hon. Dudley Pelham and, in 1924, Walter Lambert, all of whom had married into the Sibthorps in the early twentieth century.

The signatures of the Sibthorp women are entirely absent from the shooting books. Neither the wives of Charles or Montague Sibthorp nor any of their female kinfolk signed the books. There were no other female guests traced either. Shooting was a particularly male-dominated sport for much of this period, unlike foxhunting, which had allowed women hunters onto the field from the mid-nineteenth century onwards. This does not preclude the likelihood that women were present during some shoots, or closely involved in the peripheral sociability that was attached to shooting. For instance, earlier in 1858, Constance Amcotts, the sister of Louisa Cracroft-Amcotts, took the role of an interested observer when she reported on a shooting party at the house of her future husband, Captain C. E. Tenant, in Staffordshire.[39] Although more women were generally given access to shooting into the inter-war period, there was no evidence of this in the Canwick shooting books.

The shoot also formed an important centre of sociability for other gentry landowners and their families dispersed in estates around the county. Edmund Turnor and his son, Christopher, consecutive owners of a 20,000-

acre estate centred on Stoke Rochford, were frequent guests between the 1880s and the 1920s. The Corbett family, landowners in Elsham, near Brigg, were also regularly invited up to the First World War. Both of these parishes were over fifteen miles away and families such as the Huttons of Gate Burton and the Hotchkins of Woodhall Spa, travelled similar distances. Other gentry guests came from the surrounding or nearby parishes. These included the Jarvis family, of Doddington, the Couplands at Skellingthorpe, and the Hood family, who were landowners in Nettleham.

In total, members of 16 different gentry families had signed the shooting book. Between them, these families owned around 100,000 acres of agricultural land in Lincolnshire in the early 1870s. This represented over six per cent of the total land in ownership in the county, and over thirty per cent of the land owned by the gentry.[40] Very few aristocratic visitors seem to have been invited, or accepted invitations, to the Canwick shoot, although there was a visit by the fourth Earl of Liverpool in 1924. He had recently purchased land in Lincolnshire.[41] Overall though, a significant section of the Lincolnshire landed society were shooting at Canwick during this period.

Most shooting guests outside the Sibthorp family and landed society were Canwick residents of various social and economic sorts. Until at least 1914 they generally lived and worked within five miles of the estate, either in Canwick village itself or one of the nearby parishes. Gamekeepers, beaters and other staff necessary for shooting signed the book in most seasons. The gamekeeper, J. Hodson, of Pitts Cottage, was regularly present during the 1884 season. From the late 1890s, a new resident gamekeeper, William Musson, had taken over and he can be found in the books up to the First World War.[42] An estate worker, 'Black', also signed the book between 1884 and 1894. Like the gamekeepers, he was there mainly to service the shoot. Individuals of this type generally signed the books on the same occasions as the higher status guests and may well have had some sport of their own during the listed shooting parties.

The signatures of tenant farmers and rural craftsmen at Canwick are also commonly found in the shooting books. In 1884, this included William Robinson, the estate carpenter and tenant of Mill House, and George Sleightholme, a farmer at Sheepwash Grange. George also shot during the 1894 season. During the 1904 and 1913 seasons, two different farmers, Herd and Davidson, signed the books. Herd had taken over from George Sleightholme at Sheepwash Grange in the late 1880s.[43] By 1913 another tenant farmer, Henry Neesham, was also a regular attendee. He had lived in Asylum Lane in the village in 1901 but, at some point in the inter-war period, took over Sheepwash Grange.[44]

Farmers and craftsmen from the surrounding parishes were another important group at Canwick shoots. In 1884, a farmer, 'Battle', signed the shooting book. This was most likely to have been Charles Key Battle, a farmer of almost 3,000 acres in St Catherine's, on the outskirts of the city of Lincoln, although there was also a smaller farmer, John Battle, in Potter Hanworth, another nearby parish.[45] It is impossible to distinguish the two since no initial was entered into the book, but these are the most likely candidates and both were the sorts of people that would be expected to have shot at Canwick. Additionally, the farmer, Frederick Scorer of Bracebridge, and Charles Wray, a boatbuilder at Burton Stather, were also guests at Canwick.

There were a number of other residents of the Canwick area of a higher social and economic status who were invited to the shoots. These were mainly local professionals of various kinds. In 1884, the auctioneer and land agent to the Sibthorps, Samuel Ogelsby, of the Estate House, signed the books several times, although did not appear later despite his continued employment into the 1900s.[46] The agent who took over the management of Coningsby Sibthorp's estates from Oglesby, Walter Meyrick, lived nearby at Sudbrooke rectory.[47] He shot at Canwick on many occasions during the 1913 season. Also during 1913, another land agent, listed as residing at Gautby and in the employ of Montague Sibthorp and Lady Alwyne Compton-Vyner,[48] was a frequent guest. Similarly, the clergy of Canwick and surrounding parishes were regular guests of the Sibthorps. In 1894 and 1913 Rev. H. Watney, the vicar of Canwick, signed the shooting book. Since the shoot took place at Sudbrooke and Washinborough as well as Canwick, the clergy of these parishes were also involved. Rev. Charles Ellison, a close relation of the Sibthorps and the incumbent at nearby Sudbrooke, was also a frequent guest. Later, in 1913, Rev. Burland, the vicar of Washinborough[49] shot at Canwick on a fairly regular basis.

The guests were not limited to those working in the rural economy. One especially interesting name in the shooting book is William Richardson, who was invited a number of times during 1894. William was a listed as a manure manufacturer and agricultural merchant in the census of 1891 and was a partner in a milling business on the waterside in Lincoln.[50] He had formerly resided at New Hall, in Canwick, but from the 1890s through to 1905 he was a tenant of the Dower House.[51] Newer types of wealth were also represented by the visits of guests such as Claude Pym, who shot at Canwick during the 1904, 1913 and 1926 seasons. He was a banker in Lincoln with Smith, Ellison and Company. He resided at Canwick House and, after the Sibthorps purchased it in 1914, became one of their tenants.

In some ways, Richardson and Pym were unrepresentative of the guests at Canwick. The two main occupational groups from which city guests to the shoot derived tended to be solicitors and retired army officers, with a smaller smattering of other professionals. Amongst the more regular visitors before 1914 were the solicitors William Danby, Frederick Larken and William Toynbee, all of who lived and practised law in the city. Charles Scorer, of

Stonebow, Lincoln, was also a regular guest from the 1894 season onwards. Other military officers who shot at Canwick included Colonel Mason of Lincoln.

However, those who derived their wealth from manufacturing industry and the commercial sector were also invited. On several occasions in 1884 and 1894, both Alfred Shuttleworth and Nathaniel Clayton-Cockburn, engineers, manufacturers and partners in the Stamp-End works at Lincoln, were invited to Canwick. Alfred was the son of Joseph Shuttleworth and Nathaniel the co-heir of Nathaniel Clayton: they had both retained family control of the Lincoln company until the early twentieth century.[52] Shuttleworth's son, Major Alfred, was also a guest there. Finally, the brewer and spirit merchant, Anthony Soames, who was based in Lincoln, Louth and several other Lincolnshire towns and cities, was a guest at Canwick in the 1894 and 1913 seasons.[53]

Overall, the shooting books uncover a fairly broad and varied group of guests in social and economic terms, from farmers to city professionals, merchants, manufacturers and the wealthier Lincolnshire gentry. There were few major changes in the type of guests invited to the shoot throughout the period. The inhabitants of the parish of Canwick, the city of Lincoln, and the landed families of the county continued to be well represented in the books, even into the inter-war period, although they did not dominate the parties to the extent they had previously as the numbers of guests from beyond the county boundaries rose. However, the guests are highly revealing of relations between different types of Lincolnshire elite and of the nature of the sociability centred on Canwick Hall. It now remains to explore the nature of the social network in more detail.

III

There were a number of different types of relationship between the Sibthorps and their guests, ranging from dependency to gentlemanly equality. The nature of all of these associations would have varied according to the relative status of the guests and the limits of Sibthorp patronage and power. These, no doubt, reflected different types of visit, from a simple days shooting to a longer-term invitation to the house for a weekend of the family's hospitality. The presence of estate workers at the shoot has been discussed earlier. This section will examine the elite guests in more detail and the sources of their shared identity and sociability with the Sibthorps.

Those invited to the shoot were a very small group given the size of Canwick and the surrounding urban and rural society. For instance, in any single shooting season, around seven or eight Canwick residents were invited, most of whom were of independent status. Likewise, the solicitors invited were a very small proportion of those listed as living and working in Lincoln across the period and it should be presumed that they had a personal connection with the Sibthorps. In this numerical sense then, the Canwick shoot was an elite activity, available to a small and select male group deemed to be suitable company and acceptable 'society' by the Sibthorp family.

Many of those invited may be considered to be 'traditional elites' and their relationships to the Sibthorps of a 'traditional rural' nature. The frequent presence of members of other landed gentry families should hardly be a surprise to social historians of landed society. As wealthy landowners, the Sibthorps would have had an identity of social, economic and, in some cases, political interests with other gentry families. The landed gentry had monopolised elite positions of authority in rural society during much of the nineteenth century. As we have seen, many were related by birth or marriage. Similarly, the local clergy were considered part of this established order. The family did not own the clerical living in Canwick and so did not have the power to appoint the vicar.[54] Thus, Rev. Watney, who often shot at the house, could not be considered to be directly dependent on the Sibthorps in the sense of employment, as some of the other local residents were. However, the local clergyman at Canwick would have depended on the social patronage of the family for beneficial access to local society in and around Canwick and Lincoln. Equally, the local landowner relied on, and expected, the established church to provide a level of social control in the parish, to maintain acceptable levels of deference and respect for the social order. Thus, there was an identity of interests between the Sibthorps and their local vicars, and a level of social equality as 'gentlemen' that explains these visits.

However, the social basis of the political and administrative elite of Lincolnshire was widening during this period in rural and urban society; the guests invited to the Canwick shoot reflected these changes. Frederick Scorer, a farmer at Sudbrooke who shot with the Sibthorps during the 1904 season, was the chairman of his parish council.[55] It was these positions of authority that served to bind the diverse and varied 'society' found at Canwick. This is supported by the way high status office connected both the rural and urban elites.

Scorer's relative, the solicitor Charles Scorer, was the clerk of the peace for Lindsey, the pinnacle of the Lincolnshire legal profession. Charles' salary for this post was £2,500 per year and it was highly likely that his realisable wealth compared favourably with some of the lesser landowners and wealthier farmers at Canwick shoots.[56] The majority of the Lincoln professionals who shot at Canwick held positions of authority and responsibility in the administration and judiciary of the city and the county. Edmund and Frederick Larken, for instance, both occupied public positions in Lincoln, Edmund as the clerk to the commission of income and land tax for the city[57] and Frederick as the city sheriff from 1886 onwards.[58] Similarly, Walter Toynbee, a partner of Frederick Larken's, was the clerk to the West Drainage Commission.[59]

The presence of two members of the Shuttleworth and Clayton families, Alfred and Nathaniel, are particularly revealing examples of the way the crème of local manufacturing wealth was gradually accepted into elite landed social circles, on the much the same basis of service and authority as other social groups.

Their fathers, Joseph and Nathaniel had relatively modest family origins, but amassed great wealth through their partnership begun in the 1840s so that, by the time of their deaths, Nathaniel Clayton and Joseph's son, Alfred, both left over one million pounds each.[60] During the 1840s controversy over the Corn Laws, while they were establishing their business in the city, the Liberals, Joseph and Nathaniel had been outspoken about the power and grip that the Tory agrarian interest had on Lincoln society and politics. They were referring, of course, to the Sibthorps and a small group of other protectionist Tory landed families, including the Ellisons, who dominated Lincoln politics during the early and mid-nineteenth century before the Liberals gained a foothold in the 1880s.[61] Later, in 1862, Clayton and Shuttleworth became involved in a dispute with the Conservatives over the Tory candidate for Grimsby, a member of the gentry Moore family, who was rumoured to have owned slaves in Rio de Janeiro.[62] In addition, a leading Lincoln radical and the owner of a flourmill in Lincoln, Charles Seeley, became business partners with Clayton and Shuttleworth in 1848.[63] Seeley was hardly the toast of Lincolnshire landed society and, no doubt, if the shooting books had covered this earlier period it seems fair to assume that Clayton and Shuttleworth, the elders, would not have been invited to Canwick.

However, as with many other businessmen in Lincoln and in English society generally, the Clayton and Shuttleworth families became increasingly 'acceptable' to Lincolnshire landed and elite society through their adoption of the necessary status symbols.[64] They had reached the higher positions in the city and county official hierarchy from the 1840s onwards. Nathaniel Clayton was a city and county magistrate during the mid-nineteenth century. He was mayor of Lincoln in 1857 and high sheriff in 1881. Joseph Shuttleworth had a similarly impressive record, having been Mayor in 1858 along with various other roles. They became involved in philanthropy, through their funding of the parish church near Stamp-End Works, St Swithin's, and their contribution to the funding and administration of schools in the city. By 1868, both had disassociated themselves from Charles Seeley, although Clayton did vote for him in the elections of that year.[65]

Additionally, both Nathaniel Clayton and Joseph Shuttleworth bought landed estates in Lincolnshire, at Withcall and Hartsholme respectively.

Nathaniel preferred to reside in his city mansion, Eastcliffe House. In the 1870s, Joseph leased his estate, at Hartsholme, to Lord Liverpool and moved to the Old Warden estate, in Bedfordshire.[66] Clayton's estate at Withcall was an experiment in mechanised and capitalised farming rather than a context for entertaining and socialising and could be seen as an extension of his business interests in agricultural machinery rather than a reflection of social aspirations.[67] However, the purchase of rural land of any kind was a significant statement in an agrarian county such as Lincolnshire and by securing property in the countryside, both Nathaniel and Joseph were clearly attempting to send certain signals to the established elites of Lincoln in the late nineteenth century.

These patterns of behaviour were repeated in the lives of their children, including the two businessmen that appear in the shooting books: Alfred Shuttleworth and Nathaniel Clayton-Cockburn. Nathaniel Clayton-Cockburn, the co-heir and son-in-law of Nathaniel Clayton, bought Harmston and became the lord of the manor there after marrying Nathaniel's daughter. Nathaniel's other daughters married into the Swan and Shuttleworth families, thereby entrenching their wealth within the two families as well as becoming family relations of some elite Lincolnshire landed clans.[68] Both Nathaniel Clayton-Cockburn and Alfred attained high positions in Lincoln society. Nathaniel, for instance, became a commander in the Lincolnshire Yeomanry.[69] Similarly, they both continued to associate the Clayton and Shuttleworth family names with philanthropic activities in the city by providing the funds for the repairs to the church at St Peter-in-Eastgate in 1894.[70]

The frequent visits for shooting by Alfred and Nathaniel were, thus, the result of an accumulation of status gained through the adoption of the recognisable signs of wealth and social standing. Equally, their presence at Canwick illustrates the open nature of gentry sociability in his period, as they merged socially and culturally with the upper sections of the middle classes in an increasingly varied, diverse and complex gentlemanly milieu.

Many guests shared the office of magistrate with the Sibthorps in the same administrative divisions. Nathaniel Clayton-Cockburn, Alfred Shuttleworth and Colonel Mason, amongst a number of other landowners who frequently shot with the family, were all magistrates for the Lincoln Petty Sessions.[71] Coningsby was a magistrate for the Lincoln South Petty Sessions, along with Henry Hutton, and other guests he invited to the shoot.[72] Charles Scorer, who was a frequent guest of the Sibthorps and a city solicitor, can be linked to the Sibthorps through his father, William, an architect. He was the surveyor of the Lawn Hospital, in Lincoln, in 1885, when Coningsby Sibthorp filled the post of treasurer there.[73] Francis Larken's brother, Rev. Edmund, was the chaplain at the Lincoln lunatic asylum when Coningsby Sibthorp also performed the role of treasurer.[74]

The social circle outlined above was even more complex and interwoven than this suggests. The Sibthorps were an important part of this network and many lines of association lead back to them, but the family and the estate were merely one nodal point within a wider system. This can be shown by the connections between the guests themselves. For instance, Charles Scorer, the high-flying solicitor mentioned earlier, was the under-sheriff of Lincoln city at the same time that Edmund Turnor, another guest, was the sheriff.[75] Robert Toynbee, a relation of Walter Toynbee, another guest at Canwick, was clerk to the visitors at the County Lunatic Asylum in 1885 at the same time that Rev. Charles Ellison was the chaplain.

As kin relations of the Sibthorp family, the Ellisons were important connecting nodes within this network and many guests can be linked with them in a number of ways. There is a probable link between the visits of Rev. Charles Ellison and another guest, Claude Pym, the banker mentioned earlier. Claude was a banker at Smith and Ellison's, in Lincoln, which was part-owned by Rev. Ellison's family, kin relations of the Sibthorps. The manager of the Smith and Ellison bank, Alexander Leslie-Melville, also visited the Canwick estate in 1904. He was the son of a Scottish Earl who had married the daughter of Abel Smith, Richard Ellison's partner.[76] The Shuttleworth family were also related to the Ellisons through Joseph's marriage to his second wife, Caroline Ellison, the daughter of Lieutenant-Colonel Richard Ellison, of Boultham, in 1861.[77] Given the regular attendance of the Ellisons at Canwick and their family connections it seems likely that the Sibthorps regarded the Shuttleworths as distant kin.

The interconnections go on. Both Edward Larken and Walter Toynbee, two solicitors invited to the shoot, were, at different moments, secretaries of the Burton Hunt. There is no doubt that many of the landed families who visited Canwick, including the Sibthorps, as well as many of the other urban guests, rode to the hounds with the Burton Hunt. Another example was Charles Scorer, who served as clerk of the peace and returning officer for the Lindsey division of Lincolnshire County Council.[78] The alderman of the council was Robert Sutton-Nelthorpe, a kinsman of the Sibthorps who regularly shot at Canwick himself.[79] Scorer was also the clerk of the endowed grammar school at Heighington, four miles south-east of Lincoln, where Coningsby Sibthorp, Alfred Shuttleworth and the Coupland family were the main landowners.

Many further connections of various kinds can be found. G. Drake, who visited in 1913, was the land agent to Robert Sutton-Nelthorpe, as well as a relation of another gentry family.[80] In other cases, social relationships may have been established or developed through the residence of certain members of the Sibthorp family in the city of Lincoln. In the 1880s, for instance, Louisa Waldo Sibthorp, the widow of Gervase Tottenham Waldo

Sibthorp (1815–61), was living in Minster Yard with her cousin, Mary Esther Sibthorp.[81] This was part of 'uphill Lincoln' that was inhabited by the middling and upper-middling elite of the city,[82] many of whom were invited to Canwick. These included the manufacturer, Alfred Shuttleworth, the solicitor, Francis Larken and the retired Army colonel, Edward Mason.[83] The close spatial proximity of sections of the Canwick network in Lincoln underlines the complexity and density of elite social circles in the area.

As this analysis suggests the connections and interconnections between those who shot with the Sibthorps at Canwick could go on much further. These ties were of a social, political, economic and cultural kind involving a series of relationships that varied from those of family and kin to those of business and politics. This network is partly a product of the insular nature of Lincolnshire society in this period. Many of the newly wealthy families, such as the Claytons and the Shuttleworths, originated from within the county. However, the Canwick shoot undoubtedly reveals some of the more general patterns to be found in the rural-urban sociability of the landed gentry.

It should be borne in mind that the social horizons of the Sibthorps were not limited to Canwick and their main estates. Canwick Hall was the main residence of the Sibthorp family and, as such, formed one of the main centres for sociability and social interactions based around pursuits such as shooting. However, it was merely one residence amongst a broader property portfolio since, as was the case with many other wealthy gentry families, they owned a series of houses. For instance, in the mid-nineteenth century they had owned a house in London, in Eaton Square, nearby other Lincolnshire landowners such as the Cholmoleys, the Turnors and the Welby Gregory's.[84]

Equally, there were other centres and occasions for sociability in and around Lincolnshire. Shooting and other field sports were social activities of a reciprocal nature and it should be expected that the Sibthorps received these kinds of invitations. There were opportunities for shooting in the north-west of the county and for hunting in the south with the Cottesmore hounds. As young men, Montague and Coningsby were, according to their uncle, famous for their shooting and riding skills, which suggests a very active level of involvement in the broader field sports community that they probably carried into their adult lives.[85] Indeed, one of the guests at Canwick, R. H. Rimington-Wilson (1852–1927), invited Montague Sibthorp and Alfred Shuttleworth, to a grouse shoot at his estate at Broomhead near Sheffield in 1905.[86] For those more interested in the 'thrill of the chase' there were the Burton, Brocklesby and Belvoir hunts and, from 1871, the Blankney hounds under the Chaplin family. There is no doubt that the Sibthorps would have attended these hunts.

Those who shot at Canwick socialised together at other types of sporting events. In 1883, the year before the shooting books were begun, Montague Sibthorp formed part of the 'Gentlemen of Lincolnshire' cricket team. A number of the guests at Canwick also played in this team. These included Walter and Robert Toynbee, Samuel Hood, Louis Marsden and Montague's cousin, Hugh Sutton-Nelthorpe.[87] Social occasions of a more sedate nature also were available to wealthy elites such as the Sibthorps. The Lincolnshire season, which ran for a few weeks each autumn, centred on the races, the 'stuff' or 'colour' balls and the assembly rooms near the cathedral.[88]

Furthermore, the enthusiasm of the Sibthorp family for sport did not end at the butt of a shotgun in Lincolnshire, but rather followed a seasonal pattern of movement and residency. The shooting at Canwick generally occurred between September and December. At other times in the year the Sibthorps made use of other properties for field sports. Between 1884 and 1914, Montague Sibthorp leased a stretch of the river Sand, in Norway, from a banker, Walter Archer, where he built a thirty-room 'fishing lodge', called Lindum.[89] Each year, at various points between May and August, Montague and his family, as well as his brother Coningsby and family, travelled to Lindum to fish for salmon. Montague also hunted for elks and stags further inland, at Steinkilen. The family was accompanied, at various points during the year, by a number of guests whose identity, as with the shooting parties, was listed in a guest book.[90] A full analysis of these signings is beyond the scope of this paper. However, it is worth briefly mentioning the types of guests that were invited for the sake of comparison.

Kin relations were equally as prominent in the guest books as they were at the Canwick shoot, and the Sutton family were amongst the most regular visitors. There were also a number of other types of wealth represented, such as the Clayton-Cockburns, of Harmston. Unlike the Canwick books, no tenant farmers or others of similar social standing were invited, illustrating the more elite nature of the Lindum fishing parties since higher levels of wealth and status would have been required to be invited or, indeed, to be able to finance travel and sport of this kind. However, there were a number of entries by a few of the Lincolnshire professionals who shot at Canwick. One name that appears repeatedly, for instance, is Louis D. Marsden, along with his wife and children. He was a surveyor, from Louth, in the north of Lincolnshire, who held a number of senior posts in the county and had shot at Canwick. Thus, the society gathered for Canwick shoots was merely a single manifestation of a wider and multi-centred culture of sociability, although it appears to have been largely representative of the Sibthorp's social universe. At least until the First World War, it was an essential, meaningful and active component of that intricate web of associations.

IV

The pattern and frequency of shooting altered quite substantially during the war years when there was a sharp decline in the numbers of shoots and, consequently, the number of game killed. Between 1914 and 1918 there were a mere seventy-six shoots during five seasons and only four thousand head of game was killed. There was a slight rally following the end of the war and up until 1921, and again in the late 1920s. However, from 1922 onwards, the frequency of shoots never fully returned to pre-war levels and this proved to be the pattern for much of the interwar period. This numerical decline was obviously mirrored by the declining numbers of guests at Canwick for shoots, and in their type. The 1913 shooting season at Canwick attracted sixty-six guests over three months. The 1921 season involved similar numbers. Thereafter, numbers declined. In 1924, a mere twelve guests were invited and even in 1926 when the number of shoots increased slightly, the shoot could muster no more than twenty.[91]

There were a number of reasons for the decline in the shooting and sociability at Canwick into the interwar period. The pre-war shoots had taken place in the five parishes of Canwick, Hatton, Washinborough, Sudbrooke and Heignton. However, due to debts incurred by an earlier generation,[92] as well as problems caused by the decline of agricultural prices and rents in the late nineteenth century, the Sibthorps were forced to sell large portions of their estates, thus reducing the opportunity for shooting.

The exact magnitude of the effect of the depression on the family's income from their Lincolnshire lands would require far more detailed analysis. It can certainly be stated, though, that Canwick was located in one of the areas of the county worst hit by the depression and that the Canwick estates had never been the most profitable in the Sibthorp property portfolio, even in the nineteenth century.[93]

The sale of the Sibthorp estates had begun with their land in the Lincolnshire marshes, and outlying properties in Oxfordshire and Hertfordshire in the 1870s and 1880s. In the interwar period the sales were extended to the Lincolnshire estates close to Canwick. In 1919, they sold their land in Sudbrooke.[94] Partly as a result, after the war, Canwick and Hatton were the only shooting grounds frequently used by Sibthorp parties. Another reason was that, from around 1918, the shooting at Hatton was leased, first to Mr Thomas Sheffield and, later, after 1922 to Mr Langham Panton.[95] Hatton was sold later, in 1936, along with Langton, the original Sibthorp estate in Lincolnshire.

In addition to fiscal problems, the family was suffering from an absolute demographic decline by the turn of the twentieth century. Coningsby and Montague had both married in 1876. However, Coningsby's marriage was childless and Montague's produced three daughters. On Coningsby's death in 1932, after Montague's in 1929, there were no male heirs to carry on the family name or the small amount of land left in their possession.[96] Of the two daughters of Montague that survived until this period, Evelyn Pelham continued to live in Canwick, at the Dower House, with her husband the Hon. Dudley Pelham.[97] What underlay the decline in the scale of the sociability centred on the Sibthorp shooting parties at Canwick was also an ageing family that was losing its physical and authoritative presence in the parish more generally.

On top of all this, it was becoming increasingly difficult and expensive for families such as the Sibthorps to obtain and retain domestic servants, both indoor and outdoor. This was due partly to out-migration from rural to urban society, partly to a rise in the wages of servants. This resulted in a general reduction in the scale of hospitality and entertainment at country houses. Given the expenses associated with shooting and the country house sociability that went with it, it seems logical that it was these kinds of pressures that also played a role in the decline of the Sibthorp's shooting parties. Ultimately, the combination of these financial and demographic pressures led to the sale of the Canwick estate, in 1940, to Jesus College, Oxford, the last year in which any entries appear in the shooting books. This signalled the end of the Sibthorps as landowners in the area, and, consequently, of the shoots that had formerly centred on the family and on Canwick Hall.

The Sibthorp experience of change in this period can be taken to be representative of many other landed families. However, despite these strong intimations of decline and retrenchment, we should be careful not to generalise too carelessly from examples of gentry families such as this and refrain from assigning their experiences to 'the decline of the landed gentry'. The lack of male heirs and the financial problems that had hung-over from earlier generations were common amongst the gentry throughout their history since the medieval period, although the long-term depression of agricultural rents created additional problems and led to far higher numbers of sales.

Equally, historians should resist the temptation to reach deterministic conclusions as to the meaning of this type of sociability between the gentry and other social groups, based on the substantial problems the gentry encountered later. The presence of large numbers of non-landed gentlemen at the Canwick shoot was not necessarily a reflection of the declining status of landownership, or, indeed, the rise of the middle classes. Rather, this reflected an active and meaningful culture of sociability in which the gentry were mixing with elites that shared many of their privileges, responsibilities and preoccupations. Certainly until the First World War, as the spending on Lindum and other concerns shows, there was little sense of inevitability about the declining position of the family and it is on this basis that their history should be evaluated.

V

The shooting parties at Canwick in the late nineteenth and early twentieth centuries offer a number of insights into gentry life and rural society in Lincolnshire during this period and indicate probable patterns amongst other families and locales of a comparable kind. They illustrate how field sports such as shooting formed a context for sociability in rural society, between various different social types, as well as providing an opportunity for the gentry to project their wealth. An invitation to shoot at Canwick was clearly a mark of elite status and acceptance by social peers, at least in the eyes of the Sibthorps. Handling and shooting a gun with reasonable skill and accuracy were considered skills common to male social elites of various kinds and, of course, formed a link with sections of the lower rural orders. Thus, as with other rural sports, shooting parties were a means of defining 'society' and, at least during this period, underpinning the local social structure.

The Canwick shoots show how rural and urban elites could be brought together, physically and socially, by such leisure activities. The books cover a period when the gentry were becoming more open to the 'society' and sociability with new wealth, and when the upper middle classes were spending increasing amounts of time and money engaged in leisure pursuits such as shooting.[98] Where an opportunity for social mixing of this kind arose through the close proximity of city and parish and where there was a high probability of such interactions, as in the case of Canwick and Lincoln, it generally occurred.[99]

This, in turn, illustrates the contours of a very fluid local elite social order in which the source of one's wealth was not of paramount importance. Service to the county and the state were considered to be at least as important as the ownership of property in defining elite status. This situation was the by-product, at least partly, of a decline in the status attached to landownership. But overall, the Canwick shoots reveal how well gentry families, such as the Sibthorps, adjusted to the changing social and economic structure, and how a pejoratively 'landed lifestyle' could impact and influence the leisure cultures of newly established wealth. Field sports, such as shooting, were both a facilitator and a lubricator for such processes.

Appendix *The Canwick shooting parties, 1884–1927*

Year*	Shoots	Game killed [†]	Guests [‡]
1884	45	4458	36
1889	47	6012	41
1894	44	6336	30
1899	50	6511	47
1904	44	9624	66
1909	48	9850	52
1913	37	8919	49
1914	17	1464	20
1915	19	1412	19
1916	14	777	12
1917	14	604	14
1918	12	757	17
1919	20	3516	28
1920	19	3650	30
1921	28	5235	33
1922	5	1356	15
1923	4	549	15
1924	9	951	12
1925	8	853	13
1926	13	1105	20
1927	11	1033	16
Total	**508**	**74972**	**587**
mean [§]	**24.2**	**3570**	**27.9**

Source: LA, SIB 1/5, Canwick Shooting Book, 1883–1940.

Notes

* The data here have been sampled at five-year intervals for the long period between 1884 and 1909. Between 1913 and 1927 the data are supplied for each year.

[†] The main types of game bird shot at Canwick were pheasants and partridges. Rabbits were also shot, although in smaller numbers according to the lists.

[‡] This refers to the total number of guests invited to the Canwick shoot over the season, not the number of guests at each shoot. However, many guests visited more than once during each season and, thus, the figures for guests do not refer to the total number of visits as a whole.

[§] Mean of 21 seasons.

CHAPTER FIVE

Wildfowling: its evolution as a sporting activity

by John Martin

WILDFOWLING involved the pursuit of migratory species of ducks, geese and a multitude of wading birds which resided in Britain during the autumn and winter months in coastal marshes, tidal estuaries and mudflats. Historically it was undertaken both to secure meat for individual needs and for sale. Unlike game birds, which were protected by a succession of game laws, wildfowl were regarded as common property. Their large size, excellent flavour and abundance made them a highly desirable quarry. Professional wildfowlers, those who pursued the activity for a living, employed a wide variety of methods ranging from duck decoys to shooting to secure the birds. Technical improvements in firearms meant that by the late nineteenth century, wildfowling had assumed the status of a field sport with the participation of increasing numbers of amateur wildfowlers. Throughout the twentieth century it experienced challenges from environmental groups, with periodic attempts to undermine the viability of the sport. Contrary to other field sports, the relationship between the practitioners and the conservationists has evolved into one of mutual respect, or at least tolerance. This chapter will explore the metamorphosis of wildfowling from a livelihood to a sporting activity dominated by amateurs.

I

In the nineteenth century innumerable wild species of geese, ducks and small wading birds were regarded as legitimate quarry by wildfowlers. Mute swans were considered prized game, despite the fact that they had been granted Royal status in the twelfth century, and a complex system of marking of beaks had been developed to denote the owner of the birds. Restrictions on the ownership of the birds was imposed in 1482/83 when all swans owned by those who held less than five marks a year in freehold land were forfeit to the King.[1] In the medieval period, swans were regarded as a delicacy and owners of manorial rights had the right to collect cygnets which were pinioned in order to prevent them from escaping from their designated ponds and fattened for ceremonial dishes at banquets. Even as late as 1874, Prince Leopold, Queen Victoria's youngest son gifted a swan to his Oxford tutor, Dr Ackland for Christmas dinner.[2]

Among the waders, partly because of its size, the Curlew was a valued source of meat in the early autumn, as epitomised in the rhyme: 'The curloo be she white, be she black, / She carries twelve pence on her back.'[3] Plovers of all kinds, as well as their smaller brethren the Knot and Dunlin, provided excellent eating and an attractive quarry when the opportunity arose.

Geese and ducks were attracted to coastal areas of Britain by plentiful food and safe roosting sites. Amongst the most favoured areas were the Fens, the low marshy lands which surrounded the Wash in the east of England. But migration levels were dependent on the vagaries of the breeding season in Arctic tundra regions such as Spitzbergen, Iceland and Greenland. Of the wild geese recorded as frequenting Britain's shores, seven belonged to the genus *Anser* (Grey geese) and four of the genus *Branta* (Black geese), although only three of each genus migrated here regularly. Amongst the genus *Anser*, which included the Pink Footed Goose, Bean Goose, White Fronted Goose and the Grey Lag Goose, only the latter was resident. However, the numbers of Grey Lag geese breeding in Britain declined sharply from the eighteenth century, becoming increasingly localised in Caithness and Sutherland. Overwintering Black geese, in particular Barnacle geese and Brent geese, were primarily maritime birds, only going inland to feed in exceptionally adverse weather conditions. These two species of birds, which lived in lower estuaries and flew mainly over water, were rarely shot by shore gunners. The behaviour of these species of Black geese was in stark contrast to that of the Canada goose, which resided primarily inland, remaining in Britain throughout the summer breeding season. This behaviour reflected the fact that the Canada Goose was descended from stock originally imported from America which had assumed a feral lifestyle.[4]

Ducks can be divided into four groups. Shelducks (including its namesake), distinguished by their large goose-like carriage and rarity; surface feeding ducks including the Mallard, Teal and Wigeon; diving ducks including the Common Pochard, Tufted Duck and Scaup Duck; and the sawbills including the Goosander, the Red-breasted Merganser recognised by its long slender bill, and the Smew. The most numerous and important species of duck from the wildfowler's point of view were the surface-feeding ducks and, in particular, the Mallard, which was the most ubiquitous and abundant species of duck in Britain at all times of the year, and denoted by the Victorians as the 'wild duck'. Large numbers of the species resided permanently in Britain and they were more frequently found inland, although coastal populations were swollen in the autumn by an influx of winter visitors. In contrast, the

Wigeon was almost exclusively a winter coastal visitor, first recorded as breeding in Scotland at the beginning of the nineteenth century, and in England towards the end of the century. However, the size of the resident breeding population of Wigeon was inflated by the presence of birds known to have escaped from collections.

II

FIGURE 5.1
The Duck decoy: 'The mouth of a pipe, showing drop-net'. From Earl of Suffolk and Berkshire (ed.), *The Encyclopaedia of Sport* (4 vols, 1911), II, p.74.

Prior to the advent of efficient, smooth-bore guns in the nineteenth century, wildfowl were captured by a variety of methods. For example, duck catching using hand nets was a favourite sport of Japanese aristocratic families although, by the onset of the twentieth century, it was confined mainly to the Imperial family.[5] In Britain, as early as the thirteenth century, ducks were caught by driving them into specially constructed tunnel nets during the summer moulting season when they were unable to fly. This practice was well established in the Fens, where the birds were most plentiful, and enabled many of the local inhabitants to make a living by a combination of fowling and fishing. Summer netting became so destructive of wildfowl that the Government passed an Act of Parliament in 1534 prohibiting 'commoners to take fen wildfowl with nets and other engines' during

the moulting season. Catching the birds by dragging a long net over the quarry when the birds were asleep, or using a baited cage in which to lure the quarry, continued to be practised.[6] But the reclamation of the Fens for agricultural use in the seventeenth and eighteenth centuries undermined wildfowling as an economic activity in this area.[7]

The best documented method of taking surface-feeding ducks was the use of decoy ponds, which were constructed in secluded spots where the birds would suffer minimal disturbance. These were wide-mouthed, open-ended tunnels which looked like a transparent circular pipe, gradually decreasing in size, and covered by thin netting (Fig. 5.1). Food was used to entice birds into decoys, often in combination with tame ducks. Decoymen exploited the fact that ducks were prone to follow small dogs trained to run alongside the pipes, appearing and disappearing behind specially constructed screens, thus luring the birds into the narrow end of the pipe until they reached the end (Fig. 5.2). Once sufficient ducks had been enticed inside the tunnels, the entrance was closed by the decoyman, who then drove the birds deep into the tunnels in order to catch them.

Sir William Wodehouse is credited with establishing the first decoy of this type at Winterton in the seventeenth century.[8] By the early eighteenth century, there were more than one hundred duck decoys in the eastern counties and two hundred or so nationally. Calculating the numbers of ducks

FIGURE 5.2 The Duck Decoy: 'Keeper and dog working a pipe. This clearly shows the construction of the screens'. From Earl of Suffolk and Berkshire (ed.), *The Encyclopaedia of Sport* (4 vols, 1911), II, p.75.

captured in these decoys is problematic because, in a similar way to other crafts, there was an innate aversion by the decoymen to disseminating trade secrets to their competitors. According to Payne-Gallwey's classic study, *Duck Decoys*, in the early 1880s each of these decoys secured, at a conservative estimate, an average of 5,000 ducks annually.[9] By the date of publication of his book in 1886, the number of decoys in existence had fallen to 47, while a follow-up study in 1918 revealed a further decline to 28 decoys.[10]

By the outbreak of the Second World War, there were only four decoys in full-time use, plus one which was used exclusively for the ringing of ducks and functioned as a sanctuary. In addition there were six decoys which were used spasmodically during the autumn and winter season. Throughout the years 1924–35, these ten operational decoys trapped on average about 11,500 duck per annum, more than 10,000 of which were accounted for by the four in full-time use.[11] However, the numbers caught in Britain were dwarfed by the estimated one million birds entrapped each year in the 150 full-time decoys which operated in Holland prior to the Second World War.[12]

The main reason for the decline in this method of wildfowling was the increasing expense of maintaining and operating decoys. Indeed, according to Marchington's exhaustive account, it was a combination of 'increased taxation and higher wages' that resulted in the virtual extinction of the decoys, 'dinosaurs in the sporting scene'.[13] This trend was accelerated by the sale of landed estates after the First World War and the agricultural depression. As a result, many decoys were allowed to fall into disrepair, for the new estate owners were often unwilling to find the investment needed to renovate them. A small number of decoys continued to operate throughout the Second World War and its immediate aftermath. One of the most enduring of these was Borough Fen Duck Decoy in Peakirk, Cambridgeshire, which was worked continuously by the Williams family from its establishment in 1670 until the death of Billy Williams in 1959.[14]

Decoys were also increasingly made obsolete by the developing technology of shooting. At the start of the nineteenth century, the pursuit of wildfowl using shotguns was a rapidly expanding activity encouraged by the growing popularity of wildfowl as a delicacy. But the muzzle-loading flintlock guns of the period were crude, cumbersome and often dangerous. Powder, shot and wadding had to measured and loaded in the field. Exploding barrels, damp powder and 'hang fire' bedevilled early wildfowlers.[15] Muzzle-loading hand guns were not only cumbersome but were also capable only of killing individual birds.

In order to facilitate the killing of more birds with a single shot, some fowlers began to experiment by mounting extra large guns on specially constructed rafts or shallow bottomed boats called punts (Fig. 5.3). In turn, this led to the introduction of large bore guns weighing between 130 and 150lbs, with a barrel length of over eight feet, and capable of delivering up

to 32 ounces of shot at a single discharge.[16] (The more usual size for a single-handed punt gun used by a professional wildfowler was a 60–70lb, 1¼ inch bore gun, firing about 12 ounces of swan shot.) These new guns were capable of turning on their balance by means of a swivel attached permanently to the barrel (hence their other name, swivel gun), or they were positioned in a crutch or loose swivel, like the rowing spur of a boat. Guns might also be mounted on sledges which could be pushed over ice (Fig. 5.4).

FIGURE 5.3
'The punt
gunner takes
aim ...'
From
J. N. P. Watson,
*Victorian and
Edwardian
Field Sports
from old photo-
graphs* (1978),
p. 102.

One of the earliest technical innovators was Colonel Peter Hawker (1786–1853), widely acclaimed as the father of wildfowling, whose famous double muzzle-loading gun is still preserved.[17] Weighing 193lbs and with 8 foot long barrels, the gun was capable of firing one pound of shot in each barrel, approximately fourteen times that of the typical 12 bore shotgun. With Hawker's gun, one barrel was ignited with percussion and the other with flint, thereby ensuring a brief interval between the two discharges, which not only reduced recoil, but ensured that the first shot hit the fowl when they were stationary, and the second one when they were rising and presenting larger targets.[18] This technique, he claimed, allowed him to bag nearly one hundred Brent geese at one go.[19] Expensive, custom-built guns of this type were almost invariably purchased by wealthy, amateur wildfowlers and used primarily in wide estuaries where flocks of wildfowl congregated.[20] Their limited popularity reflected not only the high capital cost of the initial purchase, but also the fact that the effectiveness of the gun decreased with the size of the bore. Hawker's technical legacy to the sport was the invention of a recoil spring system, which helped to absorb the shock when the gun was fired.

This period also saw the development of, both single and double punts, which lay close to the water line and were camouflaged by being painted pale grey, mimicking the colour of a Kitiwake's back. In order to make the punt as inconspicuous as possible, variations of colour could be used depending upon the visual appearance of the estuary in which they were employed. Punt-gunning was a physically demanding, tactical sport, necessitating the meticulous control of the punt in order to ensure minimal levels of noise and movement which might unsettle the birds before they came into range. Boats were navigated over the submerged mudflats using very short oars and, by lying out of sight, punt-gunners could steal up or stalk the fowl where they congregated.

FIGURE 5.4
'The punt
gun mounted
on a sledge.'
Courtesy of
Getty Images.

Shooting a group of birds using a large bore, long-barrelled gun was a technically skilled task requiring accurate judgement of the firing range and the precise timing of the discharge. The most successful shots were made just as the fowl started to lift from the water, with their wings outstretched, which provided a larger target area. Once the shot had been fired, the punt was navigated as quickly as possible to collect the dead birds and to allow wounded birds to be dispatched with a cripple stopper, a conventional shotgun. These activities were more easily undertaken on double punts, where the puntsman could concentrate on manoeuvring the punt while the gunner, or the person in charge, could devote his attentions to the fallen birds.

Shooting at flying birds had been revolutionised by the development of more effective and safer shotguns following the invention of percussion caps in 1820. As the nineteenth century advanced, further improvements in gun technology, particularly the introduction of breech loading in 1850s, led to shooting becoming reasonably safe in mechanical terms. Given that wildfowl presented high, flying and difficult targets, use was made of heavier shotguns, with bores ranging from ten to four, which could fire considerably larger loads than those used for game shooting.[21]

Unlike other forms of game shooting, and especially battue shooting where the birds were driven to waiting guns, wildfowling demanded a considerable amount of expertise in terms of field craft and stealth. Navigating a punt within range of the birds was a highly skilled operation. Similar demands were also required of shore shooting shooters, who needed extensive local knowledge and good fortune as they waited in anticipation of ambushing the birds as they flew to and from their feeding grounds. Flight shooting was considerably more productive at dusk and dawn, particularly during periods of high winds and gale conditions, when the birds in seeking suitable shelter were forced to fly closer to the ground.

Flight shooting was undertaken not only in coastal areas but also inland on marshes, meres and ponds. In the case of wild duck or Mallard, static hides were constructed close to especially preserved flight ponds, which were extensively baited with wheat and barley to encourage the ducks to use them.[22] But specialised inland duck shooting was not extensively pursued by most game shooters until after the First World War.

III

As the popularity of wildfowling increased in the nineteenth century, it was possible to discern two groups of wildflowers who, at their polar extremes, might be described as professionals and amateurs. Professional wildfowlers resided permanently in coastal regions and saw wildfowling either as a means of eking out a precarious living, or of supplementing their income during the winter months by harvesting an important food source. Amateur wildfowlers were outsiders who visited the coast to shoot simply for the sport it provided. In between were a collection of part-timers who shot wildfowl when favourable opportunities presented themselves, in particular, at the beginning of the season when the birds were plentiful and more likely to come within range. Whether or not these individuals constituted professional gunners is a moot point. What differentiated amateur wildfowlers from the professionals who needed to make a living from the activity was their approach to the size of the bag. As Sir Ralph Payne-Gallwey had poignantly noted, wildfowling was

> a healthy and interesting pursuit and one in which little success gives
> much content; for the pleasures of fowling are to no degree relative to
> the numbers slain, as three or four duck killed after a deal of thought

and trouble, may give you greater satisfaction than, perhaps thrice this number obtained without difficulty.[23]

Wildfowling was portrayed not only as a platonic activity of sophisticated live target shooting but also a sport which was pursued for altruistic reasons. As J.Wentworth Day acclaimed

> The true philosopher of the gun is the wildfowler, for he must have the sensitive eye of the artist, a love of solitude and lonely places. He measures beauty by the flash of a bird's wing by the glint of dawn on sliding waters, by the march of slow clouds. He is the son of solitude, the lonely one.[24]

All wildfowlers appreciated – to a greater or lesser extent – the rigours, dangers and tribulations of their activity but, for those who perceived it primarily as an economic activity as opposed to a sport, they valued the work for the independence it gave them, and for the opportunity to earn a living in wild, open spaces.

In the nineteenth century, wildfowling, like many other trades and crafts, was an activity wherein sons learnt the trade from their fathers or other close relatives. Each coastal resort had extended kinship groups who earned their living in the autumn and winter months primarily from wildfowling and shooting birds for naturalists. Family dynasties in this category included the Nudds at Hickling, the Longs at Blakeney, the Cringles at Wells and the Thomases at Breydon.[25] In the spring and summer months, many professional wildfowlers supplemented their income by selling fish and eels caught not only by inshore sea fishing using long lines but also by coarse fishing and plover netting.[26] Other seasonal activities of note, particularly in the Fens, included peat cutting as a source of winter fuel, collecting Samphire from the mudflats to sell as a delicacy, and collecting plover eggs in the spring.[27] According to the season and weather conditions they aspired to be punt-gunners, rabbit catchers, long shore fishermen, cockle-gatherers and netters.

The rewards from participating in the sport, in terms of the number of birds shot, were dependent on a number of factors many of which, such as the weather, were outside the control of the wildfowler. The pursuit of wild geese in particular was typified by fruitless expeditions leading to the term 'wild goose chase'.[28] Ironically it was during spells of inclement weather that wildfowling was most productive. In order to exploit these fleeting opportunities when it was possible to get very close to the geese, professional wildfowlers on occasions used short-barrelled punt-guns, with guns mounted on sledges when the water was frozen (as in Fig. 5.4).[29]

Nineteenth-century wildfowlers also supplemented their income by trying to shoot rare birds or unusually coloured variants of common species. There was a growing demand from naturalists and ornithologists who required specimens of wildfowl to examine and record, partly because of the difficulty of observing the birds in any other way. Field glasses or prism binoculars did not become widely available until the closing decade of the nineteenth century, and they remained inordinately expensive until well after the Great War. With photography still in its infancy, the task facing ornithologists was a challenging one if they were to meet the expectations of science in terms of being able to classify the birds precisely. Shooting appeared to be the most appropriate method available of providing specimens for scientific examination and satisfying the needs of naturalists who had a predilection to amass personal collections of stuffed bird.

Wildfowling as a sport, rather than a mere economic activity, had originally been popularised in the early part of the nineteenth century by a number of writers, principally Colonel Peter Hawker (1786–1853), who has been widely acclaimed as the father of wildfowling. He did much to disseminate the pleasures of the sport to a wider audience through his book *Advice to Young Shooters*, initially published in 1814, which ran to nine editions in his lifetime, and to two more posthumous editions published by his son.[30] However, rather than being credited as the originator of this form of shooting, Hawker's contribution was more mundane, in that he was the first to describe the activity as it then existed 'with such enthusiasm and lucidness'.[31] Another important contemporary account of the emergence of wildfowling as a sporting activity was W. B. Daniel's *Rural Sports* published in 1801. The author was an indefatigable but rather enigmatic Church of England clergyman who had been appointed private chaplain to the Prince Regent.[32] His two volume text, written in a more prosaic style than Hawker, provides a detailed record of wildfowling prior to the advent of breech loading guns. The contemporary popularity of the book was marred by the well-publicised, contemptuous critique of the author by a correspondent in *Gentleman's Magazine*: 'I can not help thinking that he is fitter to act the character of Nimrod than that of a dignitary in the Church of England.'[33] It was not until the 1880s that the historical significance of the book was acknowledged as 'one of the earliest, if not the earliest, authentic accounts of wildfowl shooting'.[34]

Following the improvements in firearm technology in the early Victorian period, game shooting achieved the gentlemanly aspirations of being clean, consistent, predictable, highly social and modern but in keeping with rural English traditions.[35] Its popularity grew amongst gentlemen of high social status and independent means, and those wealthy enough to participate in organised battue shooting. In contrast wildfowling appealed more to those wishing to engage in a manlier, less predictable shooting activity. As Wentworth Day wrote,

> I may be prejudiced, but somehow I think that wildfowling is one of
> the last forms of strenuous relaxation left to the man whose heart and

soul are so essentially masculine that he must by necessity escape from the shams, conventions and orthodoxies of modern life.[36]

It also offered a more varied activity in which the pursuit of wildfowl at dusk and dawn could be interspersed with daytime activities such as rabbiting and rough shooting.[37]

One of the leading icons and most prolific writers on the sport was Sir Ralph Payne-Gallwey, head of a wealthy aristocratic dynasty, who was enthralled with wildfowling. Between the springs of 1891 and 1892, he travelled more than 7,725 miles in pursuit of wildfowl, an incredible achievement in an age of horse-drawn carriages and railways.[38] He was a role model for other members of the leisured aristocracy and the upper classes who could afford to visit coastal areas, have their own yachts and employ a puntsman to undertake the more mundane aspects of the sport. Payne-Gallwey's classic texts included *Shooting: Field and Covert* (1886) and *Shooting: Moor and Marsh* (1887), both written with Lord Walsingham, which, between them, covered all aspects of shooting. The latter provided basic designs for the construction of both single and double punts.[39] His most detailed account of the sport was *The Fowler in Ireland* (1892) and *Letters to Young Shooters* (three volumes, 1891–96). Other evocative writers of note in this period included John Guille Millais, who was the author of *The Wildfowler in Scotland* (1901), *Natural History of British Feeding Surface Ducks* (1902) and *British Diving Ducks* (2 volumes, 1913). He was the classic sporting gentleman, encompassing naturalist, artist and writer who had the time and resources to be able to meander at leisure around the Scottish coast directing his puntsman in pursuit of surface-feeding and diving ducks.[40]

Another acclaimed wildfowler who came from a similar aristocratic background was Abel Chapman, author of the seminal *Tales of a Wildfowler* published in 1896. Like Millais, he was able to afford his own personal entourage of assistants to support his wildfowling and hunting excursions.[41] Nineteenth-century writers on wildfowling were almost without exception of a similar genre, upper-class men who had sufficient wealth and income to pursue the activity as a sporting adventure. These individuals popularised the sport in books which provided compelling, almost primeval accounts reflecting the glamour, the trials and tribulations and physical dangers of traversing tidal estuaries in pursuit of exclusive quarry. Virtually unrestricted in the birds, mammals and fish which they pursued on the foreshore and sea, wildfowlers achieved the mantle of individualistic, romantic and iconic figures.

IV

By the late nineteenth century, punt-gunning was regarded by gentlemen wildfowlers in Britain as the cream of wildfowl shooting. In practice it was a dangerous activity which claimed the lives of numerous participants every year. But the constant threat of being capsized by the tide and navigating by moonlight seemed only to add the spice of danger, particularly for those who indulged in wildfowling for sporting purposes.

The record bag is usually credited to have occurred in the 1880s off the Essex coast, by a flotilla of nineteen (some authorities suggest twenty-four) single-handed punts commanded from a double-handed punt by a Colonel Russell. According to Wentworth Day, this armada killed 704 geese in a joint discharge.[42] Given that three of the principles that guide the historian in evaluating the reliability of sources are internal consistency, independent corroboration and the degree to which a source reports contemporary events, Day's account remains very suspect. For example, elsewhere in same book he claims that as many as 850 birds were killed during this sortie. An account of the incident by Payne-Gallwey suggests a total kill of fewer than 300 birds.[43] Wentworth Day also claimed a few years later that another group of punts at Goldhanger, higher up the Blackwater estuary, had, at an unspecified date, secured a bag of what is recorded in some of his sources as 200, and in others as up to 500 geese.[44] Such an assertion is, however, uncollaborated.

A more authentic insight into the numbers killed can be gleaned from the diaries of individual wildfowlers. The most comprehensive figures are provided by Colonel Hawker who, from 1802 to 1853, records 17,753, of which 4,488 were wildfowl. Even these figures were not necessarily the number of birds despatched by the author alone, but were probably accounted for by other members of his shooting party who were not always acknowledged.[45] The wildfowl killed amounted to, on average, fewer than 100 per season.

Another amateur wildfowler famed for his exploits with the gun was Victor Octave Alfred de Morton, denoted as Count de la Chapelle among the French nobility.[46] In 1907, the Count, who was a London barrister, established his wildfowling headquarters at Tollesbury, Essex, where he was renowned as an intrepid shooter and comrade to fishermen and gunners at the mouth of the Blackwater estuary. His shooting was undertaken chiefly at weekends, and usually one day a week, from about 1 August to the end of February, the contemporary start and end of the wildfowling season. Surviving records of the Count's wildfowling covering the period July 1904 to December 1918 provide an informative insight into the meagre but varied rewards he managed to secure. During this 14-year period he shot 4,243 birds, including about 74 different species. His bags amounted to slightly more than 300 a year, equivalent to little more than ten for every day's shooting. In terms of Brent geese this amounted to ten over 14 years, equating to less than one a year, while he bagged 105 Mallard, or fewer than nine a year. Clearly if he had pursued a more aggressive approach to shooting on the feeding grounds used by Brent geese and Widgeon, he might have secured substantially larger bags, but he considered these species were the heritage of the fishermen-fowlers who depended on wildfowl for a living.[47] What is noteworthy is the relatively large number of waders (854 Redshank, 570 plover and 1,322 Dunlin) that he shot.

The rewards for those who endeavoured to make a living from wildfowling declined throughout the nineteenth century. According to Daniel, one wildfowler made £50 during the five-month season.[48] In numbers of wildfowl, this amounted to about 2,600 birds, or roughly half those caught by the average duck decoy. But a bag of this size was an exceptional achievement.

On average punt-gunners fired their guns about once a day throughout the season, killing in the region of ten birds per shot. According to Payne-Gallwey, who wrote at the end of the century when wildfowl were certainly less plentiful, a double-handed punt did very well to secure 700 ducks and geese in a season. Few shooters came anywhere close to the 1,800 Brent geese which E. T. Booth claimed were bagged in a ten-week period by a single punt gunner in Ross-shire.[49] Accounts of this nature, however, were unauthenticated and reminiscent of the proverbial fishermen's tale about the size of the fish that got away. Even professional punt-gunners who went wildfowling for a living had difficulty in securing consistently high numbers of birds from year to year. The highest number recorded in a single season during the twentieth century amounted to 1,500 ducks and geese shot by four men using the same double punt.[50] The largest documented bag made in a single year by a single-handed punt was in the winter of 1917–18, an exceptional year not only because of the weather but also because the fighting on the Western Front had encouraged large numbers of wildfowl to flee their wintering grounds in France. Even this amounted to slightly in excess of 1,000 birds, while the same man's annual bag over a much longer period was 152 birds.[51] More recent studies by the Wildlife Enquiry Commission suggest that the average annual bag of a good punt-gunner working in a favoured locality was in the region of 400 ducks and geese.[52] Their study of 26 punts going out regularly over several years and covering all the coasts of England found an average bag of 287 ducks and geese per annum, and for all the punts in Britain an average of a little more than 100 ducks and geese.

By the inter-war period it was commonly accepted that punt-gunning was an increasingly precarious financial activity. In the mid-1930s, at a time when Widgeon sold for between 1s. 3d. and 1s. 9d. each and Mallard for 2s. 6d., the hundred or so ducks and geese secured by the average punt-gunner were little more that the equivalent of four weeks' wages for an agricultural labourer. This was irrespective of any allowance made for the cost of maintaining the punt, or the cost of powder and shot for the gun. Given the amount of time which would have been invested in the number of excursions which would have been needed, wildfowling as a means of making a living from the sale of birds was perilous in the extreme.

Statistics for the actual number of sportsmen participating in wildfowling as punt-gunners are scanty. The most detailed and probably most accurate assessment was provided by Brian Vesey-Fitzgerald in his *British Game*. According to his calculations, by 1939 there were fewer than one hundred punt-gunners in England and Wales and fewer than twenty in Scotland. Of these 120 punts, about forty were used no more than twice in a season, while the number of fisher-fowler punt-gunners was fewer than fifty. The true professional wildfowler had virtually ceased to exist, and the five who remained increasingly acted as guides to wealthy amateurs. However, there were an additional fourteen power-driven boats mounted with punt-guns, owned almost exclusively by wealthy individuals who had little real understanding of the craft of punt-gunning. Using a motorised boat to get within range of the birds was considered unsporting by most wildfowlers.[53] Once disturbed in this way, birds became increasingly wary, which spoilt the shooting for other participants.

Constant shooting from shore gunners also adversely affected the migration patterns of wildfowl, encouraging them to move to quieter estuaries where they would be under less pressure. The most persuasive exponent of this view was Wentworth Day who complained in many of his writings that the increase in the number of amateur shore shooters had led to a marked reduction in the size of bags in areas such as Wells.[54] This view was endorsed by Savory in 1953:

> In the end, it was overdone. A morning flight at Holkham was a thing to avoid. There were shooters behind every tree, and hidden all along the sandhills. When the geese came over everyone fired. But the great birds stuck it out, until some people who should have known better, started digging in on the sandbanks where the geese rested at night, and plastering them by moonlight. That finished it.[55]

According to the leading naturalist and wildfowler J. C. M. Nichols, the number of Pink-footed geese that frequented the immediate neighbourhood of Wells was, by the late 1940s, barely a tenth of the number which had traditionally overwintered in this area. Shooting pressure had not necessarily led to a decline in the number of migrants to Norfolk and South Lincolnshire, but had dispersed them over a much larger area. Even resident shore gunners were now unlikely to secure more than half a dozen in a season, whereas previously they may have shot sixty, seventy, or even eighty birds in a good season.[56]

But shooting pressure was not the only reason for the fall in the number of certain species of wildfowl such as Brent geese. After 1933 the wider leaved species of Eel or Widgeon grass (*Zostera marina*) on which Brent geese and Widgeon had traditionally fed, succumbed to disease. Even the narrow leaved species of *Z. angustifolia* had been badly affected by a wasting disease, characterised by brown and black patches which gradually overwhelmed the plant. *Zostera* beds were replaced by the more aggressive Cord grass (*Spartina*) which has no value as a food plant.[57] Widgeon responded to this food shortage by increasing their use of salt marshes for food and also by flying up to several miles inland to glean cereal grains and graze cereals and grassland.[58] In contrast, the Brent goose, which in the nineteenth century was probably the most numerous goose frequenting British coastal waters, was considerably less successful in adapting to these changes, a factor which precipitated a long term decline in their numbers.[59]

V

During the nineteenth-century there were few restrictions on the species of wildfowl which could be legitimately shot. This was in stark contrast to the administration of game shooting, where the Game Laws of 1831 and 1832 ensured that game birds were rigorously preserved for the landed aristocracy. Under this legislation, specific permission had to be sought from the landowner by tenants or occupiers of the land before they were legally entitled to shoot game.

Wildfowling was also a considerably cheaper sport to indulge in than game shooting. It was widely assumed that shooters had the unrestricted right to shoot below the high water mark.[60] There was little incentive for conservation in this period, given that the birds were non-residents and the numbers bred each year depended on factors completely outside the control of the shooter. More importantly, the fact that there were no formal bag restrictions on the numbers shot meant that professional wildfowlers were not inclined to restrict their activities. Rare species of birds or those which were infrequent visitors to Britain's shores such as the Stork, Ibis, or even smaller birds such as warblers and buntings, merited particular attention because of the premium prices they commanded from naturalists and ornithologists.[61] The response of the shooting fraternity to the challenge of how to protect their sport was left to a few pioneering individuals, while the most systematic and co-ordinated response was the establishment of the Southport and District Wildfowlers' Association in 1887.

By the onset of the twentieth century, increasing drainage of coastal areas and marshes and the loss of vast tracts of wildfowl habitat to development was raising concern amongst the shooting fraternity about the future of their sport. In response, the Wildfowlers Association of Great Britain and Ireland (WAGBI) was founded in 1908 by Stanley Duncan, who conceived the idea in the infamous Black Hut at Patrington Haven on the Humber. An engineer by trade, and an experienced wildfowler and naturalist, he was concerned about the future of the sport and the growing pressure for the protection of wild birds. He also wanted to help professional wildfowlers who, by this time, were struggling to eke out even a meagre living.[62]

Sir Ralph Payne-Gallwey was elected founding president, while Duncan became the Association's Honorary Secretary, a position he retained for the next forty years. With the aid of a small committee, the Association began to develop a presence in every wildfowling district, where officials could provide advice and represent amateur and professional wildfowling interests. Duncan also did much to popularise the sport through his book *The Complete Wildfowler* (1913) which he compiled in conjunction with Guy Thorne. He was an ardent conservationist and in the mid-1920s employed a man full-time to assist his three sons and their friends in hand-rearing wild geese and ducks for release on the 500-acre shoot which he rented.[63]

By the inter-war period the ranks of amateur wildfowlers were swollen by members of the middle classes. Having other forms of employment, their opportunities to pursue the sport were often constrained by work commitments. These part-time shooters avidly read books to obtain an insight into the mystique of shooting on marshes and the sea in contrast to professional wildfowlers who had, for the most part, learnt their trade first hand from older practitioners. Articulate members of this group of wildfowlers also supplemented their living by writing about their exploits. Sporting literature abounds with descriptions of isolated coastal saltings adjacent to mudflats, iodine-scented air and hardy men pursuing wild ducks and geese with punt and shotgun.

The most notable inter-war advocate of wildfowling was J. Wentworth Day, 'a doughty fighter for high Tory causes and any scheme which he believed would preserve the wildlife and countryside of Britain'.[64] A versatile and volatile individual, he was some-time editor of *The Field* magazine and a prolific writer on all aspects of shooting. In his book *Wild Wings* (1948) he described wildfowling in particularly evocative terms.[65] A staunch Royalist, Day eulogised George V's role as both a shooter and a bird conservationist. As he explained in *The Field*:

> I cannot help emphasizing the fact that, since so much fuss is made about bird protection nowadays, that more than half the wealth of bird life in North Norfolk is due very much largely to the wise protection and encouragement given to it by such landowners as his Majesty the King [and others].[66]

Day's sycophantic approach to George V culminated in the publication of his book *King George as a Sportsman* in 1935 in which he declared that 'His Majesty's principal delight is wildfowling'. He contrasted the King, desk-bound, coping with the 'solemn and tedious business of kingship' in London, with the 'plain squire of Sandringham' flighting in 'the snow and mist of a

January day ... under the sea wall of the north Norfolk coast'.[67] Ironically, the accession to the throne of King George VI following his brother's abdication heralded a new approach to wildfowling on the Sandringham estates.[68] Specialised duck flighting at dawn and dusk became an integral part of the shooting itinerary with the construction of new ponds and the intensive feeding of the birds to retain them in the locality.[69] These innovations unfortunately coincided with a general waning of Day's reputation in the late 1930s as a result of his pro-fascist sympathies. His growing disillusionment with royalty meant that these developments passed largely unchronicled by him.

VI

The wildfowling interest had to contend with an increasingly powerful, influential and articulate lobby interested in the preservation of ducks and geese. Species of birds which had once been a free resource became protected by law. Increasing international concern over declining numbers of wildfowl led to the establishment of the Wildlife Enquiry Committee in 1936 under the auspices of the British section of the International Council for Bird Preservation (ICBP). The Committee was instrumental in bringing about the Wild Birds (Ducks and Geese) Protection Act 1939, which limited imports of wildfowl during the close season. The legislation altered the date of the start of the close season to 1 February from 1 March, while the opening date was put back to 12 August instead of 1 August. These amendments, which were not well received by British wildfowlers, were intended as a gesture of reciprocation to the Dutch, who agreed to close their decoys during the spring migration, when large numbers of ducks had previously been captured immediately prior to migrating to their nesting grounds in Arctic regions.

In addition to these practical achievements, the Wildlife Enquiry Committee published two volumes of a proposed trilogy, *The status and distribution of wild geese and wild duck in Scotland* (1939) and *The factors affecting the general status of wild geese and wild duck* (1941). The third volume of the series – covering England and Wales – was delayed by the war and eventually superseded by the monograph *Wildfowl in Great Britain* (1963).

One of the most significant developments in the protection of wildfowl was the creation of the Wildfowl and Wetlands Trust in 1946 by the artist and naturalist Peter Scott (1909–89) on seven hectares of wetland at Slimbridge in Gloucestershire.[70] This was intended to act as an observation and research centre, enabling the study of both captive wildfowl within the collection and of wintering wildfowl on the Severn estuary. In order to gain a better insight into migration patterns, live ducks were captured in decoys for ringing. The reserve provided a unique opportunity for visitors to get closer to wetland birds and to enjoy spectacular wetland landscapes, but the educational success the project achieved was probably of greater significance than its research effort. The Trust constituted the first and most successful of the post-war organisations which were committed to the conservation of individual species or groups of species. In 1956 the Trust established its second centre at Peakirk in Cambridgeshire, providing the public with access to an extensive collection of birds in order to finance its operation of the Borough Fen decoy, which was used for capturing and ringing wildfowl. A further centre at Welney was established in 1967. The Trust became the largest international wetland conservation charity.

In 1947 the far-sighted leaders of the British section of the ICBP were involved in the formation of the International Wildfowl Research Institute, later to become known as the International Waterfowl and Wetland Research Bureau. It was established as an information unit and research body, running international conferences on the study and conservation of wildfowl. In the same year the ICBP embarked on the ambitious task of ascertaining the status of wildfowl in Britain, with a view to determining long-term trends in population. Synchronised monthly counts were undertaken over a prolonged period and over as wide an area as possible. In 1954 the responsibility for the winter monthly counts was transferred to the Wildfowl Trust. A more systematic approach was adopted, although practical field work was still carried out primarily by unpaid volunteers who were ornithologists skilled in the identification of wildfowl, and who were selected and, for the most part, trained by the Regional Organisers.

After the Second World War, the drive for conservation increasingly began to dominate the political arena and the government was finally persuaded to set up its own agency, the Nature Conservancy, on 1 November 1948. Its duties outlined in the National Parks and Countryside Act 1949, were 'to provide scientific advice on the conservation and control of the natural flora and fauna of Great Britain'. The Nature Conservancy provided grants to cover the administrative and salary costs of the permanent regional organisers and staff involved in the wildfowl survey.

Pressure from environmental groups culminated in the government introducing a bill for the protection of birds in 1953 which, in its draft format, had profound implications for wildfowling. Members of WAGBI, which remained a voluntary organisation at this time, devoted their time, energy and funds to support the interests of wildfowlers. Meeting were arranged, thousands of letters written, and extensive lobbying of members of both the House of Commons and Lords undertaken. The campaign led to the bill being substantially amended before it reached the statute book. The Protection of Birds Act marked a significant turning point for wildfowl conservation in Great Britain. It redefined the maximum length of the open season which now started on 1 September as opposed to the 12 August, and was extended by three weeks at the end of the season. These changes were designed to ensure that immature ducks were not killed in August, while the extension allowed wildfowlers, who were by now predominantly weekend amateurs, to have more opportunity to participate in the sport.[71]

The act also specified the species of wildfowl could be killed, which included the Bean goose, Pink-footed goose, White-fronted goose, Greylag goose, Canada goose, Pintail, Teal, Mallard, Gadwell, Wigeon, Gargency, Shoveller, Pochard, Tufted duck, Scaup, Goldeneye, Common Scoter, Velvet Scoter, Longtailed duck, Gooseander and Red-breasted Merganser. One of the most significant clauses of the Act was that granting protection to maritime species of geese such as the Brent, which had once been the most popular quarry, but whose population levels were now contracting rapidly. The legislation had less effect on the most common species of duck, in particular Mallard, Teal and Widgeon, but it did extend protection to a number of rarer species which occasionally graced the bag of the shooter. It also made it technically illegal to shoot indiscriminately at flocks which contained protected birds.

The debate on the act was characterised by frequent references to the ravages inflicted on wildfowl by punt-gunning, with grandiose claims about the number of birds killed. Lady Tweedsmuir, who had sponsored the bill, was keen to castigate the alleged slaughter of 2,000 geese by punt-gunners in a single afternoon. Excessive shooting of this kind was repeatedly deplored by WAGBI in their journal, but strenuous efforts to verify the perpetrators and location of this particular 'massacre' failed.[72] While not formally prohibiting the sport of punt-gunning, the Act did outlaw the use of motorised boats to chase and shoot wildfowl, a course of action which was widely welcomed by large sections of the shooting fraternity.[73] An amendment was proposed prohibiting the use of decoys or stuffed geese to attract birds within range.[74] This was eventually withdrawn after a lengthy and, on occasions, acrimonious debate.[75]

The conflict and in-fighting which had characterised the legislation turned out to be therapeutic, encouraging co-operation between environmental and wildfowling interests. One of the most important developments was the establishment, under the chairmanship of the Director General of the Wildfowl Trust, of informal representative meetings. These gatherings were eventually formalised into the Wildfowl Conservation Committee, encompassing representatives from WAGBI, the Wildlife Trust and the Nature Conservancy. Its terms of reference were 'To consider all matters directly affecting wildfowl and wildfowling, in particular to the establishment of a national system of wildfowl refuges and to advise the Nature Conservancy accordingly'.[76] The first refuge was unanimously agreed in January 1955 as the Humber Estuary. Sanctuary Orders followed for Southport in Lancashire, Wicken Fen in Cambridgeshire and Hamilton

Low Parks, Lanarkshire. Other European countries became involved with this movement towards the international conservation of migratory wildfowl.

Independently of this, WAGBI initiated breeding programmes for certain species of ducks for release into the wild and designated a number of local reserves by private agreement. In an era of rapprochement, WAGBI and the Wildfowl Trust united in undertaking a seven-year project to study the food preferences of British ducks, establishing in 1956 a reserve on a gravel pit in Kent to extend their research. The threat to wildfowling posed by the 1954 Act was also instrumental in promoting the establishment of new wildfowling clubs. The five affiliated organisations of the Southport and District Wildfowlers Association (1887), Morecombe Bay Wildfowlers' Association (1929), Blakeney and District Wildfowlers' Association (1927), Frodsham and District Wildfowlers' Association (1938) and the Tay Valley Wildfowlers Association (1949) in existence in 1950 had increased to more than twenty-five by the end of the decade.

WAGBI's conservation credentials were impressive. In 1966 it hand-reared and released about 8,000 ducks, more than any other body in the country. WAGBI also established three main wildfowl reserves where birds could not be shot or disturbed, including a reserve in Buckinghamshire devoted primarily to educational and scientific purposes.[77]

The sport again came under attack in 1967 and WAGBI, under the leadership of its Director, John Anderton, with the widespread support of punt-gunners, fought a three-month battle to save it from extinction.[78] One of the main threats from the Protection of Birds bill was an amendment to limit the size of punt-gun to a maximum bore of one inch, which was the largest size capable of being used as a shoulder gun.[79] This, if it had been carried, would have led to the disappearance of punt-gunning. The proposal was not only opposed by wildfowlers, but also, for entirely different reasons, by environmental groups. The Scottish Office Advisory Committee considered that the amendment could be counterproductive as it might simply serve to awaken interest in a sport that was already dying out. This view was also shared by English Nature which argued that 'the surest and least troublesome method of achieving a cessation of punt-gunning is to let it die quietly'.[80]

Since the 1970s wildfowl have increasingly been recognised as an international natural resource. Cooperation between countries was actively promoted by the International Wildfowl Research Bureau through the establishment of the annual mid-winter census of palaearctic ducks and swans. These censuses, initiated in January 1967, provide detailed accounts of the number and distribution of the species which occurred in Europe, North Africa and the western half of Asia. By the 1970s records had been collated from over 8,000 sites in 44 countries.

An international conference on the conservation of wetlands and waterfowl was held at Ramsar, Iran, in early 1971. Attended by delegates from more than fifty countries, the Ramsar Convention led to an inter-governmental treaty providing the framework for international cooperation on the conservation and appropriate use of wetlands. Under the terms of the treaty, each participating country was obliged to designate at least one wetland for inclusion in the Ramsar list, based on areas of significance in terms of ecology, botany, zoology, limnology or hydrology. There was also a general obligation for each country to include wetland conservation in their national land-use planning.

In Britain, following entry into the EU in 1973, thirteen sites were named for the conservation of wildfowl, most of which were already protected in other ways. But Britain was slow to comply with its European obligations on environmental issues and, out of a potential 218 Ramsar sites, only 44 had been officially designated by 1990.[81]

European legislation intended to maintain populations of all 'species of naturally occurring birds in the wild state, was introduced in April 1979 as the Directive on the Conservation of Wild Birds. Part of the directive's aim was to enhance habitat conservation through the provision of Special Protection Areas (SPAs). In an effort to bring British conservation law up to European standards, an announcement was made on 20 June 1979 of the government's intention to promote a new Bill concerned not only with the protection of individual species but also habitats and their management.

The Wildlife and Countryside Act 1981 was a monumental piece of legislation, the initial drafting of which took seventeen months. Part I of the Act extended the protection offered by the Protection of Birds Acts of 1954 and 1967. In line with the EU Directive, it also instituted SPAs for birds, of which 107 had been designated by 1995. In terms of wildfowling it seriously reduced the number of species of birds which could be legitimately shot. The existing protection of the Brent under the 1954 act was extended to all species of Black geese, with the exception of the Canada goose. Protection was also extended to Curlew and Redshank, the only two species of shore waders which, until then, could be shot. The rationale for this, according to the amendment inserted by the House of Lords, was that, as waders in flight are difficult to identify, it would ensure that other protected species of the same genus were not killed in error.[82] This proposal received a mixed reception having been hotly debated in the shooting press.[83] The shooting of wading birds was confined to Snipe, Woodcock and Golden Plover.[84]

The legislation was also accompanied by changes in the administration of wildfowling. In 1981 WAGBI changed its name to the British Association for Shooting and Conservation (BASC) in recognition of the growing pressure for all types of shooting to be represented by a single body. Surrendering its wildfowling identity in this way and assimilating its activities within a broader conservation movement proved to be a major landmark. The organisation which had pioneered wildfowl conservation, the brainchild of Stanley Duncan, finally became integrated with conservationists of other denominations. BASC continued to play a key role in representing the interests of wildfowlers, not only through wildfowling Associations but also through individuals.

<h1 style="text-align:center">VII</h1>

That wildfowling dramatically altered in the mid-decades of the twentieth century was due not only to legislative changes which protected individual species, but also to the continuing changes in feeding habits which had been initiated by the loss of Eel or Widgeon grass beds in the 1930s. Other behavioural and habitat changes encouraged an increase in the number of inland wildfowl. The descendants of feral geese which had lost their migratory instincts, in particular the Canadian variety with their distinct black and white markings, began to breed inland in significant numbers. This trend was facilitated by the provision of additional protected inland sites and by the increase in the number and size of man-made reservoirs for water storage.

The extent to which wildfowl conservation has affected the migratory patterns of geese is a moot point. The National Waterfowl Counts organised by the Wildfowl and Wetlands Trust (the name the Wildfowl Trust adopted in 1989 to reflect its broader concerns), have revealed that numbers fluctuate significantly from one year to the next without necessarily any apparent explanation.

Professionals who previously depended exclusively on shooting wildfowl for a living have all but disappeared.[85] One of the best documented of the legendary 'Fen Tigers', the elite breed of men who earned their living in this way, was Ernie James. As early as the 1950s he became a media personality, being interviewed by personalities including Dave Allen, David Bellamy and Harry Secombe, as well as having a documentary about his life made by Anglia Television in 1975. Some professional wildfowlers evolved into guides for amateur shooters or to aid birdwatchers shoot geese with a camera rather than, as in the past, with a gun. While it is a question of semantics whether birdwatchers can be considered wildfowlers in the traditional sense, it is evident that these amateurs developed a new role.

By the early 1980s, wildfowling clubs had generally developed the ability to regulate their activities through voluntary codes of conduct and to ensure that abuses were dealt with internally, rather than becoming matters for the media as in many other field sports. Wildfowling associations accepted membership applications from a wide cross-section of society who wished to participate in the sport on the marshes and foreshore they controlled.

Newcomers, however, were required to join as either associate (non-shooting) or probationary members, and to pass a club proficiency test demonstrating their safety with a shotgun before progressing to full membership. The associations also required all members to book in with a designated officer and to file monthly returns.

Inland wildfowling, or to be more specific, duck shooting, had also started to expand as a result of large-scale, artificial breeding of Mallard, which substantially increased the number of birds available to shoot. Mallard proved easier to breed and rear than Partridges, and regular feeding ensured that the ducks usually remained close to their point of release, even if occasionally they appeared unwilling to take off on shooting days.[86] The flying performance of these birds was sometimes lamented in the shooting press but they provided more predictable bags and, by the early 1980s, duck shooting on flight ponds had become widespread.

VIII

Since the emergence of wildfowling as a sport in the mid-nineteenth century, the activity has witnessed more profound challenges and changes than possibly any other form of shooting. The key to this continuing metamorphosis is that wildfowling has adapted quickly to new policy initiatives and the growing need for conservation, ensuring that the threats to its future which characterised the late nineteenth and early twentieth centuries have substantially diminished. As a sport, the challenge to its very existence developed earlier than for other field sports, culminating in the Protection of Birds Act of 1954. Since then the sport has provided one of the best examples of professionally coordinated integration of the needs of its practitioners and conservation. This rapprochement – which has been distinctly lacking in many other field sports – was prompted by amateurs who regarded wildfowling as a sport rather than an activity to be pursued for commercial reasons.

Professional wildfowlers who made a living from coastal shooting have been replaced by guides ferrying shooters to inland feeding grounds or flight lines to shoot. Punt-gunning, one the most popular forms of pursuing wildfowl in the past, has virtually disappeared. Amateur wildfowlers have increasingly dominated the sport and, as in the past, it is they who continue to write about their achievements in glowing terms. One of the ironies of wildfowling is that it was the amateurs, the part-time wildfowlers, who pioneered the technical improvement in the sport and, more importantly, launched the organisation of the sport along professional lines. No doubt this has largely contributed to the continued popularity of the sport not only amongst British shooters but also for many foreign visitors, ensuring that wildfowling does not necessarily end in the proverbial wild goose chase. The principles on which the sport is undertaken have, in essence, remained the same since the emergence of fowling in the mid-nineteenth century. It is tempting to concur with Eric Bergie's view in *Fowler in the Wild* that

> As a shooting sport it is unique in that success depends more on the wildfowlers knowledge of the habits and habitat of the quarry than on his marksmanship skills. It is, however, more than just a sport. For those of those of us who have responded to the call of a wild estuary, fowling can become a way of life, a consuming passion.[87]

CHAPTER SIX

A delightful sport with 'peculiar claims': the specificities of otter hunting, 1850–1939

by Daniel Allen

> Otter-hunting has peculiar claims upon the sport-loving tastes of the English people.[1]

> The tyro at otter-hunting who has previously been out with foxhounds, harriers, and beagles will be a little bewildered when he attends his first meet of the otter-hounds.[2]

AT THE END of the nineteenth century otter hunting experienced a renaissance in Britain. In its revived modern form, the activity was 'more popular than ever amongst the small clique of sportsmen … privileged to enjoy it'.[3] According to contemporary commentators such as L. C. R. Cameron and H. A. Bryden, this 'new phase of existence'[4] was 'received with the heartiest zest and welcome'.[5] Organised at a regional scale, this purely pedestrian sport hunted designated river valleys from April to October. These districts or 'countries' often had far-reaching boundaries that spanned several counties. The most established historical centres for otter hunting included Wales and the Welsh Borders; south-west and north-west England, and, southern Scotland. Each of these areas had had a number of packs based there since the 1830s. In other regions, such as the eastern counties and southern England, new packs did not spring into existence until the 1880s: Courtenay Tracy OH (established 1887); Buckinghamshire OH (1891); the Essex OH (1897) and Crowhurst OH (1903). In 1880, there were 15 packs of otter hounds in Britain. Of these, four were dual packs (that is, they also hunted other animals); two were hunt clubs financed by subscriptions;[6] and one, Mr Collier's OH, still used the spear. From the mid-nineteenth century, there were ongoing internal debates concerning the use of the spear. The mere mention of spearing in *The Field* invariably riled its readers, and provoked a series of impassioned responses. Despite opposition, the discontinuation of the spear was a gradual process. Its use dwindled and its adherents disappeared as hunts disbanded and packs changed hands. As new packs emerged each clearly set themselves apart from those that employed the spear. In 1884 the use of the spear was discontinued. This standardisation of killing saw otter hunting re-codified as a modern form of sport and leisure.

By 1910, there were 22 packs of hounds in existence. Fifteen of these were founded after 1880, nine during the Edwardian period. All but four were financed by subscriptions. 1910 also saw the formation of The Masters of the Otter Hounds Association. This was formed to promote the sport and preserve the otterhound breed. In the years to 1939 the number of Otter Hunts fluctuated between 19 and 23. In terms of followers, each of these packs generally had between 100 and 300 subscribers. On special occasions *crowds* of over 500 people were recorded.

Although these trends nicely illustrate the growing popularity of the activity, they do not account for the particular fashion and vogue otter hunting had achieved by the early twentieth century. Nor, do they explain why 'tyros' to otter hunting chose to participate in *this* particular sport. This chapter considers how otter hunters styled themselves and how they presented their activity in relation to other types of hunting. To tease out the specificities of otter hunting, this paper discusses in turn the three principal peculiar claims[7] made by otter hunters about their sport; summer hunting, its horselessness and the science of hunting, which in turn is divided into three parts: the unseen quarry, techniques for finding, and participatory practices.

I

> There is no need for any genuine lover of the chase to find the spring and summer dull if he has the means of transferring himself to the land of the otter ...[8]

The season for hunting otters was the seven months between April and October. Unlike other forms of hunting, this season was not shaped around the breeding habits of the quarry; it was chosen as it was attuned to the physical disposition of the human body. The chapter dedicated to otter hunting in *British Rural Sports* (1856) reaffirms this point: 'No other season but the summer will suit this sport, because the cold water of early spring, winter, or autumn, will chill and cramp hounds and men to a dangerous degree.'[9] As the only form of sport with hounds in progress during the spring and summer months, otter hunting held an exclusive position in hunting culture. Yet despite its unrivalled status on the hunting calendar, otter hunting did not procure a pre-ordained fan-base from alternative hunting communities. According to the unpublished diaries of the Crowhurst Otter Hounds, for practically nine-tenths of the sporting fraternity, hunting came to an end with the return of the violets.[10] Why did otter hunting remain very much a minority sport? Who were the one-tenth of people who chose to participate and what particular attributes did they possess?

For some otter hunting presented itself as an attractive seasonal stand-in when fox hunting was unavailable. One such enthusiast who found this feature particularly appealing was Captain Newton Wynne Apperley. In his hunting diary, Apperley candidly wrote: 'it is very good fun when no other sport is to be had, and serves to fill the gap that would otherwise yawn in summer when it is impossible to hunt either hare or fox'.[11] Apperley was not alone in endorsing the activity as a fun solution for the gap between fox hunting seasons. In The Sportsman's Library volume on *Beagling and Otter Hunting*, Robert Colville acknowledged similar advocates: 'I have met many people who consider otterhunting to be a useful but rather easy way of passing the summer'.[12] Distinguished from those who followed otter hounds for an 'easy way of passing the summer' were those to whom the summer was the all-important season. Choosing to follow otter hounds, they were not merely a hybrid of otherwise inactive hunters, but individuals who sought a sporting identity they could claim as their own. For these followers, otter hunting afforded a kind of sport 'superior to any other in the known world'.[13]

During much of the nineteenth century otter hunting started at daybreak. This early start was informed by the otter's nocturnal behaviour. At this hour, the animal's overnight wanderings endured on the land as a fresh trail of scent. Mid-Victorian publications such as *British Rural Sports* insisted that 'hunting must be over by nine or ten o'clock' as 'the rays of the mid-day sun' were 'inimical to the scent'.[14] For James Lomax, whose otter-hunting diary was privately published in 1892, 'four in the morning was about his usual hour'.[15] 'Modern' meets, on the other hand, could commence any time between six and eleven. Later meets gradually became the rule rather than the exception[16], and as will be shown, the daybreak meet became a nostalgic reference point of bygone days. To understand why such importance was placed on the temporal variations of meets, we must consider how huntsmen, hounds and followers were transported.

Owing to the size of otter hunting territories, regions tended to be divided into districts and hunted in sections. The district close to the kennels was known as the home waters. In pre-motor days the hounds reached these meets by foot. The hunt staff would walk, jog, cycle[17] or ride alongside the pack at a 'hound trot'. Earlier meets naturally meant earlier starts as the distance from the kennels could take several hours to traverse. The following account concerning the Cheriton Otter Hounds exemplifies this point: 'The meet was at Woodford Bridge on May 28th [1890] at 6 a.m., which necessitated starting at 4 a.m. to cover the extremely hilly seven or eight miles to the meet.'[18] To reach the more distant localities, the hunt staff and other ardent followers travelled with the hounds by horse-drawn van or train. Here they would 'lie out' overnight at a wayside inn, farm, or some other available homestead. 'Lying out' provided the opportunity to hunt a selected district for several days without returning to the kennels.

The later meet was a manifestation of modern innovations and modern tastes. As technology transformed modes of transport, travel became more affordable, places became more accessible, and, social movement became more prevalent. Such changes activated and assisted the growing popularity of the activity, and led to a broader grouping of interests within otter hunts. During Fred Collier's mastership (1891–98) at the Culmstock Otter Hounds, for example, a meet at 6.00 a.m. was considered 'damned late'; yet it became the regular time as his field 'would not tolerate an earlier hour'.[19] This notion of 'tolerance' is rather significant. Firstly, the intolerance of the field suggests a disparity of views on what otter hunting should be. This is tied to developing ideas about lifestyle and leisure. Secondly, the fact that Masters were forced to alter their practices to meet such views indicates that the field was considered to be both influential and important. The tolerance of a Master was in part due to the socio-economic circumstances of the period, and organisational restructuring of hunts. As otter hunting became more popular, the members who provided subscriptions, and followers who paid caps, became increasingly valued for their financial contributions. The majority of MOH openly acknowledged this: 'I quite agree with Mr Wardell that late meets are more popular, and in these days of hard times one has to consider the interests of one's subscribers and fix one's meets to suit them'.[20] To maintain the interest of 'one's subscribers', packs of hounds had to gather at more widely accessible locations. By the twentieth century it became increasingly common to arrange meets to suit the arrival of trains. Otter hunting experienced further changes with the arrival of motor vehicles. Horses and bicycles were replaced by cars and buses; hound vans became motorised; and railway travel was no longer a necessity. Such changes meant the hounds and the field could travel considerable distances to a fixture on the morning of a meet.[21]

Meets at 6.00 a.m. were replaced with meets at 8.00, 8.30, 9.00, 9.30; some were even as late as 11.00 a.m. Although these modifications became standardised, they were not graciously received by all otter hunters. On 6 October 1906, for instance, an article appeared in *The Field* proclaiming 'The decadence of Otter Hunting'. According to the lady author who wrote under the initials 'MEHC', late meets were at the core of this decadence: 'To my mind the hunting has deteriorated; ... I blame the late meets that now seem to be an almost universal rule for many of the blank days.' This criticism is grounded on the age-old assumption that an animal's scent or drag deteriorates over time. For 'MEHC', early morning hunting – when the drag was fresh – increased the chances of sport, and provided a higher standard of hunting. This perceived standard was not, however, just about scent. If we look more closely at her article, there is a real sense of resentment about the changing composition of the field, and the field's attitude about the activity. 'Granted it is nice to wait and give every subscriber a chance of being in time,' she states, 'even though some of them do look on otter hunting as a novel kind of picnic.'[22] In these terms the perceived decadence of otter hunting is more concerned with what otter hunting was becoming – that is, a modified form of leisure – and who it was attracting rather than the time *per se*.

Otter hunters were fully aware that in the broader context of hunting, blank days were an unfavourable feature. As W. H. Rogers acknowledged: 'to come out perhaps two or three days and have nothing but blanks' was 'of course very disappointing for a novice'.[23] For cynics, however, 'nothing but blanks' was more than 'disappointing'. Hunting without an otter was a sport without a purpose. It was an activity to be smugly disregarded: 'why bother about an otter at all; an aniseed rag can provide plenty of excitement of a sort'.[24] And perhaps more damagingly, a practice to be parodied. The satirical press readily exploited this situation. In *Punch* magazine, for example, the 'glorious uncertainty' of the sport became a reliable source of ridicule. The following cartoon published in *Punch* in 1902 (Fig. 6.1) clearly illustrates this point:

> *Diana.* 'I'm sure I don't know why you call this otter-hunting, Major. Here I've been out four times, and never seen an otter.'
> *M.O.H.* (an enthusiast). 'Ah, there you are you see! That's just where the hunting comes in!'

Here the dialogue alone is a self-explanatory source of humour. The accompanying illustration is also rather revealing. In the foreground of the riverside scene, a wise old huntsman is set against a young, naïve and inquisitive lady. The former is the figure of authority; maintaining traditional hunting knowledge, this male form is also an embodiment of stability. The naivety of the latter, on the other hand, implies a fad-like follower attracted to the activity for reasons other than hunting. This uneasy interplay between these masculine and feminine figures can be interpreted as a subtle commentary on the activity's position as both a traditional form of sport and a modern form of leisure. A closer inspection of the 1902 extract, suggests that beyond the literal reading of the pessimistic female follower, *Diana* also represents the Roman Goddess of the Hunt; praised for her strength, athletic grace, beauty, and hunting ability. In this context, Diana's sceptical remark,

Diana. "I'm sure I don't know why you call this otter-hunting, Major. Here I've been out four times, and never seen an Otter." M. O. H. (an enthusiast). "Ah, there you are, you see! That's just where the hunting comes in!"

FIGURE 6.1 Diana and a Master of Otterhounds. From *Punch's Almanac for 1902* (1901), unpaginated. Courtesy of Punch Cartoon Library.

'I don't know why you call this otter-hunting, Major,' satirically questions the position of the activity as a form of hunting in its traditional sense.

This combination of public perception and personal disappointment no doubt discouraged many a novice from persevering with the sport, and frustrated many a Master who yearned for their subscriptions. The high expectations of newcomers, unwilling or unable to persevere, was certainly a problematic issue which required careful consideration. Although otter hunting literature rarely alluded to this, in certain instances the issue did arise. In *Collections and recollections of natural history and sport* (1886) for example, Reverend G. C. Green recognised this problem and suggested a solution:

> ... the chances of a blank day with otter-hounds are always considerably more than even ... if a man wishes to show his friend from a distance what the sport is like, it is very unlikely that he will be able to do so unless the friend can stay for several weeks and be content to be present at every meet until the lucky day shall come.[25]

By urging the tyro to 'stay for several weeks', the chances of experiencing otter hunting in its entirety was assured. During this extended period, high expectations would not only be met; they could also be deemed irrelevant. This idea of otter hunting as a holiday was by no means confined to the published diaries of ardent sportsmen. On occasions, publications with a much larger readership advertised the activity in this manner. On 7 April 1909, an article in *The Field* entitled 'Otter Hunting from London', styled otter hunting as the ideal 'pick-me-up for the jaded City man'. Although the author initially claims that 'should he strike a good day ... he is converted for life,' the core of the article suggests that one day was not enough for such a conversion:

> ... when he gets his annual holiday of two or three weeks in the summer, instead of going year after year to some seaside resort, which he continues to do because he knows of nothing better, let him find out the meets of some pack of otter hounds, and follow them round the country for a week or two, as long as it pleases him. He will get constant change of scenery, good exercise, and stay at old-fashioned country hostels, where great four-posters and lavender-scented sheets may be still be found.[26]

Whether this advert managed to persuade many readers to exchange their 'annual holiday' on the beach for 'two or three weeks' following otter hounds in the country is uncertain. What is quite apparent, however, is the author's awareness of public perception, and associated efforts to articulate an agreeable version of the activity. In this version, the regularity of blank days are concealed and the strenuous aspects of the sport are played down. Instead, otter hunting is promoted as an 'old-fashioned' alternative to the popular modern 'seaside resort' holiday. This in itself was a rather extreme strategy to secure the interest of newcomers. The broader notion of otter hunting as a leisurely pastime, on the other hand, was a recurring theme. Such themes had the ability to deflect attention from disappointing features and re-shape the expectations of potential followers. Indeed, even on the most uneventful day 'the pleasures of social intercourse' could be 'freely and almost uninterruptedly enjoyed' 'more than in any other branch of chase'.[27] The seasonality, settings, time of meet and pace of pursuit were all conducive to such enjoyment. An important dimension to this was the picnic.

This coupling with picnicking is rather intriguing. The associated activities of eating, relaxing and social intercourse were the antithesis of sport and the epitome of unwelcome change. From this seeming incompatibility it would appear that the idea of 'otter hunting as a novel kind of picnic' was a relatively new-fangled association, but was this really the case? Evidence dating back as far as the 1830s would suggest not. In July 1835 for instance, a member of the Dartmoor Otter Hounds wrote in his diary: 'found above Plym Bridge and had him up two or three hours, but did not kill, as the pretty girls and the picnic spread engaged the hearts of the gallants and the hungry ones'.[28] If 'picnic spreads' and 'pretty girls' could be welcome distractions from 'killing', it could be assumed that food and fraternising were integral aspects of otter hunting rather than a mere novelty. Such an assumption is periodically reinforced throughout otter hunting literature. In 1886 for example Rev. Green openly accepted and embraced the picnic as an important part of the sport: 'a meet of the otter-hounds at Flete very often resembles a gigantic picnic. But although this may not sound business-like to hunting-men, I have seen as good sport at Flete as anywhere, and as good as I ever wish to see.'[29]

After long summer mornings afoot, a short break for food and light refreshments was an eagerly awaited event in itself. Although this was unscheduled, blank mornings, long drags and kills were all suitable circumstances for such an interval. During this pause, the river provided all the essential amenities for resting (Fig. 6.2). The lunchtime interval undoubtedly marked otter hunting as a 'more leisurely and less serious pursuit'[30] than other forms of hunting. This distinction certainly influenced the composition of the field. For 'hunting-men' such as those mentioned by Green, the 'un-business-like' character of the activity wholly detracted from the sport. Newcomers on the other hand were often 'surprised and perhaps a little amused' by this difference.[31] For others, however, the leisurely dimension of otter hunting was the sole attraction. This point is underlined by Jack Ivester Lloyd in his 1952 publication *Come Hunting!* 'In the days before 1939, when food was plentiful and in amazing variety, I believe that a few people actually paid their subscriptions, drove many miles to meets, wandering down mill lanes and over hump-backed bridges just because the sport gave them an excuse to picnic by the river with other cheery folk.'[32]

Otter hunting is sometimes decried by hunting men – by men that is to say, who only hunt to ride – but never, I think, by genuine sportsmen.[33]

Among the followers of a pack of otter-hounds you will find men who never go a-horseback after stag or hind, fox or hare, yet who will trudge mile after mile in the wake of rough sultan or Welsh Hamlet when questing for 'the sly goose-footed prowler's' trail.[34]

Those who hunt 'a-horseback' or 'hunt to ride' were clearly set apart from otter hunters; whose selected mode of movement was distinctly two-legged. As a purely pedestrian pursuit, this sense of horselessness was undoubtedly a distinguished trait of otter hunters and an indispensable characteristic of the sport. Indeed, sporadic accounts from *The Field* magazine reveal how growing attempts to ride to otter hounds were firmly denounced as inappropriate and unacceptable behaviour. On 15 May 1897, for example, one correspondent noted that 'at least one master of otter hounds had issued a notice to those who come out with him that no riding to his hounds will be permitted'. This was reiterated on 31 March 1906: 'riding to otter hounds ... is never required and masters are acting in their own interests when they discourage such an encroachment'.[35] Branded an 'encroachment', horses were not only an unnecessary hindrance to the proceedings; they were also, perhaps more damagingly, a figurative infringement on their identity.

Otter hunting was always presented as an affordable and inclusive activity, which cost barely more than a little fatigue. Often heralded as 'a poor man's pastime',[36] the expenses required to hunt on foot were 'trifling compared with that incurred by fox hunting'.[37] This was down to the cost of the kit and equipment needed for the sport. Cameron dedicates a chapter to these requirements in his book of 1908. The following is a good example of the advice he gives.

The kit necessary for Otter-hunting is by no means so elaborate or expensive as that worn by sportsmen who regularly subscribe to and follow packs of staghounds, foxhounds, or harriers. It need not cost more than the clothes worn by those who hunt with packs of foot-harriers or beagles ... A short serge jacket ... flannel shirt, loose knickerbockers of strong woollen serge, thick woollen hose, and shoes or Highland brogues ... form the most workmanlike costume for Otter-hunting.[38]

The elaborate and expensive kit of mounted sportsmen is set against the inexpensive and workmanlike costume of otter hunters. Clad in woollen garments from head to foot, otter hunters clearly emphasise the functional over the aesthetic, and perhaps more specifically endorse the aesthetic of the functional. In terms of equipment horses, which required stables and grooms, were extravagant accessories compared to the 'good pair of legs', 'thick pair of boots'[39] and serviceable pole required for otter hunting. In order to maintain this cultural distinction and safeguard the identity of the sport, it was essential that otter hunting forbade the presence of mounted sportsmen. This in itself was an effective way of keeping the field select. In *Hunting England* (1936), the foxhunter Sir W. Beach Thomas noted: 'the votaries of otter hunting are relatively few, for the very good reason that in fox- and stag-hunting the horse is at least as important as the hound or the quarry'.[40] This kind of criticism typified the views of those who would 'hunt to ride'. As the archetypal model of hunting, alternative cultures of hunting not only had the near-impossible task of disproving such notions, but also of persuading those who subscribed to them that such thoughts were untrue. Otter hunters therefore had to cultivate complex counter claims to ensure self-definition. In this process certain characteristics gained a heightened appreciation and importance.

As otter hunting was conducted entirely on foot, it was invariably promoted as a 'healthy and invigorating sport'.[41] This claim was directly tied to the distances over which hounds led followers and the duration of hunts. Frequently lasting between five and seven hours, the distance travelled varied greatly. Where the longest drag on one otter was recorded at 23 miles, for instance; the longest time recorded to hunt one otter, 10¾ hours, covered only four miles.[42] Certain authorities who hunted in the 1870s had even maintained 'it was no uncommon thing to walk thirty miles during a hunt'.[43] Later reports in *The Field*, however, suggest that distances of six to twelve miles were more common. In terms of physical exercise, it therefore required varying degrees of exertion that could prove both demanding and relaxing.

Another distinguishing feature of this sport was that the actual pursuit was not merely confined to the banks of the waterside. Hounds frequently led followers through and across watery channels. A day's otter hunting could therefore include stomping through uninviting undergrowth abounding with thistles, thorns, nettles, and densely wooded foliage; leaping over brooks and dykes; standing in streams; and wading through rivers (Fig. 6.3). The more precarious prospect of getting stuck up to the waist in mud, or worst still, losing balance and becoming completely submerged in treacherous waters, were also distinct possibilities. In 1862 Plunger proudly publicised these requirements in *The Field*:

> If ... [an individual is] worthy of being enrolled as a member of the
> doughty fraternity of otter-hunters, he must not only regard a thirty
> miles tramp over rocks, swamps and bogs, precipitous banks, and
> through tangled woods, at a pace of eight miles an hour, as a mere

FIGURE 6.3 The Hawkstone Otter Hounds drawing rough country in the River Teift, near Lampeter. From Coventry and Cameron, *Otter Hunting* (1938), plate facing p. 50.

trifle, but at the same time he must be nearly amphibious in habit, and as proof against influenza and rheumatism, as his game, and think no more of standing for hours together in a pool up to the arm-pits than he would be of tossing down a dram of Glenlivet.[44]

The idea that otter hunters were 'doughty' individuals, who not only encountered extreme conditions but more importantly excelled in them was regularly mobilised to define proponents of the sport. Importantly, these distinguishing features were still being celebrated in the middle of the twentieth century. In 1939, the July edition of the *Picture Post* had an article by Douglas Macdonald Hastings called 'Hunting the Otter'. The author reiterated the aforementioned requirements in a style more suited to the times: 'To qualify as a follower of otter hounds, it is necessary to be blessed with seal-like imperviousness to water; an affection for muddy places; and the urge to out-walk a hiking club.'[45] For proponents of the sport only the most ardent individuals could rise to the demands of otter hunting.

As well as defining the otter hunter, horselessness also informed the pace of the pursuit. As 'nothing' could 'be more fatal to the success of otter-hunting than hurry,' the exhilarating speeds inherent to riding to hounds were replaced with 'a reasonable walking pace.'[46] Following otter hounds at a slow speed ensured that the field remained at close proximity to the hounds. This was significant as the interaction of hounds in the landscape – known as houndwork – was highly valued throughout hunting cultures. If houndwork could be differentiated through proximity, then ideas about what hunting should be could be challenged. Rogers eulogised houndwork and horselessness in this way in his reflective *Records of the Cheriton Otter Hounds*.

> A lady complains: 'It's such slow sport.' Yes, Madam, it is, if your one idea of sport is rapid movement through the air on the back of a horse. But if you are interested in hounds, and can learn their names and different characteristics, what each hound is doing and why it is doing it, even a 'sticky' hunt will present points of interest to you which you would never otherwise perceive. I wonder how many people who ride (or motor) to hounds in the shires know more than a couple of hounds at the outside by name, or even care to do more than have a good gallop and a kill at the end of it. With otter-hunting houndwork is everything ...[47]

In this rather resentful outburst, the heart of the foxhunting fraternity is presented as a centre for self-indulgent thrill seekers demanding instant gratification. For Rogers the rapidity of riding to hounds generated a blinkered view of hunting which devalued the importance of houndwork. Horses had essentially led foxhunters to lose sight of the foundational process that gave rise to the activity and facilitated their enjoyment. Set against these claims, otter hunters styled themselves as perceptive individuals, who not only appreciated but also understood an older more authentic style of hunting, and more detailed engagement with nature.

III

> So far as the science of hunting goes, the pursuit of the Otter demands at least as much knowledge, skill, and experience as the pursuit of the fox.[48]

In *Beagling and Otter Hunting*, Colville went out of his way to explain that there was much more to otter hunting than 'simply putting hounds in a river and setting out for a pleasant walk in the country'.[49] The very fact that he felt the need to make this point in the middle of the twentieth century tells us a great deal about the public perception of the activity. For proponents of the sport, otter hunting was an unpredictable science in an uncontrollable environment. Its practitioners had to take into account a whole range of interrelated factors. This section will investigate how these factors shaped hunting practices and procedures, and informed the identity of otter hunters.

(a) The Unseen Quarry

> No man can hunt a wild animal with success if he is not fairly acquainted with that animals habits and mode of life ... I believe [the otter] to be the least known and most inscrutable of all our wild animals; so much so that its very existence is widely doubted in districts where otter hounds are never seen.[50]

The perceived absence of the otter from the landscape was an integral aspect of otter hunting. It not only provided the foundation for the process that aimed to bring about the presence of the animal; it also enhanced the perceived complexity of the activity, and, elevated ideas of the skilled sportsman. What really set this form of hunting apart from all others was the 'inscrutable' ways of the otter. Unlike the deer, fox and hare, the otter was 'a thing of mystery'.[51] With no fixed home, it was always on the move. Often roaming many miles in a night, it generally retired to a sheltered hollow beside the water during the day. Typical haunts ranged from tree roots, dried-up drains and stick heaps, to piles of rock, thick vegetation, and rabbit burrows. As otters showed themselves so rarely, even their presence was often doubted. Bryden emphasises this point: 'until quite lately any countryman would have scoffed at the idea of such an outlandish beast being found at all'.[52] Cameron extended this notion in 1908: 'even among Otter-hunters comparatively few have observed their quarry except when he is in process of being hunted'.[53]

Owing to the combination of traits that sanctioned its unseen status, an otter's whereabouts could only be confirmed by tracing remnants of its former presence. For the practised eyes of otter hunters, this included the five-toed impressions of webbed feet ('spur', 'seal' or 'mark'), the animal's excrement ('spraint', 'wedging' or 'coke'), and the remains of partially eaten fish. Although it was possible that other predators were responsible for this, such remnants were invariably attributed to the otter. In 1861, for instance, William Turnbull wrote: 'We had ample evidence that the midnight wanderer of the deep had in his wanton destruction killed some of the fish, as the dead were seen by the shore of the lake'.[54] It was this 'wanton destruction' which positioned the otter as the principal enemy of broader riverside cultures.

Although each of these visual clues helped to prove that an otter had been in the vicinity, they did not reveal precise locations. The only way that an otter could be found was by means of its enduring trail of scent ('line', 'drag' or 'trail'). The question of scent was (and still is) a mystery shared by all practitioners of hunting. The widely held view was that climatic conditions effected its quality. High winds, cold air, direct sunlight, and high humidity were all said to account for bad scent; the opposite conditions maintained the contrary; and, all scent deteriorated with time. Owing to the animal's interdependence with both land and water, the *actual* scent of the otter was, to a certain extent, less mysterious than that of the fox and the hare, the explanation for this being that movement between the two, left drops of scent-carrying water ('*wet* scent') on the land. According to Arthur Heinemann this residue could impregnate 'even the most sun-parched ground with a perfume so ravishing that the delicate nose of the pure, rough otter-hound' could 'own it even though eight-and-forty hours have elapsed'.[55]

If scent on the land was considered to be relatively reliable, its relationship with water was rather less predictable. The element in which the otter moved, was not only watery, it was a landscape in motion. Abounding with currents and erratic flows, this fluid constitution had the capacity to conceal an otter's movements, and, confuse the noses of the hounds. Heinemann reflected on this situation:

> … it is no child's play to circumvent an animal who is thoroughly at home in and under water, who knows every hide and holt and hover for miles, and whose scent, as the water washes over his back, flows away from him, leading hounds full cry down stream further and further away from their quarry.[56]

Although traces of scent remained strongest at the waterside, along banks, in foliage, and on rocks, flowing water carried scent away. If an otter had crossed a river or swam downstream overnight, the olfactory remnants of these aquatic movements could prove incoherent, if not irretrievable. Indeed, the buoyant scent described by Heinemann was at once confirmatory and inconclusive, providing guidance yet misdirection. The end of a trail did not necessarily provide an otter, just as its pursuance did not ensure that the hounds were getting closer to their quarry. Every possible situation involving the movement of the unseen quarry, water and scent was translated. If the trail did not lead to an otter, the hounds might have 'flashed over' or 'passed over' the drag, leaving the otter undisturbed in its holt. This could happen through the pack's eagerness, with hounds over-running the drag at speed. Alternatively, the quarry could be 'out of mark', that is, residing in a holt with an underwater entrance which concealed its scent from the outer air. Failing this, the otter may have travelled a considerable distance in the water, or swum across to the adjacent bank. Then again, the hounds could have followed the 'ream', and thus been 'swimming the foil'. Or followed the drag in the reverse direction, and be 'hunting the heel'. The experienced huntsman could interpret these possibilities through the sounds and movements of the dogs.

(b) Techniques for Finding

Before you can hunt him you must find him.[57]

After the pack had been taken to the chosen riverbank, the hounds would be put to water and led either upstream or downstream. Unlike foxhunting, where it was a heinous form of misconduct for anyone to be in front of the pack, in otterhunting the whipper-in was expected to lead the hounds. The duties of the whip were by no means easy. The job commanded an intimate knowledge of 'every hound in the pack by name, sight, voice and reputation'.[58] For this level of understanding to be reached, it was widely held that 'a whip must have taught hounds respect in the kennel' and even 'lived amongst them'.[59] Alongside these skills, the whipper-in 'required keenness, commonsense and physical fitness'.[60] These were essential qualities when the job description demanded being 'here, there, and everywhere, no bank too steep, no river too rough, and hardly any too deep'.[61] In most – though not all – cases, 'an athletic young man in good fettle' occupied this role.[62] As the primary aim of the pack was to search for ('draw') and detect ('own') an otter's drag, the whip would encourage the hounds 'to examine … every likely looking place … over and over again'.[63] During this thorough examination of the river, the huntsman followed closely behind. This rearward position was ideal for observing the working pack and controlling their rate of advancement. This holt-to-holt system of finding was often referred to as the 'needle in the bottle of hay method'.[64]

During this process, followers also had important roles to play. According to Jack Ivestor Lloyd the way that individuals interacted with the landscape whilst searching for the otter helped to define them as otter hunters. Lloyd divided the field into three specific categories:

> There are the 'Tree-men', the men who can never pass a tree without belabouring the trunk and pushing their poles into any cavities among the roots … Another type is the 'White Hunter' who, bent nearly double, walks the river bank, eyeing and sniffing stones and tufts of reeds. He goes ahead of other followers, not far behind the huntsman … He it is who spots the seal or finds the spraint … In another age and land he would have been an Indian scout … When the otter stows itself away under a culvert, in a drain or under an overhanging bank, the amphibian follower is always at hand, ready to plunge in, no matter how deep the water, and to 'progle' with his pole, however chilly the day.[65]

The more popular otter hunting became, the more pressure huntsmen were put under to perform. A consequence of this was that different huntsmen developed different techniques for finding otters. These divergent techniques were often the subject of discussion. The main point of contention was the speed at which hounds advanced. Cameron, for one, was highly critical of fast-drawing huntsmen. In *The Otter-Hunters' Diary and Companion for 1910* he stated: 'Don't "kill" your field on a "blank" day by setting the pace at five miles an hour. It may possibly be your own fault that the day is a "blank" one, and you have no right to "take it out" of the ladies of your field.'[66] Here Cameron sets the authority of the huntsman against the importance of the field. In these terms, the pace itself becomes a vehicle for criticism and an indictor of compromise. One such huntsman who was criticised in this manner – albeit not by Cameron – was Mr Fred Collier of the Culmstock Otter Hounds.

> Mr Fred Collier had learned his otter hunting in a hard school under his uncle William, but though he inherited his uncle's lovely note on the horn, he was never as good a huntsman. He was an athletic type, and an untiring walker, and used to draw very fast. He did not sufficiently consider his field, either out hunting or in the matter of publishing fixtures, with the result that both followers and subscriptions fell off.[67]

This suggests that the ability of huntsmen was not only rated in relation to practical and physical qualities, but also their broader level of regard for followers. As packs became increasingly reliant on subscribers, it became increasingly important that the huntsman's methods met their expectations. Although this reliance was widely recognised, certain huntsmen would not pander to such demands. Major Geoffrey R. Mott, who mastered the Dartmoor Otter Hounds in 1927–28, was one such huntsman:

> I always maintain that the most useful huntsman is not the man who succeeds in getting the highest 'tally', but one who *passes over the fewest otters*. The great art of otter-hunting consists in drawing closely, yet wasting as little time as possible when hounds shew [sic] that no otter has been on the water recently. It is the height of foolishness to criticise a huntsman – as one has so often heard done – for drawing too fast …[68] A good voice, and a good note on the horn are admirable qualities, yet of little value unless combined with a real instinct and exceptional powers of observation.[69]

It is quite apparent that Mott did not associate the pace that huntsmen set with ability. Instead, the efficient use of time was more important. For this, instinct and intuition were of real value. If a huntsman possessed these 'inherent' characteristics, then all decisions on whether to draw fast or slow would be vindicated. A prime example of a huntsman that reaped the rewards from this kind of vindication was Mr Sandy Rose of the Essex Otter Hounds. In 1909 an article appeared in the *Sporting and Dramatic Magazine*, hailing Rose as an innovator of the 'modern methods of otter hunting'. The article reads:

Under the able Mastership of Mr L. Rose, the Essex Otter Hounds have again resumed that career of super-excellent sport, which has so rapidly placed them, though comparatively a modern pack, in the front rank among otter hunts ... Mr Rose is not content to hunt the otter after the old-fashioned methods only too common in the south and west of England, putting hounds to water on a given river, making it good above (or below) the place of meeting and then going on down (or up) stream even without a drag of any sort until, the hands of the clock pointing to some hour past midday without a find, it is time to go home after an undeniably 'blank' day. That sort of hunting was only too familiar to a generation of otter hunters past, but it does not satisfy the present generation, and it is still more unlikely to prove acceptable to a future race of sportsmen. They are no longer content to go forth merely for the pleasure of seeing the reeds shaken with the wind. Sport is what they have paid their money and given their time to enjoy, and sport it is that modern Masters of Otter Hounds must be prepared to show their subscribers under every condition.[70]

This idea that people paid money to see action really cuts against the view that they were only attracted to the activity for picnicking purposes. In turn, it also makes the assumption that in the old days people did not mind if an otter was not found. Interestingly, the innovative feature that Rose introduced to 'satisfy the present generation' was the motor car. If, after drawing a given river it became evident that an otter had not been present, Rose would motor several miles downstream with a single couple of hounds. These hounds would then draw the river. If a drag was then owned, the pack and field could be relocated and hounds put back to water. Although this fusion of modern technology with traditional hunting methods may seem rather unusual, according to the article the proof of their justification was the results. Indeed, the 1909 season was the most successful on record for the Essex OH. In 76 days it produced 39 kills out of 57 otters found.[71]

A complicated figure of the huntsman, made up of attributes such as efficiency, display and practicality, was produced in relation to these diverse techniques for finding. When these traits were suitably coupled, the huntsman was judged to be exemplary. If, however, an insufficient number of otters were killed, there was always the danger that display could turn into showiness and the huntsman would be looked upon in a less favourable light. It was in an attempt to satisfy subscribers and to uphold their own reputations that huntsmen devised novel new methods and reinvented traditions.

(c) Participatory practices

> … no Huntsman of Otterhounds seconded only by his staff account for
> an average otter unless aided by his field.[72]

Once an otter had been 'put down' and given several minutes 'law', the
actual hunting would commence. At this stage of the hunt, the function of
the hounds was to tire out, capture and kill the quarry. The otter's role was
to evade the hounds for as long as possible. As the otter had the opportunity
to disappear back into its watery environment, otter hunting was often
likened to 'a glorified game of hide and seek'.[73] Lasting any time from several
minutes to many hours, the otter could be 'out of touch' for long periods;
'fresh found' by the pack, only to be lost again moments later. Essentially,
the scenting quality of the hounds alone was not enough to seek out and
account for an otter. Instead, additional aid was required from the field.

Participatory practices clearly set otter hunting apart from other forms
of hunting. Cameron underlines this distinction in *Otters and Otter-Hunting*:
'… in stag-hunting, fox-hunting, or hare-hunting the Field is sometimes the
greatest obstacle to a proper enjoyment of the sport, whereas with Otter-
hunting the success of the day depends to a large extent upon the presence
of a knowledgeable and hard-working Field.'[74] A 'knowledgeable and hard-
working field' would consist of individuals with a clear comprehension of the
importance of seeing, and the importance of doing. The chief requisites of
such an understanding included the visual appreciation of the otter in the
landscape, and a degree of familiarity with the formalities of otter hunting
etiquette. The former demanded that all eyes focused strictly on the water.
The latter often required individuals to render their bodies as components
of collective hunting devices in the water.

The *practice of seeing* was taken extremely seriously. The huntsman would
instruct the entire field to spread out along the riverside, stand still, keep
quiet, watch the water and wait. Whilst waiting, there were a number
of signs to watch for. If the otter was swimming deep under water, air
bubbles from its fur often rose to the surface and produced a 'chain' of
bubbles. When swimming closer to the surface, such movements were more
likely to cause a wave. It might 'vent', that is, take in air by pushing its
snout above the water. It might be viewed in clear water, or even take to
the land. Actually knowing whether the otter had really been 'gazed' was
often considered as one of most difficult parts of otter hunting. Indeed, after
informing followers: 'When "looking out" keep your eyes on the water: otters
never fly', Cameron asserts: 'If you are *sure* you see the otter, and no one else
does, shout "Tally-ho!" – and risk the consequences if it was only a fish or
a water-vole.'[75] Such a risk was an alluring feature as the dexterity attached
to this practice could be transferred to any individual; at the same time,
myopic lapses could easily taint that same person's reputable character in the

field. Prolonged periods of watching in silence no doubt induced momentary blunders by impatient followers.[76]

The participatory *practice of doing* which the majority of otter hunts readily employed was the 'stickle'. Introduced in the early 1800s, the main purpose of this device was to prevent the otter from escaping into unhuntable waters.[77] This was important as such conditions made hunting a more difficult procedure for the hounds, and a more lengthy process for the followers. When an otter had been viewed, members of the field would wade into the river and stand conjoined in a line from one bank to the other (see Fig. 6.4). This bodily barrier could prevent the otter from going upstream ('top stickle') or downstream ('bottom stickle'). In certain circumstances both a top and bottom stickle would be formed. A newspaper article recounting a day's hunting with the Eastern Counties Otter Hounds in 1905 provides a good example of what a stickle entailed.

> Once again viewed above the shallow, a stickle was quickly formed, Miss Gravell, Mrs Runnacles and Miss Goring being among the first to get in; and may I say here that they, with others, guarded this post of danger (and discomfort) for over three hours and thoroughly deserved the praise the Master gave them.[78]

In these terms, the stickle resembled a militaristic manoeuvre. Regimented by the Master, a series of battles were to be overcome. Not only was the field set against the dangerous quarry; man was set against nature. The

FIGURE 6.4
Followers of the Culmstock Otter Hounds forming a stickle. From Rod Adair, *Reflections along a chain* (2000), p. 82.

FIGURE 6.5
A whipper-
in bringing
a dead otter
ashore after
a kill. From
Coventry and
Cameron,
Otter Hunting
(1938), plate
facing p.34.

field's preventative action became an empowering instrument towards the visceral engagement between the cultured hounds and the gallant sporting adversary.

In bringing about the presence of the otter, these participatory practices not only heightened a sense of belonging, they also positioned the bodies and prepared the eyes for 'the kill'. Marking the end of the cultural event, the kill was a particularly inclusive spectacle. First, as the Master needed to bring the carcass ashore, hunt staff would pull the hounds off the dead otter with their hands, knees and flashing steel-capped poles (Fig. 6.5). Once retrieved, the huntsman then ceremoniously raised the otter above his head in full view of the Field. By this stage, a crowd of spectators would have collected around him. After the weight of the otter had been recorded, the carcass was then dismembered; the 'trophies' (head, 'mask'; tail, 'rudder'; and, feet 'pads') each cut off in due form and ceremony. This was a moment of elevated symbolism for 'new entries' as the visceral ritual culminated with a ceremonial blooding of cheeks, forehead and chin with a small piece of the otter's flesh to 'enter' him or her into the otter hunting community. The body would then be tossed to the eagerly expectant pack, to the cries of: 'Hi, worry, worry, worry', 'Who-whoop! Tear him up and eat him'. At the finish, a 'Recheat' or 'Rattle' was finally blown on the horn to signify that a kill had been scored.

> ... in otter hunting, the hounds, the invigorating air of the early morning, and the superb beauty of England's valleys and dales constitutes the chief attractions ... the quarry itself is quite a secondary consideration.[79]

Although in some cases the kill was the most climactic constituent of the hunt, this was not necessarily the most appealing aspect for all followers. For many, the preceding aesthetic of otter hunting wholly supplanted the visceral spectacle. Thomas Littleton Powys, the Fourth Baron Lilford, was one such individual. When he followed the Buckinghamshire OH in the 1890s he insisted that the drag-hunt was the prettiest part of it, and that many regretted the kill.[80] Interestingly, this kind of sentiment was more commonly articulated in response to external criticism. In the summer of 1905, for example, several readers of *Madame* magazine took umbrage at the thought of ladies killing otters. Fortunately, the pen of J. C. Bristow-Noble (a member of the Crowhurst OH) was at hand to pacify the situation. Aware of the importance of positive public perceptions, he reassuringly wrote: 'In my article on otter hunting which appeared in *Madame* for July 22, I mentioned the names of several ladies, who participate in the sport. On behalf of some of these daughters of Eve, I have now to state that it is their opinion that the quarry, as is frequently the case, should always be allowed to escape.'[81]

As the introductory citation from the unpublished diaries of the Crowhurst Otter Hounds reveals, this relegation of the quarry as 'a secondary consideration' was also surprisingly prevalent amongst otter hunters. The following passage from a history of the Wye Valley Otter Hounds reaffirms this point. Written in 1935, the author explains that: 'Beyond the possibility of a good hunt and a close view of hound work, the field, even on a dragless day, is enchanted by the beautiful scenery through which these rivers run.'[82] Here, the importance of the riverside landscape is emphasised over all other claims. Now, this alone is not necessarily peculiar. Participants of other rural pursuits also appreciated their surroundings. Anglers and ramblers also encountered and experienced the same spatialities of landscape.[83] Yet despite this, otter hunters still maintained that their sport had sensory dominion over the countryside. According to commentators such as Cameron, the reason for this distinction was the combination of the sport's peripatetic character, its demands of physical exertion, and of course, the river itself:

> Otter Hunting is, of all the various field sports pursued in the British Isles, the one most marked by those pleasures to be derived from the beauties of nature, and from hours spent in the most picturesque and soul-solacing scenes which the countryside has to offer ... [W]hile the angler is tied by the necessities of his sport to one place ... the

otter-hunter, owing to the exigencies of his sport, traverses, perhaps, ten or a dozen or even more miles of riverside scenery.[84]

In these terms, otter hunting is styled as an expansive engagement in a variety of surroundings and range of scenes. Through the pedestrian diligence of pursuit 'every type of river' was 'open to exploration'. For those who elected to follow otterhounds, 'fascinating new tracts of country hitherto inaccessible and unexplored' were opened up.[85] The meandering courses of rivers, streams and brooks would guide hounds through valleys, dales, meads, moors, combes, glens and pastures, and immerse otter hunters in picturesque, placid, wild, romantic and smooth scenes. It was this endless variety which led many otter hunters to conclude that 'Much of the joy of otterhunting comes … from its association with river valleys'.[86]

This heightened appreciation of the landscape was also directly tied to the unseen status of the quarry. This chapter has clearly shown that otters were not always found; houndwork could not always be seen; the field did not always have a part to play; and, the quarry was not always killed. If we add to this the fact that the weather did not always facilitate picnicking, it becomes quite obvious that each of the aforementioned peculiar claims were by no means guaranteed. In order to maintain the interest of would-be otter hunters, and safeguard the sport's reputation, it was therefore essential that authors emphasised the sport's most permanent feature. For this reason, the riverside landscape could be regarded as the most powerful peculiar claim that otter hunting could possess. If the landscape through which otter hounds guided its followers was the activity's chief attraction, then the tyro to otter hunting could never be disappointed.

CHAPTER SEVEN

❧

Science, sport and the otter, 1945–1978

by Charles Watkins, David Matless *and* Paul Merchant

O TTER HUNTING remained contentious throughout the post-war period until it ceased when the otter became a protected species in 1978. The hunting debate was given purpose by the increasing realisation from the late fifties that otters were becoming rarer. In the early 1950s naturalists still knew little about otters, partly because of their elusive, evasive quality; a series of post-war studies began to uncover their ecology and life history. The otter became better known through the 1950s and '60s through study by hunters, naturalists, and scientists. It became a focus of public interest with the continued prominence of Henry Williamson's *Tarka the Otter* (1927) and the publication and filming of Gavin Maxwell's *Ring of Bright Water* (1960 and 1969). As otters became more popular, concern over a decline in the otter population grew, and hunting statistics became a key resource for the documentation of the decline. The precise cause of the decline in otters remained a mystery until the very end of the period.

While the Nature Conservancy and others studying the otter understood themselves as concerned strictly with scientific research, issues of value judgment are clearly bound into efforts to understand the otter, most notably where scientific study meets the practice of otter hunting, whether in the use of hunt data or the questioning of hunting knowledge. This chapter examines the debate over the decline of the otter 1945–78 through a study of contemporary sources and records including scientific reports, hunting books, novels and public records. The paper draws also on studies of the broader cultures of nature in Herefordshire and Norfolk, areas where otter hunting continued through the period, but through different landscape ecologies and social environments.[1] Local study has given access to renderings of the otter in private as well as public circulation, and such observations of animal behaviour help us to draw out conclusions on hunting, the otter's public image, and the affinities and differences being detected between human and animal.

I

As hunting continued in the post-war period, debate is stalked by a number of accusations concerning the behaviour of otters and their pursuers. Was the otter an animal usefully part of the landscape's ecology, or a ruthless predator wilfully disturbing the balance of rivers through the plundering of fish stocks? Were otter hunters a traditional group usefully part of the landscape's ecology, or ruthless barbarians indifferent to cruelty and out of place in a modern world?[2]

For more than thirty years after the Second World War otter hunting remained a legal activity. It was defended stoutly by its adherents, although these were always a small minority of enthusiasts. Indeed, for most of the post-war period there were no more than thirteen organised otter hunts. During the war otter hunting was curtailed, but meets soon restarted. In April 1945 the *Hereford Times* noted that 'The Hawkstone Otter Hounds will meet (waters permitting) on Saturday 21st April at Craven Arms, and on Saturday, 28th April at Arrow Green, both at 10.30'.[3] The same paper reviewed a hunt on the River Teme in August 1945. The Hawkstone Otter Hounds with Captain R.E.Wallace, as master had met at Burford Bridge and 'the pack soon found the otter, which made up-stream, and went to earth in a holt on the side of the bank. The terriers did some spade work, soon dislodged it, and it took to the water. After an exciting hunt hounds killed it in mid-stream.'[4] The tone and content of this does not suggest that the author, or the editor of the *Hereford Times*, regard otter hunting as in any way problematic or unpopular. The Hawkstone Otter Hounds continued to announce their appointments in the *Hereford Times* through the 1950s and 1960s.[5]

Robert Colville, hunting editor of *The Field*, reviewed the state of otter hunting in Britain in *Beagling and Otter Hunting*, published in 1940. There were seventeen packs of otterhounds, two composed of 'pure bred' otterhounds, the remainder a mixture of 'pure-bred, foxhounds, staghounds and cross-bred hounds'.[6] Rivers in Herefordshire were hunted by the Wye Valley Otterhounds and the Hawkstone Otterhounds, those in Norfolk by the Bure Valley Otterhounds and the Eastern Counties Otterhounds. Otter hunting was a practice through which otters became known, in a number of senses. The hunt made the presence of otters in rivers visible; hounds and people, several in striking uniforms, marked out the elusive animal. It was claimed that being able to find otters and then to hunt them relied on intimate knowledge of their habitat and behaviour. Colville wrote that 'the Master of otterhounds must know every place in which an otter is likely to be found. The spot chosen for the meet will depend on this knowledge.'[7] L.C.R.Cameron wrote on 'The science of hunting the otter' in 1936, asserting that the Master should 'know every certain holt on his various rivers' and describing the science of finding (marking) an otter by a close examination of the ground and a search for spraints.[8] This attempt to follow signs and tracks is echoed in the efforts of naturalists and scientists to study otters. Colville noted that the 'appearance of the otter is, of course, well known to otterhunters, but I find that many other people would be hard put to make an adequate description of it'.[9] In his chapter on 'The Otter' he places it taxonomically and combines careful description with average measurements and comments on behaviour and life cycle. The killing of the otter is viewed as an opportunity to see it closely, to handle it and to record its size and weight. In *Deer, Hare and Otter Hunting* (1936), the Earl of Coventry, then Master of the Hawkstone Hounds, wrote a detailed chapter on the otter, including average measurements and descriptions of its life cycle and 'habits'.[10]

Other sporting naturalists also offered their insights into the otter's life, though not always in association with otter hunting. Thus Norfolk sporting naturalist and conservationist landowner Anthony Buxton, influential in the Norfolk Naturalists' Trust, discussed otters on his Horsey estate in *Fisherman Naturalist* (1946). In this 'paradise for otters', animals learned that the sound of Buxton shooting duck meant 'a cheap and appetising breakfast': 'I feel no resentment if they give me an occasional view of their graceful antics in the water. After all they have a far longer title than I to the sporting facilities of the place.'[11] In a May 1947 BBC radio broadcast Buxton reflected that some of his favourite birds and animals were those 'with a taste for sport, because I've got that taste myself'. Buxton pointed out that 'an otter catches a fish or a duck, so do I. A jay eats other birds' eggs – so do most people when they can get them. And why not? Anyhow we shall all go on doing it.'[12] Buxton's presentation of the otter as (like him) a sporting animal included emphasis on play: 'I believe that there is nothing that gives an otter greater pleasure than snow'. Otter tracks revealed enjoyment of snow slides: 'One of them had made six slides, with only one galloping stride in between each slide'.[13] The sense of the otter as playful and intelligent could bolster arguments against hunting; the otter as playful, intelligent *and sporting* could give it equivalent footing to the sporting human. For some this implied hunting was a noble battle, for others that the otter did not deserve the hunt. Buxton himself began his account with a mildly critical recollection of following otterhounds in Essex, where he felt the odds were too heavy against the animal.

The relationship between otter hunting and fishing remained problematic, with considerable divergence of views as to the diet of the otter. Colville noted that the 'fisherman maintains that the otter eats all his fish while the otterhunter argues that its range of food is much wider'.[14] The Earl of Coventry felt that fishermen usually claimed that the otter took 'the best salmon and trout' and that 'the poor old otter gets all the blame for the harm he does, and very little thanks for the good'.[15] Yet Colville and others claimed hunting as a vital form of country management through knowledge about diet. Colville considered that the amount of damage caused by the otter 'fully warrants the keeping down of its numbers by hunting. A favourite habit of the otter is to catch a fish, take two bites from the shoulders and then catch another one.'[16] Cameron used a similar argument when he pointed out that hunting 'serves a utilitarian purpose' in controlling the number of otters in 'waters now so valuable to an ever-increasing number of anglers of every class'. However, he is keen to distinguish hunting as a field sport from a grubby kind of extermination: otter hunting, he argued, was not 'a spurious, poaching, rat-catching species of amusement' because the 'sporting odds are on an average more than three to one in favour of the otter'.[17]

The fisherman's view of the otter as fierce, and relations between otter hunting and otter extermination, appear in Thomas Davison's *Angler and Otter* (1950), an account of fishing on the River Lune in the 1930s and 1940s. Here the otter appears to threaten the fisherman: 'I fished down to the Suspension Bridge without getting a rise … I still had that uneasy feeling concerning the otter, which caused me to keep looking behind as though I was being stalked by some monster.'[18] Davison later hooks the otter, which breaks his line and causes him to flee: 'I have never really forgotten that scare and I have had a nasty dream through it also'.[19] Later he organises a 'private otter hunt', and discovers a number of 'partly eaten' salmon with 'flesh eaten from the shoulders and back'. Davison decides that 'there could only be one culprit – the otter' and alerts his brother and a friend, who in turn recruit another man with 'a terrier and an Irish Setter' and a local farmer. The four set off with the dogs and three guns and kill two otters: 'there were no more dead salmon'.

Through the accounts of fishermen, water keepers and otter hunters recurs the motif of the fish found on banks or rocks, with bites taken out of the back or shoulder. Like a gangster's calling card, these seem to advertise the presence of the otherwise invisible otter. In 1953 Norfolk wildfowler and naturalist Alan Savory described 'War with the Otters' preying on his ornamental duck, extending the image of the otter killing without the intention to eat: 'Some of them were found lying wounded on the banks, with half their bills torn off. Some had a great bite out of their breasts. Some were found dead and mutilated out on the marsh.'[20] Savory killed three otters by trapping and shooting, though his account also registered admiration: 'He was a beautiful animal, and he stared me out as I shot a .22 into his brain'. Savory considered otters to be 'lovely animals' but argued that for their own benefit they should remain 'behind that secret curtain of the wild', and not threaten wildfowl or fish: 'when otters go in for robbery and violence and try conclusions with the human race it can only end one way'.[21]

In 1950 there was considerable public debate on the relation between otters and fishing in the letters pages of the *Hereford Times*. Following the reported hooking of a female otter near Wye Bridge in Hereford, Captain H. A. Gilbert wrote a 'plea' for the 'protection of otters'. Gilbert, 64, was a well-known naturalist and ornithologist who was perhaps most famous for having first filmed the Golden Eagle at its nest. He was also a keen salmon fisherman who had published *The Tale of a Wye Fisherman* in 1928.[22] Gilbert represented otters as an interesting sight and sound, especially unusual and valuable close to the buildings and people of the city: 'Very few cities can boast a pair of otters in the vicinity of an old bridge and an ancient cathedral'. He claimed, from a lifetime of fishing experience, that otters did not often attack valuable fish: 'I have only twice seen a dead salmon on the rocks with a piece bitten out of the shoulder which is always said to be the trade mark of the otter'. Gilbert went on to emphasise the delight of leaving otters alone and watching them: 'Last year, just above the Scar, at Monnington, my wife and I watched an otter fishing the shallow. She brought out four eels at to the bank and ate them ... Then having had enough slid into the water with that mysterious way that otters always use. We enjoyed the interlude in fishing.'[23] The angler who hooked the otter, P. G. Eaton, of Hereford, replied the following week stating that 'The same otter was fishing as usual the following morning. I myself watched it catch five eels.' Eaton noted that this was 'the first otter I have seen in its wild state, and I for one am very interested in their behaviour', but hoped the otters would move to Monnington to 'remain as the fishing guests' of Gilbert.[24] The following week, Gilbert confirmed that he did not regard otters as threats to fishing, pointing out that he had recently stocked his waters with small trout and the otters that he saw at dusk were 'catching eel not trout'.

Increasingly, however, knowing otters through hunting them was under threat. Colville thought that 'No one can long be unaware that there is a growing section of the untutored public which would, in its ignorance, make otterhunting illegal to-morrow'. He thought that 'hunting people' had 'no idea of the vast and ceaseless propaganda which is being waged against them'.[25] In the late 1940s arguments against otter hunting gained national prominence. In 1949 a Parliamentary Bill was introduced into the House of Commons to prohibit hunting with hounds of deer, otters and badgers, and the coursing of hares and rabbits. It was defeated, but led to the setting up of a Home Office Committee on Cruelty to Wild Animals, chaired by John Scott Henderson KC.[26] The Committee was composed of various otter authorities, including members of hunts, other sportsmen, an angler, the editor of *The Countryman*, the Secretary of the Transport and General Workers Union and a zoologist.[27] A key finding in its report published in 1951 was that otter hunting 'does undoubtedly involve suffering for the otter' and crucially, that 'the degree of it is rather greater than in most other field sports'. It considered that the future of hunting depended on 'the need for control' in relation to the harm otters caused to fisheries and that more needed to be known about the 'habits and way of life of the otter'. The report recommended that research should be commissioned by the recently established Nature Conservancy, 'or some other suitable body', into the feeding habits and natural history of the otter.[28]

II

The Nature Conservancy was established in 1949 under the chairmanship of Sir Arthur Tansley. In that year Henry Maurice, Secretary of the Society for the Preservation of the Fauna of the Empire wrote to Cyril Diver, Director General, that he had 'some hope that your Conservancy may eventually promote legislation for some of our wild mammals, especially the Pine Martin and the Polecat; to which, I think, the otter and the badger might well be added.'[29] He enclosed a letter from one of his members, Lt. Colonel D. G. Moncrieff, asking the Society to instigate 'a close season for the otter' because they 'get no peace and are victims for slaughter throughout the year'.[30] Diver's reply indicated that the Conservancy was interested and that 'reliable information on the otter would be very helpful to us'.[31] The Conservancy collected articles, letters to editors of newspapers and other mentions of otters, all in relation to otter hunting. The 'cruelty' of otter hunting tended to be stressed: 'Many of us hope that public opinion will demand the abolition of the cruelties of otter-hunting'.[32] The Secretary of the League Against Cruel Sports wrote to the editor of the *Cornish Post*: 'We would appeal to humane landlords to follow the example of others and ban the hounds, which would go far to put a stop to this cruel sport.'[33]

At this time the otter is not an animal that scientists and scientific organis-ations could confidently claim to know. While the Nature Conservancy and others understood themselves as concerned strictly with questions of scientific value, knowledge and judgement became mixed in efforts to know the otter scientifically. In particular, the study of otters is bound up with judgements on otter hunting. In July 1951, a parliamentary question asked for 'the Nature Conservancy or the Bureau of Animal Population to investigate the habits and abundance of the otter, with a view to ascertaining whether, or to what extent and by what means, its numbers should be controlled.'[34] The Home Office asked the Conservancy whether an investigation was 'practicable', adding: 'As you know, the Committee … recommended that a thorough investigation should be conducted … into the natural history of the otter and the result of this enquiry should be taken into account in deciding whether or not otter-hunting should be permitted to continue.'[35] Scientific knowledge is seen as central to decisions over the control of human and animal behaviour. The Conservancy's reply to the Home Office stressed the lack of knowledge about and experience in studying otters:

> I should … be misleading you if I gave you the impression that people sufficiently qualified to undertake and to supervise such an intricate and difficult piece of work would be readily found. The otter is far from easy to observe and very little is known about its life history, even by those most directly affected … There are very divergent opinions upon such a basic fact as the period during which it breeds.[36]

An Otter Committee was established in 1951 to promote the investigation, consisting of Dr E. Hindle (Chairman), Dr L. Harrison Matthews, FRS (Hon. Scientific Director), Richard Fitter (Secretary), H. N. Southern, H. V. Thompson, and Professor A. N. Worden.[37] This committee was given funding in 1952 from a very wide range of bodies to enable research to be undertaken. The principal funding of £700 was from the Nature Conservancy, renewed in 1953 for a further year. Smaller amounts were given by the Universities Federation for Animal Welfare, Camberley Natural History Society, the Fauna Preservation Society, the British Trout Farmers' Association, the British Field Sports Society, the Fishmongers Company and the Masters of Otterhounds Association.[38] Marie Stephens was appointed 'investigator' to the Committee. Between October 1952 and the end of 1954 Stephens studied otters by reviewing literature and oral evidence, through fieldwork in Shropshire and Cardiganshire, through feeding tests on captive otters, and by the examination of samples, collected by herself and others:

> I have been fortunate in receiving co-operation from River Board officials and others, who have sent in specimens of dead otters and samples of their faeces, or spraints, for laboratory examination: 46 bodies and 109 spraints or collections of spraints have been received, and I have also collected 184 spraints in the field; 168 of these were from specially studied stretches of river …[39]

Speaking on the radio in 1955, the Committee's Secretary, Richard Fitter, the well known naturalist and author, described the work of the Committee as an attempt to be more certain about what otters are and do:

> … we know very little really about this animal. And it's certainly true that about no other animal have I found so many contradictory statements by apparently well-informed naturalists and sportsmen. Some will tell you that it eats salmon and trout for preference, others that it eats them only when it can't get eels. Some will tell you that otters breed only in the spring or at some other season, others that they breed all year round.[40]

He stressed that the study was informed by natural history expertise: 'we've had the aid of such well-known naturalists as Fraser Darling, Frances Pitt, Mark Southern, Michael Blackmore and Dr Harrison Matthews'. A draft of the *Otter Report* was circulated in 1955, but the final report was not published until 1957 in six chapters: 'description of the otter', 'distribution and habits', 'reproduction and breeding habits', 'parasites and diseases', 'captive otters' and 'feeding habits'. The *Report* attempted to provide a comprehensive natural history of all aspects of otters on the basis of thorough new research and a review of existing knowledge. It confirmed established perceptions of the janus-like nature of the otter. They were characterised as 'full of fun and have often been observed playing in the water with a pebble or an old tin can, or just rolling over and over like a log'. Yet they could be 'very fierce if cornered or attacked, and more than one hound has been pulled under by an otter and drowned'.[41]

There were several key findings in relation to the issue of hunting. Stephens compiled a table of 'birth months of otter cubs', based on 'unpublished diaries and records of otter-hunters and naturalists'. The results were interpreted in relation to the potential for otter hunting to kill bitches with cubs. Stephens observes that 'the calculated dates of births are spread out remarkably evenly throughout the year' and concludes: 'This irregular breeding makes it impossible to fix a close season for otters, and the hunting season – April to October – has been arranged mainly for the convenience and comfort of the follower.'[42]

Stephens was dependent to a large extent on second-hand observations and claims, including information provided by hunts and anglers. Her acknowledgements thank 'Fishery Officers, water-bailiffs, keepers and others too numerous for individual mention' not just for samples but for 'valuable information about otters'. However, she often steps in as investigating scientist, and judges the quality of local knowledge:

> otters may go unobserved by people actually living on the spot. At one village the local people told me, quite genuinely and regretfully, that no otters had been seen or heard of there for over twenty years. Immediately afterwards I found fresh spraint under the village bridge, and that proved to be one of the most consistently worked stretches of the whole well-populated river![43]

Stephens attended three hunts as part of the research and relied on huntsmen to confirm thoughts about otter density, but regarded them as an unreliable source of information about numbers.

> The population of otters is never very dense. Hunters estimate that the average number frequenting most rivers within the boundaries of the hunt is about one per six miles of water … They claim that the number is much lower on virgin (unhunted) rivers, possibly one per ten

miles or less, owing to the greater amount of trapping and shooting carried out there. This is definitely not so in every case, and I have come across several otter 'sanctuaries' which are always well populated and where the hunt is practically unheard of.[44]

Stephens estimated contemporary distribution density by river board area based on river board estimates. Thus the Wye River Board was awarded four stars ('very numerous'): 'There are plenty of otters on all the rivers. They are said to be numerous on the Lugg'.[45] Norfolk fell within both the Great Ouse RBA (three stars – 'numerous') and the East Suffolk and Norfolk RBA (four stars – 'very numerous'). The view of national otter population was generally very positive.

Stephens describes her observational fieldwork on two rivers. For 'a short preliminary period', helped by a 'well-known local naturalist', she collected sprints and practised mapping the signs of otters on a stretch of the Camlad (Shropshire). Longer term collection, observation and mapping focused on a three-mile stretch of the Clettwr, a tributary of the Teifi in Cardiganshire, characterised as 'a fast-moving trout and sewin stream', thought to contain 'five or possibly six holts … two of which showed signs of regular use'. The stretch was divided into three sections and routinely examined:

> Each day one section was covered minutely and all fresh signs of activity, such as tracks and seals, were plotted on to a new daily map. Sprints were collected and recorded and their positions were plotted also.[46]

Stephens' efforts to see otters largely failed. Even under sustained, scientific study, the otter retained its elusiveness and seemed to be in control:

> Occasionally I watched for otters at dusk here, but without much success … a mist comes down early in the valley of the Clettwr and it is impossible to see much on the water even before it gets really dark … from their signs it is obvious that they are always close by … Occasionally I found very fresh sprint, still in a pool of urine, even on hot sunny days, indicating that an otter had been there in daylight not very long before me.[47]

She concluded that, 'By far the best way to see otters is to take up fishing and not deliberately to watch for them at all'. This echoed the comments of natural historians, hunters and anglers.

Another key part of the investigation was to gain an understanding of the threat that otters posed to fisheries. Stephen's field report noted, 'Not once did I come across a partly eaten fish on the bank'. Much of the *Report* considers the otters' diet; it participates in debates over the conduct of otters in relation to valued fish. Stephens makes reference to a range of views: that otters favour eels and coarse fish over trout and salmon because the former are easier to catch; that otters are quick and agile enough to catch easily the faster trout and salmon; that frightened trout and pike are easy to catch because they hide under banks and stones with their tails sticking out; that otters spoil fishing by disturbing fish; that they help fishermen by 'stirring up' fish; that otters often catch more fish than they eat, that they wound for fun, that they are blamed for the predations of herons and human poachers, that they improve fish stocks by eating predators of the spawn and fry of valued fish, such as eels, frogs, waterfowl and 'cannibal trout', that they eat mainly old and diseased fish. Through experimentation Stephens attempted to show what otters ate. Richard Fitter described this work in a BBC Radio programme in 1955:

> One of our main methods has been to examine and analyse the contents of the otters' spraints ... We were also lucky to have a pair of cubs which Peter Scott gave us ... we were able to feed fish to them in the ordinary way and were then able to see what came through at the other end so that we were able to tell what chance there was of various kinds of fish bones coming through and being identified in the spraint of wild otters ...[48]

Stephens' two 'captive' cubs, 'thought to be' two months old, were kept in the Zoological Society's sanatorium at Regent's Park. They were first fed on milk and live eels, 'eels remained their favourite throughout'. After two months 'the bulk of their diet consisted of whiting and herrings, and very seldom was it possible to give them river fish'. They also 'loved frogs, alive or dead', 'enjoyed mice and rabbits; but not horse meat', 'liked' baby chicks but not pigeon and ate forty crayfish and mussels. The 'feeding tests' were also carried out on two Indian dog otters. However, the *Report* noted that the analysis of spraints as indicators of diet was inconclusive and had significant limitations:

> Where only one or two bites are taken from the back of the neck and shoulders of a victim no evidence at all is likely to appear in the sprain ... In the case of very large fish a good meal could be had from the flesh alone, and it is doubtful is any of the bones would be eaten ... No bones from large fish have been recorded in any of the samples examined during the present study.[49]

Those opposed to hunting were able to draw some strength from the results of the *Otter Report*. The National Society for the Abolition of Cruel Sports (NSACS) soon published, in 1956, a modified version of *A Vile Sport: Facts about Otter Hunting* by Bertram Lloyd, naturalist, co-founder and first Secretary of the Society. The aim of the NSACS was 'the legal abolition of all forms of killing for sport; its immediate object is to educate public opinion to demand the suppression of the hunting and coursing of our native wild animals – Deer, Fox, Otter, Badger, Hare, etc.'[50] Otter hunting is styled in the pamphlet as a form of landed barbarism: 'There is no romance or glamour about the hunt for the otter. For him (or her) it is a ruthless, cruel, torturing, bloody pastime … And it is indeed a sorry, stunted mentality which can derive pleasure from the deliberate, planned, organised infliction of pain on a lesser being.'[51] A UFAW summary of Stephens' *Otter Report* is quoted to support the argument that otters eat a varied diet that includes predators of the spawn and young of valued fish, salmon and trout.

The government response to the report was deadening. The Nature Conservancy sent a draft copy of the *Otter Report* to the Home Office in 1955 and the reply stated,

> There has been very little interest during the last Parliament in the question of field sports … I think it is most improbable that we shall see any legislation on this subject for some time to come … if the question of otter hunting should become a live issue again, we may have to ask you for some further help.[52]

Charles Hume of the UFAW, which published the report in 1957, noted that it was 'selling pretty well and a good deal of interest has been aroused'. He was impatient for more research on the otter and asked the new Director General of the Nature Conservancy, Max Nicholson, whether the research could be carried further.[53] Nicholson replied:

> While we would … always be ready to consider a fresh application for renewed research on this interesting beast, it was our impression that lack of co-operation by otters was at least as serious a difficulty as the two which you mention, and that it would probably be more profitable to concentrate for the time being on more easily studied predators such as the Pine Marten and the Fox.[54]

Nicholson's reply echoes recent analyses of animals as (often awkward) agents in heterogeneous networks of scientific knowledge.[55] The otter slips out of sight, and out of government interest.

III

Marie Stephens' research may have pointed to the difficulty of capturing a sound, scientific natural history of the otter, but the otter certainly continued to catch the public imagination. Other cultural practices are pertinent here. Throughout the period Henry Williamson's *Tarka the Otter: His joyful water-life and death in the country of the two Rivers*, first published in 1927 and including otter hunt scenes, continued to be significant in the popular image of the otter. Williamson, author of novels and nature books, had moved to Georgeham in north Devon in the 1920s. His wife, Ida, was a daughter of a keen hunter with the Cheriton otter hunt. *Tarka* was awarded the Hawthornden prize and became enormously popular. John Galsworthy called Williamson 'the finest and most intimate living interpreter of the drama of wild life'.[56] *Tarka* continued to be popular throughout the post-war period and was reprinted by Puffin Books in 1949, 1951, 1955, 1959, 1961, and 1962 with revisions by Williamson, and in 1963 with a map of Tarka's journey. Eleanor Graham, in her introduction to the 1963 Puffin edition considered that 'Tarka the Otter is a true story – as true as a man's account of the life of a wild animal can possibly be'.[57] She stressed that Williamson's knowledge of otters was based not on attempts at domestication, but fieldwork, thus claiming a realism for the account above supposedly sentimental description of otters as pets. Williamson had reared an otter cub in Devon, but stressed that his knowledge came from work in the field, a distinction he commented on in 1938 when noting how a 'lady writer and rider to foxhounds reviewing *Tarka the Otter* in a weekly' had disputed his description of otter behaviour, which 'I had observed in their native waters', on the basis of the behaviour of her 'tame otter'. This 'interesting criticism' did however set Williamson wondering 'what was the distinction between knowing an otter intimately and knowing it personally'.[58]

Personal intimacy with the otter became a touchstone of accounts published in the post-war period, as works by Gavin Maxwell, Ernest Neal, and Philip Wayre, made the otter a literary and filmic star.[59] This provided a further challenge to hunting's claim as the only way to bring the otter to visibility. As in programmes produced through the BBC Natural History Unit, accounts combined science, education and entertainment,[60] using otters domesticated or reared in captivity to negotiate paradoxes and contradictions of wildness and tameness, nature and learned behaviour, in the name of otter conservation. The most influential work was Maxwell's famous trilogy *Ring of Bright Water* (1960), *The Otter's Tale* (1962) and *The Rocks Remain* (1963). The film version was released in 1969. The books describe his life with two otters, one of which he had brought home from Iraq, on the coast at Sandaig, near Glenelg, Inverness-shire.[61] Ernest Neal, housemaster at Taunton School, keen naturalist and co-founder of the Mammal Society of the British Isles in 1954, produced a popular account of *Topsy and Turvy: My Two Otters* in 1961. A few years later, Philip Wayre in his autobiography *The Wind in the Reeds* (1965) described the setting up of his Norfolk Wildlife Park that displayed otters among other animals.

Ownership and living with otters became a way of studying them, a source of observation beyond the work of hunters or of scientists such as Stephens, patiently waiting in vain on the riverbank. Careful records were made. Ernest Neal remembers first hearing of his opportunity to rear Topsy and Turvy: 'It was exciting news. For years I had wanted to find out more about otters, because so little was really known about the habits and the life cycle of these fascinating creatures.'[62] He weighed the cubs when they arrived as 'a start to the complete records of their progress that I intended to keep'.[63] He also tape-recorded Topsy and Turvy's various calls: 'we spent an amusing hour catching all the sounds we could'. All three authors wrote detailed descriptions of the appearance and actions of their otters. There are accounts of playing, hunting, swimming, calling, biting, sleeping and so on. For example, Maxwell, at his fictional home, Camusfeàrna observed his first otter:

> Mij ... caught a number of fish on his daily outings ... In the burn [river] he learned to feel under stones for eels, reaching in with one paw and averted head ... Near the edge of the tide he would search out the perfectly camouflaged flounders ... and farther out in the bay he would kill an occasional sea trout.[64]

Many of the descriptions in the books are of otters playing in domestic spaces, written to entertain but also to record how otters moved and thought. Intimacy, detached observation, knowledge and entertainment are bound together. Maxwell described how Mij 'slept in my bed ... on his back with his head on the pillow, and in the morning he shared my bath ... and while I shaved he would swim round me playing with the soapsuds'.[65] Intimacy, study and entertainment are combined too in Wayre's attempt to tape-record mother and cub in 1970. He fixed a microphone in the otters' shed and was able to listen to them from the comfort of his sitting room 200 yards away. 'The microphone was so sensitive I could hear Ginger breathing if I turned up the level sufficiently ... One could clearly hear the cub suckling.'[66]

The books provided much new information about the life of otters together with informal anecdotes; science and entertainment are inseparable in these efforts to record the intimate. This is brought out especially in the authors' efforts to record otters swimming underwater. The clear waters at Camusfeàrna allowed Maxwell to observe and record Mijbil's secret underwater movements: 'I could watch him as he dived down, down, down through fathom after fathom to explore the gaudy sea forests at the bottom with their flowered shell glades and mysterious, shadowed caverns'.[67] Similarly, Neal watched and filmed Turvy in a friend's swimming pool where his movements could be observed: 'I could see, for instance, how his nostrils closed but his eyes stayed open when his head went under the surface'.[68] Turvy's underwater movements were filmed by Tony Soper from the BBC's Natural History Unit. In 1962 Maxwell installed a glass tank eight feet long by three feet wide and deep in the garden at Camusfeàrna. Two otters, Mossy and Monday, were observed, and their swimming carefully recorded by Maxwell. The metaphors are again those of entertainment and spectacle: 'They began to evolve endless and intricate games together

– water-ballets, which started in slow motion and worked up gradually to a long crescendo of movement.'[69]

These domesticated animals allowed public access to the formerly secret life of the otter through the texts and photographs produced by their keepers, but also through the developing natural history television of the 1950s and '60s. Television allowed the British public to see this elusive animal moving. The dust jacket of Neal's *Topsy and Turvy* commented that, 'Many people will remember the appearance of Topsy and Turvy on television, which gave viewers the opportunity – unique for most of us – of seeing live otter cubs'. When about 22 weeks old Turvy was filmed 'for his first television appearance' on the lawn outside the BBC studios at Bristol in an edition of Winwood Reade's *Outdoors* programme. The hutch and run, 'his favourite log, his zinc bath', was brought from Taunton School to make him feel at home. Neal's account of the day plays on the sense of staging. There was 'a rehearsal in the morning, during which the cameramen were able to get some idea of the possibilities, and of the positions Turvy might take up'. Neal was pleased that the otter behaved, did not hide, run away or do something unpleasant during the filming. About a year later, Neal's third otter, Topsy the Second, appeared on a BBC children's television programme with one of the Taunton schoolboys 'talking about his experiences with her', broadcast live from the Bristol studios.[70] Maxwell's Edal was also filmed for a BBC programme in April 1960.[71] But such publicity could bring problems, as when Maxwell and his work became a spectacle in its own right. By Spring 1961 Camusfeàrna had become a tourist destination and Maxwell, who hated being observed in this way, wrote bitterly of people claiming his home and the otters as public objects. Parties of tourists settled on the 'hilltops' around the bay and watched the otters: 'from these vantage points they would scrutinise the house and its environs with field-glasses, telescopes and long-focus ciné-camera lenses'.[72]

Philip Wayre, in contrast, well known as a presenter on Anglia Television and BBC Natural History Programmes, set out to attract visitors to his Norfolk Wildlife Park at Witchingham established in 1961, and later his Otter Trust at Earsham in Suffolk. Here otters were shown at sites which did not unnaturally confine the animal. Otters sliding and diving for visitors were offered as natural performers. Here, as in other accounts of the tame yet lively otter, a complex anthropomorphism was at work, which aimed to understand the domestic animal yet allow it to retain its wildness, producing an epistemological landscape other than that of otter hunting, and which could reshape the otter's cultural status. Wayre's first otter was a Canadian female otter, Limpet, purchased from breeders in America. Sometime in 1961 Limpet escaped and a fortnight later 'the otter hounds arrived in our area and were due to meet the following day at Lyng bridge on the River Wensum, scarcely a mile away'.[73] Concerned about Limpet, Wayre attended the meet of the Eastern Counties Otter Hounds and the Master agreed to call off the hounds if Limpet was spotted. Wayre's description of the hunt emphasised chaos and absurdity: 'The followers lined either bank gossiping. They were an odd assortment of young and old; some in hunt dress, blue jackets and knickerbockers with deerstalkers, were leaning on tall ash staffs; others displayed a remarkable diversity of muftie.' Wayre's analysis of the day led him to call for the protection of otters: 'To me it was all rather pointless, the otter was so much more beautiful and interesting alive'. He could see no reason for wanting to kill otters. 'They are enchanting, beautiful creatures who by their specialised requirements of food, habitat and living space are never likely to become numerous ... the more logical course would be to give them total protection.' [74]

These very public renderings of the otter were reinforced by private studies of naturalists and nature conservationists. In December 1962 and 1963 Dr Charles Walker, a Herefordshire doctor and important naturalist and nature conservationist, used snow to study animals.[75] His notebook for 1959–64 recorded his attempts to reconstruct the movements of water voles, hares, foxes, deer, rabbits, wood mice, grey squirrel, badgers, stoats and otters by following tracks. A sighting of otter tracks in January 1963 is underlined: 'Tracks of hare, rabbit, fox & near water otter'. On 20 January 1963 Walker attempts to read off from tracks the behaviour of an otter.

> Whoopers heard going past whooping while I was in thick bush and tree roots under bank, into which otter seal went – ?holt. The tracks went both in the snow at field level & also on the river ice of Wye and Lugg – quite a long distance. At several points the bank had been descended or climbed between field & river ice. At one place the otter had slid down bringing a lot of soft drift snow down with him & at others he had climbed up & down at places where bush roots had given foot holds. At one point he had crossed the Lugg & then ice at the middle had given way & he had to swim to get over.

The movements of the otter were recorded in detail. The otter was so elusive and invisible that this rare recording (in snow) of its movements, however mundane, were taken down in full. The movements gained interest because they were not seen, but reconstructed and in that sense imagined. Walker returned to the site several times and on the 23 January noted that going downstream from Mordiford Bridge: 'had otter track all the way, plodding along the ice or the bank at the water's edge, & sometimes scrambling up the bank or coming up at slopes, sometimes sliding down to river level'.[76]

IV

By the mid-1960s the otter had achieved a strong position in the public imagination through appearances on children's television, natural history radio and television programmes, and novels. The otter was perhaps better known than at any time in the past. This popular knowledge was backed up by the scientific knowledge gathered by Marie Stephens in the mid-1950s and by the continuing interest of hunters, anglers and natural historians. But the otter did not seem to respond to this burst of human interest. Indeed, the elusive otter increasingly began to disappear. In 1967 a parliamentary question asked whether the Minister was 'aware that the otter is becoming extinct and what action is he taking to prevent this?'. A Nature Conservancy 'note for the file' recorded that 'no member of the Conservancy staff is presently engaged on work on the otter' and that the Minister should reply that he 'was not aware that the otter was becoming extinct'. However, a new otter survey was to be carried out 'by the Council for Nature in association with the Mammal Society [which] should throw further light on the population levels of the otter'.[77]

The new survey was conducted under the auspices of otter hunters and nature conservationists who were both alarmed by an apparent rapid disappearance. It was carried out by the Mammal Society of Great Britain at the request of a 'working party on mammalian control' organised by the British Field Sports Society (BFSS) and the Council for Nature. Preliminary results were not published until 1969. In the interim, the National Trust, Peter Scott (of the World Wildlife Fund) and the RSPCA were among those who asked the Conservancy for information about the number and distribution of otters. They were also asked whether otters had been affected by the recently introduced mink or by habitat change or pollution, and whether they needed to be protected. Peter Scott, perhaps the most influential contemporary conservationist, told the Conservancy that 'he was under pressure in his World Wildlife Capacity to do something about the conservation of otters in Britain'. He noted that concern came mainly from people 'in the South East who are complaining that they never see an otter these days' and wondered if the Conservancy had any 'reliable information on the distribution and numbers'.[78]

Replies from the Conservancy stressed uncertainty about numbers and whereabouts. To the National Trust, for example: 'I doubt whether anyone can tell you authoritatively whether otters are becoming rare in the country at the present time'.[79] In the context of anxious speculation about how many otters were left, otter hunting received renewed attention. Chris Fuller, one of the Conservancy's Assistant Regional Officers reported that there had 'been a new wave of protest against otter hunting, especially near my home in Cardiganshire'. He attended a protest in September 1968 to 'to get some ideas of the issues involved' and reported that the main objections to hunting were 'on the grounds of cruelty and bloodsports'. He noted that 'apart from holding personal convictions, we in the Conservancy are not concerned with this aspect of the matter. We are however surely concerned with the conservation aspect.'[80] In this way cruelty and blood are very consciously expelled from the Conservancy's self-understanding as scientific. The official reply to Fuller did not mention hunting, but pointed out the need to assess reasons for any decline: 'there may well prove to be pockets of recession elsewhere: if so, we shall want to know the causes before we can take action. How much is due to habitat change, pollution, river 'improvement', or the presence of mink?'[81]

The otter was very much in the limelight in 1969 with the release of the film *Ring of Bright Water*. In January of that year the Mammal Society also produced their 'Interim Report' of their Otter Survey.[82] It made use of two distinct kinds of data: figures from thirteen otter hunts (solicited by question-naires circulated by the BFSS); and statements from River Authorities (15), individual investigators and societies (160). The report divided England and Wales into fourteen research areas 'based on river basins and having some regard to the distribution of available data'. Otter hunters were regarded as skilled trackers and observers of otters, and their observations were valued over those of the River Board officials, naturalists and others. The report noted that 'since the O.H. [otter hounds'] data were the only figures available they have been treated as the most objective material and submitted to simple mathematical treatment'.[83] It argued that the returns by River Authorities and by individual investigators did not, in any area, contradict the findings based on the Otter Hunt returns'.[84] Data from otter hunt returns for the years 1900, 1937, 1947, 1957 and 1967 were provided. A comparison of the figures for 1957 (71.6 finds per hundred days hunting) and 1967 (43.6) are interpreted as 'very significantly different' indicating 'a considerable decrease in the population'.[85]

The Report offered various possible 'causes of the decrease' including increased trapping, increased disturbance to rivers by fishing and 'increased tourist and pleasure boat pressure on the eastern and southern rivers'. Other potential causes were the 'destruction of the riparian habitats in the interests of drainage', the severe winter of 1962–63 followed by 'the incidence of a high level of pesticide pollution' affecting 'the reproductive potential' of otters 'so that a return to normal numbers was prevented'.[86] An attempt was made to relate different causes of the decline to the different regions. In the area around the Wash, for example, it was thought the decline could be due to insecticide pollution and pelt trapping.[87] The effect of otter hunting itself on the decline in otters is not clarified. It concluded, however, that while the cull of otters by hunting did not appear 'to cause any decrease in the population between 1900 and 1937', the 'greatly reduced numbers of the

'60s' might mean hunting had an effect'.[88] The report recommended that 'For at least the next ten years or so therefore the killing of otters and further pollution should be avoided as much as possible'. This, it hoped, would 'at best … allow the otter to re-establish itself and adjust to the increased human disturbance'.[89]

In February 1969 the BFSS and Council for Nature issued a statement based on the Interim Report. This stressed the non-hunting causes of decline and attempted to place otter hunting within a scientific effort to track the otter. The hunters' intimacy with the rivers, their ability to spot signs and follow was worked into a wider scientific effort to observe an elusive subject. The statement noted that the 'scientific assessment' of the data from otter hunts concluded that it was 'intrinsically accurate as a measure of otter populations'. It argued that 'to call a stop to all Otter Hunting would remove the one reliable source of information on otter populations'.[90]

The statement asserts that under 'normal circumstances Otter Hunting does not significantly affect the numbers of otters' but proposed that 'at the present reduced level of otters in some areas, the pattern of otter hunting should be amended'. A scheme is outlined involving new 'patterns' of hunting. Certain rivers in the Norfolk areas, for example, would not be hunted but 'drawn by packs of Otterhounds at the request of Mammal Society in order to obtain information for the next survey'. Others would be 'hunted, but no kill will be made unless considered necessary (e.g. a sick or maimed otter)'. By contrast, in an area such as Herefordshire the number of days hunted would simply be reduced.

This attempt by the otter hunts to become enmeshed in a programme of otter conservation has parallels with the way in which wildfowling and game shooting became key players in the investigation and practice of conservation management in the same period.[91] But this was not to be, and in May 1969 a determined 'campaign' to ban otter hunting, led in Parliament by Labour MP Edwin Brooks was initiated. Brooks was supported by the League Against Cruel Sports. Arguments over the cruelty, clumsy violence and barbarism were rehearsed; as well as claims that otters eat diseased and predatory fish, and should not be 'vermin'. However, a reading of the Interim Report as scientific evidence that otters may become 'extinct' was central to this campaign. A *Guardian* headline relied on the word 'extinction' to produce feelings of existential anxiety – 'MP campaigns to save otters from extinction' – and continued: 'British wild life is in retreat or dying and unique and delightful species face extinction'.[92] The *Morning Star* reported 'Otters are in danger of extinction in Britain … Mr. Brooks, whose Bill would make all otter killing illegal, said that the animals had been declining "catastrophically" over the past ten years.' Brooks had described otter hunting as indulged in by perhaps not more than 1,000 people in Britain, and as 'the most offensive and cruel of all blood sports, and utterly useless'.[93]

In June 1969 the Natural Environment Research Council (NERC) asked the Nature Conservancy for comments on the Otters Bill. Drawing on the Mammal Society's Interim Report, officers advised that 'the otter is not seriously threatened', that 'habitat destruction, pollution and the human population explosion have greater effects on otter numbers than hunting', and that 'the Bill as a conservation measure (as distinct from humanitarian) was premature'.[94] A 'Parliamentary note' held by NERC at this time reported that a Commons Motion, signed by 109 Members, suggesting that appropriate legislation to protect otters and ban hare coursing should be introduced as a 'contribution to European Conservation Year'.[95] The Conservancy sought to distinguish 'conservation' from attempts to prevent perceived cruelty to animals and noted that it 'would be a great pity if the important matters to be dealt with under ECY were to be blurred by minor and sectional interests of this type'.[96]

In May 1969, at the time of the first and second reading of Brooks' Bill, 'leading figures in the otter-hunting world in Wales and the border country' met at Llandrindod Wells 'in an attempt to restore their public image in the face of threatened legislation'.[97] The *Hereford Times* reported the event in some detail. Some participants argued that otters were not dying out, but merely lying low as usual. N. E. Hill-Trevor, a member of the British Field Sports Society otter committee stated, 'Because they [non-hunters] don't actually see otters in the river, they think they are desperately scarce. But I've lived beside a river all my life and have actually seen an otter only twice – other than when hunting.' Captain R. E. Wallace, Master of the Hawkstone Otter Hounds for thirty years, stated that he 'had also seen only two in the same circumstances' while the current Master, Mr Michael Downes, had only seen one otter 'except when hunting'. The elusiveness of the otter was used to dispute worries over extinction.

Another argument was that the nature and value of otter hunting could only be understood by people who had a deep understanding of rural life. Otter hunting was an expert practice that was intimately connected with a wider economic management of flora and fauna. Mr Downes argued that if 'there is a glut of otters, some must be destroyed. They create havoc in a trout hatchery, damage water-cress beds and kill salmon'. Captain Wallace said, 'I've never met a genuine farmer type who was against otter hunting on ethical grounds'. The representatives presented hunting as a precise, discriminating form of control, against visions of it as crude, primitive, brutal. The President of the Masters of Otterhounds Association argued that hunting was 'so much more decent than trapping, which is indiscriminate and can leave a trapped otter to starve or be brutally beaten to death with a stick'. The field secretary of the BFSS stressed that hunters were eager to contribute to study and conservation as 'The people with the strongest vested interest in the preservation of the otter are ourselves'.

The contentious nature of otter hunting meant that the report of the Llandrindod Wells meeting initiated a spate of articles and letters in the *Hereford Times* through May, June and July. Letters often refer to studies on the otter, including the Mammal Society's Interim Report and Stephens' *Otter Report*. Geoffrey Smith, of Mill Street, Hereford, set the clear certainty of scientific study against the clumsiness and muddiness of hunting. He argued that the Mammal Society and amateur and professional naturalists had proved 'beyond doubt' that otters had 'decreased to an alarming degree'. On the contrary, he asked, how could how could 'huntsmen know that the quarry is a bitch otter when hounds are plunging in full pursuit into a river or reed bed?'[98] Another letter argued that the British public had never known so much about otters and 'never has so large a majority opposed the particularly pointless, cruel and vandalistic pastime'.[99] In June, the debate featured on the front page of the paper when otter hunting was condemned by a vet from Leominster. He had been approached by 'a number of people ... in view of the decreasing number of otters in the Leominster area'.[100]

The Herefordshire and Radnorshire Nature Trust (HRNT) responded to the concern over the future of the otter by gathering more information about sightings. In June 1969, T. H. R. Owen, vice-chairman of HRNT wrote 'Nature Trust Notes' on 'Badger and Otter' for the *Hereford Times* and argued that the otter – 'once common in Herefordshire' – was indeed 'reduced here and over nearly all England to a fraction of its former numbers'. He argued that 'Hunting ... is the least cause' and pointed to disturbance by visitors, dogs, picnickers and canoeists, river drainage and the removal of old willows and alders as likely causes. He also thought that 'pesticides are a most likely factor'.[101] Owen invited readers with 'information on otter or badger' to write to him or Dr Charles Walker. Walker wrote to the *Hereford Times* in July 1969 outlining his and the Trust's 'attitude' to otter hunting. He stressed that otter hunting 'was not the cause of the drop in numbers', but the tone and content of the letter asserted the Trust and scientific study as authorities in decisions over county nature, otters specifically. He noted that 'our Trust has had discussion with Mr Michael Downes, Master of the Hawkstone Hounds, and we are satisfied that the hunting is now being conducted in a greatly modified manner'. However, if the decline in the otter population was not halted, he argued that otters should be protected like birds, this 'would make the killing by any method illegal'.[102]

Walker collected data from informants such as water bailiffs, keepers and otter hunters in a large notebook from 1968 to 1977. Most thought otters were getting scarcer. R. A. Bufton, a water bailiff at Glasbury of Wye for 45 years, for example was 'certain the otter has become very scarce ... has looked for pad-marks and droppings, latterly more and more hard to find. The big reduction in otter is since the war.'[103] C. Jones, the keeper at

Garnons, reported that 'there used to be otters, but he has not known of any for years. They used to be at Monnington falls and he saw their tracks in the snow there in winter, but not for many years now.' By 1975 the decline in the number of otters was so apparent that the Hawkstone stopped hunting.[104] Walker had become more critical of hunting and wrote on 19 December 1976 to the Hawkstone's Master, Mr Andrews, concerned about 'outside' hunts disturbing local rivers, suggesting hunting would hasten extinction, and accounting for popular debate:

> The truth is that the general public has ceased to look upon otter hunting as a harmless sport, and regards it more as something which is out of date, and justified formerly by its votaries by the untrue claim that the otter is a menace to fish and therefore worthy of death.[105]

Walker argued that while he was aware that the 'strong public reaction against otter-hunting' had been 'largely stimulated' by books such as *Tarka the Otter* and *Ring of Bright Water*, he considered that there was a 'strong distaste for the killing of harmless wild animals', and noted 'the inability of the uninitiated to understand the mentality of the killers'. Walker thought that the opponents of otter hunting were not 'all cranks, actuated by envy and "leftist" principles' such as those opposed to fox hunting, but rather the 'ordinary citizen – town and country – who has come to deplore the continual persecution of the otter'.[106] Walker here carefully defines to the hunt master the proper grounds on which opposition is justified, distancing himself and the Trust from particular politics and literary suasion, and suggesting anti-hunting views stood on firm and ordinary local ground. The wandering otters of the Wye and Lugg should be left to hunt and play, spotted occasionally by the citizen, and tracked only by the naturalist.

V

This analysis of a wide range of sources, including scientific reports, government records, novels, diaries, interviews and local papers has indicated that the way that different groups and individuals came to know and understand otters changed dramatically in the thirty years or so following the Second World War. Traditional understandings of the otter as a menace to fishing, as vermin to be trapped, as an entertaining opponent to hunt became increasingly marginalised. The enormous success of works such as *Tarka* and *Ring of Bright Water*, reinforced by a series of less well-known works and television programmes, gave presence and voice to otters. The previously little known animal became for many an attractive and loveable creature. This new way of knowing the otter was increasingly at odds with older understandings. The contentious debate over hunting produced two studies of the natural history of the otter which, drawing on scientific analysis and reviews of hunting statistics, allowed different understandings of the number, distribution and habits of the otter to emerge. It also, albeit briefly, allowed a rapprochement between hunters and some nature conservationists and officials, as hunts were able to provide the only reliable statistics for change over time. The killing of individual otters allowed the documentation and estimation of trends in the overall population of otters.

And it was these trends in the 1970s, researched at the suggestion of Lord Cranbrook by scientists employed by the Nature Conservancy Council, which identified the now largely accepted key reason for the collapse of the otter population in the mid-1950s. Drawing on hunting records, Paul Chanin and Don Jefferies, in a paper published in 1978, analysed all the possible causes and found that the immediate cause of the decline was the large number of deaths of breeding adults otters from pesticide poisoning.[107] The 'only new factor' which could be correlated in time and place with the decline was the 'introduction of the persistent insecticides, dieldrin and aldrin, as cereal dressings and sheep-dips in 1955 and 1956'.[108] This was not to say that the otter hunts themselves were not implicated in the decline. It was likely that they contributed to the 'weakened status of the otter population of southern Britain' by the early 1950s, just before the population crash.[109] One outcome of this research was that a case could be made by the Nature Conservancy Council for the otter to become legally protected under the Conservation of Wild Creatures and Wild Plants Act 1975.[110] The otter was placed on Schedule 1 of that Act, and became legally protected from 1 January 1978, and in anticipation, the Masters of Otter Hounds Association announced the suspension of otter hunting in 1977.

CHAPTER EIGHT

The development of salmon angling in the nineteenth century

by Harvey Osborne

T HE FARMING of Atlantic salmon on an industrial scale, has, in recent years, diminished the cachet of the 'king of fish' in the minds of the British consumer, albeit that the inexpensive 'product' available on supermarket shelves bears little comparison to its wild counterpart. The latter remains both relatively exclusive and expensive, a reflection of limited supply, seasonal availability and superior quality. Equally while rising incomes and the greater commercialisation of the sport have made salmon angling much more accessible, sport fishing for salmon, on the best beats and at the best times, remains the preserve of the relatively well-heeled and well-connected. In this regard salmon angling continues to retain some of the elite credentials first established in the mid- to late-Victorian era. This chapter focuses on the growth and development of salmon angling during the nineteenth century and seeks to explain why the salmon and the sport of salmon fishing came to be so heavily associated with the middle and upper classes, in contrast to 'coarse' fishing for other freshwater fish and sea angling where working-class participation was not only more typical, but predominant. It will argue that, alongside technological and cultural developments, the emergence and direction of salmon angling as a sport was shaped by environmental factors and that the growing exclusivity of salmon angling, real and imagined, was in large part a consequence of a catastrophic decline experienced by the British salmon fisheries during the early to mid-nineteenth century.

I

Fishing for salmon using an artificial bait or lure has a long history in Britain. Legionnaires used plumes or streamer flies to fish for salmon on the Thames, Tyne and Severn during the Roman occupation.[1] *The Treatise of Fishing with an Angle* (1450) included recommendations for the strength of horse hair line required for salmon fishing and discussed the possibility, among other methods, of taking salmon with a 'dubbed hook [artificial fly] in the same styles and manner as you catch a trout or a grayling'.[2] However, prior to the seventeenth century, angling for salmon was limited in both practicality and appeal since virtually all forms of angling featured the use of a solid, or two-piece, rod with a fixed length of line affixed to the tip. The limitations of tackle and particularly the inability to extend and retrieve line for casting and retrieving was a particular problem for the salmon fisher for two reasons. First, as the *Treatise* highlighted, without the ability to cast and control line over long distances, it was difficult to present a bait or lure effectively to salmon on larger rivers, since 'for the most part he keeps to the middle of the water: that a man cannot come at him'.[3] Second, even if hooked, a salmon on a fixed line was extremely difficult to land. Without the ability to pay out line in response to the run of hooked salmon, efforts to play and subdue a fish renowned for its fighting abilities and weighing on average 7–10lbs were often doomed to failure (Fig. 8.1).

The development and adoption of the fishing reel was therefore perhaps more significant to salmon angling than any other branch of the sport. Only with the ability to allow the fish to take line during its powerful runs and to gradually retrieve it as the fish tired could salmon angling truly become a practical proposition. The first references to fishing reels, or winders or winches as early models were termed, can be found in the seventeenth-century works of Thomas Barker and Col. Robert Venables.

> I will now shew you the way to take a Salmon. The first thing you must gain must be a rod of some ten foot in the stock, that will carry a top of six foot pretty stiffe and strong, the reason is, because there must be a little wire ring at the upper end of the top for the line to run through, that you may take up and loose the line at your pleasure; you must have your winder within two foot of the bottom to goe on your rod made in this manner, with a spring, that you may put in on as low as you please.[4]

Venables, like another contemporary writer and fellow Cromwellian soldier Capt. Richard Franck, undoubtedly caught lots of salmon using primitive 'winders' or 'winches', and significantly also with artificial flies.[5] However, as Andrew Herd has demonstrated, early reels of the seventeenth and eighteenth centuries had a number of serious weaknesses, particularly apparent to the salmon angler, including narrow spindles, an absence of a check or drag mechanism and only a single action for retrieval.[6] Furthermore, reels made from brass alloy, the commonly used material of the time, were prone to break easily and knotted horsehair line did not pare off spindles smoothly and was prone to stick or jam. The development and emergence of the multiplier reel after 1770, alongside the introduction of manufactured

FIGURE 8.1
'Game to
the Last': an
illustration of
a heroic battle
between
salmon and
fisherman
from the
1890s
by C.H.
Whymper.
From H.
Cholm-
ondeley-
Pennell,
*Fishing: Salmon
and Trout*
(1895), p. 244.

knotless horsehair lines, theoretically represented a vast improvement over these single action reels and also provided for a check mechanism, but even these advancements could not conceal weaknesses, related to the new multiplier technology itself, which were most apparent to those who pursued the largest and most powerful fish in British freshwaters, the salmon. The internal gears of eighteenth- and early nineteenth-century multipliers, manufactured of soft brass, tended to fail under stress and such was the likelihood of reel failure that contemporary experts advised anglers to revert to a form of hand-lining to recover line if faced with a salmon. Bainbridge advised, 'should a salmon of tolerable size be hooked, and the line attached to a multiplying reel, it will require the utmost skill and attention of the Angler, by occasionally drawing up line with his left hand, and then winding it, to secure the fish.'[7]

It was in part because of the limitations of fishing tackle that participation in salmon angling lagged behind other branches of the sport, such as trout and coarse angling where fish species were, relative to the salmon, smaller, easier to subdue and pursued in less challenging environments. Herd has suggested that even 'in the early years of the nineteenth century, salmon fishers were still few and far between' and the observation by Francis Frances in 1840 that 'something like killing a gorilla was this killing of a salmon with a fishing rod' underlines how far the inadequacy of tackle contributed to the minority appeal of salmon angling.[8]

Nonetheless, distinctions between salmon angling and other forms of pleasure fishing had already begun to emerge, at least in terms of end tackle and tactics. While the boundaries between trout and salmon angling were often blurred, with those angling for the former often becoming unintentionally attached to the latter, it was evident even from the seventeenth century that the construction of artificial flies for salmon was assuming a noticeably different direction. Early evidence for this is provided by Barker who recommended 'if you angle for him [the salmon] with a flie (which he will rise at like a Trout) the flie must be made of a large hook, which hook must carry sex wings, or four at least'.[9] The tendency toward a larger hook for salmon is understandable, but perhaps more significant was the emergence of the 'salmon fly' based on distinct tying styles and materials; in itself perhaps an indication of a wider, if tacit, awareness that provocation was more important than imitation when seeking to tempt salmon to take.

Venables and Franck provided some of the earliest descriptions of salmon flies. In both cases, a tendency, which would be firmly reasserted in the late nineteenth-century, towards a brightly coloured and heavily winged fly was detectable. Venables, for example, instructed his readers 'that the salmon flies must be made with wings standing behind one another, whether two or four; he also delights in the most gaudy and orient colours.'[10] Some indications of the origins of these 'gaudy and orient' colours are provided by Franck. Despite the fact that he had also used relatively sombre local creations to great success north of the Border, *Northern Memoirs* instructed anglers in the use of 'the feather of a moccaw, phlimingo, parraketa or the like'.[11] The materials potentially available to the fly-tyer speak well of seventeen-century trading links and adventurousness of the flourishing hat-making industry, but these were still descriptions of salmon flies rather than established 'patterns'. It is clear that salmon fishers had local styles and preferences and the absence of nationally recognisable and transferable patterns indicates something of the infancy of salmon angling, particularly with the fly.

The first transferable patterns for salmon flies were identified in print by Charles and Richard Bowlker, but it was not until the late eighteenth and early nineteenth-century that the emergence of a distinct salmon fly-tying industry is first evident and the development of a recognisable catalogue of patterns gathered pace.[12] Existing regional and localised fly-tying styles and preferences both contributed to, and in some cases were supplanted by, the emergence of dominant styles and patterns. Early nineteenth-century distinctions between Irish, English and Scottish styles of salmon fly were highlighted by Williamson, who observed that 'English anglers make a great fuss about the proper flies for salmon; whereas the Scotch anglers content themselves with either a heron's or a bittern's hockle.'[13] Similarly Bilton, writing shortly afterwards, suggested that the 'Limerick flies are almost always very gaudy ... those tied in Dublin are usually of mohair or fur, and much more sober in their colours, although infinitely more showy than Scotch salmon flies.'[14]

It was the gaudier and more systematically constructed salmon fly associated with Ireland that became the dominant influence on national trends during the nineteenth century, supplanting many pre-existing regional styles. Herd identifies the influence of Irish specialists, such as O'Shaughnessey who established his fly-tying business in Limerick in 1795, and later William Blacker, a native of County Wicklow who emigrated to England to establish a tackle and fly-tying business in the early nineteenth century.[15] The first 'Irish' flies hit the Tweed in the 1810s and soon replaced older native patterns in the affection of anglers, to the consternation of some local traditionalists. Thomas Tod Stoddart, for example, called on Scottish fishers, 'Answer me, where in thy day was the Doctor? Where the Parson? Where the Butcher? Where the Childer? Where in short all those prismatic rarities that stock so amply the tin ... of the modern salmon-fisher? You possessed them not. It was neither your wish nor your interest to employ them.'[16]

William Blacker died in 1856, but had helped set in train the development of a new generation of salmon flies, named patterns of complex design, albeit with echoes of the flamboyance of those deployed by Franck. Significantly, these flies were as distinct from trout flies as chalk from cheese, and bore little resemblence to the plain and utilitarian offerings of decades past. This shift accelerated under the influence of celebrated angling publicists and fly-tyers such as the Jermyn Street tackle dealer John Jones and Major John Traherne. As the author of *A Guide to Norway and Salmon Anglers Pocket Companion* (1848) and a purveyor of tackle and advice to leisured London society, Jones was in a unique position to promote the cult of the gaudy salmon fly and included exquisitely detailed hand-coloured plates of his creations in his publications. Traherne was one of the country's most experienced salmon fishers and seems to have cast a line over almost every major river in England, Scotland, Ireland and Norway, at one time also holding the world record for distance fly casting. In 1883 he exhibited a case of flies at the International Fisheries Exhibition in London, attracting the attention of one George Kelson who subsequently celebrated Traherne and his creations in Kelson's *Fishing Gazette* series 'On the description of salmon flies'.

Ultimately, it was George Kelson himself who wrought the most influence on the cult of the fully dressed 'gaudy' salmon fly that reached its apogee in the last decade of Victoria's reign and on salmon angling more generally. Under the influence of Kelson and like-minded zealots, salmon fly design reached its zenith in the last two decades of the century, at least in terms of the complexity and artistry of patterns, materials and construction. Kelson's belief that salmon angling was a science, governed by rules that he was able to interpret based on years of observation, led him to promote his own 'methodical, organised and precise system of fishing' which not only involved devotion to incredibly sophisticated and ornate fly designs, but an astounding range of them, with different patterns for individual rivers and a bizarre range of river conditions.[17] Kelson's flies and theories were ultimately published in *The Salmon Fly* (1895), a 500-page manual with some 200 detailed salmon fly patterns and instructions on when and how to fish them.[18] The complexity of the fly as it had emerged by the end of the century is shown in Figures 8.2 and 8.3.

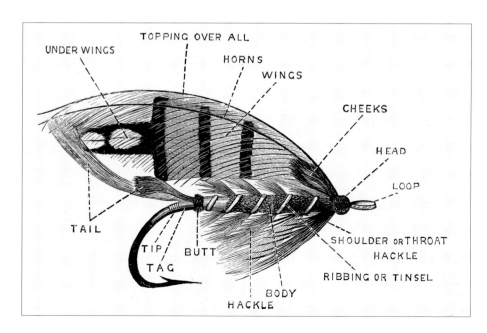

FIGURE 8.2 The anatomy of the 'fully-dressed' salmon fly. From H. Cholmond-eley-Pennell, *Fishing: Salmon and Trout* (1895), p. 177.

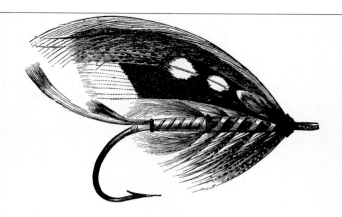

THE 'JOCK SCOTT.

Tag: Silver twist and light yellow silk.

Tail: A topping and Indian crow.   *Butt:* Black herl.

Body: In two equal sections, the first light yellow silk ribbed with fine silver tinsel ; above and below are placed three or more toucan's according to size of hook, extending slightly beyond the butt and followed with three or more turns of black herl.   The second half black silk with a natural black hackle down it and ribbed with silver lace and silver tinsel.   *Throat:* Gallina.

Wings: Two strips of black turkey with white tips, below ; two strips of bustard, and grey mallard, with strands of golden pheasant tail, peacock (sword feather), red macaw, and blue and yellow dyed swan over ; having two strips of mallard and a topping above.

Sides: Jungle fowl.   *Cheeks:* Chatterer.   *Horns:* Blue macaw.   *Head:* Black herl.

FIGURE 8.3 George M. Kelson's instructions for tying the 'Jock Scott'. From H. Cholmond-eley-Pennell, *Fishing: Salmon and Trout* (1895), p. 207.

Kelson's supreme self-belief, or perhaps dogmatism, extended well beyond fly design. He was also the inventor and patent holder of the Kelson Salmon Rod, Kelson Gaff, Kelson Salmon Line and Kelson Lever Winch Reel and even invented a gadget to assist the one-armed angler to fish with a double-handed salmon rod. Kelson was also never hesitant to propound his own particular view of salmon angling etiquette. In responding to an article in the *Daily Telegraph* which suggested that the Princess of Wales and her daughters fished in gowns made with skirts down to the ankle, Kelson wrote with advice addressed directly to their Royal Highnesses;

[you] need a short skirt of tweed bound deeply around the hem with porpoise hide and worn over knickerbockers. This is made so it be buttoned right up, forming a sort of fishwife skirt and furnished with a big pocket for fly book and tackle. If it is necessary to wade so as to cast over a favourite hole, waterproof overall fishing boots can be put

on; but as a rule, this is not found needful and few ladies use them. A high-legged pair of porpoise hide boots and thick woollen stocking are usually sufficient as, if a fisherwoman must get wet, she will soon walk herself dry again.[19]

Parallel to developments in salmon fly design and construction, the mid-to-late Victorian period also witnessed momentous developments in rod and reel design, in part stimulated by the availability of new materials sourced from the burgeoning British empire, but also by developments in tackle manufacturing in America. During the first half of the nineteenth century most salmon rods were constructed of a combination of materials, typically ash for the butt section, with middle sections constructed of lancewood or hickory and whole bamboo cane, or cane and bamboo spliced together for the top section. Rods of this construction were much more suited to distance casting than the single piece rods used by Walton in the seventeenth century, but problems remained, principally in terms of their prodigious weight and uneven actions. However, the 1850s and 1860s witnessed a considerable advance with the introduction and adoption of greenheart, a densely grained wood native to the rainforests of Guiana. Greenheart held a number of advantages over other materials in that it was water resistant, fairly elastic, and produced a potentially slow, deliberate action that favoured the casting style of salmon fishers. Such was its popularity with UK anglers and tackle makers alike that it rapidly supplanted other materials, although, like some of the rod materials it superseded, Greenheart was heavy. A typical 18–20 foot salmon rod of the 1870s weighed between two and three pounds, a similar weight to an earlier hickory rod (Fig. 8.4). Furthermore, rods fashioned from greenheart were not particularly cheap, with a good salmon rod of the early 1870s costing between three and five guineas.[20]

During the same period rods manufactured from split cane began to appear on the market, although rods of this construction tended to be two or three times the price of those made of greenheart which retained the loyalty of salmon fishers up until the end of the century. Herd argues that British loyalty to greenheart and a countervailing failure to pursue split cane technology cost Britain its lead in the development of fishing rods, primacy in which shifted to the United States where rod-making pioneers Samuel Phillipe and Hiram Leonard led the development of the first six-strip split-cane rods and provided the catalyst for the emergence of the American rod-making industry, centred initially on Vermont. Nonetheless, British tackle makers did adopt the new technology and split-cane rods from home and abroad were widely available to domestic anglers by the mid-1880s. Allcocks were marketing some of the first 'hexagonal built or split-cane' rods in 1879 and their 1881 catalogue included a collection of trout and salmon rods ranging from 10 to 18 feet in length.[21] Hardy Bros. of Alnwick won first prize at the International Fisheries Exhibition held in London in

FIGURE 8.4
River keeper
John Cragg
fishing down
the Cottage
Stream Pool
of the River
Test with an
'18 footer'
in the early
1900s. From
A. Grimble,
*The Salmon
Rivers of
England and
Wales* (1913),
p. 4.

1883 for their split-cane rods, although it is said that this owed something to espionage, since Hardy's employees had allegedly used a steaming kettle to prise apart an American 'Leonard' split cane rod a number of years earlier to discover the secrets of its manufacture. However, although split-cane rods were widely adopted by trout fishermen, they made less impact on salmon fishers. Part of the reason was cost, allied to concerns over the casting power and reliability of split cane. For example, an 18-foot split-cane salmon rod manufactured by Allcocks in 1881 retailed for £12, compared to £5 for a comparable hickory or greenheart model. Even as late as 1898 the fishing author Sir Herbert Maxwell argued that, 'in the larger sizes of salmon rod it is not very easy to discern any superiority that split-cane possesses over greenheart, except perhaps in appearance, and the cost is at least three times as great'. Maxwell went on to observe, 'Let every man please himself in the matter; if he chooses to give ten or twelve guineas for a split-cane salmon rod, instead of three or three and a half for a greenheart, nobody but his wife has any right to complain.'[22]

Rapid advances in rod technology after 1860 were matched by those in the design and manufacture of salmon fishing reels. Manufacturers and anglers moved away from the multiplier technology that had often failed salmon fishers earlier in the century toward a simpler winch with an adjustable drag check mechanism (Fig. 8.5). Brass was still widely used, although by the 1880s aluminium and hard rubber-based synthetics marketed as Ebonite and Vulcanite were increasingly replacing heavy metals in reel manufacture. Three models in particular came to dominate the salmon angling scene; the 'Kelson Patent Lever Winch' introduced in the early 1880s and manufactured by Farlows of the Strand, London, the 'Sun and Planet' manufactured by the Perth firm of P.D.Malloch, and the Hardy Bros. 'Perfect' which was introduced in 1891 (Fig. 8.6). These late-nineteenth century models were a great deal more reliable than earlier brass-geared reels and significantly lighter. They also offered greater ease of disassembly and all included adjustable drag systems to assist in the playing of large salmon. The advances in reel design and manufacturing during this period were such that there have been few major design changes since the introduction of the Perfect in 1891. Nonetheless, these pieces of Victoria ingenuity were expensive. The Kelson Patent Lever Winch cost 70s. in brass with a 25 per cent premium for aluminium, whereas the alloy Hardy Perfect retailed at 60s.[23]

Advances in reel and rod design during the nineteenth century made salmon angling incrementally more possible, practical and pleasurable, although arguably less accessible given the cost of reliable salmon fishing tackle. Perhaps just as significant, however, at least in terms of accessibility, was the late-Victorian cult of the fully dressed gaudy salmon fly. The mid- to late nineteenth century witnessed a shift away from the simplistic, locally rooted, creations of earlier years towards nationally and internationally recognised patterns of enormous complexity and no small cost, in terms of materials and construction. More than advances in rods, reels and other equipment, the cult of the gaudy salmon fly marked the growing singularity and separateness of salmon fishing (at least with the fly) from other branches and served to imbue the sport with a degree of complexity and mystery not previously present. Under the influence of Kelson and others, the cult of

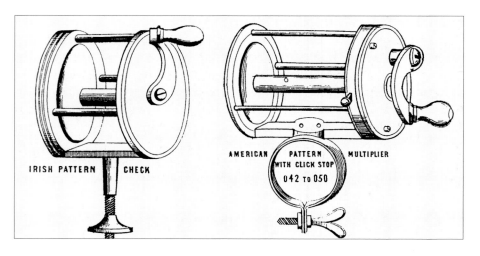

IRISH PATTERN   CHECK

AMERICAN   PATTERN   MULTIPLIER
WITH CLICK STOP
042 TO 050

FIGURE 8.5 (Left) A 'winch' from Allcock's fishing tackle catalogue of 1866 designed to be secured to a rod by a spike through the rod butt. (Right) A 'multiplier' from the 1866 Allcock catalogue with a 'collar' rod fitting. From N. Dowden, *Old Fishing Tackle* (Shire Publications, 1999), p. 8.

the gaudy salmon fly helped to cement the separation of salmon angling from other branches of angling, made it more expensive, more complex and seemingly less accessible.

Andrew Herd argues that the division between game (salmon and trout) and coarse angling, with the upper and middle classes associated with the former and working-class participation confined to the latter, began in the middle of the nineteenth century. Certainly during the period 1850–1900 there is a sense in which the technologies and methodologies of salmon angling, and therein the sport itself, were appropriated by the middle and upper classes. Nonetheless, at the beginning of the nineteenth century, the appropriation of the salmon, alongside the stag and grouse, by middle- and upper-class field-sports enthusiasts as a sporting icon may have appeared unlikely. Despite the growth of salmon angling throughout the nineteenth century, and

FIGURE 8.6 The Hardy 'Perfect' Salmon Reel, 1891. From H. Cholmond-eley-Pennell, *Fishing: Salmon and Trout* (1895), p. 57.

the emergence of complex angling methodologies and culture, for much of this period the salmon was still primarily considered a foodstuff, and a commonplace and ordinary one at that. Equally, most salmon fishing was commercial rather than sporting, and most salmon caught and consumed in Britain met their ends in nets or traps, rather than as a result of a blow from an angler's priest. Some of this was to change rapidly, particularly the relative abundance of salmon, as the British salmon fisheries experienced a sudden and catastrophic decline from the beginning of Victoria's reign. This decline had a number of effects and implications. The relative scarcity of salmon eventually contributed to a growing sense of exclusivity, which was compounded by the introduction of new controls on some methods of fishing as legislation was introduced to protect and preserve dwindling salmon populations. In the long term, a diminution in the availability and commercial importance of salmon increased its value and status as a sporting commodity.

II

Concerns about the failing productivity of the British salmon fisheries first began to emerge in the 1820s and 1830s and heightened significantly in the mid-Victorian era. The presence of voluble landed riparian owners in both Houses of Parliament ensured that the issue received increasing amounts of parliamentary attention in the 1840s and 1850s, so too concerns that, in Ireland at least, falling catches of salmon and disputes between commercial fishing interests were, in some areas, contributing to a heightening of social tensions.[24] Equally, and also because of contemporaneous Irish experience, concerns about the productivity of the salmon fisheries were sharpened by wider mid-century anxieties over the nation's capacity to feed an expanding population.[25] As a result a Royal Commission was appointed in 1860 to investigate the sudden decline of the salmon fisheries of England and Wales; its members included Sir William Jardine, the principal Victorian scientific authority on the salmon, William Ffennell, chief fisheries inspector at the Irish Board of works and architect of the 1848 Irish Salmon Fisheries Act, and the political economist, Sir George Kettilby Rickards. Aside from their professional interest in the salmon, both Jardine and Ffennell were 'ardent' anglers.[26]

As the Commissioners were soon well aware, the decline in both the supply and availability of salmon had an enormous impact and resonance both materially and psychologically, particularly since during the eighteenth century the fish had been commonplace enough to be considered a mundane staple food of the poor. The commissioners heard reports that groups as geographically diverse as the inmates of Romsey workhouse and the apprentices of London and Lancaster had demanded not to be fed salmon more than twice weekly such was its familiarity to the public palate during the reign of George III.[27] Some of these accounts were exaggerated, but not apocryphal. In Daniel Defoe's time the river Tamar (Devon) had been 'so full of salmon ... that the country people cannot take too many', while even the Mersey was reported to 'greatly abound with salmon'. Further north, the naturalist Thomas Pennant, writing in the last quarter of the eighteenth century, witnessed enormous landings of salmon on the Tees at Dinstall, with fishermen paid 5s. for every 12 fish.[28]

By the middle of the nineteenth century salmon had become both relatively scarce and expensive and recent memories of past abundance only served to sharpen concerns about the sudden fall in catches. The price of the fish to the urban consumer increased almost twenty-fold between 1820 and 1850. Such was the novelty value of one of the last salmon captured in the Thames in 1830 that George IV reportedly bought it for a guinea a pound.[29] By the 1860s, at anywhere between 2s. and 10s. a pound, a prime salmon could be as valuable as a Southdown sheep.[30]

Salmon populations have always experienced both short and long term fluctuations according to a range of natural factors, including weather and changes in their marine environment. Human exploitation of the British fisheries, ever since Roman garrisons on the Thames and Severn first named the salmon 'Salar' (the leaper), has also long had some impact. However, the decline of the salmon fisheries during the early to mid-nineteenth century was something altogether different. Not all rivers were equally affected, but between the end of the Napoleonic wars and Victoria's accession to the throne most had experienced the beginnings of a massive and prolonged drop in productivity. On the Hampshire Avon, for example, the overall catch fell from 1,160 salmon in 1816 to 68 in 1860.[31] The fishery at Boulter's landing on the Thames at Maidenhead had produced 72 salmon in 1804 and 60 in 1806, but fishing ended here in 1821 after only two salmon were caught.[32] On the Lune (Lancashire) the value of salmon caught at the Skerton fishery dropped from £1,000 in 1832 to only £300 in 1859; evidence of a significant catch shrinkage given the compensatory effect of rising prices.[33] The decline in the productivity of salmon fisheries was mirrored in tumbling fishery rental values. The Kings Garth fishery on the River Eden (Cumberland) has been let at £845 per annum in 1781, but by 1850 was attracting only £55. On the Taw (Devon) the annual rental on the Wrey fishery fell from £100 to £10 in the thirty years between 1830 and 1860. On the Test (Hants.) fishing traps let annually for £100 in 1830 were returning only £18 by the 1850s.[34] This collapse in rental values had a number of implications, with the diminution in financial value and annual income borne primarily by civic, ecclesiastical and aristocratic landlords and proprietors.

From the perspective of the twenty-first century, and given what we now know about the ecology of the salmon, the fundamental causes of this decline are relatively easy to identify.[35] The Atlantic salmon (*Salmo salar*) is an anadromous fish, whose migratory life cycle is divided between sea and freshwater. This cycle begins in the upper reaches of freshwater rivers where adult salmon reproduce in the winter months by laying and fertilising eggs. It is here that the hatched juvenile fish (parr) remain for approximately two years before undergoing hormonal changes (thus becoming smolts) and migrating to the sea in spring. Once out in their oceanic feeding grounds, Greenland and the Faroe Islands for the bulk of British fish, the salmon grow rapidly. Thereafter, following between one and three years at sea (those with only one sea-winter are termed grilse), the now adult salmon return to British freshwater to spawn. Some arrive in spring, but the majority enter freshwater rivers in late summer and autumn. Virtually all return to their natal freshwater river to reproduce, guided by the individual chemical scent of each river, the memory of which is thought to be imprinted in the brain of the fish as parr and smolts. In the subsequent winter months the returned adult fish breed and the cycle is repeated.

It will be clear, therefore, that the ability to move freely between freshwater and sea habitats is a fundamental requirement of the species. Furthermore, salmon require water of relatively high purity in order to breed and migrate effectively. During the first half of the nineteenth century these fundamental requirements were being undermined with severe and often almost immediate consequences for the ability of the salmon to migrate and reproduce. Of the many factors responsible, perhaps the most damaging but often the least understood was the damage caused to the salmon's freshwater environment by rapid urbanisation and industrialisation. The heightened use of rivers as sources of power and to convey both industrial and domestic pollution had disastrous consequences for the species.[36] Mining was particularly destructive. In much of the south-west, south Wales and the north-east, deposits from clay, slate, coal and iron-ore mining simply choked the rivers of life. Silt ruined the texture of gravel spawning beds and altered the chemical constituency of the waters to such an extent that sometimes few forms of life could flourish. For example, in the 1830s coal washings became so pervasive in the rivers Ystwith and Rheidol (Ceredigon) that even cattle, sheep, geese and hounds died after drinking from their waters.[37] Similarly, on the Tees, the periodic flushing of lead mines was said to result in the immediate death of every fish within a mile downstream of the mines.[38]

Throughout much of the industrial North, the Potteries and West Midlands, new mill-dams, pollution from manufacturing industry and domestic effluent similarly ended the salmon's presence. The rivers of the West Riding and south Yorkshire were among the first to relinquish the fish to pollution from textile mills, tanneries and mines. The Ribble (Lancashire), whose watershed encompassed the streams of Blackburn and Darwen, was badly affected by waste from textile, print and paper works by the 1850s.[39] Other forms of exploitation were equally destructive. The increasing extraction of gravel from riverbeds, under special or local Highway Acts, for road building and ostentatious private driveways, ruined many rivers. Major spawning areas were lost on the Dee near Chester and on the Severn at Shrewsbury where over twelve miles of gravel bar were removed in the 1840s.[40] The abstraction and canalisation of the waterways, which reached its peak in the early nineteenth century, also destroyed many salmon rivers. By converting rivers into navigable waterways, valuable fast-running spawning areas were lost. Finally, in all areas, the almost imperceptible spread of locks, weirs and dams increasingly impeded the salmon's ability to migrate.

On top of these problems were those resulting from indiscriminate and often illegal forms of commercial fishing. Firstly, the early nineteenth century witnessed an increase in the efficiency and number of permanent coastal and estuarine stake-nets. These nets were essentially large fixed structures, with net material laid over and around wooden frameworks, into which the salmon swam and became trapped. Some certainly enjoyed considerable antecedence, but the wider growth in estuarine netting during the early part of the century was almost certainly stimulated by an increased demand for fish foods, related perhaps to population growth. As the Royal Commission discovered, many of these so called 'fixed-engines', were often operated contrary to existing fishing laws, working almost continuously and in such a way as to prevent sufficient numbers of adult fish reaching their breeding grounds upriver.[41]

Commercial and leisure fishing practices inland were often little better. Here other types of fixed-engines, such as permanent fishing weirs and coops, also often worked without adequate periods of cessation. Legal restrictions on fishing seasons were often ignored or misunderstood. Immature salmon were killed in large numbers both by netting and by fishermen with rod and line. Even if the adult salmon reached their spawning areas on the upper waters, they still faced danger from those without legal claims to fish. In much of Wales, northern and south-western England large numbers of salmon were killed annually as they assembled in winter to breed. In many upland areas this illegal activity resembled a cottage industry with black-smiths producing custom built spears and leisters for local populations long accustomed to winter salmon poaching.[42]

Despite these problems the Commissioners concluded their report in upbeat mood, declaring that 'the causes which have reduced the fisheries to their present state ... are clear and palpable, and admit, to a great extent, of being remedied by legislation'.[43] Their central recommendations included the prohibition of all fixed engines, including the estuarine stake-nets which had proved such a point of contention over the preceding decades, new restrictions on net sizes and the introduction of fish passes on all inland weirs and dams. The commissioners also called for the suppression of effluents and industrial pollution and the introduction of new, nationally uniform, weekly and annual close times for fishing. Steps to prevent the sale and possession of salmon during the winter close time were also suggested.

Other recommendations sought to deal with the problem of poaching. The commissioners called for the prohibition of the use and the possession of those instruments and baits connected in some way to poaching and illegal fishing. These included spears, gaffs, snatches, torches and salmon roe. Furthermore, it was also recommended that the killing of young fish and the disturbance of spawning salmon be made an offence. Finally the commission argued for the introduction of local river conservancy management boards for each river and its watershed. These boards were to be composed of local fishery owners and major riparian tenants, invested with the power to raise income through fishing licences and levies, and charged with responsibility for the enforcement of new close times and fishing rules and the suppression of illegal fishing engines and barriers. These recommendations passed into law in the Salmon Acts of 1861 and 1865.

Despite the merits of the new legislation, and Macleod has argued forcefully for the Salmon Acts to be regarded as part of a new generation of 'public interest' statutes, in its practical application and effects it served to reduce public access to salmon rivers and contributed to a strengthening association between the salmon and landed interests.[44] The enforcement of the Salmon Acts, and two aspects in particular, the banning of popular fishing methods and introduction of local salmon-river conservancy boards to oversee the administration and policing of the salmon fisheries and the licensing of angling, were critical in this regard.

III

The introduction of local river conservancy boards was significant in both practical and symbolic terms. On the basis of their knowledge of the 1848 Irish Salmon Act, the architects of the Salmon Acts understood that without effective administration and enforcement, any new legislation to control the exploitation of salmon would fail. The Salmon Acts sought to provide for administration and enforcement in two ways, first, through the creation of a national salmon fisheries inspectorate, based initially within the Board of Trade and subsequently the Home Office, and second, through the introduction of new local management and policing agencies, the salmon-river conservancy boards. The conservancy boards, each with responsibility for an individual river system, were granted the authority to raise revenue through the imposition of rates on individual fisheries and the introduction of licences for both commercial fishing and angling. This revenue was principally used to fund the employment of river bailiffs to enforce the Salmon Acts through the detection and prosecution of poaching and other forms of illegal fishing.

Crucially, the new conservancy boards were constituted to ensure that the largest local riparian owners received the greatest representation, and therefore enjoyed the greatest influence over all aspects of board policy. These arrangements in part acceded to the realities of local landed power and influence, but also reflected a deliberate effort on the part of the architects of the Salmon Acts to encourage a reassertion of landed influence over the salmon rivers, based on the principle that those with the greatest interest in rivers, and therefore the most to gain from an improvement in productivity, should assume much of the responsibility for implementing and enforcing the legislation of 1861 and 1865.

The character and membership of the new conservancy boards themselves helped contribute to an association between the salmon and the landed interests who were now the principal public faces of salmon protection and preservation on each and every salmon river. Consider, for example, the composition of the Derwent Conservancy Board in Western Cumberland. Like most boards, it was dominated by the largest owners, including the fifth Earl of Lonsdale, Lord Lieutenant of Cumberland, whose 67,457 acres in Cumberland and Westmorland included over four miles of the Derwent as well as holdings on the rivers Eden, Ehen, Duddon and Lune;[45] Sir Wilfred Lawson, Bt, JP, of Brayton Hall, Aspatria, variously Liberal MP for Carlisle and Cockermouth, who held four and a half miles of river; and Lord Leconfield of Cockermouth Castle, who lived for the most part on his estate in West Sussex, but owned 11,147 acres in West Cumberland including two miles of the Derwent plus fishing rights in Lakes Bassenthwaite and Derwentwater. Perhaps the keenest salmon angler among this group, Leconfield also made some huge rod catches as a frequent guest of the Duke of Richmond on the Spey.[46] These, and other members of the aristocratic cabal on the Derwent Board, were also often contemporaries at school (Harrow and Eton), University (Christ Church) and clubs (Carlton and Reform).

The intended effect of the local conservancy board model was, in the words of the Salmon Fisheries Inspectorate, 'the establishment of a chain of gentlemen, from the source of each river to the sea, specially responsible, from the accident of their position, for the improvement of the stream(s)'.[47] This acknowledgement of the geographic range of individual conservancy boards hints toward the significance of the new arrangements for the general public and those 'public' fisheries to which they had traditionally enjoyed access. In reality the constitution and powers of the conservancy boards represented much more than a mere reassertion of landed influence over private inland fisheries. The authority of the new conservancy boards and their bailiffs extended to every yard of river, including those areas to which the public had often formerly exercised rights to fish unimpeded (Fig. 8.7).

The introduction of the Salmon Acts, conservancy boards, new regulations and fishing licences and the activities of river bailiffs in suppressing unlicensed angling and forms of illegal fishing, contributed to a deepening association between the salmon, the salmon rivers and salmon angling with the middle and upper classes. Working-class access to salmon angling under the new boards and licensing systems was not impossible, but it was financially difficult. On the Cumberland Derwent and Eden, season tickets for salmon fishing on 'public' areas of rivers in the 1890s cost the equivalent of 2–3 weeks of average labouring wages, over twenty times the cost of an equivalent ticket to fish for trout.[48] Just as significantly, the best salmon beats were held in private hands and those riparian owners possessed of the most productive salmon fisheries were usually the least likely to grant access to a wider angling public. Cost and the realities of riparian ownership meant that the 'king of fish' usually remained the preserve of gentry and middle-class anglers on both public and private stretches.

There is plenty of evidence to suggest the extent to which the general public regarded the Salmon Acts, and the new systems of regulation and licensing under the conservancy boards as tantamount to an appropriation of fishing rights. A government enquiry into disturbances on the Upper Wye in Breconshire and Radnorshire in 1881 found that most local people thought the Acts designed 'to rob the working class of their [fishing] rights'.[49] On the Cumberland Derwent, where it was argued that 'before the boards ... a man could fish when and where he chose', the new legislation was similarly accused of being a front to restrict the access of the poor to the salmon. There was, as one local writer argued 'a big difference between protecting fish ... and restricting them for the sport and good of a few'.[50] Feelings ran equally high just across the border. In the early 1860s the Galashiels Fishery Reform League was formed with the object of repealing the fishery laws, particularly those pertaining to the Border Tweed, and making the salmon the common property of all Borderers.[51] In large part because of localised experiences of administration and enforcement, the general public came to have a very different perception of the Salmon Acts to that intended by government ministers and their expert advisors. The belief that the primary

intention of the Salmon Acts and conservancy boards was to preserve 'wild' property for the rich remained prevalent within many communities well into the next century.[52] In the public mind at least, the salmon and game laws came to be seen as analogous in many parts of the United Kingdom, despite continuing affirmations of the 'public interest' served by the Salmon Acts by government ministers and fishery inspectors.

IV

Controls on fishing introduced in the Salmon Acts of 1861 and 1865 may have been pragmatic and well intentioned, but they were also influenced by a developing ethos about 'the right way to catch salmon' which was both informed by and derived from salmon angling. The new controls introduced, principally in the Salmon Act of 1861, sought not only to differentiate between angling, legitimate commercial fishing and ancient popular fishing techniques, but also to extinguish many of the latter. Although the 1861 Salmon Act was ostensibly a measure in the national interest to protect and preserve salmon stocks, in its attitude to popular and primitive fishing practices the new legislation was indelibly imbued with notions of sporting fairness derived from angling and other field sports.

FIGURE 8.7 Commercial netting at 'The Run', a public fishery at the mouth of the Hampshire Avon. Fixed-nets here were declared illegal and removed in 1862, but commercial netting with drift nets continued into the twentieth century, albeit regulated and licensed by the Avon and Stour Conservancy Board. From A. Grimble, *The Salmon Rivers of England and Wales* (1913), p. 15.

These emerging sensibilities are evident in the ban that the 1861 Salmon Act introduced on spearing and similar practices, albeit that this measure was primarily aimed at those who targeted the spawning salmon and whose legal right to fish was often most disputed. Spearing, using single or multi-pronged implements, also known as 'leisters' or 'wasters', was the oldest method of taking salmon in British waters. Sometimes used in sandy estuaries, or at points where the salmon ascended obstacles, spearing was commonest during the winter spawning season, when the fish could be easily approached during daylight as they assembled in shallow upland waters to breed. However, perhaps the most dramatic form of spearing occurred at night when torches, often simple affairs constructed from straw, were used to illuminate the riverbed. This practice was known as 'burning the water' and usually involved relatively large numbers of participants. The hook-shaped gaff was used in a similar manner to spears, while 'snatches' and 'stroke-halls', which were essentially hand held lines with large hooks attached, were primarily used to 'foul hook' spawning fish.[53]

Parallels to this kind of legal discrimination against the hunting tools of the poor can be found in both English and colonial game legislation of the mid- to late Victorian period. The English game laws did not specifically outlaw those hunting instruments favoured by working-class hunters, but under the Poaching Prevention Act of 1862, the possession of such things as snares and long-nets became an offence in many circumstances. For example, while it was not an offence for a landowner to kill a rabbit with a snare, it was illegal for someone to carry such an implement with intent to commit a poaching offence. Clearer parallels are detectable in the game laws imposed in British colonies during the late nineteenth century, aspects of which have been explored by Mackenzie and Beinart.[54] Statutes introduced to preserve African game for sport invariably sought to prohibit the implements used by indigenous hunters. African hunting tools, such as spears, snares and nets were often explicitly outlawed, as in the Cape Colony Game Act of 1886 and the Natal Game Act of 1891. Legislation which determined that game could only be killed by shooting had a complementary effect and, allied to stringent gun laws, prevented indigenous peoples from hunting game in much of Africa.

Mackenzie contends that the prohibition of native hunting implements was linked to the development of an imperial hunting code, itself heavily informed by the conventions of domestic field sports, which increasingly defined itself against the supposedly primitive and cruel methods of native hunters. He argues that although early settlers and hunting writers had described African hunting techniques in a largely neutral way, by the second half of the nineteenth century colonists and visitors were increasingly emphasising the lack of moral equivalence between white and black methods. African hunting practices certainly varied according to the species and region concerned and the purpose of the hunt. However, by the 1880s, native techniques such snaring, poisoning and the driving of animals into pits where they were lustily dispatched with spears, were increasingly being negatively contrasted with the approach of the white hunter, who sought to administer a quick death with a rifle, often following a long and sometimes hazardous stalk.

Mackenzie suggests that the developing hunting code of the colonial elite, with its emphasis on field craft, marksmanship and above all the idea that the animal should have a fair chance, partly reflected in a reluctance to shoot young, female or breeding animals, was predicated upon functional and technical change. European hunting in Africa and India had initially been 'a subsidy for colonial expansion and exploration'. Once the need for this subsidy lessened, and the requirement for defensive or subsistence hunting by whites also diminished, 'imperial rulers began to restrict access to game … and the killing of animals lost economic and achieved ritual significance'. The emergence, in both cultural and legal forms, of the sporting ethos of the great white hunter was also facilitated by improvements in firearms technology. The high velocity breech-loading rifle of the 1880s made the 'single mortal shot for any animal, including the elephant, … not only a possibility, but the prime objective of the sporting hunter'.[55] It was primarily these developments which allowed enabled imperial hunters to distance themselves from indigenous hunters whose techniques were primitive and motives primarily utilitarian.

The plains of Africa may be long way from the salmon rivers of Great Britain, but parts of Mackenzie's thesis can be applied to Victorian efforts to curtail certain modes of popular fishing. Spearing, for example, had for a long time been regarded as an acceptable means of fishing. Indeed, up until early nineteenth century, spears were used by all social classes. Visitors to Cumberland in the sixteenth and seventeenth century, for example, noted how the Cumbrian and Border yeomanry considered it the greatest sport to spear salmon from horseback in estuary shallows.[56] Sir Walter Scott's description in *Red Gauntlet* suggests that the practice continued on the Solway Firth until at least the early decades of the nineteenth century.[57] The spear was also the traditional weapon of salmon fishermen in mid-Wales. Even 'gentlemen', when questioned by government enquiries into fishing disputes on the Upper Wye in the early 1880s confessed to past use of the spear and admitted that in the right hands the weapon was a highly effective means of taking salmon.[58] Similar indulgence characterised early nineteenth-century attitudes to spearing on the Border Tweed. Guests at Sir Walter Scott's home at Abbotsford at the turn of the century were apparently invited out nightly to view the spectacle of 'burning the waters'. Thomas Tod Stoddart, author of *The Art of Angling* (1836), described 'leistering' as a 'national amusement' whose survival into the 1830s typified 'the old spirit of the borders'.[59]

Many descriptions of spearing in these areas in the early part of the century were not just neutral, but eulogistic. Scott's depiction of nocturnal leistering in the northern border counties were both vivid and heavily romanticised.[60] Stoddart was equally enamoured and, in 1836, declared that spearing was a 'manly and vigorous sport', which he would rather see 'encouraged, within certain limits, than tyrannically suppressed'.[61] The first verse of the 'Leister song' recounted, and probably also penned, by Stoddard, underlines the sense of the noble and romantic which many observers attached to the activity.

> Flashes the blood-red gleam,
> Over the midnight slaughter,
> Wild shadows haunt the stream,
> Dark forms glace o'er the water.
> It is the leisterer's cry!
> A salmon, ho! oho!
> In the scales of light the creature bright
> Is glimmering below.[62]

However, attitudes to spearing were certainly changing during the period in which Stoddart was writing. William Scrope, author of *Day and Nights of Salmon Fishing on the Tweed* (1843), conceded that leistering might 'to the southern ear, sound like poaching of the most flagitious description', which suggests that outside Wales and the Scottish and English borders attitudes were already altering. Even within these areas there were signs of shifts during the 1840s and 1850s, even from those like Thomas Stoddart who had previously championed leistering.[63] In his later work, *The Angler's Companion to the Rivers and Lochs of Scotland* (1853) Stoddart described how in 1846, 'six thousand breeding fish', which had 'formed the hope and stay of future seasons of abundance', had been the subject of 'a massacre … by means of the same deadly instrument [the leister]' near Melrose. The Tweed, Stoddart reported, 'has not yet recovered … from the effect of this bloody onslaught'.[64]

By the 1850s attitudes to the spear were changing fundamentally, particularly among middle- and upper-class groups who were now more likely to emphasise its destructive potential than to eulogise over the wild escapades of bands of rugged leisterers. This shift culminated in the prohibition of both the use and possession of spears and such like instruments in 1861 and may be accounted for by several factors including the kind of functional developments highlighted by Mackenzie. The development of salmon angling for sport occurred alongside, and undoubtedly influenced, the marginalisation of more primitive forms of fishing, even though salmon angling itself, with flies and lures, long preceded the nineteenth-century attack on spearing. Nonetheless, as Douglas Sutherland suggests, with the emergence of a debate over the 'right and wrong way to catch a salmon' during the life times of Scrope and Stoddart, 'it may be said that the sport came of age.'[65] Amid debates over the merits of lures, flies, greased-lines, greenheart or cane rods, salmon angling gradually became imbued with an ethos, which, as with many other forms of elite hunting, distanced itself from easy and primitive modes of capture. Like any cults, the salmon-angling craze among the Victorian elite had its high priests, notably George Kelson, H. Cholmondeley-Pennell, and Francis Francis.[66] By the end of the century they had established that the 'right way to catch salmon was, indisputably, with a fly' (Fig. 8.8).[67]

Nevertheless, the emergence of a more defined code of salmon angling during the nineteenth century cannot completely explain the detachment from more primitive methods like spearing. After all, the salmon rivers were never entirely environments for sport. Indeed, the function of the fisheries remained predominantly utilitarian throughout the nineteenth century. Even before it faced the fly fisher, the salmon risked an inglorious death in the nets of commercial fishermen and even many landed gentlemen anglers also extracted fish using 'ancient' fishing traps. This suggests that the growing opprobrium attached to methods like spearing and snatching was also influenced by other factors, notably a growing concern for spawning fish. After all, vulnerable breeding salmon were the quarry most commonly targeted with snatches and spears. Furthermore, a preparedness to kill

spawning fish marked those associated with such implements apart even from commercial and sport fishermen who generally recognised some form of close time.

The influence of a hunting code, which increasingly regarded the killing of vulnerable breeding animals as unacceptable, is again apparent here, although it should be noted that English statute law had long sought to protect salmon during the winter breeding season. Indeed, the concept of close times for fishing, however badly observed, predated both the development of any nineteenth-century hunting cult or the emergence of the 'new sensibilities' which Keith Thomas suggests led to a 'new concern for the suffering of animals'.[68] The premise for this was entirely practical and based on the understanding that the cessation of fishing during the winter benefited future stocks.

What undoubtedly intensified mid-nineteenth century concerns over the use of spears and snatches on spawning fish, was the recognition that the productivity of the salmon fisheries was failing. Those communities attached to spearing had never observed close time restrictions, but, crucially, this was only an irritant to other fishery users while the rivers remained productive and the fish abundant. Tolerance for primitive fishing methods declined as the salmon fisheries began to experience problems in the early to mid-nineteenth century. Stoddart's new anxiety at the damage caused by leistering in 1846, for example, almost certainly coincided with signs that the Tweed was becoming less productive. However, although justified on conservation grounds, the attack on the spear and snatch also drew on developing notions of the rectitude of certain fishing methods over others. Since Royal Commissioners Jardine and Ffennell were anglers, likewise the subsequent Salmon Fisheries Inspectors Frank Buckland and John Archer, there is little doubt that many of the government's own fishery experts were adherents to the new ethics of salmon angling and naturally regarded the spear, snatch and gaff as unsporting.

V

The development and growth of salmon angling was part of a wider expansion in pleasure angling during the nineteenth century. Like other forms of the sport, salmon angling benefited from improvements in tackle technology, the commodification of leisure and improvements in travel that enabled easier access to the rivers of England, Scotland, Wales, Ireland and beyond. Its association with the upper classes was in part accidental and linked to wider developments in field sports, in so much as many salmon rivers, particularly in Scotland and northern England, were within the geographic areas increasingly acquired for wilderness sporting estates and exploited for other elite field sports, such as deer stalking and grouse shooting. Salmon angling offered wealthy field-sports enthusiasts an opportunity for out-door sport in the spring, at the end of the principal winter shooting season, while the main salmon runs also coincided with the periods when the sporting lodges received their owners, tenants and guests for grouse and deer shooting during the second half of summer and autumn.

To some extent, therefore, salmon angling's separateness from other fishing disciplines reflected the new realities of property ownership in the nineteenth century and particularly the acquisition and appropriation of wilderness areas for elite field-sports. However, even this physical association of salmon rivers with large, and often aristocratic, landowners was compounded by other factors, with their roots in the rapid decline of the salmon fisheries in the early to mid-nineteenth century and the remedial measures adopted in response. Victorian efforts to reverse the decline of salmon fisheries deliberately sought to reassert landed influence over the salmon rivers on the principle that property owners should assume much of the responsibility and burden of implementing and enforcing the legislation of 1861 and 1865. This reassertion of landed influence was achieved principally through the introduction and operation of local river conservancy boards, constituted and composed of the largest fishery owners. In the eyes of the public, the character and constituency of the new conservancy boards contributed to an association between the salmon and the aristocratic and landed riparian owners who were now the principal public faces of salmon protection and preservation on each and every salmon river. In many areas the introduction of conservancy boards, licences for angling, river-bailiffs, and the consequent suppression of traditional methods of fishing, contributed to the effective cessation of public exploitation of the salmon rivers.

The emergence of new legal, practical and economic barriers to popular participation in salmon angling, particularly after 1861, occurred alongside the coincident development of a particular salmon-angling ethos, based primarily around fly-fishing. Over the course of the last quarter of the nineteenth-century salmon angling 'rapidly accumulated a burden of tradition and convention' which was predominantly elite in character and origin.[69] Under the influence of figures such as Kelson, Cholmondeley-Pennell, Traherne and Francis, salmon angling methodologies became more complex and less accessible. There was a particular emphasis on the supremacy, not least in technical and moral terms, of fly-fishing for salmon over simple and primitive methods of capture. In this sense salmon angling methodologies drew on those that had developed around the other elite hunting activities where sport was celebrated over utility. The conditions in which salmon angling developed and to an extent separated from other branches of angling were complex, and given the falling productivity of the salmon rivers of England, Scotland and Wales after 1830 perhaps unlikely. But, ultimately the salmon's decline as a commercial resource and its relative scarcity increased its value as a sporting commodity and its attraction to field sports enthusiasts among the landed elite.

CHAPTER NINE

Starting a hare: exploring the history of coursing since the mid-nineteenth century*

by Ian Roberts

ALTHOUGH field sports have played an important part in country life over the past two centuries and more, far too little attention has been paid to these activities by rural historians. The same criticism may also be made about those authors who have written about the history of sport in the nineteenth and twentieth centuries, where mention of field sports is usually confined to one or two references to shooting or foxhunting.[1] And yet field sports and notions of animal rights have become increasingly live issues during the last few years. The Countryside Alliance mobilised thousands of people to protest, march and strongly indicate their opposition to proposed legislation outlawing hunting with dogs.[2] Not least among the appeals of this group is one to support countryside traditions, three of which, foxhunting, hunting deer with hounds and the pursuit of hares with dogs, are particularly threatened at the present time. But, as historians, what do we know about these traditions? What part did they play in the life of rural Britain or rural England? How widespread were they? By whom and by how many were they supported? What social and economic effects did field sports have on rural society?

This paper presents the preliminary results of an investigation into some of these questions as they apply to one particular field sport, that of coursing. Coursing is one of four ways of hunting hares. The others, shooting, beagling and hunting with harriers, are all worthy of research but coursing has a number of features which make it different from the others and mean that

* The author wishes to thank the members of the Research Seminar of the University of Durham History Department and members of the Redesdale Society who heard and commented on early versions of this paper. Personal help has been given by Charles Blanning and the NCC, Peter Atkinson, MP, Major Ronnie Hedley-Dent, Jon and Maire West, Corinne Walton, Gerry Wood, Liz Hall and a number of other coursing enthusiasts.

this field sport merits consideration in its own right. Not least among these features is the lack of easily located literature. Both beagling and hunting with harriers are conducted by established packs of hounds, many of which have been in existence for considerable periods of time. Information about these packs is readily available in *Bailey's Hunting Directory*[3] and this provides an excellent starting point for further investigation in libraries, newspaper files and county record offices.[4]

Coursing, as a form of hunting, does not figure in *Bailey's Hunting Directory*. Instead, the sport has its own discrete literature in the form of two publications, *The Coursing Calendar* and *The Greyhound Stud Book*.[5] Both volumes are produced by the National Coursing Club and circulation tends to be confined to followers of the sport. As a consequence, these publications are to be found in few libraries. General studies on coursing, beyond those written for readers who were already followers, or potential followers, of the sport, are rare.[6] The most readily available are often books detailing the origins and development of the Waterloo Cup.[7] As the most prestigious and widely followed coursing event in the national sporting calendar, such books have commanded a wider readership and are more generally available. However, even the most informative and copiously illustrated book, written by Charles Blanning and Sir Mark Prescott, provides only a glimpse of the other coursing events taking place and the numbers of followers who participated in and supported them.[8] Studying coursing with the use of such volumes is akin to trying to write a history of football based on the story of the FA Cup or of cricket from accounts of Test matches at Lord's!

Even the volumes of the *Victoria History of the Counties of England* (hereinafter *VCH*), the most generally accessible history of the localities of England, contain only short studies of coursing for particular counties, some of limited value.[9] Most of the studies appear among the early publications of the *VCH* between 1905 and 1912 and were more often written by coursing enthusiasts rather than professional historians.[10] Consequently, they tend to the anecdotal rather than the analytical and contain few footnotes to the sources used by their authors. They are also, like much coursing literature, more concerned to impart information about individual owners and the dogs that they bred and coursed rather than systematic information about the structure of the sport. In addition, the coverage given by the *VCH* is limited. Volumes have never been produced for Northumberland and Westmorland, two counties where coursing has taken place both before and since 1850.[11] In the case of some of the other counties, for example, Norfolk, where coursing has flourished and about which volumes have appeared, no article is devoted to the sport. Two volumes written in more recent times give a more analytical treatment of the sport in their counties and support entries with full sets of references.[12] Helpful though these are in providing a small segment of the national picture, they also serve to illustrate the shortcomings of the remainder of the *VCH* and indicate the considerable work which remains to be done in recovering a more complete history of coursing.

The absence of secondary sources, as well as the limited scale of these field sports in recent times, dictates the approach and content of this paper. Because the subject has received such limited investigation by historians, I shall begin by explaining what is meant by coursing and attempt to sketch its early history prior to the late eighteenth century. I shall then describe in more detail the nature and extent of the sport since the mid-nineteenth century and also attempt to assess its significance in rural society. I shall also indicate other questions that require answers and suggest an agenda for further research.

I

Coursing is a form of hunting with a specific type of hound – a dog sometimes referred to in the past as a 'gazehound' which, in Britain, is the greyhound.[13] References are made in coursing literature to the presence of coursing dogs on Egyptian tomb paintings and their importance in Greek and Roman times,[14] while a recent study of one Roman garrison in Britain has suggested that the sport was practised by soldiers stationed on Hadrian's Wall.[15] More detail is recorded about coursing during the Middle Ages. Almond, in his recent study of medieval hunting, has demonstrated the importance of the greyhound both for its quality as a hunting dog and companion as well as a symbol of the high status of its owner. Almond also indicates that during the late Middle Ages coursing began to concentrate around the pursuit by greyhounds of two animals, the deer and the hare. In the case of both species, the hunt was followed on horseback and the pursuit of both animals was continued until the quarry was killed.[16] Almond cites a number of authors who praised the greyhound and the hare. The hare not only tested the dogs fully, but it could also be hunted for a much longer period than deer without the need for some of the elaborate equipment and ritual usually prescribed for deer hunting. However, despite this enthusiasm for the sport, it was not until the sixteenth century that a set of rules emerged which regulated coursing.

During the reign of Elizabeth I, the first set of such rules was published.[17] It is known that coursing was popular in the Royal household and elsewhere in the second half of the century.[18] Tradition has it that the rules were drawn up by the Duke of Norfolk at the command of the Queen, although it seems more likely that they were issued from the office of the Earl Marshal as a result of requests for some sort of order in the sport. If they were issued by Norfolk, their likely date of formulation is between the start of the reign in 1558 and his execution in 1572. The rules stipulate that coursing would,

FIGURE 9.1
In the slips for
the Waterloo
Cup, 1898.
From
J. N. P. Watson,
*Victorian and
Edwardian
Field Sports
from Old
Photographs*
(1978), p. 58.

in future, be carried out by pairs of greyhounds. There were regulations governing the distance that the hare had to be in front of the hounds before the dogs were released. They also suggest that the hounds could be followed on horseback or on foot. However, the followers were to remain a certain distance behind the hounds in order not to interfere with the sport or the ability of the judge to see enough of the activities of the hounds to adjudicate the winner of the course.

Later writers about coursing add very little to their accounts of the subject from this point until the story is taken up again in the late eighteenth century.[19] The assumption was that the laws as set down by the Duke of Norfolk provided a general code under which any coursing that took place throughout the country was conducted. To some extent this is supported by those few accounts of coursing matches which have survived. One coursing reference from Lincolnshire describes dogs single-mindedly pursuing one hare to the exclusion of others and the chase lasting up to three hours.[20] This suggests that the hunters followed on horseback and rode freely wherever the hare led them.

The latter point is particularly important as it is embodied in the Game Laws of the seventeenth century. Under the Game Act of 1671, the pursuit of game – by which was meant hare, pheasant, partridge and moorland game – was restricted to persons with an income from property of a value not less than £100 per annum.[21] This simply reinforced a number of previous pieces of legislation which limited hunting, and the ownership of the means of hunting, including the possession of greyhounds, to the propertied members

Slipping.

Hoisting the winning color.

The first turn.

The Judge signalling the winner to the flag man.

Drinking the winner's health.

S.T.Dadd.

Driving the victor home.

Going home by rail.—
Looking after the dogs.

FIGURE 9.2
'Coursing
Matches'
Illustration
from *Illustrated
London News*
25 Feb. 1882,
p. 180.

of society and entitled anyone with the requisite qualifications to pursue game wherever it roamed. Deer and rabbits were excluded from 'game' as defined under the law but were entitled to protection because they were deemed by law to belong to the person on whose property they were found.

Towards the end of the eighteenth century, coursing underwent a number of further changes and a new form of the sport was introduced from which the present day system is descended. The originator of the new arrangements was Lord Orford who founded a club by the same name on his Swaffham estate in Norfolk in 1776.[22] It would appear that Orford was seeking to conduct a modest sized club for fellow enthusiasts and to run coursing days which were more controlled and therefore more successful in providing good coursing for the participants.[23] Orford was seriously interested in the sport and possessed a kennel which frequently contained more than one hundred dogs, most of which had been bred on the premises. All of the club members came from the same social background as Orford and all were probably qualified to hunt in their own right. The club was a great success and was soon emulated by Lord Craven, founder of the Ashdown Park Club in 1780, and by the Duke of Richmond and others when they opened the Malton Club in 1781.

Despite the new form of coursing introduced by the clubs, the rules by which they conducted their coursing were usually based on those set down by the Duke of Norfolk, but modified slightly to reflect the peculiarities of each club's founder members. There is also some evidence that the members of these clubs followed the course on horseback and that many of the runs continued for several miles.[24]

Over the succeeding forty years, the number of clubs founded on the lines of the Swaffham Club continued to grow, so that by the late 1820s there were approximately 27 in England with a further eight in Ireland, Scotland and Wales. Although many of these clubs ran the long courses mentioned above, others confined the sport to a shorter distance and began to use the form of coursing which is now used by present day coursing clubs.[25] In this form of coursing, beaters drive the hare to the running ground where it passes in front of the greyhounds. The hounds, which are concealed within a shy, are held by a slipper who releases them after the hare has passed in front of them and gained a previously determined start over the dogs (Fig 9.1). A judge, mounted on horseback, scores the resulting pursuit by the dogs and adjudicates on the final outcome of the pursuit. The organisation of the Victorian coursing match is shown in Figure 9.2 and, in the case of the Waterloo Cup, Figure 9.4.

It was at this point that two events took place that transformed the nature of coursing in Britain for several decades to come. The first of these was the publication of two important books about the sport of coursing. Goodlake's *Courser's Manual or Stud Book* came out in 1828, written by a coursing enthusiast who had established a club on his own estate at Letcombe Bowers in 1814 as well as being involved in other coursing clubs.[26] In his book, Goodlake attempted to gather together a history of the coursing clubs then in existence together with information on the pedigree and breeding of the leading greyhounds. Goodlake's book was speedily followed in 1829 by Thomas Thacker's *Courser's Companion*.[27] Thacker, an experienced follower and judge of greyhound coursing, attempted to build upon the work of Goodlake and offered some hints on the future development of coursing, together with a reformed set of rules for the conduct of coursing clubs and the running of the actual courses. In 1834 a two-volume revised edition of Thacker's work appeared, which included an important treatise on the breeding of greyhounds.[28] In many ways this book is a landmark in coursing because it recognises that coursing had ceased to be principally about the hunting of hares and had become more concerned with testing the skills of the greyhound. This element may well have drawn some participants to the sport prior to this date and could well have been one of the chief reasons why Orford started his club in the first place. Only under controlled conditions was it possible to conduct fair trials of greyhounds and these conditions could not be created under the old methods of coursing. It was, and is, this concern for the performance of the greyhound which distinguishes coursing from other methods of hunting the hare, in which the hare's death is integral to the successful conclusion of a day's hunting. In coursing, it is not. A course may be completed successfully and the hare troubled by little more than a brief run to escape from a pair of pursuing greyhounds. Although it is true that until the 1970s, the judge had the discretion to award a point for a kill, it is the assessment of the dogs during the run which is of paramount importance and victory could be awarded without a kill.

The other major event that affected coursing in the early nineteenth century was the passing by Parliament in 1831 of a new Game Act. This piece of legislation removed the former property qualification for hunting and now placed all game under the ownership of the person on whose land the birds and animals happened to be located. It also removed the previous restrictions that prevented the widespread breeding and ownership of greyhounds. At the same time, some safeguards against poaching were introduced, as a number of clauses were included in the 1831 Act to control ownership and dealing in game.[29]

The effect of this legislation on the world of coursing was considerable. The fact that the ownership of game within an estate was now vested solely in the landowner meant that efforts to preserve game could be wholly devoted to the preservation of that game for the use of the owner and his friends. Tenants could be required to assist in this process and might well be rewarded by participation in the sport while other landowners, who might previously have enjoyed sport on the land without contributing anything to its provision, were now precluded from doing so without express let or invitation. In terms of coursing, it was now possible to undertake a coursing meeting within the confines of an estate and regulate attendance and participation without fear of intrusion. Such a degree of ownership also permitted landowners to control entry to the event, charge for admission and regulate the supply of hares thus enabling the formal organisation of coursing stakes. As will be shown below, this had a profound effect on the amount of coursing that took place in Britain.

Another important effect to emerge in succeeding decades was the presence of three types of coursing in Britain: public, private and clandestine. The remainder of this paper will be devoted to a consideration of public coursing, where the event was open to the public and where the coursing was conducted by coursing clubs which were, by and large, open to a wide range of members. Although sometimes reported in the press, private coursing was usually conducted for the benefit of tenants on estates by permission of the owner and was controlled in terms of membership, participation and spectacle. It usually subscribed to the same rules as public coursing, but in other respects was a closed event that sometimes had a function in estate terms beyond the mere provision of private sport for tenants, or a personal meeting for family and friends.[30] Clandestine coursing was more the province of poachers but was known to have been carried out in many parts of Britain with greyhounds, whippets, terriers and lurchers.[31]

II

In the new climate created by the Game Laws of 1831, public coursing flourished. The number of clubs increased, as did the geographical spread of coursing. At the same time the number of coursing stakes also increased. Coursing was traditionally conducted most frequently during the winter months, but there had always been those who coursed the hare in all seasons, largely as a result of some of the mistaken beliefs surrounding the hare's production of young.[32] Hare hunting now began to be conducted from October into the following March, with some meetings occasionally organised in September or April, although these became increasingly rare. At present, it is even considered unusual to go beyond the first week in March.[33] The new clubs held meetings throughout the winter, often publishing notice of them in advance. Even the smaller clubs attempted to hold at least one meeting before Christmas and one after. At each of the meetings there was usually more than one event in which the greyhounds could compete, thus enabling the younger dogs to be separated from the older, more experienced greyhounds. In the season 1843–44, for example, 107 clubs conducted 605 prize stakes.[34]

FIGURE 9.3
Richard
Ansdell, The
Waterloo
Cup coursing
meeting, 1840.
Courtesy
of National
Museums
Liverpool
(The Walker).

As the sport spread, so there arose a necessity to report on the results of meetings and provide information about the performance of individual greyhounds. In addition, the roles of the slipper, the man who released the dogs, and the judge, who was responsible for awarding victory, became increasingly important in terms of the regulation of events and information on the conduct and performance of the officials was also required. Some meetings were reported in local newspapers, but in 1840 Thomas Thacker began the first comprehensive reportage of coursing events in his *Courser's Annual Remembrancer and Stud Book*.[35] The *Remembrancer* became the Bible of the coursing world until the formation of the National Coursing Club (NCC) in 1858 when the Club began to issue its own *Coursing Calendar* with which the *Remembrancer* was merged.

The NCC represented the culmination of a desire on the part of major coursers, like the Earl of Sefton and Edward Marjoribanks, to produce a regulatory body which would issue a revised set of rules for coursing and would act as the court of appeal for all problems connected with greyhound coursing and breeding.[36] It was a resounding success and brought order to the sport and especially the Waterloo Cup meeting. The Cup had been first coursed for in 1836 and the quality of the coursing, together with its association with the Seftons and other notable coursers, speedily led to it becoming the blue ribbon event in coursing.[37] Viscount Molyneux, who became the third Earl of Sefton in 1838, had considerable responsibility for this. A coursing enthusiast since 1825 when he was introduced to the sport by his father, he permitted the first Waterloo Cup meeting. Named after a hotel owned by the organiser, William Lynn, the event took place on the Sefton state at Altcar where coursing meetings had previously been organised by the Altcar club. As a result of the sporting success of the first meeting, Molyneux took great pains that the estate was well prepared for a second running the following year. This was an even greater success and ensured the continuance of this meeting in the sporting calendar. The aristocratic origins of the meeting at Altcar are shown in Richard Ansdell's 'The Waterloo Cup coursing meeting', commissioned by the Seftons in 1840. This also shows just how informal the early meets were (Fig. 9.3). Enlarged to a 64-dog event, later Waterloo meetings were attended by tens of thousands of spectators each year as may be seen in Figure 9.4, taken from *The Graphic* of 1882 and which shows the meeting at its Victorian apogee. It was regarded as a major social, as well as a gambling, event, and, as it took place before such a large number of spectators, the conduct of its annual meetings provided a standard to emulate. Its prizes were the most sought after in the coursing world.

One consequence of the success of the Waterloo Cup meetings was that the fourth Earl of Sefton became Chairman of the National Coursing Club on its foundation in 1858 and later its president. On his death in 1897, his son, already keenly interested in coursing, succeeded not only to the Sefton title but also to the Presidency of the Club. Thus began a tradition of participation and leadership that continued until the death without issue of the seventh earl in 1972 when the Molyneux's dominance of the sport ended after 140 years.

Set against the background of the changes in the Game Laws and the influence of the publications by Goodlake and Thacker, there is strong evidence that coursing had become more widespread before the NCC was founded. David Brown, writing in 1884, attributed this to three factors: the establishment of regular open meetings, such as those associated with the Waterloo Cup, which encouraged would-be coursers who might have been daunted by the older prestigious clubs; the rapid growth of the railway system which enabled coursers to enjoy their sport in a wide variety of venues; and the lively interest taken in coursing by the sporting press.[38] Table 9.1 supports this suggestion, but also demonstrates that an even greater expansion in coursing took place after the formation of the NCC. The NCC membership was made up of two representative members drawn from each of the coursing clubs which contributed to its expenses and there were never to be fewer than 24 members. Thus the clubs had real control over the sport and, furthermore, it was in the interests of new clubs to contribute to the NCC and send members to participate in its deliberations.[39] The Club

FIGURE 9.4
'Notes at the Waterloo coursing meeting'. From *The Graphic*, 25 Feb. 1882, pp. 174–5.

Rushing on Fate

Penny Toll

Taking Home News

A "Kill"

not only represented those who actually participated in the sport but also gained a reputation for acting in a decisive and positive manner in dealing with disputes and infringements of the rules, all of which indicated that coursing was honestly controlled and fairly conducted. Table 9.1 shows the growth of the sport up to 1880 in terms of the number of clubs identified as carrying out public coursing and whose events were reported in various publications.

Table 9.1 *Coursing clubs in the British Isles for selected years, 1829–80*

	1821	1841	1857	1871	1880
England	26	79	98	129	187
Wales	2	5	6	12	12
Scotland	6	16	17	16	25
Ireland	2	6	15	12	19
Total	**36**	**106**	**136**	**169**	**243**

Sources: 1829, T. Thacker, *The Courser's Companion* (1829); 1843, id., *The Courser's Annual Remembrancer and Stud Book* (1843); 1857, Stonehenge [J. H. Walsh], *The Coursing Calendar and Review*, I, pts ii and iii (1858); 1871, *The Coursing Calendar – Spring Season* (1871); 1880, *The Coursing Calendar – Spring Season* (1880).

Between the foundation of the NCC in 1858 and 1880, the number of clubs in England and Wales almost doubled, while there was also significant growth in Scotland and Ireland. From the same sources of data, it is also possible to demonstrate that in England, growth was not simply in the areas in which coursing was already established, but involved extension into counties in which coursing had not previously existed. The extent of this spread is shown in Table 9.2.

Table 9.2 *Counties in England with coursing clubs for selected years, 1829–80*

1829	1841	1857	1871	1880
15	25	25	28	33

Sources: as Table 9.1.

Anyone familiar with the recent research into the growth in interest among the general public in a wide variety of different sports in Victorian Britain will not be surprised by the increased interest in coursing.[40] In many respects, it mirrors the growth in foxhunting and horseracing which drew the participation of a large number of the middle classes from the mid-nineteenth century onwards.[41]

III

There are four questions posed by the growth in coursing which need to be examined. First, why did coursing expand? To some authors, hare coursing had been associated with the working class and was believed by them to have declined in the early nineteenth century.[42] The evidence presented above strongly suggests the contrary. Illegal forms of coursing may have declined, but coursing under the pre-1831 Game Laws had grown and become more organised. In the wake of the legal changes, coursing had increased steadily and experienced an accelerated growth again in the 1850s and thereafter. The growth of interest in coursing amongst the middle classes can perhaps be explained by one principal reason: coursing was a relatively cheap sport. The would-be courser need only purchase a greyhound from an approved source, join a coursing club, train the animal or have it trained and then enter it in coursing events. The cost of entry to greyhound coursing was relatively inexpensive when compared with becoming a member of a foxhunt or purchasing a racehorse.[43] The advantages were, however, similar to horseracing. Coursing was a controlled sport whose rules were carefully administered by officials whose code of conduct was regulated by the National Coursing Club and the local club of which the courser was a member. The men in charge of these bodies were usually of considerable standing and propriety in their local communities, if not nationally. Gambling and the conduct of courses were strictly controlled and the prizes were often very prestigious. For those who sought information about the sport, much was available. Goodlake's and Thacker's publications were supplemented by the writings of 'Stonehenge' (the veterinarian J. H. Walsh, 1810–88) from 1853, which contained a wealth of information about the care and training of the greyhound as well as other important information about coursing.[44] At the same time, national and local newspapers carried increasing numbers of articles and reports about coursing meetings.[45]

The second question worthy of examination is the extent to which control of coursing passed into different hands after 1850. Because of the legal standing of those engaged in hunting earlier in the nineteenth century, many people involved in coursing in the 1830s were drawn from the landed families who had previously dominated the sport. As the number of coursing clubs grew, this might be expected to diminish, but difficulties arise in adopting such a simplistic view. Land is at the centre of most field sports, and linked inextricably to ownership of property is the granting of permission to hunt over it and the preservation of the quarry being hunted upon it. Whenever a coursing club came into existence, it was necessary to have both access to a fairly extensive area of land over which to course and also a sufficient quantity of hares to make coursing worthwhile.[46] Thus the goodwill of a landowner was always a vital part of the sport even if the

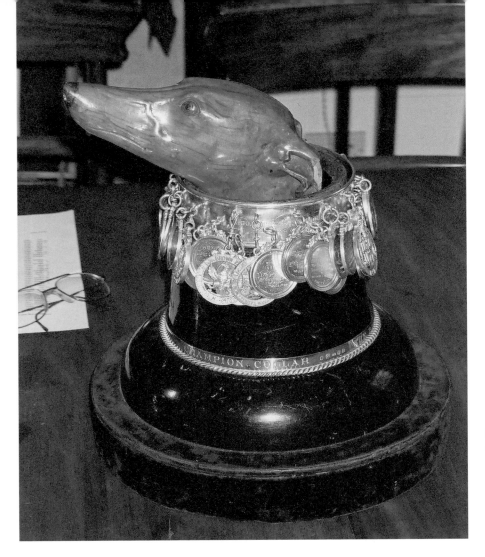

FIGURE 9.5
The Silver
Collar trophy
of the Biggar
Club. Photo:
Ian Roberts
by kind
permission
of Julian
Burchill.

landowner himself did not actually participate in coursing. It was therefore inevitable that the same landowning section of society should continue to be involved in the burgeoning sport after 1850 as previously. Thus, landowners, both titled and otherwise, continued their involvement as presidents and patrons of coursing clubs throughout the century even when they themselves did not own and course greyhounds. Should an estate change hands and the new owner, for whatever reason, be hostile to coursing, then that estate was lost to the coursing club.[47]

The third question concerns the nature of the membership of these coursing clubs. This is an area that is still largely unexplored and must be linked to the final problem discussed below. It is known that membership of the pre-1831 clubs was modest, often under thirty members. Later clubs were larger than this, but how large is still unclear. Evidence from Shropshire suggests that not all members ran greyhounds and that the real hard core of greyhound owners was quite small. The disappearance of coursing club records means that it is impossible to arrive at any general conclusions.

Stonehenge (J. H. Walsh) throws some light on the question of participation in coursing in his *Manual of British Rural Sports*, and the changing state of coursing can be followed through successive editions of this book. In 1857 Walsh stated that around 28,000 guineas was invested in coursing stakes and that, as there were around 4,000 greyhound owners, this meant that each incurred the small cost of seven guineas for the sport and exercise that they enjoyed. In the 1882 edition, he gives the stake money and the value of trophies to be won in 1874–75 as £40,000, but which, on this occasion, was to be shared among 1,000 owners. He considered that this was a modest sum and could be found by those of the middle class whom Walsh contends were now the principal followers of the sport. The growth in the value of stakes seems perfectly reasonable given the proliferation in the number of clubs, but the reduction in the number of coursers is less easily explained, particularly when set in the context of the increase in the number of clubs as shown in Table 9.2. While only more information about the membership of clubs will resolve this paradox, Walsh's point about the importance of members of the middle class in coursing is important and was a feature of the sport that was found elsewhere. In the case of one club, the Biggar Coursing Club located in Upper Lanarkshire in Scotland, it was also one that was not appreciated. The club had been founded in the early nineteenth century by members of landed and aristocratic families in Upper Lanarkshire and it flourished into the 1860s. However, members began to complain about the new breed of coursers attending meetings, owning dogs and attempting to change some of the club's traditions. The pretensions of such social inferiors caused the club to cease its coursing activities in 1867 and transform itself into a dining club where membership could be carefully regulated, in which form it survives to the present day.[48] The club still retains the silver collar trophy, purchased in 1821 and contested by its members until it ceased to hold coursing matches in 1867. A silver medal was added each year to the chain showing the names of the winning dog and its owner in a manner similar to that of the Waterloo Cup itself (Fig. 9.5).

For another club established at Bothal in Northumberland, a list of 103 members for 1887 has been preserved in a stud book.[49] From associated lists of owners entering greyhounds for races, it is possible to expand this to 125 for the period 1884–91. The patron of the club was the Duke of Portland, who occasionally ran greyhounds at club meetings and was joined in this by 62 other members. Of the remainder, 25 acted as nominators of dogs only, leaving 38 members who never ran or nominated a dog.[50] The list of members gives both names and addresses of members. By examining directories and lists of tenants on the Bothal estate, it is possible to identify the trades or professions of some of the members as well as to decide how many were not country dwellers.[51] Thirty-four members were tenants of the estate and at least 21 of these were farmers. The remainder included a clergyman, a coal merchant and a builder. The club members who were not tenants include five publicans, five farmers, three brick makers and builders, a doctor, a joiner, a carter, a butcher, an engineer, two bankers, an MP and a greyhound trainer. Together this means that it is possible to identify 46 (36.8 per cent) of the 125 members of the club of whom 26 (20.8 per cent) were farmers. It is not always easy to decide if the addresses of members are urban, suburban or rural due to the growth of urban areas since 1887 and the demolition or disappearance of some of the properties, but 34 (27.2 per cent) can definitely be assigned to urban locations.[52] How far this analysis is typical of what was happening in clubs elsewhere in the 1880s is, as yet, unknown. However, in the absence of data from elsewhere, the evidence from Bothal provides a starting point for later comparison with some evidence of twentieth-century coursing club membership given below.

Finally, there is the question of how widespread coursing was in its influence on the countryside in general. The historian of Shropshire's coursing fraternity demonstrated that many of the clubs held only one or two meetings per year and held that coursing was much less practised than sports such as foxhunting.[53] While this may be true, other clubs held more meetings and may have had more stakes at those meetings. These are questions that can be answered from published data, although retrieval is time consuming. Less easy is determining how many people were involved in coursing. Although accounts of meetings were widely published, the figures for attendance are rarely reported except for such large meetings as the Waterloo Cup. Statements such as 'thinly attended' or 'a very respectable crowd' occur frequently, but no actual figures are attached. Again, lists of approved trainers, judges and slippers were printed in the *Coursing Calendar*, but there was much more to the sport than this. Trainers and owners had kennel men and boys to assist them; large numbers of beaters were required for events and then there were those who looked after the greyhounds as pups and walked them like foxhounds around the countryside. Some of these, like the gamekeepers, can be located through census returns, but puppy walkers and beaters usually had other occupations and remain uncounted. Much information is still to be unearthed about those whose lives were touched by coursing, either as a sporting interest or as an additional casual occupation.

IV

As shown in Table 9.1, 1880 saw the high-water mark of coursing in England, Wales and Scotland. After this date, as Tables 9.3 and 9.4 demonstrate,

FIGURE 9.6
Fullerton and
his trainer,
Edward
Dent. Photo:
Ian Roberts,
by kind
permission of
Major Ronnie
Hedley Dent.

coursing went into a slow decline, but the reasons for that decline are not the same throughout the period from 1880 to the present day.[54]

Two separate factors, one internal and one external, were responsible for the decline in coursing from 1880 to 1891. During the 1870s, an alternative form of coursing had been developed by a Sussex farmer called Thomas Case at his farm near Plumpton. In this form of coursing the hares were coursed within a special enclosure having been released from a holding-pen. The hares ran the length of the course and could escape through a specially designed sough at the end of the course.[55] Close to the railway and with a grandstand and other amenities, this was a form of coursing that appealed to those looking for an opportunity to watch from a seat and within easy reach of a bookmaker. Not only was it a huge success for Case, but it spread to other parts of England in a short space of time. The most important artificial, or 'park' courses as they were called, were to be found at Gosforth, Haydock and Kempton, but there were others throughout the country. The prizes offered for the most prestigious stakes at Gosforth and Kempton were 1,000 guineas, double the prize money for the Waterloo Cup. The Gosforth meeting attracted huge crowds, many of whom were miners from the nearby Northumberland and Durham coal fields and the numbers drawn to the other park meetings were almost as large. The effect of this new form on the traditional coursing world was considerable. Attendances at meetings other than the parks were reported as falling and some clubs, such as the Ashdown Club, which had been started in the 1780s, were forced to cease operations completely.

As a result of cash problems and the decline in support for this rather predictable novelty, the park courses gradually disappeared through the 1890s and there was a revival of coursing clubs.[56] In particular the Waterloo Cup regained much of its former lustre in the 1890s probably due to the successes of Fullerton – the only dog to win the trophy four times. Fullerton was bred by Edward Dent at Shortflatt Tower in Northumberland and then sold to Colonel North, the nitrate millionaire. The dog was sent back to Dent to be trained: both dog and trainer appear in the celebratory portrait still in the possession of the Dent family (Fig. 9.6). However, the craze for park coursing had wrought significant lasting damage as its presence coincided with changes in the Game Laws which created further considerable problems for coursing.

In 1880 the Ground Game Act was passed. This piece of legislation was part of the continuing struggle over tenant right in Victorian England: its background is too lengthy to consider in this paper.[57] Essentially the Act transferred control over hares and rabbits from the landowner to the occupier of land. It prompted a fear that the hare population would be exterminated by farmers shooting them as pests and coursing would be extinguished for good.[58] Some landowners had already anticipated this and had given permission to their tenants to shoot rabbits and hares believing them to be a nuisance and also that such permission was a 'loss of sport to the landlord made up by the satisfaction of the tenant'.[59] As some landowners soon discovered, there were a number of restrictions in the Act which prevented the wholesale extermination of hares and rabbits that the Act's opponents feared. Nevertheless, other estate owners felt that the preservation of hares on their properties was no longer viable and some coursing grounds, together with the clubs that had used them, disappeared forever.[60]

The combined effect of park coursing and the 1880 Act was to diminish the total number of clubs to 183 by 1891, a fall of a quarter in a decade, as shown in Table 9.3. Although the Waterloo Cup meeting and some other coursing events such as the Border Union Cup continued to be regarded as prestigious sporting occasions and drew large crowds of spectators (as may be seen from Figure 9.4), this picture is not the same for coursing meetings elsewhere. Agricultural depression and the desire to lease land for shooting rather than preserve it for coursing combined to eliminate yet more clubs by 1911.

Table 9.3 *Coursing clubs in the British Isles, for selected years,*
1891–2003

	1891	1911	1921	1931	1961	2003
England	145	93	33	52	26	21
Wales	7	2	1	3	1	1
Scotland	15	13	3	3	1	1
Ireland	16	204	7			
Total	**183**	**212**	**44**	**58**	**28**	**23**

Sources: 1891, *The Coursing Calendar – Spring Season* (1891); 1911, *The Coursing Calendar – Spring Season* (1911); 1921, *The Coursing Calendar – Spring Season* (1921); 1931, *The Coursing Calendar – Spring Season* (1931); 1961, *The Greyhound Stud Book* 80 (1961); for 2003, *NCC List of Coursing Club Secretaries and Notification of Meetings* (2003).

Table 9.4 *The number of counties in England with coursing clubs,*
selected years, 1891–2003

1891	1911	1921	1931	1961	2003
27	23	15	25	16	14

Sources: as Table 9.3.

V

The First World War contributed to this decline as coursing was generally suspended for patriotic reasons. Some kennels were closed down in order to conserve supplies of food and to release staff for military service or other essential war work. The Waterloo Cup was not contested between 1916 and 1920. Thus, in 1921, only 33 clubs were found to be active in England and their membership was reported as being lower than in the pre-war period.[61] However, the inter-war period has been described at Waterloo Cup level as the era of 'Rolls-Royce Coursing'[62] and was marked by a revival of coursing brought about by new entrants who gave great quality to the sport. Some of these, like the Earl of Lonsdale, represented the older landed families, but others, such as the miller J.V. Rank and the Jones brothers, brought money from commerce and banking to the sport. The net result of this was that some clubs were re-founded and coursing was revived in a number of counties.[63] Although more work needs to be done on tracing the sources of the new money in coursing and their effects on the sport, the case of the Coquetdale Club in Northumberland provides an illustration of what the introduction of a new sponsor with finance from non-traditional sources could produce.

There had been coursing matches in Upper Coquetdale in the nineteenth century, but regular meetings disappeared before the beginning of the twentieth century. In January 1907 one of the local landed proprietors,

FIGURE 9.7
Major
Renwick's
kennels at
Holystone,
North-
umberland.
Photo: Ian
Roberts.

T. C. Fenwicke-Clennell of Harbottle Castle, in association with neighbouring estate owners, arranged a series of matches on his own estate.[64] High hopes were placed on the future development of the sport in the area, but only a few more coursing events were held before war broke out and the club was not listed among those registered with the National Coursing Club when sport resumed after the War.[65] The resumption of coursing and the revival of the Coquetdale Club came about as a result of the arrival in the area of a new coursing enthusiast – Major Gustav Adolph Renwick.[66]

Major Renwick was a Northumbrian by birth who had entered the Army and served in the Northumberland Fusiliers. On leaving the Army, he entered the family shipping business and took charge of operations in Manchester. He married in 1907 Mabel Deuchar, the daughter of a wealthy Sunderland brewer, James Deuchar. The couple lived at Great Budworth in Cheshire where the Major began his own greyhound stud. In 1929 he bought the Holystone Grange estate in Coquetdale and moved his greyhounds to the new property. The Major did not become involved immediately with Holystone as he continued his business career in Lancashire and was also MP for the Stretford Division of Lancashire from 1931 to 1935. However, from the mid-1930s onwards he began to expand his estate in Northumberland and revived the Coquetdale Coursing Club as well as perfecting his own Holystone greyhound stud.[67] Major Renwick eventually settled at Holystone and assisted in the conduct of regular coursing meetings, either on his own estate or in other parts of the Coquet valley such as Westfield House farm. He built kennels at Holystone village, a little over a mile from the house, which included an office for the kennelman (Fig. 9.7). His stud also proved very successful and in 1953 the Major's greyhound, Holystone Lifelong, won the Waterloo Cup. Three years later, in 1956, Major Renwick died, but his death did not curtail the activities of the Coquetdale Coursing Club.

The Club carried on under the leadership of the Major's greyhound trainer, Archie Scott. As the estate passed to members of the Renwick family, meetings continued to take place at the traditional venues that had been used for the preceding two decades. In time, some of these coursing grounds had to be abandoned as the number of hares declined, but the Club continued to thrive. New coursing grounds were obtained, some from the Duke of Northumberland, and the Club continued operating into the twenty-first century, holding four meetings in the 2003–04 season, one each in November, December, January and February.[68] The origin of the revival of the Club, which was also the basis of its future success, was the leadership and finance of Major Renwick. Although detailed information about the impact of new entrants on coursing drawn from similar backgrounds to that of Major Renwick is not available, it would seem likely that wealthy patrons such as Rank and Sir Richard Burbidge, the wealthy retailer, brought welcome patronage to both their clubs and the Waterloo Cup. The support of the new patrons undoubtedly did much to explain the increase in the number of registered coursing clubs from 33 in 1921 to 52 in 1931. However, this was still only 60 per cent of the number of clubs in existence on the eve of the First World War.

To some extent the failure to equal the number of clubs prior to the war can be explained by the prevailing economic circumstances of the depression and changes in the ownership of estates.[69] The new owners were not always as content as their predecessors to protect hares for coursing while others simply wished to preserve game for their own pleasure and not share it with others. However, in addition to these factors, two other features of the inter-war period account for the limited revival of coursing.

The first of these was the introduction of track greyhound racing in 1926 which provided an urban racing experience that drew many away from the traditional rural sport of open coursing.[70] Trials of mechanical methods of greyhound racing had taken place in the 1870s, but had proved abortive.[71] Although interest in track racing waned in Britain, it was pursued more vigorously in the United States. At first, it was introduced as a preliminary contest at horse racing meetings as a method of entertaining spectators before the first race. Although well-presented and more exciting for spectators as the greyhounds now raced around a circuit, track racing did not come into its own until it was divorced from horse racing and became an evening event held under floodlights. At this point crowds began to flock in, especially as the events were held after the working day and thus permitted urban workers to attend.

It was this form of the sport that re-appeared in Britain in the 1920s. The leading figures were, with the exception of the American promoter, Charles Munn, all members of coursing clubs, while the most enthusiastic, Major L. Lyne Dixon, was a noted coursing judge. The first meeting was held at Belle Vue in Manchester on 24 July 1926 and, although over 1700 people attended the event, it ran at a loss. Not daunted, the proprietors persisted, so that when the season concluded, on 9 October, they found that the 37 meetings they had conducted had drawn an average gate of 11,000 paying customers and that they had made a substantial profit.[72] Before the 1927 season began, tracks had been constructed in Liverpool and London and plans had been made for other cities as well. There was some rivalry between the various companies and on occasions these disputes reached the Law Courts,[73] so that two bodies, the National Greyhound Racing Club and the National Greyhound Racing Society of Great Britain Limited, were formed early in 1928 to regulate the sport. The former dealt with general policy and the licensing of clubs and tracks, while the latter dealt with the administration of events and the conduct of owners, trainers and others involved in the greyhound racing business. These regulatory bodies brought order to the sport and helped to ensure its long-term success. It also provided an accessible form of greyhound racing that was open to all and much closer to the urban sporting public than most coursing meetings, thereby exacerbating the decline of coursing.

It has also been suggested that another factor concerning the control of greyhound racing widened the gap between coursing and track racing. During the early days of track racing in 1926, it was apparent to Major Lyne Dixon and to others involved in racing that a regulatory body would be required for the sport. To the Major, the natural body to take charge of the new greyhound sport would be the National Coursing Club. All greyhounds would continue to have to be registered with the Club and entered in the Stud Book as, at this time, many track greyhounds continued to course or had been coursing dogs before they went to the tracks.[74] Thus, the Major contended that the Club should control racing as it regulated coursing. He approached the President of the Club, the Earl of Sefton, and the Committee, but, under the influence of the Earl, who had a dislike of this new-fangled popular sport, the Club refused to have anything to do with racing.[75] There is little doubt that this diminished the influence of the coursing fraternity and did damage to its popularity. Paradoxically, the NCC continued to administer the Greyhound Stud Book and to register all greyhounds irrespective of whether they were to participate in coursing or track racing. This is still the situation, as is the lack of any formal connection between the NCC and the bodies controlling racing.

Greyhound racing provided an alternative sport to coursing and drew supporters away from it. At the same time, pressure from another quarter entirely was also exercising an adverse influence on the sport. The movement against hunting in all forms on the grounds of cruelty to animals had now begun to agitate against coursing. Throughout the nineteenth century, there had been a degree of opposition to hunting but it had been part of a wider desire to create a more humane attitude to animals which began with the work of Richard Martin in the late eighteenth century.[76] For much of the nineteenth century, notions of animal rights and actions to forward them were confined to a minority of educated people and attempts to extend their influence were slow to succeed. However, there is evidence to demonstrate that in the last two decades of the century greater success was achieved as result of the efforts of reformers such as Henry Salt and Tom Mann.[77] The National Canine Defence League was founded in 1891 and another society, Our Dumb Friends League, in 1897 to provide protection for dogs. At the same time, the animal rights campaigners turned their attention to hunting and their deliberations resulted in the circulation of two public petitions to outlaw aspects of hunting, both organised by the Humanitarian League, in 1900 and 1908.[78] The outbreak of war prevented any further action on this front, particularly as many hunts suspended their activities in the war years after 1914. However, as soon as the War ended, in the words of Hilda Kean, 'Organisations established after the First World War against cruel sports significantly shifted the geographical locus of concern with animal welfare from the cities to the countryside'.[79]

FIGURE 9.8
'In the members' enclosure': the Waterloo Cup meeting, 1943. Courtesy of Getty Images.

The suffering endured by many animals in the War appeared to create a wider sense of the need for animal rights and animal welfare in the post-war world which, in turn, led to agitation for legislation to reduce or curtail hunting and other field sports. One of the earliest to be tackled was legislation to regulate rabbit coursing, which resulted in a number of prosecutions.[80] In early 1924 Isaac Foot, the Liberal MP for Bodmin, introduced a Bill into Parliament for the Protection of Animals which included clauses which would have outlawed coursing. By August the Bill had passed a second reading and was entering its Committee stage in the House of Commons.[81] It was the opinion of later anti-hunting MPs that under the MacDonald Labour Government the Bill had a good chance of becoming law,[82] but it was lost through a lack of parliamentary time in the political crisis and subsequent General Election in the autumn of 1924.

This failure to pass legislation acted as a spur to those seeking to ban hunting and in 1926 a new society, the League for the Prohibition of Cruel Sports (later the League Against Cruel Sports) was formed to act as a focus of the campaign to end hunting.[83] Efforts to introduce further legal measures against various aspects of hunting continued to be made in the years up to the Second World War.[84] These were accompanied by campaigns through public meetings and petitions, including one to the Crown organised by the Bishop of Liverpool to raise awareness of the cruelty of hunting and to seek abolition of the Waterloo Cup competition.[85] In response, the proponents of hunting sought to mount campaigns to represent their points of view and to co-ordinate opposition to legislation prohibiting their activities. In 1930 they established the British Field Sports Society to counter the propaganda disseminated by the League Against Cruel Sports.[86] In spite of this defence, no matter how strong it might be, coursing did not increase its following during the 1930s although those who participated remained fiercely loyal and did all in their power to maintain their traditional activities.

Although the spirit shown by committed coursers in the 1930s carried the Waterloo Cup through the Second World War, the numbers supporting it in wartime were small. *Picture Post* sent its reporter and photographer to the 1943 meeting to produce what it called an 'unprejudiced' account of the proceedings to stand against the sensationalist accounts which had appeared in the popular press.[87] It offered a view of a sport in decline with small coterie of committed supporters.

> They're snobbish (You and I couldn't enter a dog for the Waterloo Cup even if we wished to). They don't like outsiders (which is reasonable because, after all, outsiders haven't been very nice about them). And between you and me, they regard greyhound track-racing as rather degrading.
>
> Forgive them if they cling to a sport which doesn't suit your taste; or this new age. Time, anyhow, will work more changes than any amount

Table 9.5 *Membership of three coursing clubs in 1974*

	%
Landowners	7.3
Farmers	18.3
Professional breeders and trainers	8.3
Others (rural background)	43.5
Others (town background)	22.6
Total	**100.0**

Source: O. Stable and R. M. Stuttard, *A Review of Coursing* (1971, 1973 edition), p. 14.

of protesting letters to the papers. This is no time to waste sympathy on a handful of hares (who would almost certainly have come to a sticky end anyhow).

Look at the pictures of these very decent English people in a very comfortable English scene. Before long, you may not be able to see the like of it again.

Fearless in the offence it might cause coursings' supporters, *Picture Post* offered a view of the crowd – not, it might be said, a terribly large one (but entirely male) as may be seen in Fig. 9.8 – with the caption:

In the members' enclosure, where everyone knows everybody else. Not more than a few thousand people attend the Waterloo Cup meeting. Not more than a few thousand people are left who really understand the finer points of the course.

Picture Post spoke too soon. There was a revival of the Waterloo Cup after the war and it was another quarter century before its meets were temporarily suspended. But this was not true of coursing at county level.[88] The number of coursing clubs and the number of counties in which they were located fell to a level not seen since 1829 and thus it remained to the end of the twentieth century. After some success in the 1950s and 1960s, the Waterloo Cup also declined in popularity during the 1970s and the meeting did not take place between 1977 and the end of the decade. A new committee established under the leadership of Sir Mark Prescott resurrected the Waterloo Cup competition in 1981 since when it has regained much of its former importance and has attracted large crowds of spectators.[89] The success of the revival of the Waterloo Cup had little effect on the level of coursing in the country as a whole. Despite the development by the NCC of a web site and the posting of regular reports on coursing matters, the number of coursing clubs and followers attending meetings are similar today to those reported by Stable and Stuttard in 1974.[90] At that time there were 23 clubs in England and Scotland which had a total of 2703 members, of whom 1623 ran greyhounds and 1086 did not. A more detailed analysis of three clubs located in Hampshire, Huntingdon and Yorkshire revealed that 295 members shared 80 occupations but a broader picture is given in Table 9.5.[91]

A comparison between the figures shown in Table 9.5 with the statistics which have been recovered to date for the Bothal Club in the 1880s, show some important similarities. As all of the Bothal Club meetings were held on ground owned by the Duke of Portland, he is the only landowner known to have been a member of the Club, but further research may yield others. However, 20.8 per cent of members of the Bothal Club were farmers compared to 18.3 per cent of the members of the clubs shown in Table 9.5 and in the Bothal Club 27.2 per cent came from a town background as against 22.6 per cent of those shown in the Table. These figures would seem close enough to suggest that over the ninety years between the two surveys of membership little had changed in terms of the backgrounds of those who joined coursing clubs and that the majority of members on each occasion had a rural background. While this does not tell us anything about the more general supporters of coursing, it does suggest that in an increasingly urban society, such a rural sport might have only a modest chance of creating sympathy for its activities among the remainder of the population. Under these circumstances the coursing clubs had a difficult time defending themselves from the onslaught of those who wished to extinguish the sport.

During the same period from the early 1970s to the present day, it has been reported that stadium greyhound racing has had mixed fortunes, but it has still been a significant public attraction to the spectating and betting public. This view is supported by the number of greyhound registrations in the *Stud Book* which was reported at the beginning of the 1990s to exceed 6,000 per annum,[92] and also by the number of race meetings advertised and reported in the *Racing Post*.[93] However, greyhound racing has had few opponents and has not faced the prospect of being outlawed.

VI

The possibility of being legislated out of existence is one that has faced coursing since the late 1940s. The election of a Labour government in 1945 encouraged opponents of all field sports to believe that this might provide an opportunity for the introduction of laws against fox hunting, coursing and other sports involving the deaths of wild animals. This came in 1949 when two private members bills were introduced into the House of Commons, one of which was against fox hunting in particular while the other dealt with a number of other sports including coursing. Both bills failed to obtain support from the Government: the general bill was defeated and the bill against fox hunting was withdrawn.[94] In an effort to mollify the supporters of this proposed legislation, the Government appointed a committee under Mr John Scott Henderson, KC, to consider the question of cruelty to animals.[95] The committee reported in 1951 and recommended that, although they plainly disliked the anthropomorphism of many of those against hunting, wild animals should be brought within the scope of the law. Committee members had attended some sporting events, including the Waterloo Cup. Although they discussed hare hunting in some detail, they did not recommend that coursing should be banned, nor find that it was in any way cruel to the hares.

The recommendations of the Scott Henderson Committee were largely ignored and the return of a Conservative government in 1951 ensured that any proposals for further anti-hunting legislation had little chance of success for the foreseeable future. Thus, despite the fact that protests continued to be made about coursing and other field sports outside Parliament, it was not until the return of a Labour government in 1964 that the topic began to feature again in lengthy Parliamentary debates. Once more, in 1966, a private member's bill to ban hare coursing was introduced into the House of Commons, by Eric Heffer, MP for the Walton Division of Liverpool, and progressed to a second reading in 1967.[96] Heffer was one of the MPs most concerned to ban coursing and his name was associated with all measures to end the sport until his death in 1991.[97] His continued support, together with the agitation of other Labour MPs, persuaded the Labour government in 1970 to adopt the latest private member's bill as a government measure. From this time, until the enactment of the legislation against all hunting with hounds in 2005, the Labour party supported all attempts to ban coursing and other forms of hunting.

This is not the point to review the later attempts to outlaw coursing, nor to consider the reports of bodies such as the Select Committee on the Hare Coursing Bill (1976) or the Enquiry under Lord Burns (2001). These have been substantially recounted in the press prior to recent legislation. The position after 1970 was that it was only a matter of time before the political climate, the size of the government majority in Parliament and public pressure would put a ban on coursing and other field sports into effect. Unsurprisingly, the arguments on both sides have hardly changed over the last fifty years. Efforts on the part of coursers to accept some of their opponents' case have been ignored as only an outright ban was acceptable, while the voice of moderates, such as Jim Barrington of the 'Parliamentary Middle Way Group' have also been ignored.[98] All that remains, therefore, is to consider the role remaining for the historian.

VII

Earlier in this paper attention was drawn to some of the questions about coursing which require further investigation. There are others which can be added to this list. What do we know about the financing of coursing clubs? What was the extent of the trade in greyhounds and what did this contribute to the rural economy? How much employment resulted from coursing and how did this change over time? What are the sources for coursing history and what is being done to preserve these as coursing clubs disappear in the wake of the ban on hunting with dogs?

Coursing meetings were reported extensively in the national and local press up until the time of the First World War. Since then there has been a steady decline at national and provincial level. Even the major country periodical, *The Field*, no longer has a regular coursing correspondent and in recent years has carried few reports of coursing other than the Waterloo Cup meeting. At a local level the situation was more complex, but perhaps more encouraging. Few Record Offices have much catalogued material that refers to coursing. However, local newspapers contain reports of meetings and these usually identify the location of the coursing event with some precision. From this, and the list of local officials given for the coursing event, it is possible to search estate and census records where there often lurks material that has not yet been catalogued with the coursing historian in mind, but nevertheless contains helpful references. Oral history has also proved rewarding in capturing information and has also provided leads to caches of material that have not yet, and perhaps never will, find their way into the public records. Enough may yet be recovered to produce a substantial history of a once important and widely followed field sport.

CHAPTER TEN

Foxhunting and the Yeomanry: county identity and military culture

by Nicholas Mansfield

'LYDBURY NORTH was similar to most English villages in its condition and life. Our knowledge of geography was not great, Britain to most of us meant little more than Lydbury North or at most Shropshire.' This statement is taken from the 1919 printed war record of a parish in south-west Shropshire which lists, in alphabetical order, several dozen men from the village who had served in the Great War, mainly privates who had volunteered for the Kitchener battalions of the King's Shropshire Light Infantry in 1914. Two of their number served with the Shropshire Yeomanry. Whilst the privates were almost all farmworkers, the yeomen came from higher up the social strata. One of them, Wilfred Newill, was the son of one of the most powerful men in Shropshire, R.H.Newill, the agent for the local absentee landlord and Colonel of the Shropshire Yeomanry, the Earl of Powis. Wilfred was later commissioned into the Indian Army, but most locals would have known him as active in the South Shropshire Hunt. His regimental comrade was Jack Davies, saddler and shoemaker from Edgton, the neighbouring hamlet. Both men survived the war, with Davies dying aged 104 in 2002.

The document is quoted in my book, *English Farmworkers and Local Patriotism* as an illustration of how rural society displayed both class tensions and pride in local identity in the aftermath of the Great War, and how this tension was settled in favour of the forces of conservativism, paternalism and parochialism.[1] This chapter examines how two closely connected rural institutions – foxhunting and the county yeomanry – contributed to this process and developed from being minority interests in the mid-Victorian period to, by the 1920s, spectacularly representing their world view as the dominant cultural and political concern of much of lowland Britain, with a resonance still felt today. The paper also tentatively argues that their shared outlook had a negative effect on British military culture, which was to have disastrous consequences for many, including those on the Lydbury North list, who were not as fortunate as Newill and Davies.

Readers will be familiar with foxhunting, but it may be worth defining the yeomanry as part-time mounted volunteer soldiers, first raised in the 1790s and still in existence today. My interest in the yeomanry arose from research in the early 1980s on recruitment for the Great War in East Anglia and in more recent years on the farmworkers' union in Shropshire. In this latter research I became interested in working-class conservatism and those rural institutions which seemed to offer explanations as to why farmworkers did not join the union. The study has included interviews with seven retired yeomen, of whom five were actively involved in foxhunting. Whilst their regional backgrounds varied from Shropshire, to Norfolk, Gloucestershire, Devon and East Yorkshire and their periods of service ranged from the Great War to the 1970s, what was apparent was the homogeneity and longevity of a continuing shared culture. This oral history has been essential given the emphasis on the technical side of military history in what little literature exists.[2]

Foxhunting and the yeomanry are exemplars of what some historians have called 'invented traditions'. Both were created in the same period. Foxhunting, the slightly older activity, was mainly a mid eighteenth-century creation. Foxes, which traditionally had been regarded as vermin, were, within a generation, preserved for this activity. Although typically a gentry activity, the major winter pastime of those who did not actually have to work the land, in some parts of the country, farmers began to participate. In Shropshire, for example, a leading commentator could assert: 'that no other county showed more respect for the "noble science" or had more sportsmen and well-wishers among the "higher orders" and the Yeomen, the result being an "excellent feeling" between tenant and landlord'. Here many estates included in their tenancy agreements the requirement that wire fences were to be taken down by 1 November. In other parts of the country, farmers often continued to be aggravated by the inconveniences imposed by hunting.

Most of the rural poor were indifferent to foxhunting with the exception of the few who found some work in the sport. Aside from full-time hunt jobs (the huntsman, whipper-in and kennel hands), most employment seems to have been part-time, seasonal and transitory. Typically it was combined with a smallholding or dealing, and financial reward was secondary to a part in the thrill of the chase. Spotters for the hunt built artificial earths and fed 'wild' foxes so that the field could minimise fruitless days. Connected with them were the 'Leadenhall' men who supplied foxes to order, often imported from France or Holland. Gate openers (often seen as picturesque by-standers in hunting prints) were hunt-struck elderly labourers who perhaps earned a few coppers by saving more nervous riders from a tumble. Publicans and others connected with victualling the hunt also formed part of these supporters; as did livery men, saddlers and farriers. Terrier men who trained dogs to dislodge 'gone to earth' foxes and earth stoppers who went around before the hunt to cut off underground escape routes were also part of this group. The latter worked in conjunction with gamekeepers and were recipients, along with the other groups, of gentry paternalism, through dinners, tips, garden parties and horse races. This led to genuine working-class admiration for the 'gameness' of individual hunters, shown for example by the thousands who apparently lined the funeral procession of Jack Mytton, Shropshire MP, joker and spendthrift, who drank himself to an early grave in 1832. The real conflict was to come with the shooting interest. In Norfolk for example, the breech loading shotgun, the battue system and the lead given by the Sandringham estate meant that shooting came to reign supreme. It took decades for strategies to be evolved there which enabled both sports to harmonise their interests.[3]

The Yeomanry were first raised in 1794 as a response to war with revolutionary France, though some had some roots in earlier armed county associations and unofficial bodies. Whilst defence against invasion from the traditional enemy was one motive, their close links with conservative loyalism defined their patriotism as anti-radical. Their recruiting posters made this clear, one from the North Riding defining their role thus: 'Assist and support the legal constituted authorities of the kingdom, in suppressing any riots and tumults which may be excited by seditious and designing men'. Conservatism is also illustrated in Yeomanry songs of the period, for instance one from Hertfordshire:

> You who support our noble cause,
> Our King, our Liberty and Laws.
> Nor let the Democratic Band,
> Spread desolation o'er the Land.
> Their Treasons deep in darkness lay,
> Our course is open to the day.

By the end of the Napoleonic Wars, the yeomanry's antagonism extended to others who challenged the gentry's local authority. The early nineteenth-century radical leader Henry Hunt, serving in a Wiltshire Yeomanry troop, accused his comrades of 'keeping up the price of corn, keeping down the price of wages and at the same time keeping in subjugation the labourers and silencing their dissatisfaction.' However, as outlined before, the repression of potential subversion could be successfully combined with paternalism.[4]

Yeomanry were initially formed in all parts of rural lowland Britain, with an emphasis on the southern and eastern coastal counties nearer potential invaders and the area around Gloucester where regular cavalry had been traditionally stationed, because of good grassland and excellent hunting country. There is a certain irony in the name Yeomanry, as changes in agriculture at the turn of the nineteenth century were arguably squeezing out the small yeoman farmer. Drawn from small holders, in most rural areas the social composition of the Yeomanry became established in a way which lasted until farming was mechanised, with the gentry (and often the aristocracy) supplying the officers, substantial farmers the non-commissioned officers and the sons of tenant farmers making up most of the rank and file. Whilst some tradesmen, especially those connected with horses, were found in the ranks, farmworkers were almost entirely excluded because yeomen were expected to provide their own horses and uniforms. There is a strong sense that the possession of a horse was a clear demonstration of their physical, as well as social, superiority. The government allowed the Yeomanry to be self-governing through the Lord Lieutenants, almost like private armies. In the early period, most units consisted of single troops, often of no more than thirty to forty men, centred on a market town or a stately home. The county organisation came later. It is likely that the personnel of the yeomanry troop and local hunt were interchangeable and both were often funded out of estate revenues. The two organisations also became joint enablers of local agricultural enterprises and ancillary trades; 'natural mutual prospering', as it described by one MFH and yeomanry officer.[5]

While the Yeomanry's local social position might be superior, their poor training and their lack of opportunity to act with other units meant that their role in the Napoleonic invasion scare was limited to a reserve one. Regular soldiers treated the force with disdain: 'The [most] scurvy set as ever met', and 'Gentlemen and clowns … two legged bumpkins', are descriptions of units from Norfolk and Scotland. Whilst the Yeomanry, along with the other auxiliary forces, did turn out for false invasion alarms – most famously described by yeomanry officer, Sir Walter Scott – they would not have acquitted themselves well had they actually encountered Napoleon's veterans. It was fortunate that the Castlemartin Yeomanry only came up against a heavily outnumbered and drunken French penal unit during the incursion at Fishguard in 1797, thus winning a unique British army – and undoubtedly least dangerous – battle honour for the Pembrokeshire Yeomanry.[6]

Though the rural location of the Yeomanry was encouraged by the government because it was 'not infected with the poison of large towns', it soon found that the industrialising counties of the Midlands and North were a fruitful area of recruitment and provided a counterweight to working-class sedition. Here they acted as a semi-permanent political gendarmerie and their regiments grew enormously so by 1850, the Staffordshire Yeomanry mustered nearly 900 in 11 troops and Worcestershire 760. The activities of the yeomanry were a clear example of class warfare in early nineteenth-century British society. Every Yeomanry unit in the country was called out to aid the civil power in this period. Their duty climaxed in 1842 against the Chartists, when 84 Yeomanry units were on duty in 15 counties for a total of 338 days, some for continuous periods of over 70 days. By 1850 the North Somerset Yeomanry had been called out 64 times.[7]

The range of the Yeomanry's opponents was varied: corn rioters, 'Captain Swing' supporters, women bread rioters, Tyne Keelmen, striking Hertfordshire bargees, those asserting woodland customs in the Forest of Dean and the New Forest, resisters against the New Poor Law in Norfolk and Buckinghamshire, insurrectionary Welsh ironpuddlers, militia ballot objectors, as well as mutinous local militiamen, riotous seamen, agricultural labourers, political radicals, trade unionists, utopian socialists, turnpike protestors, bonfire night revellers, colliers, Welsh Rebecca rioters, Luddites, textile workers in Cheshire and elsewhere, those protesting against enclosure of common land in Oxfordshire, Irish Fenians, fenmen, Chartists, election disturbers, theatre crowds, coastal wreckers, smugglers, and incendiaries at government gunpowder mills. They also did garrison duty and acted as bodyguards to VIPs so that regular cavalry could be employed in more active roles.

The Shropshire Yeomanry was a typical example, being employed against striking ironworkers in the Ironbridge area in 1820, 1821 (this armed clash on the slag heaps being known as 'Cinderloo'), 1831 and 1842. They clearly relished action against to the old enemy across Offa's Dyke, seeing action against radical miners in Denbighshire in 1831 and Welsh Chartist insurrectionaries at Llanidiloes in 1839, as well as acting against local Chartists in Market Drayton and Nantwich.[8]

Some of these conflicts were bloody, with the Peterloo Massacre of 1819 achieving the highest body count and widespread notoriety for the Yeomanry. Here, despite recent revisionism, Edward Thompson's account of acute class hatred still rings true, albeit with the radicals cast less in the role of victims. There were probably a score of other under-researched incidents where the Yeomanry inflicted casualties, ranging from the Littleport insurrection of 1816 in the Cambridgeshire fens, to the shadowy radical rising at Bonnymuir, in Scotland, in 1820. The Yeomanry did not have it all their own way against determined and armed opponents. At Merthyr Tydfil in 1831, ironpuddlers and colliers spectacularly surrounded and forced the surrender of the entire Swansea troop of the Glamorgan Yeomanry. After 1815 though, radical activity enabled the yeomanry, as the only military force in much of countryside, to avoid both disbandment and interference from central government.[9]

Politics was important to the Yeomanry. Although there were Whig yeomen, and even some radicals – though most of these resigned between Peterloo and the Reform Crisis – the Tory interest gradually became dominant, especially after the Whig government reduced expenditure and disbanded some corps in 1838. There are accounts of rural Yeomanry units appearing – without uniforms – in the election processions of Conservative parliamentary candidates, and this tradition continued into the twentieth century. Hunting, though was more important. It is probably no accident that the size of the early, pre-county, Yeomanry troops was same as an average hunting field, and probably consisted of the same people. One retired Yeomanry officer (one of four MFHs serving in his unit) estimated that until the Great War the majority of the Yeomanry hunted and then most of its officers continued to do so until the 1970s. 'Yeomanry and the foxhunting' he said 'go hand-in-glove'.[10]

From the time of Cromwell, British regular cavalry had a reputation for cohesion and discipline. This tradition was continued in Marlborough's Wars and with the massed heavy cavalry formations commanded by the Marquis of Granby in the Seven Years War in Germany. The same period saw the development of British light cavalry skills, which were raised to an apogee by Banastre Tarleton, when his irregulars consistently outclassed their patriot opponents during the American War of Independence. However, by the time of the Peninsular War, British cavalry, now largely officered by men who had embraced the new sport, were notorious for charging madly, without reconnaissance. At Talavera in 1809, one regiment was practically eliminated even before it reached a French square, failing to notice an intervening ravine. In the open field, British cavalry were initially successful against their counterparts, but were then defeated by the counterattacks of French supporting reserves, which the less skilled British had themselves failed to retain. After one defeat the Duke of Wellington concluded that, 'It is entirely occasioned by the trick of our own officers of cavalry have acquired of galloping at every thing and their galloping back as fast as they gallop on the enemy. They never consider their situation, never think of manoeuvring before an enemy.' The situation was compounded by the adoption of horses of the hunter type as the main mount of the British cavalry. Wellington too was a keen foxhunter, riding behind a pack imported from Shropshire when his army was in winter quarters. It took one of opponents to make the direct connection. 'The British Cavalry officer seems impressed by the conviction that he can dash or ride over everything; as if the art of war were precisely the same as that of foxhunting.' British regiments were initially incapable of outpost duty until taught by the Hanoverians of the King's German Legion. Only in one of Wellington's victories – Salamanca – did British cavalry make a decisive contribution and even at Waterloo, the British heavy brigades were virtually destroyed by French counterattacks in the first hours.[11]

The new fad had been taken up by cavalry officers, both regular and yeomen, and the shared hunting culture created an ongoing close connection between full- and part-time soldiers. Many young aristocrats – like Lord Cardigan of Light Brigade fame – served initially in the yeomanry as a taster for service life. Many ex-regulars maintained comradeship by joining their local yeomanry after resigning their commissions. Penniless ex-regular officers often filled the junior technical jobs in the Yeomanry, as adjutants or riding masters. Cavalry officers were generally anti-intellectual and cultivated a conscious lack of professionalism. During the long wars of Victorian imperial conquest, hounds were regularly taken on campaign and at home regimental standing orders stated that 'during the hunting season officers may reckon such arrangements being made as will enable them to pursue this diversion'. The myth rapidly spread that skill on the hunting field was all that was needed for a gentleman to become an officer. It has been repeated for 200 years. In 1929, 'One [pro-hunting] speaker said that cavalry officers, who had done splendid work during the war, received most of their training in the hunting field'. In 1999, a retired Yeomanry colonel told me that 'hunting was wonderful training for an armoured car commander'. The result was a series of disasters, with Balaclava as only one example amongst several. It is worth remembering though that amongst the minority of officers whose attitude to soldiering was more professional, there could still be a passion for the hunt. This thread is traceable from Wellington himself, through Lewis Nolan, who delivered the fatal order for the Light Brigade and who authored a treatise on cavalry tactics, to Orde Wingate, the founder of the Chindits.[12]

With continuing domestic unrest in the early nineteenth century, the yeomanry's governance of its own affairs continued. Answering to the lords lieutenants, it could play the War Office off against the Home Office. The influence of county magnates was enhanced by this process and it became usual for them to consolidate their positions by assuming the colonelcies of the county Yeomanry regiment, which were created from the previously autonomous troops. The Duke of Beaufort in Gloucestershire, is a good example. Gloucestershire is perfect hunting country, with mainly pastoral farming and a damp climate to encourage scents. It is home to well-established packs like the Old Berkeley Hunt and the Duke of Beaufort's pack. The latter defined its own country – South Gloucestershire and North Wiltshire – 'Beaufortshire'. Yeomanry troops formed almost 'tribal' groupings based around the market towns – Cirencester, Stroud and Gloucester – and 'there was tremendous rivalry between troops'. With the Beaufort influence, outlying troops were formed on his Welsh (or Monmouthshire) estates in Monmouth, Raglan and Chepstow, leapfrogging the less biddable area of the Forest of Dean. Successive Dukes continued to serve as Colonels of the Yeomanry – the Royal Gloucestershire Hussars. The 10th Duke, who died in 1984, had been Colonel for 59 years and was referred to as 'Master'.[13]

After 1850, British society became more stable and with the establishment of police forces, the gendarmerie role of the yeomanry declined, although the Devon and Staffordshire forces were called out in aid of the civil power as late as 1867. With powerful supporters though, the yeomanry was able to retain its elite position even within the mass volunteer movement of 1859. It soon became apparent though that when compared to the more urban and middle-class volunteers, yeomanry were comparatively expensive and inefficient. Liberal politicians suspected that the yeomanry were using public money to support their hobby, but the county magnates could generally deflect these arguments. The Yeomanry became more of a smart *social* organisation and its events, running parallel to those of foxhunting, were the most important in county society.[14]

Fortunately for the yeomanry it was forced to be part of the Cardwell reforms in the 1870s and managed to retain some serious military purpose. Cardwell consolidated the *county* organisation of the force, often amalgamating two separate under-strength corps. Where the yeomanry was too weak to form a full county regiment, troops from adjacent counties became affiliated. So the Cambridge troop became part of the Suffolk Hussars and troops in Herefordshire, at Leominister and Ross, were placed with Shropshire and Gloucestershire. A major plank of the reforms was the strengthening of county infantry regiments, though, until 1914, many were still reluctant to get involved with 'their' counties. Regular cavalry regiments were not given county affiliations, so the Yeomanry's authority to represent their localities was enhanced. Cardwell also seconded regular cavalry officers to serve as instructors, but as they shared the same pro-hunting, anti-intellectual culture, the realities of modern warfare could be ignored. Instead the yeomanry looked gorgeous and added colour to any county occasion. The War Office's regulations were evaded as the Yeomanry designed extraordinarily elaborate uniforms. They used showy colours (sometimes based on their colonel's racing colours) and retained antique uniform affectations long after these had been abandoned by regular troops. The link with hunting was also maintained with regimental badges featuring foxes and hunting terms, regimental marches of 'De Ye Ken John Peel' and the retention of military titles by MFHs, even after they had retired from the forces.

The future Sir John French, who served as regular adjutant of the Northumberland Hussars Yeomanry between 1881 and 1884, wrote:

> If in the long years of their existence which preceded their participation in actual war they have done nothing else, I venture to think they have justified the cost of their maintenance by keeping alive a Cavalry spirit amongst the farming, hunting and racing classes of the country. They were commanded by the Earl of Ravensworth, than whom no better sportsman ever lived. The officers were all good sportsmen and fine horsemen … Two of them were prominent Masters of Foxhounds.[15]

All this fitted in with the Yeomanry's pointless but slightly comic, 'Hooray Henry' existence until the 1890s. Their wild behaviour was contrasted unfavourably with their more sober comrades in the Volunteers. At their annual camp in Lichfield in 1884, the Staffordshire Yeomanry had stormed the local theatre, threatened the performers, manager and audience, and then defaced the Johnson statue, giving their CO, the foxhunting Tory MP William Bromley Davenport, a fatal heart attack. When some members of the Liberal government voiced mild criticism of foxhunting in 1895, the Staffordshire CO (a member of the Albrighton Hunt) turned on 'grandmotherly government chiefly composed of humbugs who have their own ends to gain for limitations for the suppression of all kind of sports'. But there were also unruly incidents at their 1900 camp at Keele Park. In the same period two Oxfordshire Hussars officers, Winston Churchill and F. E. Smith, lost £1,000 in one night in camp playing chemin-de-fer with two Rothchild members of Buckinghamshire Yeomanry. As late as 1959 the new regular army CO of the East Riding Yeomanry described his new command as 'a drunken, party-going outfit'.[16]

The golden age of the country house and Victorian farming did see some changes in the social composition of the Yeomanry together with a higher turnover of personnel. The officers were still from the gentry, often generations of the same families. In Norfolk, the Birkbecks provided successive Yeomanry COs and MFHs of the West Norfolk Foxhounds, with only the recruitment of Freddie Duleep Singh, exiled Sikh prince from Elveden Hall, providing some exotic variation. In a semi-industrialised county like Staffordshire, yeomanry officers could encompass successive generations of families like the Pagets (whose members had charged at Waterloo and Balaclava), the recusant Fitzherberts, minor gentry like the Oakleys (one of whom mastered the Aetherstone Hunt for twenty seasons) as well as the Manders (paint manufacturers, Wolverhampton politicians and all-round sportsmen). In the ranks, farmers, though probably not their sons, decreased in numbers, to be replaced by the aspiring young middle class from nearby urban areas, attracted by the smarter uniforms and increased social opportunities. In addition, tradesmen supplied a higher proportion of troopers, not just from traditional equine trades – like saddlers, farriers and horse dealers. In this way the way in which the Yeomanry – along with its allied hunts, became a forum for the local economy. 'My father wouldn't have had the farm at Newton House if it hadn't been for hunting with Squire Foster at Apley Park. It was a way of doing business,' as one Shropshire MFH/Yeomanry officer described it to me. The location of the annual county Yeomanry camp gave rise to acute competition from rival market towns. Farmworkers though were still rare in the yeomanry. 'They could never be spared at the weekend.'[17]

After the British army suffered defeat in the opening stages of the Boer War, and in an extraordinary dry run of the events of 1914, a rhetorical appeal from Lord Kitchener went out to the Yeomanry for volunteers to serve in South Africa. Complete regiments did not go – 'they couldn't give up their businesses' – but affiliated companies of *Imperial* Yeomanry were raised, mainly from new recruits, with officers and NCOs from the Yeomanry. Active service, as mounted infantry, brought realism into their world. Further reform saw all regiments converted to mounted infantry, with the rifle replacing the sword as the major weapon. The numbers of new Imperial Yeomanry regiments were increased from 38 in 1899 to 52 in 1905, outnumbering regular cavalry regiments two to one. Whilst these were often raised from urban areas, the Yeomanry tradition was fostered with support from the newly established county councils and can be seen as deliberately contributing to county pride. An example of this was the East Riding of Yorkshire Yeomanry (Lord Wenlock's Horse) formed in 1903. In recruiting meetings, Wenlock built up county loyalty by suggesting that the rival Lincolnshire Yeomanry was filling up its ranks faster, using the ancient enmity for people on the other side of the Humber. The new regiment was also looked down on by the older Yorkshire Yeomanry Regiments: 'the Yorkshire Hussars thought themselves socially superior'.[18]

The incorporation of the yeomanry into Haldane's Territorial Force in 1908 should have promoted further reform, but as a trade-off, the regiments were restored to their cavalry role, joyfully receiving their arme blanche back from their hunting friends in the War Office. This process received support from cavalry officers, like Allenby, Birdwood, Gough, Haig and French, who had made their reputations against the Boers and who were now dominant on the General Staff. All were foxhunters. As we saw, French had served as adjutant to the Northumberland Yeomanry. All were to take their aggressive cavalry charge mentality and detachment from life for the infantry with them into high command in 1914.[19]

On the outbreak of war, the Yeomanry were immediately caught up in the military rhetoric in which, for the first time, sense of place and the importance of the county was stressed. Although most voluntary recruiting was concentrated on Kitchener battalions of the county infantry regiments (it was these that mainly absorbed the 250,000 farmworkers who volunteered), Yeomanry regiments were also increased. Whilst, initially, 'There was no difficulty in obtaining recruits, but it was not easy to find men of the right stamp for a Yeomanry regiment,' it was also 'difficult to obtain clothing big enough for these country bred yeomen.' Social exclusivity continued as Yeomanry preferred 'farmers' sons ... every man had to supply his own horse ... they considered themselves a cut above the normal infantry regiments like the King's Shropshire Light Infantry', particularly as 'enormous numbers of rank and file, being officer material, were commissioned in the early years of 1914–1918.' Siegfried Sassoon (from the Sussex Yeomanry) was the archetype of these gentleman rankers who officered the mass armies.

The world of foxhunting was also part of this military rhetoric.

There has been prompt and loyal response from the Hunts both with horses and men … of the 10,000 or more hunting men with the colours we need not write, for they shall do and they shall dare, as becomes their blood and breeding. A great number of Masters were already officers in the Yeomanry of Territorial Forces. The masters lead … with a tale of over 80% of their number, the Hunt Secretaries following with over 50%, while the Hunt Servants with over 30%.

Recruitment techniques made specific reference to the historic military prowess of particular counties. So, Shropshire men were characterised as 'proud Salopians, bulwark against the Welsh'. As one Yeoman said, 'Shropshire border people were always very wary of Welsh people you know … we didn't trust them somehow … there was something underhand about them'. Yet there was a sense in the farming part of the Yeomanry/foxhunting community that this rhetoric did not apply to them.[20]

In addition, the Yeomanry's amateurism was still apparent. One sergeant serving in a newly mobilised Yeomanry brigade recalled:

> I was unlucky enough to appointed NCO in charge of the guard on the maingate, with strict orders not to allow anyone through without a special pass … a mighty roar broke out from the Cheshire Yeomanry lines, followed by a rush of troops for the main gate. We tried to bar their way, but were powerless … the Denbighs began to follow. 'What is the trouble?' I asked. It was the grub they said. They were going to Chester for a decent feed.[21]

There was no legal requirement for the Yeomen to serve abroad and although the majority did volunteer, there was an accommodation with the military authorities who allowed some Yeomen to carry on farming whilst serving at home. A Shropshire yeoman interviewed in the 1970s claimed 'the half of the Yeomanry that were grass farming could go home for the hay harvest and the arable yeomen could go home for the corn harvest'. This was formalised as the Yeomanry regiments were ordered to raise a second line unit to act as a reserve and to accommodate the sizeable minority who choose not to volunteer for overseas service. One eager subaltern in the home service unit of the North Somersets wrote: 'the life is ghastly. No training only odd jobs and standing about amongst half dressed farmers who've refused to go abroad and only want to get back to their farms.' Another regular officer complained:

> they [were] always going home for a bit and turning up again. I heard the other day of a B[attalio]n where 79 disappeared one night without leave. They turned up again in three days to a fortnight, quite calmly saying that they had been home to do a bit of work on the farm and seemed to think it quite natural.[22]

After the initial enthusiasm and the departure of the first line Yeomanry, it soon became clear that their natural rank and file constituents – the farmers and their families that remained – perhaps prompted by labour shortages, were not inclined to volunteer. The failed appeal in January 1915 of Lord Kenyon, CO of the 2nd Welsh Horse, for volunteers is typical. 'Rightly or wrongly it has been said that recruiting has not been as active as in other parts of the country and more especially has this been said of the farming class, the mainstay of my regiment.' As the war continued, this became part of the general opinion that farmers were shirking and doing well from the hostilities. The solution was to recruit from further down the social structure. So the Wiltshire Yeomanry took in 'railway trainees, local teachers, clerks, shop assistants … who had never ridden a horse. The feeling was it was going to be a jolly sporting show and that we'd see some fun with the Yeomanry'. Even working-class men began to be accepted, mostly useful tradesmen like Jack Davies, the Shropshire saddler mentioned at the beginning, but others like my uncle Charlie Crouch, a railway plate-layer from the east end of Cambridge, sneaked into the Suffolk Hussars.[23]

Some Yeomanry regiments served bravely abroad. In the Leicestershire Yeomanry – crack hunters of the Quorn and Belvoir – 94 per cent volunteered for general service as did 85 per cent of the Gloucestershire Yeomanry, veterans of the Berkeley and Beaufort Hunts. Parted with their horses temporarily at Gallipoli, they had the difficult task of defending the same length of trench as a full infantry battalion. They were re-mounted for full-scale cavalry operations in Palestine, where the Duke of Beaufort's whipper-in won the Military Medal with the Gloucestershire Hussars. As casualties mounted and horses were found to be irrelevant to the slaughter on the Western Front, other Yeomanry regiments were converted to infantry. They retained what they called the 'Yeomanry spirit', their cavalry uniforms (illegally) and an interest in hunting. A pack from the Quorn was hunted behind the lines in France by the Leicestershire Yeomanry, hounds were taken to the Salonika front by Scottish Yeomanry, and to Egypt by the Hertfordshire Yeomanry.[24]

In Britain hunting continued throughout the Great War, even after rationing had been introduced. In the Albrighton Hunt, Mrs Mayall, wife of Major C.G. Mayall, took over as MFH 'During his absence in the Dardenelles'. It was also claimed that 'the farmers, nearly to a man, have all joined forces in keeping the organisations going'. However the overall shortage of labour caused difficulties. 'Still another source of trouble was that no wire was removed and that this very often allowed of hounds getting clean away from their attendants'. Again there was the stopping difficulty. Like the hunt servants, all the younger gamekeepers were serving, and the veterans who took their places were not probably very keen on turning out at night. In the autumn of 1916, whilst stationed at Huntingdon, the CO of the Hertfordshire Yeomanry defied Government orders that regimental horses should not be used to follow hounds: 'The officers … managed to get a lot of hunting with the Cambridgeshire and Fitzwilliam'. When the South Shropshire Hunt applied for exemption from conscription for their kennelman, the chair of the tribunal said 'the military had no objection at all to the application. It was a recognised that hunting should be kept up'.

Sassoon's memoirs give an indication not only of the morale-raising effect hunting could give officers on leave or convalescence but also the way it became an absent representation for 'Englishness' and all that they were fighting for at the front. *Country Life* reflected the same sentiments.

> How many of them writing from the front, have referred to the sport they love, and have expressed the wish that they may find it going strong when they return … leave barbed wire for its fit use – to protect war trenches and trip up enemies, not friends, nor gallant lads who are fighting and dying for our homes and country, the home of the finest sport on earth.

Such sentiments were probably not shared by the infantrymen ordered over the top, following the attacking strategy of Douglas Haig – cavalryman and foxhunter. The same month that the South Shropshire Hunt secured deferment for their hunt servant, Lord Hastings was promoted to be CO of the 2nd Norfolk Yeomanry, despite having refused to go on foreign service. Although his appointment attracted much criticism, including hostile Parliamentary questions, it was confirmed. By this stage in the war, some farmers were sacking their workers and moving their sons into their places, allowing the former to be conscripted. All of this contributed to class conflict and a wave of protest from farmworkers' unions, ex-service organisations and the newly formed rural Labour Party.[25]

After the Armistice, the Yeomanry had a problem in recruiting in the face of anti-war feeling, compounded by the temporary success of rural radicalism. However, in most of rural Britain, the elite rapidly recovered their political hegemony by establishing new paternalistic institutions like village halls, Women's Institutes, the British Legion, war memorials, and Young Farmers Clubs. These had the purpose of genuinely wishing to improve the quality of rural life and deflecting rural depopulation. Older institutions like foxhunting and the Yeomanry, which seemed to symbolise the national unity of 1914 and local county pride, also played a part in this self-conscious post-war reconstruction. There is some evidence that with increasing involvement of women and children, that hunts became more diverse and 'democratic' after the war. The Yeomanry, per force, were required to be less flexible and they could still play a policing role as in 1921, when they were indirectly called in 'to assist in the preservation of civil order' during the coal strike. In Shrewsbury, MFH Colonel H.H.Heywood-Lonsdale raised the Shropshire Dragoons from Yeomanry volunteers.[26]

But the Yeomanry's main enemies were not organised labour or mass pacifism but the 'Geddes Axe' of inter-war parsimony and modern mechanised warfare. Even, ex-Yeoman Winston Churchill at the War Office could not save sixteen regiments – mostly from the urban fringes – from being disbanded in 1921. Many of the others were converted to artillery or armoured car units. Fourteen regiments, almost entirely from counties whose landed magnates could influence their foxhunting friends, retained their horses. This pecking order amongst Yeomanry regiments (with Gloucestershire, Yorkshire and Cheshire at the top of the heap) is emphasised by the inter-war military deficiencies, which pre-occupied the mechanised regiments, with which they coped through borrowed farmers' tractors and improvised armoured cars. The regular cavalry were reduced even more drastically and by 1939, they retained only four mounted regiments compared to the Yeomanry's eight.[27]

The latter took their horses to Hitler's war, affected full dress and continued to hunt. The North Somerset Yeomanry hunted jackal in Palestine – 'We soon clobbered them' – and the Yorkshire Dragoons made the last mounted charge of the British Army in 1943 against Vichy French in Lebanon. The 3rd Gloucestershire Hussars was a 'phantom' unit based in Scotland whose official mission was 'the sending of misinformation to the Germans', but according to its CO – one of three MFH officers – the main function was to 'entertain the troops with a foot pack of beagles'. In the Western Desert some of the Yeomanry were fighting a sterner war – although the 'regulars looked down their noses at us a little bit'. Their high casualty rate against German 88s might be attributed to the forward 'Yeomanry spirit' learnt on the hunting field. The Warwickshire Yeomanry were left with seven out of 60 tanks after El Alamein. Although Yeomanry regiments did receive conscripts, it is likely that they maintained a higher percentage of volunteers and a local identity with 'their' counties than any other army units.[28]

Hunting at home seems to have continued during the Second World War for the benefit of officers on leave – this time involving all three services – and there is some evidence that RAF officers took over the elite status previously held by the cavalry. However the post-war settlement seemed likely to offer little comfort for both institutions. Clearly the social composition of the Yeomanry changed after 1945. According a retired Gloucestershire CO:

> Recruitment went further into urban areas as the century progressed. Though some officers were landowning farmers, the junior officers were young professionals, land agents, self-employed. The NCOs were skilled self-employed people like plumbers, or lower GPO management. The soldiers had left the land and were postmen or worked in Walls

Ice Cream factory in Gloucester; tractor drivers were quite rare. Very few were unemployed.[29]

Although members of the same landed family were involved in the regiment (this interviewee was the fourth generation), the role of the landed estates declined. 'No longer was the landowner taking out his troop at the weekend though the link allowed use of the grounds for training and functions. The direct link with hunting declined' although 'Yeomanry by and large were supporters of the hunt'. Hunting continued to be practised by the officers in regular cavalry regiments. One of my interviewees was given three months hunting leave a year whilst serving with the 9th Lancers in the early 1960s, as well as a soldier groom to clean his kit. Another was sent on a prestige riding course run by the French Gardes Republicane as late as 1974. The Yeomanry though survived successive reorganisations until the 1960s and even after disbandment some units soldiered in a semi-official capacity. The hunt still played a part in preserving prestigious regiments like the Gloucestershire Hussars from the effects of successive defence cuts. 'Where there are strong links with hunting the Yeomanry kept the nearest thing to a cavalry armed role. They made a nuisance of themselves with the War Office.' As the regular army regiments weakened their county structures, the Yeomanry took it on themselves to represent the old counties. It even lobbied, unsuccessfully, against the local government changes of 1974. 'We were very conservative to the county of Gloucester, the Duke of Beaufort never forgave Peter Walker for putting Badminton in Avon.'[30]

In the 1980s, landed influence managed to get most Yeomanry units re-established, albeit as cadres with back-up roles, though the number of what they still describe as 'sabre squadrons' is remarkable. The direct link with hunting has declined, according to one retired Yorkshire officer and ex-MFH:

> In the 1960s squadron leaders were owners of the large estates and practically every officer used to hunt. Since then everything has changed. The estates are still important but their sons go into the city, they don't join the Yeomanry. Farming people don't have the time. In 1971 the regimental race had 17 competitors – all foxhunters – (on horseback). We couldn't hold the race in 1998 as there were only two. Officers are now solicitors and accountants. Nowadays no-one can ride a horse. The Yeomanry are a bit of an elite in the TA. Where there's landed gentry it still gives a bit of influence. It's a bit difficult to knock the Duke of Westminster on the head!

In 1994 the Yeomanry celebrated 200 years of existence with royal patronage under the slogan 'We welcome the opportunity of supporting local communities in our counties'. By then though, the county community which they and the hunts had tried to define, seemed under threat. Yeomanry soldiers and even officers were recruited from an urban world. Foxhunting, rarely having had to justify itself politically, similarly found that the strength it had always gained from both the landed establishment and the *nouveau riche*, was outweighed by a more cosmopolitan urban view which regarded the practice as barbaric. The following year, the formation of the Countryside Movement (soon to be Alliance) – bankrolled by an ex-Yeoman, the Duke of Westminister – formalised the defence of similar shared values against this perceived outside threat.[31]

CHAPTER ELEVEN

The fortunes of English foxhunting in the twentieth century: the case of the Oakley Hunt*

by R.W. Hoyle

H OW DID FOX HUNTING survive the twentieth century to be a matter of political debate and contention in the first years of the twenty-first? Despite all the heat and controversy that hunting with hounds has provoked over the past fifty years and more, it remains largely unexplored by historians as a rural social phenomenon.[1] There is no shortage of questions to be asked, about, for instance, hunting's declining public standing and its transformation from a sport which epitomised Englishness to a minority pursuit of toffs. For the poet John Masefield in the 1920s, hunting brought all ranks of society together on equal terms in a shared venture.

> ... in the English country, during the autumn, winter and early spring of each year, the sport is fox-hunting, which is not like cricket or football, a game for a few and a spectacle for many, but something in which all who come may take a part, whether rich or poor, mounted or on foot. It is a sport loved and followed by both sexes, all ages and all classes ...

And,

> ... it is a social business, at which the whole community may and does attend in vast numbers in a pleasant mood of good-will, good humour and equality and during which all of them may go anywhere into ground otherwise shut to them.[2]

* The assistance of Barry Stephenson at Bedford Local Studies Library was invaluable in preparing this paper. Dr Kyle Jones undertook some of the initial research. Extracts from Pearl Lawson Johnston's memoir are published with the permission of Bedford and Luton Archives and Records Service (hereafter BLARS). All references to X213 are to the records of the Oakley Hunt deposited in BLARS.

Wilson Stephens, the Editor of *The Field*, acknowledged in 1961 that hunting was seen to be sectarian.

> In the minds of some rather vocal non-hunting people there seems to be a rather strange image of the hunting field as being composed mainly of barons, some of them doubtless bad, and nearly all wearing monocles, whilst around them is an aura of snobbery and money and down-trodden peasantry. It is doubtful if such a picture ever had any relation to the truth, and it is certainly not true nowadays.[3]

On this occasion, we broach a different question. How did hunting survive in conditions which, in so many ways, seemed so hostile towards it? How did it cope with the disappearance of the aristocracy, the relative poverty under high tax regimes of those which remained, disadvantageous landscape changes, the disappearance of riding as a normative skill and repeated attacks, whether in the parliamentary forum, in the local press or from the direct-action wing of the anti-hunting movement, the Hunt saboteurs? What transformations did it undergo to ensure its survival?

I

One of the few academic studies of foxhunting, David C. Itzowitz's *Peculiar Privilege*, draws a picture of hunting in grave difficulties at the end of the nineteenth century. Hunts were making serious losses, beyond the ability of masters to sustain or hunts to guarantee. At the end of the century, in the late Victorian recession in agriculture, some landlords who were well known for their support of the hunt found that they had no choice but to retrench. The Earl of Rutland had to cut back to four days a week in 1891. Lord Lonsdale was forced to retire from the mastership of the Quorn in 1898 on the instruction of his trustees. Lord Spencer declined a fourth term as master of the Pytchley in 1900 because he was unable to afford it. Lord Yarborough sold his hounds – retaining only the bitches – in 1895. Hunts could not cope with the numbers who came along for a free day's entertainment in the field but tried to turn this demand for sport to their advantage by asking non-subscribers for day fees ('caps'). Farmers, themselves under pressure, became less accommodating to the hunt, increasingly looking for compensation for their loss of poultry and seeing barbed wire as the means by which economies could be made on the labour employed in hedge maintenance. Churchward, writing in the early 1960s, recalled that the generation of huntsmen active before the First World War had seen barbed wire as eventually curtailing and preventing hunting, never imagining how arrangements might be made for it to be taken down during the hunting season. Moreover, the vulnerability of the hunt when confronted by rural communities hostile to landlordism had been revealed by the disruption inflicted on Irish hunts during the land war of 1881–82.[4]

So, if at the end of the nineteenth century, the prospect for hunting was none too rosy, it is hard to see any change in the twentieth-century countryside which improved the prospect of its survival. The first half of the century saw the collapse of the old landed society and the disappearance, in many districts, of the country house as the focus of rural life. Those families who survived without selling up were certainly straitened under the high tax regime which characterised most of the twentieth century. That hunting survived probably reflects the influx of new men and new money. *The Country Gentlemen's Estate Book* for 1921 mused that

> Although it was prophesied that hunting would take a new lease of life after the war, and that fields would be greatly augmented, little difference in numbers has been experienced. Certainly a good number of the profiteer class have taken to sport, to whom it was previously foreign, but at the same time it must be remembered that may hunting people have retired from active participation in the fields altogether or have considerably curtailed their number of hunting days per season, on account of the increased expense, the result of taxation and inflated prices.

Comments about the withdrawal of the pre-war aristocracy and squirearchy were commonly made and are found in accounts of inter-war shooting too.[5]

Whilst hunting may well have found a new personnel, alterations in the countryside all worked against the sport. There was an appreciation that the very extent of the countryside was shrinking. Carr quotes an observer who, returning from the First World War, saw to his dismay 'in the Nottingham, Derby and Burton-on-Trent areas the spread of shoddy building over some of the best of the heart of England'. (Or as one writer said in 1936: 'Lamentations arise. Depressed conditions and barbed wire and bungalows are alleged to threaten the life of the hunt'.[6]) In addition, land which had been open to hunts was often withdrawn for shooting and managed by gamekeepers who would not tolerate foxes.[7] The countryside, having been divided up by canals in the eighteenth century (which pessimists though marked the end of hunting) and railways in the nineteenth (ditto) was further segmented by fast roads before the Second World War and motorways after it. But fast roads (and faster cars) probably continued a benefit started by the railway: it brought a weekend's sport (and perhaps a country cottage too) within the reach of men and women who spent their working hours in a completely different environment. Overall, the car and the motorised horse box was a mixed blessing.[8]

The collapse of aristocratic ownership had further implications for hunting and hunters. Where once the farmers had little alternative but to tolerate their landlord's hunt (and the nuisance of his foxes), farmers who had bought their own farms in the fire sales before and after the First World War and now had mortgages to meet and banks to satisfy clearly felt the need to make economies where possible, and to maximise their income. To this was added the rapid landscape change seen in war-time conditions. As Higginson wrote in 1948:

> men have purchased the farms which they formerly rented, and the sense of ownership has brought with it a new responsibility to see that every acre is utilised for production to its fullest extent. Unhappily, intensive farming and foxhunting do not go hand-in-hand, the rolling pasture land, with its acres of sound old turf which supported the grazing herds in the Midlands have been ploughed up because of the need to grow grain ... Even in parts of the country where there were many acres of rough pasture, dotted here and there with gorses which formed wonderful covert for the foxes, a change is noticeable; for the modern farmer, with newly invented mechanical tools, has grubbed up the gorse and made what was once a sportsman's paradise into an agriculturally productive domain. The hedges which bounded the fields and furnished cover – not only for foxes, but also for the rabbits which provided them with food – have in many cases been destroyed: their place being taken by wire fences, often stretched along concrete or iron posts.

In a sense farmers became more pivotal in hunting once they became independent occupiers. Higginson, for example, was keen to stress the importance of keeping farmers sweet. 'The existence of pleasant and personal relations with the farmers and landowners of the country is very important and no one should become Master of a pack of hounds unless he is very keen and prepared to devote practically his entire time to it.' Or, as Clayton put it forty years later, 'Masters have to be exceptionally tactful and diplomatic in their dealings with farmers and land-owners within their country. Keeping the country "open" for hunting is the greatest responsi- bility undertaken by a Master.' It was achieved by offering 'a vast amount of unofficial hospitality to farmers, covert owners and many others', to the point where Clayton saw alcoholism as one of the dangers faced by the master of foxhounds (another was adultery).[9] The need to maintain cordial relations with farmers is reflected in the many injunctions that hunters should buy their horse provender locally.[10]

One may suspect that a further element in the estrangement of farmer came from the fact that many of those hunting were no longer locals.[11] One wonders too when farmers stopped owning hunters; as horses disappeared from the farm, the means and skills to keep a stable turning over were also lost. Indeed, horse riding skills disappeared from society as a whole:

where once the ability to handle a horse was as ubiquitous as the capacity to drive today, by the middle of the twentieth century it was very much an acquired skill. The hunting community recognised this early on with the establishment of Pony Clubs in 1928: 'each generation of young riders was automatically introduced to foxhunting as part of its education in horsemanship'.[12]

And we should also note that any form of hunting became a minority sport, not only practised by a minority but approved of by a minority. Men in red coats lost their resonance as an emblem of bucolic Englishness. They disappeared from Christmas cards, and hunting scenes in general disappeared from the decoration of county pubs.[13] These were all symptoms of a growing divide – in sentiment and understanding – between town and country. The hunting fraternity could both acknowledge their otherness and be patronising about it. So, for Stephens in 1961,

> Hunting has become a freemasonry of countrymen who recognize the lamentable truth that the population of Britain now constitutes two nations. One through no fault of its own, is town-based and, also through no fault of its own, cannot know the facts of life in the fields and woods and farmsteads which lie beyond the points where the pavements end. Ignorance is generally the breeding ground of disapproval and intolerance.

Although the case against fox hunting was first made in the eighteenth century, it was most notoriously articulated by E. A. Freeman in his essay of 1869. Fox hunting was not merely a way for the indolent to waste their time: it was cruel. Its abolition was sought by its opponents for over a century. The League against Cruel Sports was founded in 1924, its alter ego, the British Field Sports Society, in 1930.[14] A sort of high watermark was reached with the private members bills introduced in 1949. Whilst the anti-field sports lobbies were handsomely trounced, and their cause received little support from the Home Office Committee established under John Scott Henderson KC, localised opposition to hunting, especially stag hunting, continued through the fifties and sixties. Overall, the anti-hunting groups seem not to have made major advances before 1970.[15] The abolitionists then secured a number of victories which, even if they fell well-short of illegalising any of the field sports, redrew battlelines and showed just how little support there was for hunting in some constituencies, even in the shire counties. The 1970s were marked by struggles to control the policies of the RSPCA with accusations of entryism being made by both the pro- and anti-hunting lobbies against the other. The Labour Party was intensely lobbied during the 1974–79 government, not to introduce government bills, but to include the abolition of some or all of the field sports as a manifesto commitment in the next election. The policy document *Living Without Cruelty* of 1978 came out against field sports but contained no promise as to when a new Labour government would implement any ban. The party accepted a substantial donation (£80,000) from the League against Cruel Sports in 1978 but the 1979 manifesto still contained no commitment to act. The 1983 manifesto did, and the abject failure of Labour in that election perhaps gave fox hunting (in particular) an additional two decades of life. The League against Cruel Sports developed a new tactic in the late '70s and early '80s. It began a campaign of persuading landowners, starting with the Co-operative Wholesale Society, to institute bans over their farmland and during 1981–83 a number of local authorities did bar hunts from their land after rancorous debates. It also bought land itself, notably in the West Country, to hinder hunts, passage through the countryside and provide a refuge for animals. The League's caravan then moved on to the National Trust which was convulsed by pro- and anti-factions throughout much of the 1980s. Whether these bans did a great deal to inhibit hunting remains to be established. Clayton refers to the Fernie as particularly hard hit by the county council land ban:[16] but the way in which League-inspired motions were accepted by some predominantly rural county councils must have left no one in any doubt that the standing of hunts in the shires was much diminished.[17]

So far this reads like an exploration of why hunting disappeared. But of course it did not. By the 1970s even the most determined opponent of hunting would have to admit that the sport did not lack eager participants, perhaps even too many of them. The 1972–73 edition of *Baily's Hunting Directory* contained an editorial entitled 'The price of popularity'. 'Fox hunting is becoming more popular each season' it began. 'The large mounted fields attracted to the remaining grass counties are part of the evidence of the sport's popularity ... A waiting-list of would-be subscribers has to be drawn up this season by one of the most famous of the Shires packs ... The growth and activity of hunt supporters' clubs is further evidence of foxhunting's popularity'. The price was that 'in some counties the size of Saturday mounted fields have become so unmanageable that Masters of Foxhounds have real problems in providing worthwhile sport for the foxhunter who can only follow hounds at weekends'. In 1977 J. N. P. Watson, *Country Life's* hunting correspondent, assessed 'The future of foxhunting in Britain'. He identified a great many looming problems, but membership was not one of them.

> All through the present century, the army of foxhunters has shown a steady increase, and many of the hunts are more and more embarrassed by the size of their fields. Some see fit to confine their membership and following to those who live and keep horses in the hunt country concerned. For, besides the sport itself, it is the land that inevitably suffers from too many horses: ... Membership of hunt supporter's clubs – the foot, car and bicycle brigade – also swells ...[18]

It was the proud boast of the Duke of Beaufort in 1987 that 'we have to turn away a lot of people who would like to hunt with us, we simply cannot accommodate them in the interests of farmers and landowners'.[19] The combination of buoyant arable agriculture and the penetration of the shires by professional couples all seem to have contributed to foxhunting going from strength to strength. Of course, one would like to know how easy a time smaller and less fashionable hunts had in the seventies and eighties.

For all there were queues wanting to join, establishing the changing character of hunt membership is far from easy. Watson thought that 80 or 90 per cent of the strength of many of the swollen fields were farmers and their families. As a general rule, this seems doubtful. Wilson Stephens, editor of *The Field*, gave his impressions in 1961.

> Hunts vary in their character. In the small valleys of the West Country where Hunts are numerous and small, it is probable that 90 per cent of the followers are farmers and their families. In a wealthy Hunt, situated, say, between London and Birmingham, 70 per cent of the Hunt followers may be businessmen and industrialists. In an average Hunt, half the mounted field are likely to be farmers and their families, one-quarter businessmen from a distance and serving officers who have somehow contrived to save a bit of money, and the remaining quarter are doctors, lawyers, auctioneers and agricultural merchants of the neighbourhood.[20]

In his review of Itzkowitz's *Peculiar Privilege* in 1977, Raymond Carr quoted the President of the JCR of Christ Church Oxford as calling foxhunting 'a bourgeois sport'. 'But', he went on,

> embourgeoisement was the price of survival when the landed aristocracy could no longer afford the pace. The secret of survival of foxhunting is its power of social absorption: it captures new recruits lower down the social scale.[21]

One has to concede that there is something in this: in fact this paper may be taken as illustrating the point. For a certain sort of person, membership of a hunt was plainly aspirational: along with a good horse, the right school for the children, it conferred social cachet for the arriviste. Hunting though contained its own class divisions, between those who were mounted and those who followed the hunt, between the field and its followers who were destined to be not followers even, but 'supporters'.

Informed opinion could be disparaging about the field, implying that they were not well versed in the ways or traditions of the hunt. An Essex farmer was quoted as saying (in 1959) that 75 per cent of the followers of one of the Home Counties hunts were Londoners who did not know the difference between wheat and grass.[22] Those who did know were increasingly the followers. The stalwart of the Oakley, Pearl Lawson Johnston, wrote in her memoir of 1996 that

> Gone are the days when the Oakley was the preserve of experienced and hard-riding members who met regularly and knew their sport. Today's riding population is ever changing and lacking in knowledge of cross country hunting ... [t]here are numerous car or foot followers, some of whom are very knowledgeable, who spend several days a week in pursuit of their spectator sport, either with the Oakley or other packs. The foot followers are, in comparison with either the Oakley or other packs, an unchanging band of devotees who know their country intimately

even if they might be an unruly element as an account by Caroline Blackwood reveals all too clearly.[23] An estimate of 1983 by the Standing Conference on Countryside Sports suggested that 214,000 people *hunted* with hounds, but of these only 50,000 *rode* to hounds.[24]

And yet one senses that by the 1980s hunting went on in an environment that was fundamentally hostile to it. There was a well-organised anti-hunting lobby and many hunts found that their meetings were impeded by direct action. Reports of hunting generally disappeared from newspapers except on those occasions when things went wrong – huntsmen striking hunt saboteurs, the hounds catching a domestic cat. By the early 1980s there seems to have been doubts about hunting in even conservative circles. At the height of the campaign to bar hunts from county council land, Raymond Carr published a somewhat desperate piece in the *Spectator* under the title of 'Fox-hunters, unite'. A fortnight later this was answered by two letters, both anti-hunting. Other columns mentioning hunting in the *Spectator* about this time were, at best, diffident.[25] Under this pressure, hunting reversed its position and began to justify itself not as a sport or recreation, but as a means of controlling vermin.

This paper considers the fortunes of a single hunt – the Oakley in Bedfordshire – which by not being greatly fashionable, is perhaps more representative of fox hunting as a whole than the hunts of the Midland shires such as the Quorn, the Belvoir or the Cottesmore.[26] Occasionally it draws on Dorian William's account of being Master of the Grafton and Waddesdon Chase in the early 1950s, both packs lying adjacent to the Oakley on its south-west side.[27]

II

First we need to explore in general terms the means by which hunts were financed in the twentieth century. There are three broad models of hunt organisation and although exceptions are myriad, it may be suggested that the majority of hunts passed through all three sequentially. They are, respectively, the private hunt, the subscription hunt in which the Master of Foxhounds met shortfalls in subscriptions and other income out of his own pocket, and the subscription hunt with a salaried master. In the first model, the hunt was the possession of a single landowner who, at his expense, provided sport for his guests, neighbours and tenants. In this way the private hunt may be seen as an extension of the hospitality of the country house and one of the ways in which the ties of neighbourliness were maintained. 'Hunt servants in private packs wore six buttons on the tails of their coats, a reminder that they were, like footmen, part of the household of the owner of the hunt and not employees of a hunt committee'.[28] It followed that the landowner was normally the master of fox hounds: he owned the hunt stables, kennels and hounds and employed the hunt servants. In its origins the Oakley conforms to this pattern.[29] In 1793 the fourth Earl of Bedford established a pack of hounds at Woburn Abbey and built stables to accommodate thirty-six hunters, kennels for 70 couple of hounds and a covered riding school.[30] Bedford, like other landowners, quickly found that it was beyond their ability to fund a hunt entirely from their estate revenues. By the end of 1797 he was trying to place the Oakley on a new financial footing. He limited his contribution to a subscription: on 20 March 1798 the Duke wrote to Samuel Whitbread: 'I will continue my subscription of £500 so long as the hounds are kept at Oakley and Mr. Pitt leaves me the money'.[31] He was joined as subscribers by Whitbread and Mr Lee Anthony who became master. Anthony too found the cost hard to carry. In 1809 the Duke of Bedford's eldest son, the Earl of Tavistock, came to the rescue of the hunt when the estimated expense of the hounds was £2,850. 'You will be glad to hear Tavistock has determined to undertake the arduous task,' the Duke wrote to Whitbread on 4 April, 'although it is rather hard on him to exact the sacrifice of half his income for the gratification of a few gentlemen who are unwilling to contribute anything towards their own amusement'.[32] The Oakley was placed on a more formal basis as a subscription hunt in 1814

It might be added that it was not until 1876 that the Oakley owned its own hounds. The early nineteenth-century masters brought their packs with them (and took them when they left). Robert Arkwright, when he became master in 1850, bought the pack from his predecessor for £400. Arkwright had a considerable reputation as a breeder of hounds, but when he too came to find the Oakley a financial struggle, he sold the pack to the ninth Earl of Bedford (for £1,500) and Bedford placed them in the hands of the hunt committee.[33] Thereafter the pack was, in effect, lent to masters for their period of office with covenants that they were to return the same numbers to the hunt committee at the end of their term.

The general tendency was for private hunts to mutate into subscription hunts although a few private hunts survive to the present day. Subscriptions hunts became dependent on their subscriptions but also their ability to find a master of fox hounds backed by wealth. The system emerged by which a master – appointed by a hunt committee – was responsible for the organisation of the hunt and the provision of its sport whilst carrying the costs of the hunt less an agreed subvention. A master whose investment in sport was judged to be inadequate or could not command the support of hunt's members was likely to be invited to make way for someone who could.[34] Alternatively it might be suggested that he should employ a professional huntsman who could improve the sport. This was an insulting suggestion to make to a master. In 1920 C. B. Kidd, in his second year as master of the Oakley, resigned, writing in the following terms:

> Dear Fraser,
>
> Frank Thompson told my wife out hunting yesterday that, at the general meeting, I was to be asked to keep a professional Huntsman. I can only see two reasons for this request: either people are not satisfied with the sport I have shown or they wish for my resignation by making a request, which they know I shall grant. I think therefore under the circumstances the best thing I can do is to tender you my resignation and I should be glad if you will lay this letter before the general Meeting …

Kidd went off to become master of the North Cotswold.[35]

There is general agreement in the literature that the post of Master of Hounds was a full-time one with demanding responsibilities. Higginson, writing after the war, described how

> A master is responsible for the sport, be it good or bad. He is in complete charge of everything pertaining to the hunt – servants, hounds, horses, kennels, stables, country – everything; and he must be a master of organization as well as a master of detail in order to achieve success. This may sound like a pretty tall order, but is nevertheless absolutely true. There is some which needs his attention every month in the year. A busy man might argue that the minor of details of kennel and stable management, pup rearing, earth stopping, damages, poultry claims, etc., etc., could be attended to either by his huntsman, the Stud Groom or the Hunt Secretary. In a way, that is quite true, but someone must instruct the Huntsman and the Stud Groom; some one must dictate, to a great extent, the policy to be followed by the hunt secretary; and, after all, since it is the Master who is Commander-in-Chief and who is responsible for the quality of the sport shown, he is the man to do it.[36]

And, as we noticed, he had also to maintain good relations with the local farmers.

The basic relationship between the hunt committee and its master was regulated by contract. In the specimen contract printed by Higginson, the master agreed with the committee that he would hunt their country 'in a fair and sportmanlike manner' for a specified number of days a week. In return the committee undertook to pay a specified sum towards the expenses of the hunt. They also agreed to shoulder a range of incidental costs (including insurance, taxes, rates and repairs). The master acknowledged the loan of a specified number of hounds and agreed to return as many at the year's end. The contract was to run until notice was given on 1 February by either party, the contract to end on 1 May after.[37]

Arrangements like this continued through most of the last century. They were, of course, financially open ended.

> The Master is elected by vote of the Hunt Committee prior to the annual Subscribers' Meeting, and is normally expected to make up any financial deficit between the sum voted by subscription and the cost of the upkeep of the hunt; which is another way of saying that he had to dig very deep indeed into his private resources, and accounts for the fact that a number of hunts have several joint-Masters who share the responsibility and the burden of the costs.[38]

If costs ran away, as they did in the inflation of the 1970s, then they could find themselves severely out of pocket. Clayton, writing in 1987 estimated that the master of a four-day-a-week pack was likely to be paying £10,000 towards the pack and thought that the figure could reach £16,000. For these reasons a ceiling was increasingly placed on the master's contribution. Instead of the hunt offering a sum of money to the master, in a reversal of the previous arrangements, his costs in excess of a fixed amount were met by the hunt committee. But increasingly a third model emerged in which hunt committees employed a master who ran the hunt for it in return for a salary and expenses. Looking to the future, Clayton thought that amateur huntsmen would become increasingly rare as masters of fox hounds unless they had a private income, and that more and more professional huntsmen would take over as masters.[39]

For most of the nineteenth and twentieth centuries the success of hunts depended on the supply of committed, wealthy individuals willing to spend their own money providing sport for the other members of the hunt. The reasons why masters of fox hounds wished to take on such apparently onerous duties and spend their money on the sport remain to be analysed: but other than the sport itself, it was certainly a way of securing local social prestige (although much less in the twentieth than in the nineteenth century).[40] As a result of these structures, the majority of foxhunters through these centuries had their sport for less than it cost to supply. Individual subscribers were further subsidised by a range of other activities developed by hunts. Visitors could pay what was in effect a day subscription or 'cap'. But hunts worried about people paying caps swamping the subscribers and sought to limit the number of caps sold, both in terms of the number of people paying caps attending any meet, but also by limiting the number of days an individual could pay for a cap before he was asked to contribute a subscription.[41] The definition of the hunt became further fudged by the proliferation of car followers: not members, not directly participants, but plainly of the hunt in loyalty and sentiment.[42] Hunts also developed supporters' clubs and a range of fund-raising activities such as point to point races and country fairs, all of which contributed both to the gaiety of the countryside and hunt finances. Their real contribution lies outside the range of this paper, but it needs to be noticed that hunts were the foci of a wider range of rural leisure pursuits than merely hunting.

III

The Oakley's country is a roughly oval area 25 miles north to south and 22 miles east to west centred on Bedford, stretching in the west to a little short of Northampton and in the south-west to Milton Keynes and Bletchley. Although the Woburn connection is prominent in the hunt's early history, Woburn itself is well to the south of the country and is now separated from it by the M1. In 1959 *The Times* reported that the Oakley had agreed to secede this land to the Whaddon Chase 'because the new London to Yorkshire motorway has cut across their land, and the speed of the traffic using the road will make it dangerous to hunt across it'. When the Oakley hunted from Woburn in 1979, it was said to have been for the first time in 20 years.[43] The M1 apart, landscape change did not pass the Oakley by. The annual returns in *Baily's Hunting Directory* gave a sense of how changes in farming damaged the interests of the hunt. In 1907–08 it was reported that 'about one-half of its area is pasture, 40 per cent plough and the remainder woodland'. When the first *Baily's* appeared after the Second World War, the territory was 20 per cent pasture, 70 per cent plough and the remainder woodland. When *County Life's* hunting correspondent had a day with the Oakley in 1981, he thought 95 per cent of the land was arable 'with winter wheat and rape, not stubble, composing most of the pattern'. And he drew attention to one element of landscape change not noted by *Baily's*: that during the war, the fog-free climate of the district made it suited for air fields, and no fewer than eight were constructed within the Oakley's boundaries.[44] In a newspaper interview in 1973, the then Master, Lord Denham, reflected that the switch into wheat had forced the end of the season to be brought forwards from the end of April to the second week of March as it was impossible to ride through wheat without doing damage.[45]

Pearl Lawson Johnston, writing in 1996, but whose recollection went

Table 11.1 *The health of the Oakley, 1876 to 1974/75*

	Master	number of days hunted	Guarantee	number of hounds (couples)
1876	Captain Browning	4	1800	
1885	J. Butt Miller	4	1700	58
1886	J. Butt Miller	4	1700	58
1897	P. A. O. Whitaker	4	1800	58
1902–03	P. A. O. Whitaker		2300	
1903–04	P. A. O. Whitaker		2300	
1904	Esme Arkwright	4	1800	58
1907	Esme Arkwright	4	2,000	58
1920–21	C. B. Kidd		2000	
1921	Esme Arkwright	3	2800	50
1922	Esme Arkwright	3	2800	35
1923	Esme Arkwright	3	2800	40
1932	Esme Arkwright	3	2700	35
1933–34	Esme Arkwright and Captain B. Hudson	3	2700	
1935–36	Lord Melchett and Misses Farrar	3	2300	50
1938–39	Pearl Lawson Johnston and W. H. F. Brunskill	3	3,600	45
1945				14
1947–48	Lord Luke	2	1,200	20–30
1949	Lord Luke	2	1,200	25
1962–63	J. G. Harris (acting master)	3		25
1975–78	H. Bowley and D. Barney	3		34

Source: Baily's Hunting Directory, various years, except 1933–34, BLARS, X213/246; 1938–9, X213/59, 254; 1947–8, X213/60.

back well into the 1930s, admitted all these problems, but added the loss of woodland had diminished the covert for the fox whilst also reducing the interest of the ride by leaving the landscape devoid of hazards. Another difficulty which she identified was the loss of land to shooting syndicates. Their keepers were willing to shoot foxes, and the hunt itself was banned from entering shooting woods until the season had ended and then permitted only one visit a year.[46] In writing this, she was almost certainly referring to the acrimonious and dispute between W. R. N. (Dick) Sanders of Snelson near Lavendon and the hunt which reverberated through the late 1950s and early 1960s and was the subject of both a public correspondence and reports in the *Bedfordshire Times*. Sander's father Cecil (d. 1953) had been a long-time member of the hunt (indeed he helped Esme Arkwright from his horse when he died in the field in 1934) and Dick Sanders himself was a member of the hunt committee from 1945 to his resignation in 1960. Sanders, it is clear, was acquiring and developing shooting in coverts which the hunt had traditionally entered. On several occasions the hunt took the lack of any instruction not to enter this land as a permission to hunt, and there were allegations about damage to wire. Sanders came to feel that the hunt (as his solicitors told the hunt in 1965) 'demonstrates a continual disregard of the rights, comforts and convenience of farmers, landowners and other members of the public'. By 1965 he was refusing to open his land until the management of the hunt changed: the acting Master J. G. Harris resigned in early 1965 with effect from the end of the 1965–66 season. A new master was appointed and a concordat formulated between Sanders and the new master in early 1967.[47]

Landscape change and changing land use therefore conspired against the Oakley. Table 11.1, which is based on a number of sources, printed and manuscript, traces a different sort of decline. It presents a number of indicators which collectively we make take as revealing the financial health and activity of the hunt. The first is the number of days hunted: consistently four before the First World War, three between the Wars and two after the Second World War, rising to three again in the 1960s. At the same time one can see a tendency for the guarantee offered to the master to grow. By the last year of P. A. O. Whitaker's mastership, it had reached £2,300. Esme Arkwright ran it for less in his first few years of mastership, but it crept up and came to exceed pre-war levels, albeit for a day less in the field. By the eve of the Second World War the guarantee had reached £3,600. Lord Luke accepted much less: but after his two years as master, the mastership passed to the committee and no new master was appointed until 1966. The number of hounds kept by the Oakley also diminished over time, most abruptly and severely during the Second World War when the hunt, in effect, disbanded for a time.

The accounts show that the master's guarantee was the major charge on the hunt. As he was, in effect, responsible for all disbursements except for the few which custom held were the hunt committee's to meet, the few surviving accounts – all from between the wars – cannot begin to give a realistic assessment of the hunt's financial state (Table 11.2).[48] Nor do the printed accounts tell us anything about the hunt's reserves although they do notice income from consols and the 'Reserve hunt dividend'. And some of the hunt's money was held by the Oakley Club (founded in 1814). But a few useful points can be made. For one, the hunt was plainly in some difficulty in the years immediately after the First World War. The situation would have been much worse had it not been for the sale of land (for £207) in 1919–20. One notable cost was that of repairs to the kennels which had been rented to the War Office during the war. In 1924–25 the hunt plunged severely into deficit, caught between a collapse in subscription income and the increase of Captain Arkwright's guarantee to £2800. By 1932 there were signs that the hunt was beginning to look to other sources of income. Capping first appears in the accounts in 1924–25. In 1932–33 it yielded £88, which was treated as subscription income. An annual point to point race existed by the early 1920s (although this income does not appear in the accounts until 1932–33) and the hunt ball was expected to turn a profit.

Table 11.2 *The Oakley Hunt accounts, 1919–1933*

	1919–20	*1920–21*	*1921–22*	*1924–25*	*1932–33*
***Income*:**					
Subscription fees	£2,239 0s. 0d.	£2,324 5s. 0d.	£2,557 19s. 0d.	£1,928 6s. 0d.	£2,655 11s. 0d.
Other receipts	£398 0s. 0d.	£29 9s. 8d.	£29 9s. 8d.	£178 19s. 4d.	£233 16s. 8d.
Total income	£2,637 11s. 2d.	£2,509 5s. 8d.	£2,601 4s. 2d.	£2,148 2s. 7d.	£2,889 7s. 8d.
***Expenditure*:**					
Master of Foxhounds	£2,000 0s. 0d.	£2,000 0s. 0d.	£2,800 0s. 0d.	£2,800 0s. 0d.	£2,700 0s. 0d.
Kennel repairs	£359 13s. 8d.	£369 15s. 1d.	£104 13s. 4d.	£54 4s. 8d.	£117 4s. 9d.
Kennel insurance	£10 4s. 1d.	£5 13s. 3d.	£5 13s. 3d.	£5 13s. 3d.	£5 13s. 3d.
Hounds Insurance		£22 11s. 0d.		£70 1s. 0d.	
Rent of kennel drain	£1 0s. 0d.	£1 0s. 0d.	£1 0s. 0d.	£1 0s. 0d.	£1 0s. 0d.
Printing and postage		£1 10s. 6d.	£13 11s. 2d.	£4 2s. 0d.	
Tax for the year	£67 7s. 3d.	£70 3s. 8d.	£72 12s. 10d.	£29 19s. 7d.	£64 18s. 1d.
Other	£7 7s. 0d.	£15 14s. 6d.			
Total expenditure		£2,416 4s. 4d.	£2,924 17s. 9d.	£2,935 0s. 11d.	£2,823 18s. 0d.
Balance brought forwards	(£32 6s. 9d.)	£159 1s. 3d.	£26 17s. 11d.	£40 17s. 0d.	
Surplus/(deficit) for the year	£191 8s. 0d.	(£132 3s. 4d.)	(£410 1s. 11d.)	(£857 15s. 2d.)	
Retained surplus/(deficit)	£159 1s. 3d.	£26 17s. 11d.	(383 4s. 0d.)	(816 18s. 2d.)	
Surplus/(loss)	£155 11s. 0d.	£13 17s. 8d.	(£396 4s. 2d.)	(£811 0s. 1d.)	11s. 7d.

Source: BLARS, X213/232–233; 1921–22, BLSL. I am grateful to Dr Margaret Lyle for recasting these accounts for me.

Table 11.3 *Analysis of selected Oakley subscription lists, 1902–03 to 1932–33*

	1902–03	*1917–18*	*1918–19*	*1920–21*	*1921–22*	*1924–25*	*1932–33*
Subscribers paying ≥ £50							
number	9	5	8	13	12	9	8
total paid (£)	800	490	575	1245	1407	992.5	742.5
%	34.0	37.4	38.0	53.6	55.0	51.9	28.9
subscribers paying ≤ £10 10s.							
number	38	32	32	40	42	28	33
%	41.3	56.1	53.3	48.2	50.1	45.9	34.3
Total number	**92**	**57**	**60**	**83**	**83**	**61**	**96**
Total subscription income (£)	**2352.75**	**1311.2**	**1511.25**	**2324.25**	**2557.95**	**1913.6**	**2566.6**

Source: BLARS X213/211, 232, 237, 212, 238, 239.

The clear reliance on subscription income prompts a much closer examination of the few extant subscription lists (Table 11.3). The gross numbers reflect the pattern remarked on elsewhere, of the numbers of subscribers halving over the years of the First World War. In the immediate post-war years they bounced back, but fell precipitately in the post-war depression. In fact subscriptions are more complicated that the bald figures might indicate. There was no fixed subscription rate: it was customary for hunt subscriptions to be negotiated according to the number of days the subscriber wished to hunt, whether the subscription was to cover one, two or more family members and whether the subscriber was a local resident or not. Hence the subscription list for 1919–20 contains 16 names paying £50 or more, but 31 names paying £10 or less.[49] In 1924/25 the richer subscribers plainly rallied around to contribute more. Mr Donald Fraser, who paid £150 in 1920–21, headed the list with £200, matched by Major Hulse (£60 in 1920–21). Sir George Lawson Johnston raised his subscription from 50 guineas (£52 10s. 0d.) to £150. The hunt secretary, A. F. Thompson, went from £50 to £100. Others, however, were cutting their subscriptions – most noticeably, but representative of many, the Marquis of Northampton (down from £100 to £50) and as the overall figure shows, somewhere in the region of a quarter of the subscribers of 1920–21 did not renew in 1924–25. By 1932 the subscription base had returned to something nearer the pre-war levels and some of the prominent individuals took the opportunity to reduce their subscriptions, Hulse to £80, Thompson to £50, whilst the Marquis chipped in a useful £100 again. This behaviour is further confirmation that the Oakley – and doubtless hunts generally – were simply not run as a commercial enterprises. People paid what they could: when there were difficulties the wealthier members could be called upon to pay more. In these circumstances, A. F. Thompson wrote to a new committee member in January 1925.

Dear Lawson Johnston,

You were duly elected to the Oakley Hunt Committee of Friday. So of course you would like to know the exact position of the hunt. I therefore enclose a copy of this season's subscription list which I hope is plain. I am not a good accountant.

You will see that there is a deficit of £811. I hope to get between £400 and £500 more in subscriptions. The Oakley Hunt Ball profit of £200 is still in the club account. With any ordinary luck the point to point and the ball should bring in between them at least £300. We should therefore clear this season without any call on the reserves.

As to reserves, there is £1684 in consols value at £58, £976 0s. 0d. [and] £650 in War Loan Bonds, £650, total £1626 0s. 0d. There was a balance of about £1,000 in the club on 1 November before this years subscriptions were paid. Of course I did not produce all these figures at the general meeting on Friday. It might discourage some of the subscribers.[50]

Much of the success of the hunt therefore depended on it being able to secure a master who was prepared to bankroll its activities and supporters who were willing to pay substantial subscriptions in order to see hunting carried on at an acceptable level and with a degree of style.

The Oakley's master throughout most of the inter-war years was Captain Esmé Arkwright. His grandfather, Robert Arkwright had been master between 1850 and 1876 and joint master 1876–85. Esme Arkwright became Master in 1904 at the age of 22 having been educated at Eton and seen service in the Boar War. War service apart, the Oakley seems to have been the major preoccupation of his adult life: he gave up the mastership in 1915 to return to active service, took it up again in 1921 and died in the field early in the 1934–35 season. Arkwright was plainly a man of independent means (he was a descendent of Sir Richard Arkwright's youngest son) whose lifestyle revolved around field sports. His obituaryist in *The Times* recorded that

> Esmé Arkwright was a good shot, when he had the time to snatch a day: a keen fisherman; and he possessed an intimate knowledge and love of nature in general. With all that he was a very well-read man.[51]

His death – or rather his funeral in Bletsoe parish church – marked the end of an era. The Oakley turned out in force. Representatives from 19 other hunts attended. The Oakley never found anybody else whose commitment and willingness to spend their money for the purposes of the hunt matched Arkwright's.

That said, in the absence of accounts, there is no way of knowing just how much his Mastership cost him. It was reported after his death that he resigned in 1927 but was persuaded to carry on; resigned again in 1931 when a collection solicited money to paint his portrait, and then became joint master with Captain Barton Husband in the 1932–33 and 1933–34 seasons. He had just entered into a new arrangement with the Misses Farrar of Chicheley Hall when he died. Arkwright may well have been physically worn out (his Doctor told the inquest that less than 10 days before his death he had told Arkwright to give up hunting), but the recourse to joint masters also suggests that financing the hunt had become a struggle. Until the war, the mastership remained in the hands of joint masters, none of whom lasted long. The Misses Farrar of Chicheley Hall near Newport Pagnell carried on with Lord Melchett (who moved from the Tedworth). In 1938, after Melchett resigned through ill-health, Pearl Lawson Johnston became joint master with W. H. F. Brunskill. It was agreed that the hunt committee would put up £2,500, Lawson Johnston would add in £500 to make £3,000, and then match the committee pound-for-pound until £3,600 was reached.[52] This, it was felt, would finance six or seven days a fortnight in the field, but it makes the point that Arkwright could easily have been spending £1,000 per annum of his own money a decade earlier. Then the war overtook everything.

Arkwright was 'old' industrial money: Melchett, the son of Henry Mond, chemist, founder of ICI and Liberal MP (d. 1930) may be counted as new 'industrial' money and this was true of most of those who subvented the Oakley in these years. Douglas Fraser, who acted in Arkwright's absence and immediately after the first war (1915–19) was said much later to have had 'very considerable interests in South Africa'. He was also known as a racehorse owner.[53] C. B. Kidd (d. 1966), who served as master in 1919–21, graduated from Cambridge with a fourth-class degree in 1899. He held a succession of masterships (the West Kent, 1910–13, the Southdown 1913–14) before war service. He moved from the Oakley to the North Cotswold. In 1953 when he must have been past seventy, he retired as master of the North Warwickshire. He was the son of C. N. Kidd of Dartford (d. 1917), brewer and maltster, owner of the Steam Brewery there and a director of the Dartford Gas Company. It must have been his father's money that allowed him to dedicate his life to hunting.[54] The Misses Farrar were the daughters of Colonel Sir George Farrar who made his money in South African mining. Managing Director of the East Rand Proprietory Mines Ltd, he had been sentenced to death for his role in the Jameson raid, was leader of the Transvaal opposition and died on active service in 1915 in what is today Namibia (German south-west Africa). He was buried at his property, 'Bedford Farm', in the Witwatersland. His widow evidently returned to his English property where she died in 1922.[55]

The Lawson Johnstons who, in the 1930s, emerged as the leading figures in the Oakley, represented new commercial money. George Lawson Johnston (1873–1943), created Lord Luke of Pavenham in 1929, was the son of John Lawson Johnston (1839–1900), a Scot, who having developed interests in the Canadian canned beef trade, devised 'Johnston's Fluid Beef' which from 1886 was sold as Bovril. George Lawson Johnston developed the Bovril company's cattle ranching interests in the Argentine and Australia, and also acquired two other household brands, Marmite in the 1920s and Ambrosia (originally a manufacturer of milk-based baby foods). In 1936 Ambrosia creamed rice was launched. According to his biographer, Lawson Johnston was an extremely directive manager, taking personal control of finance and the management of raw materials, vetting all advertising and tasting every batch of Bovril before he would allow it to be bottled. Amongst other financial interests he had a substantial shareholding in the *Daily Express* to 1917. He served on government committees in the First World War and chaired the Advisory Committee on Nutrition from 1937. He was also a committed benefactor to hospital charities and, when ennobled, took the title of Luke from the dedication of his local church in London, but also because Luke was the patron saint of medical practitioners.[56]

The first Lord Luke ran a notable food-processing company and was actively engaged in a range of charitable activities. He exemplifies the way in which successful industrialists moved from commerce to county. He married a younger daughter of Lord St John of Bletsoe in 1902 and this may well have been his introduction to Bedfordshire. He bought an estate at Pavenham and purchased Odell Castle in 1934. He first appears as a subscriber to the Oakley in 1917–18 paying £20: this he raised incrementally to £150 in 1924–25 and he was elected to the hunt committee (as we saw) in 1925. Luke certainly hunted: but it was the next generation who were prominent in the hunt between the 1930s and 1950s. His daughter Pearl Lawson Johnston appears in the subscription list for 1932 paying £15. As we saw, on the eve of the war she was joint master as well as bankrolling the hunt to the tune of at least £500 per annum. Her brother, the second Lord Luke, was master in 1947 and joint master with Pearl in 1948. Thereafter the hunt was run by a committee, which Lord Luke chaired at some periods, Pearl Lawson Johnston acting as secretary and Hugh Lawson Johnston served as Treasurer from 1955.[57] For all their commitment, the Lawson Johnstons blanched at the cost of subventing the hunt at the level it needed in the post-war years, but in the absence of accounts or subscription lists in the public domain, it is impossible to say how far Bovril contributed to the survival of the Oakley.

IV

Looking back over half a century, Pearl Lawson Johnston described how hunting was forced into change after the Second World War.

> This system [of masters financing hunts] worked well between the two wars, for there were still leisured young men around with money in their pockets (much of it derived from family fortunes created during the industrial revolution), who welcomed the opportunity of indulging in their favourite sport. By 1946, when hunting slowly began to revive after the war years, the scene had changed dramatically. Gone were the young men with money and gone also was the industrial wealth which, from the early nineteenth century, had to a large extent financed fox hunting. Gone too was the wealth of the aristocracy, now faced with heavy death duties and the cost of repairing the ravages the war years had wrought on their estates. Land and stately homes remained, but cash abruptly vanished, thus precipitating a totally new approach to hunt finance. The owners of packs found it increasingly difficult to meet the cost of maintaining their hounds single-handed and they were forced to rely more and more on additional funds provided

by hunt subscribers. Masters could no longer undertake an open ended financial commitment. They were less able to afford financial contributions beyond, perhaps, the cost of mounts.

The signs are that the as the war ended, the Lawson Johnsons stepped in to revive the hunt under traditional arrangements but by December 1948 there was plainly a degree of debate as to how to proceed. Hugh Lawson Johnston, writing as a subscriber 'and one who has always held, and still does hold, the interests of the Oakley Hunt very much at heart' put his thoughts for the future in writing. There was, at that moment, a very strong – and 'very ignorant' – opposition to foxhunting (this being the moment of the private member's bills against hunting).

Foxhunting is branded in the minds of many ignorant people as a rich man's sport – the pastime of the wicked capitalists who can afford to pay for their pleasures. Amongst those who know and appreciate foxhunting, it is an accepted fact that since the war such a picture of foxhunting is largely misleading, and it is the opposite picture – that foxhunting nowadays is run by the farmers for the good of the farmers – which must be put over to the masses, if foxhunting is to survive.

Many hunts are, I believe, alive to the necessity of making this picture real, but for it to be real, the farming community in a hunting country must be able to say that it can maintain a pack and carry on hunting without any outstanding backing from an individual, whether outside or within the hunting country.

For too long, in my opinion, the Oakley country has clung to the idea that it cannot carry on without a substantial contribution from a master or masters. Such individuals who can still afford to pay large sums towards the maintenance of packs of hounds in these days of Income Tax at 9s. in the pound, surtax at 8s. 6d. in the pound and special contributions, can, I should imagine, be counted on the fingers of one's two hands. If the Oakley is fortunate enough to be able to find one to carry on over any length of time, good luck to them! But I am convinced that a time will come fairly soon when the Oakley hunt will have to be run wholly by the farmers – financially as well as otherwise. In taking this view, I am, of course, counting in Ian [Lord Luke], Pearl and myself as farmers in the Oakley country, though not active one's like the majority of the Hunt's supporters. When that day comes, I feel, and hope, that none of us will be backward in contributing our share (as, I think you will agree, my family has done in some measure in the past) both financially and also in placing our land, such as it is, at the disposal of the Oakley for hunting purposes.

What Lawson Johnston sought was a debate within the Hunt committee as to how the hunt could be run without subventions from individuals.[58] It was in these conditions that the Lawson Johnston mastership ended. They were replaced by a committee with Mr James Harris, who farmed at Newton Bromswold, acting as field master. In the early 1950s he became acting master and his son ('young Jim') became field master and then, in 1962, acting master.[59] It has to be wondered whether the farming community reached for their cheque books in the way Lawson Johnston hoped. In December 1951 a circular was sent to subscribers asking then to send in their subscriptions urgently. While costs were running at three times the pre-war level, the minimum subscription remained unaltered at £25. Since the beginning of the financial year on 1 May, expenditure had reached £2066 but the 37 subscriptions received totalled only £922 10s. and total income to date, including £52 8s. for caps, was only £1,068 13s.[60] Writing to Hugh Lawson Johnston the following July, the secretary said that the 'financial position is bad, far worse than is shown in the 1951–52 accounts, because so many things cannot be put on paper'. The costs of feeding stuffs was understated badly because most, together with all the hay and straw, was donated; the hunt had had to borrow £1,000 from the Oakley club to keep going and the point to point had lost money in 1951.[61] When Hugh Lawson Johnston was elected treasurer in 1955, he found the books were not quite as bad as he feared: he had a balance of £13. There was around £450 in the Oakley Club reserve fund and Lawson Johnston wanted to put back something of the £1500 drawn on from that source over the previous two years. He also had £200 from the Hunt Supporter's Committee 'which is doing such splendid work'.[62]

The following January, 1956, Hugh Lawson Johnston wrote a note to Lord Luke and his sister Pearl weighing the immediate options for the hunt. They could (a) continue as at present, with a committee and Jim Harris sen. as acting master or (b) they could ask his son, Jim jun. to take over from his father; they could (c) invite Dick [Sanders] to take over as master; or (d) they could 'bring in a master either by advertising or personal contact, such as Lord Beatty (he is a possibility but I doubt if he would be interested to that extent in the Oakley)'. Financially (c) and (d) were the most attractive although they carried with them the fear of unsettling some of the existing subscribers and followers; Harris might continue for a further year. The choice of Jim Harris jun. was 'least attractive from the financial angle as the committee would have to find the bulk of the money and probably a great deal more than at present ... There would be no question of young Jim having to provide a lot of finance in the same way that his father has been doing'. As it happened, Jim Harris sen. volunteered to carry on for another year and then the acting mastership passed to his son.[63] These arrangements seem to remained in place until 1966. Harris resigned in early 1965 for reasons not unconnected with the Sanders feud, and the following year the hunt appointed Henry M. Stockdale, the son of a Northamptonshire farmer, as master.[64]

For all Pearl Lawson Johnston's optimistic recollections of the 1950s and 1960s, reports of the Hunt's AGMs from the early 1960s suggested that it lived in a hand to mouth fashion, never raising adequate amounts through subscriptions and increasingly reliant on the subventions of the hunt supporters' club. In 1960 Hugh Lawson Johnston reported that hopes of £2,000 from subscriptions were not likely to be met. The hunt supporters though had given £1,000 and more was expected. In 1963 Lawson Johnston reported subscription income of £2,337 but a deficit on the year's account of £906: £1,060 had been borrowed from the reserve account. He deplored those members of the hunt 'who wait to see what sort of hunting season they have had before they pay up'. In 1964 he reported a deficit of £1,286 in the previous year and that subscriptions had fallen short of the target of £3,000. In 1968 the hunt decided to reduce its days from three a week to five a fortnight.[65]

The Treasurer's comments at the AGM, in the years they are reported in the *Bedfordshire Times*, are a poor substitute for accounts and minutes. But they do show how the hunt failed to charge its members at an appropriate level for their membership. Instead, it became reliant on the hunt supporters' club. Pearl Lawson Johnston dates the formal establishment of the club to 1955. Fund-raising events – whist drives, darts and skittles competitions – had started in the thin times after the war, but it was only after the Oakley heard that the Pytchley had started a supporters club that steps were taken to create an Oakley counterpart.[66] The supporters first major event was an open day at the kennels but the programme became ever more elaborate to include terrier shows, clay pigeon shoots, and barbecues.[67] The fortunes of the supporters varied over time. They raised over £1,000 in 1960, but by the time of their annual meeting in March 1964 they had raised only £450 out of a promised £1,000. In July 1964 they launched a Field Fair held at Melchcombe Park: this failed to match expectations but it was reported at the 1965 AGM that they had, nonetheless, donated £900 to the hunt in the previous year. At the 1966 AGM it was reported that they had raised £850 in the previous year from a variety of activities – the point to point, a terrier show, clay pigeon shoot, a 'footsloggers supper'.[68] They also served the Hunt as a pool of people who could be called on to help set up the point to point and act as hunt stewards. The hunt supporters went some way to making up for the lack of a rich individual who might take the mastership. In the early 1960s they were contributing about £1,000 per year when subscriptions brought in between £2,000 and £3,000. If, though, these figures are about right, the hunt in the 1960s was probably existing on much the same sums of money as it did in the 1930s when the rule of thumb was that a day a week throughout the season cost £1,000.[69]

Stockdale acted as Master for three years after which the mastership was shared between joint masters, in the 1971 season four, in 1972 five. On a few occasions a single master was appointed including, in 1982, an American from North Carolina, Tom Wright, who had previously been Master of a hunt there. He had, he told the *Bedfordshire Times*, merely applied to an advertisement.[70] The *Bedfordshire Times* reported in 1971 that the Oakley met three times a week: 'as many as 100 cars have been counted as spectators drive for miles to watch them move off'. According to Pearl Lawson Johnston, the Hunt Committee came to recognise the burden that was placed on the masters when they had to

> make good shortfalls in their annual budgets. The responsibility for financing the pack was, therefore, shifted squarely onto the responsibility of the shoulders of the committee, who undertook to pay 90 per cent of the master's costs. Nevertheless, the Oakley was fortunate at this time [1970s and 1980s] in that it still possessed some masters willing and able to subsidise the pack.[71]

In 1971 the supporters' club donated £1,000 per annum towards the costs of the hunt: in a report of the following year, it was said to have 600 members. A decade later it was 300 members and a contribution of £2,000 annually.[72] At the end of 1982, the County Council barred the Oakley from hunting over its land.[73]

V

To have merely survived the difficult years after the Second World War may be counted as an achievement. There was a clear reversal of role: the inter-war master accepted a fixed sum towards his costs: once masters were reappointed after 1966, they were much more constrained by what the committee could give them. The hunt moved towards a position of self-sufficiency, learning to live without rich patrons but also drawing on the supporters' club for a sizeable part of their income. It may well have become much more a hunt for farmers by farmers as Hugh Lawson Johnston predicted its future to be in 1948: it might equally be said that the majority of the field continued much as before, but the wealthy subscribers as a category disappeared.

In a sense the Oakley had two enemies, one indifference, the other active hostility. The first is seen in the changing attitude of the *Bedfordshire Times*. In the 1930s it would print accounts of individual meets. In the early 1960s it would still carry photos of New Year day meets, of dignitaries at the hunt ball (no fewer than five Lawson Johnstons in one photograph in 1961 but six and two guests in 1964!) and print a list of those attending, and it would send a reporter along to both the Hunt and Supporters club AGMs.

Bedfordian's Diary contained little snippets about the past years of the hunt. As late as the 1966 the paper maintained a hunting correspondent who wrote under the name of 'Almanack'. By 1970 this had just about ceased, as indeed had the *Bedfordshire Times'* coverage of agricultural and rural matters generally. From about 1964 the paper was printing anti-hunt letters, some of which originated with the expected readership of the paper, but others clearly came from determined anti-hunt agitators from outside the district. In February 1964 an aside in a letter in the Sanders business was answered by a letter from Dorset ('The fact remains that, shorn of its out-of-date social trappings, the hunting and hounding of animals in this country of ours is a beastly and bloody business') followed the following week by letters from the League against Cruel Sports' stalwarts Gwendolen Barter of Broadstairs and Mrs Vera Sheppard of Solihull, who was to Field Sports what Mrs Whitehouse was to the rest of the 1960s.[74] In the 1960s at least, the Oakley seems not to have been troubled by the Hunt Saboteurs.[75]

At the 1961 annual meeting Lord Luke urged members of the Oakley to join the RSPCA and to help defeat a motion to be discussed a general meeting later that year. Luke it might be noticed, was also county president of the RSPCA. In 1963 he was reported as observing that not much had been heard of the anti-hunt lobby of late.

> 'Perhaps they are biding their time and thinking up the next move,' he declared, 'I would like to make a strong plea for the supporters of hunting, shooting and fishing to weld themselves together into a firm triple alliance in defence of the countryside'. It should be borne in mind, he said, that as soon as the anti-hunters secured a success against any of the three, they would start picking off the remainder.

Luke's comments were seconded by the chairman of the Supporters, T. H. K. Berry who was quoted as saying

> The only reason there is so much anti-hunting feeling in this country is that in the past our public relations have not been what they ought to be. It is up to the supporters and foot-followers to remedy this. So far as the general public is concerned there really is very little opposition to hunting.[76]

These ideas clearly developed over the next year. At the 1964 AGM it was announced that there was to be field sports fair '… an event at which every form of country life will be represented'. At the same meeting Lord Luke was canvassing the idea of a television sportsman of the year.[77] The field sports fair idea caught fire: the sportsman of the year became something else. Although an initiative of the Oakley Supporters Club, they were joined as sponsors by the North Buckinghamshire beagles and by March 1964 it has been decided to create a Field Sports Fair Society (membership subscription £1) to promote interest in all field sports within the county.[78] Held in the grounds of Hugh Lawson Johnston's house at Melchbourne Park on 4 July, it offered displays (inter alia) of archery, fencing, fly fishing, tractor driving, clay pigeon and small-bore shooting; there was to be a terrier show, gymkhana, military band and morris dancing. The *Bedfordshire Times* reported than 5,000 people had attended. The following year it transpired that the day had not brought the hoped for financial rewards. The *Bedfordshire Times* reported that the fair had been a 'flop': Berry had a letter published the following week saying that he had never used this word but admitted that the effort put into the fair had not been commensurate with the financial reward.[79] This though was not what the day was finally about: it was a device to encourage understanding and win friends for embattled pursuits.

The chill of these years brought about a further change: a reversal of the justifications used by the hunt to justify its existence. At one level hunting is about reducing the levels of a species of vermin. In 1964 a correspondent in the feud over Sanders, who bred 'rare ornamental pheasants and waterfowl' asked 'when the hunt is going to kill the foxes which swarm about the Stagsden and Bromham area. Their barking at night is rapidly turning me grey'.[80] In this respect the hunt offered a 'public' service to farmers and others. But the hunt, in order to be financially viable, also needed to attract subscribers and caps who paid for the chase. If the sport was bad, then subscribers grew disillusioned: some would fail to renew their subscriptions and all grumbled at their Master of Foxhounds. Of course, the danger was that the fox, as a mammal could, like any other, be overhunted. Hunts therefore took steps to maintain their numbers. Here the artificial earth has a particular part to play in the argument: it served no purpose other than to increase the number of foxes in a locality by giving them niches in which to breed. The consequence was that hunts were open to the accusation that they were deliberately breeding vermin for hunting purpose and that the animals they hunted were semi-domesticated.

The acceptance of the Oakley – even in the early 1960s – was such that even in the *Bedfordshire Times* there was no occasion (that I have discovered anyhow) in which the hunt justified its purposes. It is in this light that we must read what in retrospect are the unguarded comments of W. R. N. Sanders made in 1960. This was prompted by an odd letter printed by the *Bedfordshire Times* on New Year's Day in which the author, a Mr Cook, wondered

> one wonders what will become of the foxes now that their vital food, the rabbits, are being destroyed [by myxomatosis]. They must be having a lean time. What the future holds for hunting no one can tell unless the foxes' food is guarded.

A week later Sanders replied that the foxes were getting on perfectly well as they

> have always had a very varied diet and for the last five years they have had to do with a little less rabbit in their diet. If Mr Cook were to handle a fox these days he would be surprised at its healthy and fat condition, and if he would care to visit a litter of fox cubs with me in the spring he would be amazed at the different foodstuffs on which a vixen will rear her young.[81]

To admit that he could show Mr Cook fox cubs suggested a degree of cultivation, if not domestication. A few weeks later he made this admission concrete. There was some alarm about a mystery disease of foxes which had caused a heavy mortality amongst the fox populations of East Anglia and was believed to be spreading westwards. Sanders was interviewed by the *Bedfordshire Times*: he told them that on his own land he had 11 artificial earths, most of which were used quite regularly. He had received no reports of dead foxes from his keepers.[82]

It was possible to admit to the existence of artificial earths – whose sole purpose was to maintain the sport – in 1960. The League against Cruel Sports worried away at the Warwickshire hunts a few years later, asking them to sign a declaration that they had no artificial earths or other devices to maintain fox numbers: they refused. They did say though that artificial earths served a useful purpose 'by allowing foxes to breed under natural conditions in parts of the country where there are no natural earths'.[83] By 1980 such an admission as Sanders made would have been wholly imprudent. In 1973 Lord Denham, interviewed by a kindly reporter from the *Ampthill News*, spoke of the exhilaration of riding over open country. 'The pleasure of foxhunting is entirely the pursuit'. Draghunting was of no interest to him. Asked how he justified chasing foxes to their death, Denham expounded his case.

> Foxes have got to be killed because if there are too many they do considerable damage to poultry, pheasants and young lambs. Once you accept this premise then you have got to decide how to kill them – the alternatives to hunting are gassing, which is not very easy, shooting or poison.

And he added

> We do it because we get fun out of it, but we are justified in doing it because the foxes have got to be killed in some way. This particular way of doing it is arguably kinder to the fox. Of course they could be all killed, but a lot of people would be sorry to see a species of wild life wiped out together.[84]

Or Tom Wright, incoming Master in 1982.

> He makes no apology for hunting. Foxes, he declares, are vermin and a
> kill by hounds is virtually instantaneous ... To conservationists he says
> that if there were no hunts ... the fox would have been eliminated long
> ago by gamekeepers – shot, snared or poisoned.[85]

which is perhaps an indirect admission that that the fox had not gone the
way of the wolf because it was protected, encouraged, even bred, by hunts.

VI

What the Oakley also had to contend with was not only changing
circumstances but a perception that the glory days were over. *Bedfordian's
Diary* by 'Touchstone' in 1962 had an piece recounting a conversation with
'an old sporting friend' who remembered the pre-war days of the Oakley.
Under the heading 'Is foxhunting doomed?', Touchstone's companion
expounded.

> 'But,' said he, 'nobly as the present people in charge of hunt are doing
> to show sport and maintain efficiency, the great days have gone and
> will not return. There simply aren't the "people" in the country now
> and mere money won't make up for the loss of them. And as for the
> "anti-cruelty" campaigns they needn't worry – hunting will die a
> natural death.'

'Touchstone' was not quite as pessimistic. But he appreciated that Lloyd
George, excessive taxation and the break up of big estates made it impossible to replace the personalities of the hunting field who had dominated
fifty or sixty years before. Added to that, there was no longer the country to
gallop over.[86] A fortnight later Hugh Lawson Johnston replied.[87] There were,
he admitted, no longer names in the Oakley like Esme Arkwright. But the
hounds, the turnout of the hunt servants, the discipline of the kennels, all
were every bit as good as in his day. It had become more difficult to hunt
over land 'soiled by every type of fertiliser' and given the increase of the
motoring population 'and the replacement of county lanes by motorways,
the performance of the hounds is every bit as creditable'. As to the charge
that there were not the names, Lawson Johnston was 'happy to be allowed
to hunt among the farmers of the Oakley country.' 'The majority of those
on horseback on any hunting day are themselves farming folk – and very
rightly so.' Backing them up were the followers from towns. 'The support
of the Oakley hunt is more broadly based than ever.'

> Members of my family have hunted with the Oakley since the first
> world war. I myself can only claim to have done so for 28 years, but I
> can honestly say that I enjoy it far more today than ever I did before the

war. There is no recreation I know of which helps one so rapidly forget for a few hours the problems of life today … I can reassure Touchstone – and I am sure that he will be pleased – that the Oakley Hunt will not die a natural death while it continues to enjoy the support of the many sporting people it has today.

If this was a different sort of account, then many of those who were associated with the Oakley would be named. Not only Masters, but secretaries, treasurers, field masters and kennel staff would be named and praised for their devoted service. Enough has been said to show that the Lawson Johnstons kept the Oakley alive through thin times: but Pearl Lawson Johnston herself pointed to the Harris family for their pivotal role over three generations. The Oakley survived because a small number of people in every generation were devoted to it, were prepared to spend substantial sums of their own money and give freely of their time to ensure its survival. Before 1939 they were men and women whose money came (originally) from non-agricultural sources. After 1945 there were fewer footloose men and women of wealth who could support a hunt as master or pay a disproportionately large subscription and the Oakley seems have lived in a very hand to mouth fashion. It is not impossible that it had less money *c.*1960 than it had had thirty years previously. Subscription income was close to £2,500 in 1902–03, 1921–22 and 1932–33, but not as much as £2,000 in 1960, £2,337 in 1962–63 but not as much as £3,000 in 1964.[88] In 1951 the Oakley's Treasurer thought that costs had trebled since before the war: 1959 Williams thought that costs had between doubled and trebled between the 1930s and then and suggested that a three-day-a-week pack then cost about £7,000 a year to run.[89]

So how did the Oakley survive? Without post-war accounts it is hard to say for certain. In part the hunt got by by reducing its activities. Some of the shortfall in subscriptions was made up by the subvention from the supporters' club. And it is an unavoidable conclusion that most of the hunting fraternity probably had their days in the field for much less than their real cost. Without the contribution of a rich MFH, the Oakley must have met Lawson Johnston's expectation that it would become a farmer's hunt, run by them, for them. It came to include, in a very real sense, not merely its subscribers but also the much larger body of people who followed and supported it, many of whom gave gifts in kind. As voluntary societies, the enthusiasm of their members allowed hunts to be immune to the hard laws of economics.

This seems to be true of hunts as whole. Dorian Williams, attending the Grafton in 1950 for the first time since the war, and having bought a horse for £300, asked at his first meet what the subscription was for a single man hunting one day a week and was told it was £35. 'It seemed to me most reasonable. A whole season's sport for £35. I could remember occasions when I had spent the best part of that on a night out in London!' Within a matter of months it was being suggested that he might like to become master: an arrangement emerged in which he would be one of three joint masters, with most of the costs being carried by the third of the three, a man described as a big landowner with 'vast business interests'. He was killed in a shooting accident shortly after, and although his widow met his share of the costs, Williams was forced to sell some land which he had inherited and realise a life insurance policy to meet his share. The two remaining joint masters were helped financially by an older friend who set about dining the better-off hunt regulars and raising money from them. Oddly, Williams never connects the 'very reasonable' subscription he was asked to pay and the somewhat desperate attempts he and his friends made to raise the funds they needed to operate as masters.[90]

In another passage, Williams also tells us about the weight of tradition and the pressure that he and others came under to ensure the survival of the hunt into another generation. As he dithered over whether to accept the Grafton's mastership, Williams was addressed by the professional huntsman, Will Pope, who had hunted with his father.

> Hunting's got to go on. We managed to see that it survived the war, but now its got to go on – got to continue sir. At present it's the old ones that are keeping things going. But we want you young 'uns to come and help us. Just as your father came in after the last war. It's you who want the fun now, sir. Well, unless you'll come in and give us a hand you won't get it, sir. Hunting's got to get a new look, sir, and it won't get it from us old 'uns, sir.[91]

And here, in a nutshell, we have a series of truths: the capacity of hunting to transform itself, the succession between one generation and another, the trust that reposed in each generation to ensure that hunting was passed on to the next in some shape or form. As Lawson Johnston said, with the support of such people, hunting would never die a natural death.

We can end with Wilson Stephens in 1961:

> Hunting today is on its last legs; just as it was a century ago, if the hunting folk of that period had been believed, and just as it will be a century hence. The railways, which were said to have spelled the doom of hunting in the 1840s, will of course have their successor in the shape of some unheralded menace in the 2070s. But it does not look as if anything will actually stop hunting because hunting people, who ride to hounds for the fun of surmounting obstacles, are not likely to be put off by the difficulties. They will grumble, of course. But nobody, not even other ranks in the army, can grumble better than hunting people, especially when things are going well. But do not be deceived by the small talk of the hunting field. There is a long life ahead of the countryside's premier sport.[92]

Notes and references

Notes to Chapter 1: Introduction: field sports as history

1. Guy Paget, *History of the Althorp and Pytchley Hunt* (1937), pp. 1–4: a curiously backhanded memoir; also his obituary in *The Times*, 29 Oct. 1931.

2. What follows is based on a reading of Charles H. Akroyd, *A Veteran Sportsman's Diary* (1926) supplemented by *The Times* obituary, 1 Mar. 1929.

3. I owe this to the kindness of Julie Carrington of the RGS.

4. The exception was a stint on the Severn Salmon Fishery Board (for these regulatory boards, see below, pp. 202–3). 'It struck me that most of my fellow-board members did not know the difference between a salmon and a pike'. *Veteran Sportsman's Diary*, p. 44.

5. According to the genealogy in *Burke's Landed Gentry* (sixth edn, 1882), Akroyd had two daughters.

6. H.C. Akroyd was born in Denton Park, near Leeds, of which his father was then tenant. In 1852 the family moved to Doddington Hall, Cheshire. In 1869 Henry Akroyd gave up Doddington and took a lease of Wollaton Hall, Nottingham. By 1889 he was living near Henley on Thames where he died in 1892. Henry Akroyd also had a lease of a game estate at Altnaharra/Badenloch from the Earl of Sutherland from 1856 to 1889. In 1877 he took a winter lease of Benacre near Southwold for the duck shooting and for that season and he and his son alternated between there and Wollaton. Akroyd, *Veteran Sportsman's Diary, passim*.

7. *British Sports and Sportsmen, Past and Present* (2 vols, 1908), I, pp. xvii.

8. A. Stuart-Wortley quoted by B.P. Martin, *The Great Shoots. Britain's Premier Shooting Estates* (1987), p. 14.

9. Ibid., p. 15. Joyce Lee Malcolm, in *Guns and Violence. The English Experience* (2002), app. pp. 257–9 graphs the numbers of gun and game licences issued 1871–1964 and finds the largest number of licences were granted around 1920. This data is more complicated than might seem: the purchase of a game licence was deemed to cover the possession of gun; a person with a gun licence still needed to procure a game licence in order to shoot. The data presented by Malcolm requires a fuller analysis than it receives there.

10. *British Sports and Sportsmen*, I, pp. xvii.

11. Cited in David Cannadine, *The Decline and Fall of the British Aristocracy* (1990), p. 361 (and other examples at that page).

12. Joseph Rushton, speaking in 1885 (but referring to the late '50s); B. Newman, *One Hundred Years of Good Company* (?1957), pp. 22–3, which I owe to the kindness of Peter Dewey.

13. For opposition to field sports, see E.S. Turner, *All Heaven in a Rage* (1964); and for more general questions of attitudes to animal welfare, H. Keen, *Animal Rights. Political and Social Change in Britain Since 1800* (1998).

14. J.A. Mangan and Callum McKenzie, 'The other side of the coin. Victorian masculinity, field sports and English elite education', *European Sports History Rev.* 2 (2000), pp. 62–85.

15. Lord de Grey, Marquis of Ripon, in A.E.T. Watson, *King Edward VII as a Sportsman* (1911), p. 57. This was the man Akroyd had beaten at Hurlingham in 1874 (above, p. 3). For his shooting, see *The Times*, 24 Sept. 1923, p. 15 and Martin, *Great Shoots*, pp. 222–7. Ripon claimed to have shot 556,813 head of game.

16. R.G. Verney, Lord Willoughby de Broke, *Hunting the Fox* (1920, 1925 edn), p. 6.

17. Sir Charles Frederick, 'Fox-hunting in the past' in Frederick *et al.*, *Fox-hunting* (1930), p. 17. Wroughton had been killed in the field in Dec. 1928, *The Times*, 31 Dec. 1928, p. 4, 4 Jan. 1929, p. 15.

18. I first learnt of Munnings on hearing a paper by

Nicholas Watkins, 'Alfred Munnings (1878–1959), Lionel Edwards (1878–1966) and the perception and preservation of the East Midland landscape as the international centre of foxhunting' given at the W. G. Hoskins and the Making of the English Landscape conference, Leicester, 2005. I am grateful to Dr Watkins for the loan of the text of the paper.

19. The sport of the English abroad lies outside the range of this volume. See J. M. Mackenzie, *The Nature of Empire* (1988) for an excellent account.

20. See here J. M. Mackenzie, 'The nineteenth-century hunting world', in id., *The Empire of Nature* (1988), pp. 25–53. The adolescent trait for killing can be shown from many memoirs, including Akroyd's, but see also Mangan and McKenzie, 'The other side of the coin' for schoolboy hunting and shooting.

21. First published 1853, 2nd edn 1856; the eighteenth edition (1882) is drawn on here.

22. A. Harris, 'Gorse in the East Riding of Yorkshire', *Folk Life* 30 (1991–92), p. 17.

23. Mrs Cresswell published a memoir under the pseudonym of 'Lady Farmer' entitled *Eighteen Years on Sandringham Estate* in which she recounted her dealings with the Prince of Wales and his agents.

24. *The Times*, 24 Mar. 1848, pp. 2–3.

25. Below, pp. 228–9.

26. S. Terrett, 'A study of change in a north Hampshire farm, 1890–1965, with special reference to the impact of outside influences', University of Reading, MA in Rural History dissertation, 2005.

27. MAF, *The National Farm Survey of England and Wales, 1941–43: A Summary Report* (1946), Table 1 (which I owe to Stan Terrett).

28. Paget, *History of the Pytchley hunt*, p. 23. Wroughton was master 1894–1902; 'Brooksby' was the nom-de-plume of the hunting journalist Capt. Pennell-Elmhirst.

29. Hampshire RO, 34/M68/28.

30. For some contemporary comment, see M. H. Hayes, *Riding and Hunting* (sixth edn, 1928), pp. 315–41. Some hunts took shooting rights to prevent them being exercised or found friendly tenants; cf. Paget, *History of the Pytchley Hunt*, p. 227. For a conflict in the 1960s, below p. 268.

31. Evan G. Mackenzie, *In Grouseland* (1895, reissued as *Grouse, Salmon and Stags*, 1997), p. 11.

32. T. C. Smout, *Nature Contested. Environmental History in Scotland and Northern England Since 1600* (2000), ch. 5; A. Durie, 'Unconscious benefactors':

Grouse-shooting in Scotland, 1780–1914', *International J. of History of Sport* (1998), pp. 57–73 citing figures by Orr.

33. Lord Dochester, *Sport, Foxhunting and Shooting* (1935), p. 17.

34. The following section draws heavily on F. M. L. Thompson, 'Landowners and the rural community', in G. E. Mingay (ed.), *The Victorian Countryside* (2 vols, 1981), II, pp. 459–65. For the long-term census figures, S. Tapper, *Game Heritage. A Ecological Review from Shooting and Gamekeeping Records* (1992), pp. 16–17. Since this was written. H. Osborne and M. Winstanley, 'Rural and Urban Poaching in Victorian Britain', *Rural Hist.* 17 (2006), pp. 187–212 has appeared: for numbers of gamekeepers, pp. 200–2

35. Lord Walsingham and Sir Ralph Payne-Gallwey, *Shooting, Field and Covert* (3rd edn, 1889), p. 290.

36. Tom Speedy in Earl of Berkshire and Suffolk (ed.), *Encyclopaedia of Sport and Games* (4 vols, 1911), II, pp. 300–1.

37. There is useful material on keepers in J. Ruffer, *The Big Shots. Edwardian Shooting Parties* (1989 edn), ch. 7.

38. Hayes, *Riding and Hunting*, pp. 4, 296.

39. On the latter, the recollections of H. A. Vachell, *The Best of England* (1930), p. 16; also p. 252 below.

40. 'The Shires' were the hunting territories of the Quorn, Belvoir, Cottesmore, Mr Fernie's and the Pytchley: Hayes, *Riding and Hunting*, p. 370.

41. Lady Diana Shedden and Lady Violet Apsley, '*To Whom the Goddess …': Hunting and Riding for Women* (1932), ch. 11 ('The choice of a hunting country and the life therein').

42. Lord Dorchester, *Sport, Foxhunting and Shooting* (1935), pp. 18, 35.

43. Cannadine, *Decline and Fall*, p. 363.

44. This phenomenon has never been considered systematically, but see George T. Burrows, *Gentleman Charles. A history of Foxhunting* (1951), ch. 20.

45. For J. V. Rank, D. J. Jeremy (ed.), *Dictionary of Business Biography* (6 vols, 1984–6), sub nomine; for Lord Rank, see *ODNB*, sub nomine; Martin, *Great Shoots*, pp. 165–8.

46. Obituary, *The Guardian*, 13 July 2005. Dates are taken from *Baily's Hunting Directory*: for periods King was joint master.

47. The point here is that this was excessive: Walsingham and Payne-Gallwey held that a 'good head-keeper and two under-keepers

will easily look after an estate of 3,000 acres', *Shooting, Field and Covert*, p. 292.

48. Dochester, *Sport*, pp. 186–90.

49. For an attempt to reconstruct trends in the population biology of game and predators, see Tapper, *Game Heritage*.

50. Robert Churchyard, *A master of hounds speaks* (National Society for the Abolition of Cruel Sports, n.d.), pp. 18–21; For Churchyard, below, pp. 29–30.

51. *The Times*, 14 Mar. 1848.

52. W. Rothschild, 'Pheasant: species suitable for acclimatisation', in Berkshire and Suffolk (ed.), *Encyclopaedia*, III, pp. 304–7. John Martin makes the point that there was an element of incompatibility between the best bird for the shoot and the best for the table.

53. C. C. Tudway, 'Partridge, rearing', *ibid.*, III, p. 283.

54. Walsingham and Payne-Gallway, *Shooting, Field and Covert*, pp. 18, 209.

55. Edward, Duke of Windsor, *A King's Story. The Memoirs of HRH the Duke of Windsor KG* (1951), pp. 85–7; J. Gore, *King George V. A Personal Memoir* (1941), p. 230. It was a legendary day in another respect: the King was alleged to have killed 39 birds with 39 successive cartridges. At Eleveden in Suffolk, a party including George V killed 3,247 head in a day in 1912, and 7785 over three days. G. Martelli, *The Elveden Enterprise* (1952), p. 51.

56. H. S. Gladstone, *Record Bags and Shooting Records* (2nd edn, 1930), p. 177.

57. Tapper, *Game Heritage*, pp. 36–45.

58. The committee of enquiry into Grouse Disease published *The Grouse in Health and in Disease* (2 vols) in 1911. The cost of the enquiry was £4,366 raised mostly from amongst landowners and the shooting interest (p. xvi). As a private research initiative, it predates the much more recent work of the Game Conservancy into grouse populations for which see Tapper, *Game Heritage*, pp. 46–9 and P. Hudson, *Grouse in Space and Time: The Population Biology of a Managed Gamebird* (1992).

59. M. Portal, *Partridge Disease and its Causes* (1932).

60. Martin, *Great Shoots*, p. 64.

61. Akroyd, *Veteran Sportsman's Diary*, pp. 256–6. Clouston (1840–1915) was lecturer in mental disease at the University of Edinburgh; he was President of the Royal College of Physicians of Edinburgh, 1902–04. Murray (1841–1914) sailed on the Challenger expedition and spent much of the remainder of his life writing up its results on the deep oceans and sedimentary processes. Both are in *ODNB* which gives Clouston's pastimes as shooting, fishing and golf. John Martin explained the full significance of this exchange to me.

62. *The Times*, 27 Mar. 1931.

63. See Michael Walters, *A Concise History of Ornithology* (2003), p. 167 for this; and E Huxley, *Peter Scott, Painter and Naturalist* (1993, 1995 edn), p. 95 for Scott distinguishing species of geese from shot specimens.

64. Duke of Windsor, *A King's Story*, p. 235. He was not a pioneer though: J. R. Ryan, '"Hunting with the camera"; photography, wildlife and colonialism in Africa', in C. Philo and C. Wilbert, *Animal Spaces, Beastly Places. New Geographies of Human–Animal Relations* (2000), pp. 203–21.

65. Mackenzie, *Empire of Nature*, pp. 42–3; Sir Sidney Lee, *King Edward VII, A Biography* (2 vols, 1925–27), II, pp. 411–12.

66. Aubrey Buxton, *The King in his Country* (?1953), p. 120.

67. For Gladstone, who was also President of the Dumfries and Galloway Natural History and Antiquarian Society 1909–29, a member of the county council for 40 years, its convenor for ten years and a member of the Council of the Zoological Society of London, see the obituary in the *Trans. Dumfries and Galloway Natural History and Antiquarian Society*, third ser., 27 (1950 for 1948–9), pp. 222–3.

68. Huxley, *Peter Scott*, pp. 78, 159, 164 etc.

69. David Matless, Paul Merchant and Charles Watkins, 'Animal Landscapes: Otters and Wildfowl in England, 1945–1970', *Trans. Institute of British Geographers* 30 (2005), pp. 191–9.

70. Keen, *Animal rights*; E. S. Turner, *All Heaven in a Rage* (1964); C. C. McKenzie, 'The origins of the British Field Sports Society', *International Journal of the History of Sport*, 13 (1996), pp. 177–91. For Bromley Davenport's verse, see his *Sport* (2nd edn, 1933), p. 220. Davenport was a pioneer of salmon fishing in Norway: 'I have provided myself with a dwelling and an estate [in Norway] – partly for sake of the sport, and partly to have another string to my bow – some refuge in republican Norway from the possible legislation of constitutional England, where inability to pay the heavy bill for "unearned increment", which has in my case been running for 900 years, may cause my family estates to be handed over to someone else'. ibid., pp. 82–3.

71. A. Taylor, '"Pig sticking princes". Royal hunting, moral outrage and the republican opposition to animal abuse in nineteenth and early twentieth-century Britain', *History* 89 (2004), pp. 30–48.

72. For the League, see D. Weinbren, 'Against all cruelty: the Humanitarian League, 1891–1919', in *History Workshop J.*, 38 (1994), pp. 86–105. There is also useful material on the League in M. Tichelar, '"Putting animals into politics". The Labour Party and hunting in the first half of the twentieth century', *Rural Hist.* 17 (2006), pp. 68–70. For the League's role in the campaign against the buckhounds, below pp. 215–19.

73. Tichelar, 'Putting animals into politics', p. 219.

74. Ibid., pp. 224–7.

75. See here the RSPCA's statement in *The Times*, 19 Feb. 1949, p. 4: they saw no viable alternative to hunting to keep down fox numbers.

76. M. Tichelar, 'The Labour Party, agricultural policy and the retreat from rural land nationalisation during the Second World War', *AgHR* 51 (2003), pp. 209–25.

77. *The Times*, 18 Feb. 1949, p. 4.

78. For the debate, see *The Times*, 26 Feb. 1949, p. 4; for Ministers voting against the bill, 28 Feb. 1949, p. 2.

79. For an example of this, see the exchange of letters in *The Times* between the Chairman of the Devon and Somerset Staghounds and the officers of the National Society for the Abolition of Cruel Sports, 3 Sept. 1957, p. 11, 7 Sept. 1957, p. 7.

80. Below, pp. 58–9.

81. Cited in National Society for the Abolition of Cruel Sports, *Foxhunting* (1947), p. 10.

82. Clayton, *Endangered Species*, pp. 53–8. See though the analogy between the ill-preparedness of hunting and the ill-preparedness of the country before Dunkirk in a speech of 1949: R. Carr, *English Fox Hunting, A History* (1976), pp. 247–8.

83. Robert Churchward was the nom de plume of Capt. Paul Rycaut de Shordiche-Churchward, 1907–81. For his biography, see P. Moore (ed.), *Against Hunting* (1965), p. 157 and his obituary in *The Times*, 4 May 1981. For an account of Churchward and an interview with his widow, C. Blackwood, *In the Pink* (1987), pp. 142–54. The libel action is noticed in *The Times*, 1 July 1964, p. 16. Churchward became an advocate of drag-hunting.

84. I say this on the basis of the few remnants of 1960s records in the basement of the League against Cruel Sports, inspected with the permission of the League in October 2004.

85. *The Times*, 17 Feb. 1958, p. 4; 22 Feb., p. 6.

86. There is valuable material on the early stages of these campaigns in R. H. Thomas, *The Politics of Hunting* (1983).

87. The Hunt Saboteurs Association awaits its historian. See P. Windeatt, *The Hunt and Anti-hunt* (1982), pp. 27–30. For the stimulus of the Committee of 100, see S. Poole, 'The history of the Hunt Saboteurs Association, part 1', at has.enviroweb.org/features/hist1.html, accessed Mar. 2006.

88. Nigel Gray, 'Pioneer tells story of the game fair', programme for the CLA Game Fair, Burghley House, Stamford, 26–27 July 1963 (1963); figures for attendance are given in the programme for the Woburn Abbey game fair, 1977, p. 55.

89. Gore, *George V*, pp. 229–30.

90. The Duke of Portland, *Men, Women and Things* (1937), p. 237.

91. P. Tombleson, *The Fixed-spool Reel* (1961), pp. 9–10. I owe this point to Ian Roberts.

92. Walsingham and Payne-Gallwey, *Shooting, Field and Covert*, pp. 293–4.

93. Anon., *The Private Life of King Edward VII (Prince of Wales, 1841–1901) by a Member of the Royal Household* (1901), p. 231; P. Horn, *Pleasures and Pastimes in Victorian Britain* (1999), p. 112; Gladstone, *Record Bags*, p. 205.

94. The old style of shooting is further illustrated in H. Alken, *The National Sports of Great Britain* (1825 and much reprinted subsequently). For butts, see Andrew Done and Richard Muir, 'The landscape history of grouse shooting in the Yorkshire Dales', *Rural Hist.* 12 (2001), pp. 195–210.

95. *The Times*, 11 Dec. 1828, p. 11; 6 June 1829, p. 3.

96. Walsingham and Payne-Gallwey, *Shooting, Field and Covert*, pp. 3–5.

97. 'Lady Farmer', *Eighteen Years*, pp. 99–100, 70.

98. MacKenzie, *In Grouseland*, pp. 29–30. Whilst the grand battue has disappeared, the principle of having game driven towards the shooters remains fundamental to modern game practice.

99. A. Trollope, *British Sports and Pastimes, 1868* (1868), pp. 78–9.

100. A. J. Stuart-Wortley, 'The Scotch mail' in H. A. MacPherson *et al.*, *The Grouse* (1894), pp. 83–101; also on this, Durie, 'Grouse-shooting in Scotland'.

101. C. C. Hartopp, *Shooting and Sport in England, Past and Present* (1894), pp. 126–30; Martin, *Great Shoots*, p. 234.

102. Paget, *History of the Pytchley Hunt*, p. 230.
103. Carr, *English Fox-hunting*, pp. 238–9; Dorchester, *Sport*, pp. 32–7; Hayes, *Riding and Hunting*, p. 328.
104. Martin, *Great Shoots*, pp. 163–4.
105. See here the case of Lady Ribblesdale: Horn, *Pleasures and Pastimes*, p. 112.
106. There is a useful resume in Carr, *Foxhunting*, pp. 172–5.
107. See here the comments of Lady Diana Shedden and Lady Apsley, 'To Whom the Goddess …', pp. 39–40.

108. Dorchester, *Sport*, pp. 74–5 (quotations): see also p. 38.
109. Michael Clayton, *The Golden Thread. Foxhunting Today* (1984), p. 69.
110. MacKenzie, *In Grouseland*, pp. 41–6.
111. Martin, *Great Shoots*, pp. 212–13.
112. Akroyd, *Veteran Sportsman's Diary*, pp. 317–18.
113. *The Times*, 26 Feb. 1949, p. 6. Winterton died in 1962 at the age of 79. *The Times*' obituarist said he was 'often explosively outspoken'. *The Times*, 28 Aug. 1962, p. 10.

Notes to Chapter 2: Royalty and the diversity of field sports, *c.*1840–*c.*1981

1. For the royal family's sporting activities, see Nicholas Courtney, *Sporting Royals Past And Present* (1983). Individual monarchs also had celebratory volumes on their sporting skills as follows: A. E. T. Watson, *King Edward VII as a Sportsman* (1911), J. Wentworth Day, *King George V as a Sportsman* (1935); A. Buxton, *The King in his Country* (n.d., ?1952).
2. Edward, Duke of Windsor, *A King's Story. The Memoirs of HRH the Duke of Windsor, KG* (1951), pp. 192–6, 221, 226; Courtney, *Sporting Royals*, p. 165.
3. Compare 'The Prince of Wales [Edward VII] is considered by good judges the best shot in the kingdom' (Anon., *The Private Life of King Edward VII (Prince of Wales, 1841–1901) by a Member of the Royal Household* (1901), an insider's account, written for the American market, p. 231) with 'As a shot King Edward the Seventh was somewhat variable, at times distinctly good, although never approaching the very first rank' (Watson, *Edward VII as a Sportsman*, p. 25, also pp. 76–80) or 'He did not excel as a shot in spite of assiduous practice' (Sir Sidney Lee, *King Edward VII, a Biography* (2 vols, 1925–7), I, p. 32. Such plaudits have continued into modern times: 'Prince Philip, often cited by Sandringham guests as one of the best shots in the country ("which means", they add in awed tones, "in the world") is now equally lavish in praise of his son. A. Holden, *Charles, Prince of Wales* (1979), p. 210.
4. P. Ziegler, *King Edward VIII. The Official Biography* (1990), pp. 38–9; Windsor, *A King's Story*, p. 102.
5. Pictures published in the *Sunday Mirror* on 19 Nov. 2000.
6. Wentworth Day, *George V as a Sportsman*, pp. 55–6; Watson, *Edward VII as a Sportsman*, p. 73.
7. Roger Fulford, *The Prince Consort* (1949), pp. 90–2; Watson, *Edward VII as a Sportsman*, pp. 69–71, 75–6; Wentworth Day, *King George V as a Sportsman*,

pp. 54–9 (which includes comments on the Prince Consort and nineteenth-century shooting at Windsor); Windsor, *A King's Story*, p. 261.
8. Courtney, *Sporting Royals*, p. 101.
9. Kevin Cahill, *Who owns Britain. The Hidden Facts Behind Landownership in the UK and Ireland* (2001), pp. 61–4; for the extent of the estate *c.*1910, Watson, *Edward VII as a Sportsman*, p. 112; Ralph Whitlock, *Royal Farmers* (1980), pp. 164–73. On the estate at the beginning of the new century, *Daily Telegraph*, gardening supplement, 31 Dec. 2001. For the reference to Thuringia, D. Bennett, *King Without a Crown. Albert, Prince Consort of England, 1819–1861* (1977), pp. 157–8.
10. Mrs Helen Cathcart, *Sandringham, The Story of a Royal House* (1964), pp. 28–30.
11. On Sandringham, Whitlock, *Royal Farmers*, pp. 132–63; J. D. Foster, 'Sandringham', *Agriculture* 64 (1957), p. 180.
12. J. Gore, *King George V. A personal memoir* (1941), p. 230.
13. Ziegler, *Edward VIII*, p. 262; Windsor, *A King's story*, p. 25. A constant theme of this memoir is the Duke's modernity compared to his father's outmoded attitudes.
14. Ibid., pp. 292–3.
15. These had been bought by George V on a mortgage from the Duchy of Cornwall which Edward had released to his father's estate *before* he discovered he had been left nothing in his father's will. Ziegler, *Edward VIII*, pp. 247, 261.
16. Ibid., pp. 261–2.
17. Both quoted by Cathcart, *Sandringham*, p. 15.
18. Philip Hepworth, *Royal Sandringham* (1978), p. 42.
19. Gore, *George V*, p. 379.
20. *ODNB*, 'George V'. Gore recalled that 'King George loved Norfolk frankness and Norfolk men', p. 233.
21. Windsor, *A King's Story*, pp. 32, 182.
22. Lee, *Edward VII*, I, pp. 169–70; Sir Frederick

Ponsonby, *Recollections of Three Reigns* (1951), p. 199; M. Beard, *English Landed Society in the Twentieth Century* (1989), pp. 6–7. The itinerary was also conditioned by the racing calendar and the staggered beginnings of the open seasons for game birds.

23. Gore, *George V*, pp. 188–9, 262, 273, 280, 331.

24. B. Pimlott, *The Queen. A Biography of Elizabeth II* (1996), p. 451.

25. Giles St Aubyn, *Edward VII. Prince and King* (1979), pp. 84, 87.

26. P. Horn, *Pleasures and Pastimes in Victorian England* (1999), pp. 100–1; *Private Life*, p. 128.

27. Watson, *Edward VII as a Sportsman*, p. 281.

28. Windsor, *A King's Story*, p. 254; Ziegler, *Edward VIII*, pp. 226–7. For the social life of inter-war Melton, M. Clayton, *Foxhunting in Paradise* (1993), ch. 8.

29. Lee, *Edward VII*, II, pp. 411–12: Courtney, *Sporting Royals*, ch. 9.

30. Fulford, *Prince Consort*, p. 93; Bennett, *King Without a Crown*, p. 246.

31. Horn, *Pleasures and Pastimes*, p. 112 (where she cites examples of women who did shoot).

32. 'Both the Prince and the Princess have stead-fastly set their faces against the latter-day fashion of ladies walking with the guns'. *Private Life*, p. 233.

33. *Hunstanton and its Neighbourhood, Including a Complete Guide to Sandringham* (fifth edn, 1873), pp. 32–3, an account of 'Home life at Sandringham' repr. from *The World*, 20 Jan. 1877; Ponsonby, *Recollections*, p. 201; *Private Life*, pp. 227–33.

34. Horn, *Pleasures and Pastimes*, pp. 112–13; S. Bradford, *George VI* (1993), p. 36; Windsor, *A King's Story*, p. 22.

35. Watson, *Edward VII as a Sportsman* pp. 331–2, 47–8. For crowds watching the Prince shooting at Knowlsey in 1896, H. S. Gladstone, *Record Bags and Shooting Records* (2nd edn, 1930), pp. 305–8.

36. *Illustrated London News*, 24 Jan. 1863, pp. 101–2, engraving p. 93; 21 Jan. 1865, pp. 71–2; Watson, *Edward VII as a Sportsman*, pp. 279, 281, 283, 286–7; *The Field*, 21 Dec. 1889, p. 893; Gore, *George V*, pp. 177–8; M. Clayton, *Prince Charles, Horseman* (1987), pp. 79–80

37. P. Magnus, *King Edward the Seventh* (1964), p. 92.

38. For a useful discussion of the international dimension of shooting, J. Ruffer, *The Big Shots. Edwardian Shooting Parties* (1989 edn), ch. 5.

39. Magnus, *Edward the Seventh*, pp. 127, 190–1, 210. There is, in addition, useful material on Albert Edward's shooting abroad in Ruffer, *Big Shots*, ch. 5.

40. Lee erroneously dates this trip to 1891, *Edward VII*, I, pp. 577–8; Magnus, *Edward the Seventh*, p. 211. The following January the Prince was a guest at Hirsch's house, Wretham Hall near Thetford. *The Times*, 6 Jan. 1891, p. 7; 7 Jan. 1891, p. 7. For Hirsch, see the report of his death in *The Times*, 22 Apr. 1896, p. 9; Ruffer, *Big Shots*, pp. 77–80; *Private Life*, p. 236; Watson, *Edward VII as a Sportsman*, pp. 338–9 where he quotes the game card of a four-week visit to St Johann in 1894 in which 37,654 animals were shot, including 22,996 partridge and 11,346 hares.

41. Gore, *George V*, pp. 189, 215–16.

42. Magnus, *Edward the Seventh*, p. 256.

43. Watson, *Edward VII as a Sportsman*, pp. 70–1; Wentworth Day, *George V as a Sportsman*, pp. 29–59, 60; Gore, *George V*, pp. 177–8.

44. Ian Coster, *The First Gentleman. His Royal Highness the Duke of Edinburgh* (?1952), p. 77; Mrs Helen Cathcart, *HRH Prince Philip, Sportsman* (1961), pp. 124, 127; *The Times*, 1 Nov. 1978, p. 2.

45. For Albert Edward shooting wild bulls at Chillingham, Lee, *Edward VII*, I, p. 578.

46. Fulford, Prince Consort, p. 90; E. S. Turner, *All Heaven in a Rage* (1964), p. 167; St Aubyn, Edward VII, pp. 136–7; 'The Lady Farmer', (pseud., Mrs Louisa Cresswell), *Eighteen Years on the Sandringham estate* (?1887), p. 76: in one year she secured compensation for her losses. *Private Life*, p. 232.

47. For the history of deerstalking, see the useful article by H. Lorimer, 'Guns, game and the grandee: the cultural politics of deerstalking in the Scottish highlands', *Ecumene* 7 (2000), pp. 403–31 and the references offered there.

48. Courtney, *Royal Sport*, ch. 7 gives details. For Queen Victoria keeping the stag books, Wentworth Day, *George V as a Sportsman*, pp. 76–7. 'Balmoral dilemma', *Daily Telegraph* gardening section, 31 Dec. 2001.

49. E. Longford, *Elizabeth R* (1983), p. 350. The Duke of Edinburgh's writings on conservation deserve discussion.

50. Wentworth Day, *George V as a Sportsman*, pp. 78–80.

51. A. Durie, '"Unconscious benefactors": Grouse-shooting in Scotland, 1780–1914' in *International J. History of Sport* 15 (1998), pp. 66–7.

52. 'Lady Farmer', *Eighteen Years*, p. 64; also, *Private Life*, p. 228.

53. K. Rose, *King George V* (1983), p. 293.

54. 'Lady Farmer', *Eighteen Years*, p. 71; Lord Walsingham and Sir Ralph Payne-Gallwey, *Shooting, Field and Covert* (3rd edn, 1889), pp. 3–4.

55. Rose, *George V*, p. 293.

56. Watson, *Edward VII as a Sportsman*, pp. 22–3, 46.

57. Watson, *Edward VII as a Sportsman*, p. 22; *Private Life*, pp. 232–3, W. A. Dutt, *The King's Homeland. Sandringham and north-west Norfolk* (1904), p. 109; Holden, *Charles, Prince of Wales*, p. 210.

58. Gore, *George V*, pp. 221–2.

59. For Holkham, Ruffer, *Big Shots*, pp. 61–3. Albert Edward was probably there in 1863, again in January 1865 when a major ball was held in honour of the Prince and Princess and on a single day 2,190 head were shot, of which 1,020 were pheasants, again in January 1866 and in January 1867 when his party killed 1,863 birds in a day. In December 1869 it was announced that the Prince and Princess would be making 'what may be regarded as their annual visit to the Earl and Countess of Leicester at Holkham'. *The Times*, 19 Oct. 1863, p. 9; 28 Oct. 1863, p. 9; 6 Jan. 1865, p. 9; 7 Jan. 1865, p. 7; 12 Jan. 1866, S. Weintraub, *The Importance of being Edward: King in Waiting, 1841–1901* (2000), p. 143 (1867); 23 Jan. 1867, p. 9; 30 Dec. 1869, p. 7.

60. Magnus, *Edward the Seventh*, p. 91; Cathcart, *Sandringham*, p. 88. A friendly rivalry with Holkham continued into the twentieth century, Rose, *George V*, p. 293.

61. For descriptions of shooting at Sandringham, see 'Lady Farmer', *Eighteen Years*, pp. 68–72; *Hunstanton and its Neighbourhood* (fifth edn), pp. 32–3; *Private Life*, pp. 225–33 and Weintraub, *Importance of being Edward*, pp. 157–8.

62. 'Lady Farmer', *Eighteen Years*, p. 65–6, 71–2; Magnus, *Edward the Seventh*, p. 91.

63. Ibid., p. 264.

64. Wentworth Day, *George V as a Sportsman*, pp. 23–5. Generally, this book is evasive on the king's shooting of pheasant and partridge at Sandringham. Compare Gore: 'He loved the Marshes more than the covert', *George V*, p. 231.

65. Windsor, *A King's Life*, pp. 182–4; Buxton, *King in his Country*, p. 31. For the costs of the estate and its poor wages, Rose, *King George V*, pp. 100–1.

66. Ziegler, *Edward VIII*, pp. 141, 189; Windsor, *A King's Story*, p. 235.

67. The following section is based on a reading of Buxton, *King in his Country*.

68. For this circle, see Bradford, *George VI*, p. 402–3.

69. Calculated from Buxton, *King in his Country*, who prints extracts from the king's gamebooks. In late September and early October 1941 the king took some holiday at Sandringham, and with a scratch shooting party he and his friends took 5531 birds and hares over six consecutive days. The bags could have been bigger because the guns lacked beaters and the shooting party had to do its own picking up (ibid., pp. 118–20).

70. Cathcart, *Prince Philip*, p. 121; Courtney, *Sporting Royals*, pp. 101–2.

71. *The Times*, 27 Dec. 1974, p. 2; *Sunday Times*, 10 Feb. 1980, p. 1.

72. Walsingham and Payne-Gallwey, *Shooting*, p. 18.

73. Except for the particular points referenced, see Courtney, *Sporting Royals*, ch. 8 for this section.

74. *Private Life*, p. 239.

75. Magnus, *Edward the Seventh*, pp. 54–5, 102–3, 138–9; Weintraub, *Importance of being Edward*, pp. 107, 224–6, 235; *Private Life*, pp. 117, 236–41.

76. J. M. MacKenzie, *The Empire of Nature* (1988), *passim*.

77. Windsor, *A King's Life*, pp. 87; Rose, *King George V*, p. 135.

78. Windsor, *A King's Life*, p. 221.

79. Cathcart, *Prince Philip*, p. 18.

80. *The Times*, 12 Nov. 1960, p. 5; 24 Jan. 1961, p. 7; 25 Jan. p. 7; 27 Jan., p. 10; 30 Jan., p. 8; 31 Jan., p. 8; 25 Feb., p. 6; 28 Feb., p. 11, 3 Mar. p. 9 (this last a report of a critical article in the *Church Times*); also 16 May 1962 (a denial by the Palace that the whitlow was feigned). Pimlott, *The Queen*, p. 304; Cathcart, *Prince Philip*, ch. 16. For the showing of the film in 1986, MacKenzie, *The Empire of Nature*, p. 310.

81. Fulford, *Prince Consort*, pp. 93–4.

82. *Private Life* says that a fall 'subdued his ardour in the field', pp. 192–3. The fullest account seems to be 'Sabretache', *Monarchy and the Chase* (1948), ch. X; also Lee, *Edward VII*, I, p. 80; Watson, *Edward VII as a Sportsman*, ch. 7 (Chaplain quoted on p. 289). Whether he was ever really committed to hunting may be doubted. In February 1866 *The Times* (p. 10) reported that he had shot 'upwards of 26,000 head of game' that season, which cannot have left much time for the fox.

83. Again the fullest account of his hunting and that of his brothers is 'Sabretache', *Monarchy and the Chase*, ch. XI, although this is strongest on the Shires. The Prince of Wales started with the Pytchley early in 1920 and let it be known that he would hunt with them the following season (*The Times*, 1 Mar. 1920, p. 6). In 1920–21 he hunted with a number of Shire packs

(reports in *The Times*) including the Pytchley. In August 1922 took a house near Malmesbury and that season hunted with the Beaufort.

84. Ziegler, *Edward VIII*, pp. 175–6.

85. Windsor, *A King's Story*, pp. 102, 162, 192–6, 221, 226; Ziegler, *Edward VIII*, pp. 175–6, plate opp. p. 190; *The Times*, 4 Nov. 1931, p. 5; Clayton, *Prince Charles, Horseman*, pp. 14–16; id., *Hunting in Paradise*, pp. 124–7.

86. Clayton, *Prince Charles, Horseman*, pp. 16–18; Courtney, *Sporting Royals*, pp. 22–3; Wentworth Day, *George V as a Sportsman*, pp. 258–9.

87. *NDNB*, 'Henry Duke of Gloucester', 'George Duke of Kent'.

88. [Viola] Lady Apsley, *Bridleways Through History* (2nd edn, 1948), p. 357. I know of the portrait from a paper by Nicholas Watkins, 'Alfred Munnings (1878–1959), Lionel Edwards (1878–1966) and the perception and preservation of the East Midland landscape as the international centre of foxhunting' given at the W. G. Hoskins and the Making of the English Landscape conference at Leicester, 2005, and I am grateful to Dr Watkins for the loan of the text of the paper. The portrait hung in the Duke and Duchess' Paris house and was sold at Sotherbys in 1998 for $2.3m.

89. Pimlott, *The Queen*, p. 64. Courtney, *Sporting Royals*, p. 23, confirms that the Queen never hunted.

90. National Society for the Abolition of Cruel Sports (hereafter NSACS), *Bulletin*, 163 (Mar. 1973), p. 4.

91. NSACS, *Bulletin*, 115, 116 (1955), 125 (1959).

92. Quoted by the *Daily Mail*, 14 Jan. 1970.

93. *The Times*, 20 Nov. 1972, p. 1; 8 Dec. p. 16; 14 Dec. pp. 1, 4, 17, and c.f. the letters on 17 Dec., p. 13.

94. Holden, *Charles, Prince of Wales*, p. 16; Clayton, *Prince Charles, Horseman*, chs 7–9 describes his induction into the sport in detail.

95. *The Times*, 4 Nov. 1975, p. 2; 14 Mar. 1978. p. 3; 2 Apr. 1976 p. 3; 4 Nov. 1978, p. 3; 19 Sept. 1980, p. 4. The full anecdote about Princess Anne is reported in Holden, *Charles, Prince of Wales*, p. 18.

96. Reported in *The Field*, 28 July 1981, p. 257 and Clayton, *Prince Charles, Horseman*, p. 85.

97. In 1999 it was complained that he had taken his sons hunting. In 2002 he was reported as saying that 'if the Labour government ever gets round to banning foxhunting, I may as well leave the country and spend the rest of my life skiing'. In 2004, there was a report that he had refused

the Queen's request to stop hunting although his sons has agreed to stop and it was reported that he hunted in the week before the ban came into force (*The Guardian*, 31 Oct. 1999, *Observer* 29 Sept. 2002, *The Guardian*, 6 Nov. 2004, 17 Feb. 2005).

98. Holden, *Charles, Prince of Wales*, pp. 28–30.

99. *The Times*, 29 July 1980, p. 2; 7 Aug. 1980, p. 2.

100. *The Times*, 25 Feb. 1981, p. 18.

101. *The Times*, 28 July 1981, p. 50 ('Highgrove, the (almost) perfect spot'). Holden, *Charles, Prince of Wales*, confirms that he avoided publicity about his hunting at this time (pp. 208–9).

102. The fullest account of the hounds and their practice in their last years is Lord Ribblesdale, *The Queen's hounds and stag-hunting recollections* (1897). For an earlier account of the agitation which preceded their abolition, see Turner, *All Heaven in a Rage*, pp. 230–43.

103. Stratton and the Humanitarian League produced a number of pamphlets against the sport, presentation copies of which may be found in TNA, HO 45/10122/B12657. J. Stratton, *Hunting the Carted Stag* (n.d., 1895?), p. 17. For the Humanitarian League, D. Weinbren, 'Against all cruelty: the Humanitarian League, 1891–1919', *History Workshop J.* 38 (1994), pp. 86–105.

104. *The Times*, 17 Jan. 1893 (editorial italics).

105. These instances are taken from Stratton, *Hunting the Carted Stag*, pp. 19–21.

106. Stratton, *Hunting the Carted Stag*, p. 28.

107. Ribblesdale, *The Queen's Hounds*, pp. 154, 156–7, 207–8. Sabretache, *Monarchy and the Chase*, pp. 139–40, says the Prince hunted with the Buckhounds until the early 1870s.

108. *The Times*, 8 Nov. 1892, 8 Sept., 1893, p. 6; 6 Dec., p. 6. See also the report on 1 Sept. that 'A section of the Radical members are quietly, but persistently, bringing pressure to bear upon the government in the hope of securing the abolition of the buckhounds', p. 7; their identities may be gathered from the signatories to the letter to the Prime Minister seeking the discontinuance of the buckhounds, pr. *The Times*, 3 Oct. p. 7.

109. *The Times*, 11 Jan. 1893, p. 12 (letter from Bowen May); 16 Nov. 1892, p. 5.

110. *The Times*, 11 Jan. 1893, p. 12; 13 Jan., p. 10, 17 Jan. p. 4; 19 Jan. p. 4; 20 Jan. p. 15; 24 Jan. p. 6.

111. The League published Ponsonby's letter in 1901; see clipping in TNA, HO 45/10122/B12657 (43); *The Times*, 5 Jan. 1895, p. 3; 20 Feb. p. 6 (parliamentary report); 26 Nov. 1896, p. 8; 5 Apr. 1897, p. 15; HO 45/10122/B12657 (27), (32, 36, 37, 38);

The Times, 4 May 1899, p.9; 1 Nov. 1900, p.5; 3 Nov. p.11.

112. J. Stratton, *The Royal Buckhounds. The Popular Verdict upon their Sport* (1897) quotes from 26 newspapers.

113. Stratton, *Hunting the Carted Stag*, pp.23–4.

114. TNA, HO 45/10122/B12657 (43); *The Times*, 13 Feb. 1901, p.9.

115. *The Times*, 14 Mar. p.7; 19 Mar., p.11; 21 Mar., p.4; 5 Apr, p.6; 13 Apr, p.11; 2 May, p.6, 10 May p.6; 2 June, p.9.

116. *The Times*, 4 May 1901 (letter from Sir Arthur Arnold).

117. V. Cowles, *Edward VII and his Circle* (1956), p.88.

118. Turner, *All Heaven in a Rage*, pp.179–87.

119. NSACS, *Bulletin*, 153 (Oct. 1967).

Notes to Chapter 3: Sport and the survival of landed society in late Victorian Suffolk

1. Roy Douglas, *Land, People and Politics. A History of the Land Question in the United Kingdom, 1878–1952* (1976), p.17.

2. Nicholas Everitt, 'Shooting' in *VCH Suffolk*, II, p.365.

3. F. M. L. Thompson quoted in W. D. Rubinstein, *Men of Property* (1981), pp.197–8.

4. Suffolk RO [hereafter SRO] (Ipswich), HA108/8/2 (item 10); SRO (Ipswich), HA93/5/125.

5. SRO (Bury), HA507/4/39.

6. F. M. L. Thompson, 'The end of a great estate', *EcHR* 8 (1955), pp.43–4.

7. *Hansard's Parliamentary Debates*, 87, p.544; Arthur Oswald, 'Helmingham Hall, Suffolk, V', *Country Life*, 120 (1956), p.715. The Marquis of Bristol by contrast, supported Robert Peel, *Complete Peerage*, II, p.327; Susanna Wade Martins and Tom Williamson, *Roots of Change. Farming and the Landscape in East Anglia, c.1700–1870* (British Agricultural History Society, Supp. Ser., 2, 1999), p.152.

8. James Caird, *English Agriculture, 1850–1851* (1852, repr. 1968), p.491.

9. Lord Ernle, 'The Great Depression and recovery, 1874–1914', repr. in P.J. Perry (ed.), *British Agriculture, 1875–1914* (1973), p.1.

10. D. Cannadine, 'Aristocratic indebtedness in the nineteenth century: the case re-opened' *EcHR* 30 (1977), p.638.

11. *Complete Peerage*, X, p.767; *Burke's and Savills Guide to Country Houses* (3 vols, 1978–), III, pp.232–4 and 258; William White, *History, Directory and Gazetteer of Suffolk* (1885), p.540; Anthony Dale, *James Wyatt* (1956), p.68; H. Colvin and J. Harris (eds), *The Country Seat* (1970), p.168; Richard Wilson and Alan Mackley, *Creating Paradise. The Building of the English Country House, 1660–1880* (2000), p.217.

12. Peter Thellusson (1737–97), a merchant of Huguenot origins, by will placed his fortune out of reach of his immediate descendants in a trust in which it was to accumulate until the death of the last survivor of his sons and grandsons living at his death, when it was to be divided between the three eldest male lineal descendents of his three sons then living. The will was judged legal in 1799 and 1805, but similar schemes were illegalised by statute of 1800. When it was divided in 1859, much of the fortune had been spent on litigation and the resulting fortune was modest. See *ODNB*, sub 'Peter Thellusson'.

13. Cannadine, 'Aristocratic indebtedness', pp.639–40; *Complete Peerage*, X, p.767; SRO (Lowestoft), SC/335/1. Between c.1830 and 1871 Lord Rendlesham presumably resided on his estate in Hertfordshire. Wilson and Mackley, *Paradise*, p.27.

14. SRO (Lowestoft), HA12/B3/14/17. This huge sum was cleared by Lord Waveney in 1873 through the sale of 2,800 acres in Suffolk.

15. SRO (Ipswich), HB26/412/1854.

16. Wilson and Mackley, *Paradise*, p.288; Christopher Hussey, 'Ickworth Park, Suffolk: The seat of the Marquis of Bristol', *Country Life*, 117 (1955), p.680; SRO (Bury), HA507/4/39.

17. F. M. L. Thompson, 'Landowners and the rural community', in G. E. Mingay (ed.), *The Victorian Countryside* (2 vols, 1981), II, p.459. The balance between farm improvement and house-building, in the case of the Earl of Stradbroke at Henham and Sir Shafto Adair at Flixton, is analysed in B. A. Holderness, 'Landlord's capital formation in East Anglia, 1750–1870', *EcHR* 25 (1972), p.445.

18. David Cannadine, *The Decline and Fall of the British Aristocracy* (1990), p.16.

19. Michael I. Wilson, *The English Country House and its Furnishings* (1977), pp.161–2.

20. Mark Girouard, The *Victorian Country House* (1979), pp.7–9.

21. Everitt, 'Shooting', p.367.

22. Michael Alexander and Sushila Anand, *Queen Victoria's Maharajah, Duleep Singh, 1838–1893* (1980), pp.110, 112.

23. Corrance quoted in Everitt, 'Shooting', p.367.

Exactly how this was done is is explained subsequently.

24. Ibid., p. 367.

25. Alexander and Anand, *Maharajah*, pp. 111, 133.

26. David Cannadine, 'Aristocratic indebtedness in the nineteenth century: a restatement', *EcHR* 33 (1980), p. 571. Indeed, if, as David Spring suggests, the aristocracy had in fact 'reduced' or even 'removed' the debts charged to their estates, 'one is bound to ask what all the fuss was about'.

27. SRO (Bury), 941/30/109.

28. Evidence of Sir Edward Kerrison to the *Royal Commission on Agricultural Depression*, III, British Parliamentary Papers 1882, XIV, p. 179.

29. SRO (Ipswich), HA11/C3/27.

30. Royal Commission on Agriculture. 'Report by Mr Wilson Fox on the county of Suffolk', *British Parliamentary Papers* 1895, XVI, p. 348.

31. Kenneth Clark, *Another Part of the Wood: A Self Portrait* (1974), p. 4.

32. Mark Girouard, *Life in the English Country House: A Social and Architectural History* (1978), p. 302.

33. *Estates Gazette*, Jan. 1898, p. 836. Other sporting estates on offer included the 2,854-acre Brandon Park estate, *Estates Gazette*, Jan. 1898, p. 1079 and the Depperhaugh estate *Estates Gazette*, Sept. 1894, p. 349; *Estates Gazette*, July 1902, p. 799.

34. Author's correspondence with Lord Henniker.

35. Wilson Fox, 'Report on Suffolk', p. 355.

36. Pamela Horn, *The Changing Countryside in Victorian and Edwardian England and Wales* (1984), p. 47; White, *Suffolk*, pp. 312, 318, 538; *Kelly's Directory of Suffolk* (1888), pp. 997, 998, 1000, 1078, 1104; Bramford, Hall, SRO (Ipswich). HA61/436/870–872; Broke Hall, SRO (Ipswich), HA93/3/37–8; Bosmere Hall, SRO (Ipswich), HA93/3/361–2.

37. F. M. L. Thompson, *English Landed Society in the Nineteenth Century* (1963), p. 303.

38. Everitt, 'Shooting', p. 364.

39. Wilson and Mackley, *Paradise*, p. 351.

40. Presumably the sport was better than at Hintlesham Hall. SRO (Ipswich), HA93/3/39; SRO (Ipswich), HA93/3/40.

41. SRO (Bury), 941/71/4.

42. Charles Adeane and Edwin Savill, *The Land Retort. A Study of the Land Question with an Answer to the Report of the Secret Enquiry Committee* (1914), p. 80.

43. H. Rider Haggard, *Rural England, Being an Account of Agricultural and Social Researches Carried Out in the Years 1901 and 1902* (2 vols, 1902), II, pp. 383–4.

44. Haggard, *Rural England*, II, p. 384;

E. H. Hunt and S. J. Pam, 'Responding to Agricultural Depression, 1873–1896: managerial success, entrepreneurial failure?', *AgHR* 50 (2002), p. 238 and E. J. T. Collins, 'Rural and agricultural change: the Great depression, 1875–1896' in id., (ed.), *The Agrarian History of England and Wales* VII, *1850–1914* (2000), p. 205; George Martelli, *The Elveden Enterprise. A Study of the Second Agricultural Revolution* (1952), p. 49.

45. Everitt, 'Shooting', p. 364. In 1902, on the Elveden estate, Lord Iveagh decided to take 2,000 acres out of regular cultivation. This land was left to be 'cropped occasionally as game lands'. Martelli, *Elveden*, p. 49.

46. Haggard, *Rural England*, II, p. 384; Wilson Fox, 'Report on Suffolk', p. 348.

47. Thompson, 'Landowners', p. 460.

48. SRO (Ipswich), HA11/A14/4.

49. Alexander and Anand, *Maharajah*, p. 129.

50. *Public General Statutes* (London, 1862), pp. 1337–8.

51. Russell M. Garnier, *History of the Landed Interest, The Customs, Laws, and Agriculture* (2 vols, 1908), II, pp. 470–1. Eggs were also marked with the owners name written in invisible ink to counter against egg-stealers.

52. Harrington v. Cocksedge, Stowmarket County Court, 16 Mar. 1864, reported in *The Times*, 9 Apr. 1864, p. 7.

53. Editorial in *The Times*, 9 April 1864, p. 11.

54. George Ewart Evans, *Ask the Fellows Who Cut the Hay* (1956), p. 104; SRO (Bury), 449/3/13 and J. H. Porter, 'Tenant-Right: Devonshire and the 1880 Ground Game Act', *AgHR* 34 (1986).

55. Wilson Fox, 'Report on Suffolk', p. 334.

56. *The Times*, 9 Apr. 1864, p. 11.

57. G. E. Mingay, 'The Farmer' in Collins (ed.), *Agrarian History*, VII, pp. 766–7.

58. Everitt, 'Shooting', p. 366. Corrance also explains that in the early nineteenth century there were many yeoman farmers, farming 200–300 acres who were very dangerous neighbours to highly preserved estates. However, 'these farms have been almost entirely bought up and absorbed into the large estates or their shooting hired at some cost'.

59. SRO (Ipswich), HA1/HB6/4/8.

60. Everitt, 'Shooting' p. 365. To avoid any arguments with farmers about shooting over his land, the Earl of Iveagh simply bought out his tenants on the Elveden estate and replaced them with bailiffs who kept the land in cultivation as a home for game. Martelli, *Elveden*, p. 49.

61. *Public General Acts* (1880), p. 216.

62. Martelli, *Elveden*, pp. 42, 50–1, 53–4; Jamie Camplin, *The Rise of the Plutocrats* (1978), p. 222.

63. Clark, *Wood*, pp. 16–17.

64. Grateful thanks to Harvey Osborne for his invaluable assistance in explaining how Elveden could achieve bags of this magnitude; Martelli, *Elveden*, p. 51; see also Lord Walsingham and Sir Ralph Gallwey, *Shooting: Field and Covert* (3rd edn, 1889).

65. Everitt, 'Shooting', p. 366; again, my thanks to Harvey Osborne.

66. *The Times*, 9 Apr. 1864, p. 11 (from where the following quotations are taken).

67. Walsingham and Payne-Gallwey, *Shooting, Field and Covert*, p. 211.

68. Ibid., p. 211. Presumably, this is a reference to a derivative of the Euston system.

69. Ibid., p. 252.

70. Ibid., p. 252.

71. Ibid., p. 252.

72. J. Ruffer, *The Big Shots. Edwardian Shooting Parties* (1989 edn), p. 149. Whether these prices could be realised is questionable. The Rothschilds were said to have more birds to dispose of than they could sell, so they gave them away to carriage drivers and busmen passing their London house. V. Cowles, *Edward VII and his Circle* (1956), p. 139. The market for game deserves consideration.

73. Clark, *Wood*, p. 14.

74. Pamela Horn, *High Society. The English Social Elite, 1880–1914* (1992), p. 134.

75. SRO (Ipswich), HA11/A15/7; HA11/C47/16/4. The household at Euston was equally impressive, SRO (Bury) HA513/7/8.

76. SRO (Ipswich) HA11/C8/13; HA11/C8/13. The Earl of Ashburnham, whose heartland was in Sussex, broke-up and sold for £55,616 the Barking Hall estate in 1917, SRO (Ipswich), HA1/HB4/6, 7. The outlying portions of this estate had already been sold in 1914 for £6,620. Similarly, the Duke of Hamilton sold the bulk of the Easton Park estate in 1919 for £58,000, the residue being sold in 1922. SRO (Ipswich) SC/142/5, 10.

77. SRO (Ipswich), HB416/A2/19, 20; SRO (Lowestoft) SC/335/1, p. 3; *Complete Peerage*, X, p. 768. The bulk of the estate had to be sold to pay death duties.

78. Cannadine, *Decline and Fall*, p. 438.

Notes to Chapter 4: The shooting party: the associational cultures of rural and urban elites in the late nineteenth and early twentieth centuries

1. F. M. L. Thompson, *English Landed Society in the Nineteenth Century* (1963), pp. 137–40; G. E. Mingay, *The Gentry: The Rise and Fall of a Ruling Class* (1976), pp. 132–3.

2. Thompson, *English Landed Society*, pp. 137–8.

3. Ibid., p. 140; G. E. Mingay, *Rural Life in Victorian England* (1998), p. 31.

4. Thompson, *English Landed Society*, p. 139.

5. Before the 1831 Game Act, only those in ownership of land with a value of £100 in rental each year could obtain game and gun licences for shooting.

6. See, for instance, Thompson, *English Landed Society* and Mingay, *Gentry*. The social history of foxhunting has, in fact, received more attention as a result of D. C. Itzkowitz, *Peculiar Privilege. A Social History of English Foxhunting, 1753–1885* (1977) and R. Carr, *English Fox-hunting: A History* (1976).

7. For instance, see M. Waterson (ed.), *The Country House Remembered* (1985), esp. pp. 88–98.

8. J. Mills, D. Mills and M. Trott, 'New light on Charles De Laet Waldo Sibthorp, 1783–1855', *Lincolnshire History and Archaeology* 36 (2001), pp. 34–6.

9. R. Olney, *Lincolnshire Politics, 1835–85* (1973), p. 4.

10. F. W. S. Craig (ed.), *British Parliamentary Election Results, 1832–1949* (3 vols, 1977), I, pp. 187–8, III, pp. 419–23; *Burke's Landed Gentry* (1937 edn), p. 2061.

11. *Kelly's Lincolnshire* (1896–1919), pp. 14–16.

12. R. Olney, *Rural Society and County Government in Nineteenth-century Lincolnshire* (History of Lincolnshire, X, 1979), pp. 101–2.

13. *Kelly's Lincolnshire* (1896–1919), pp. 15–16.

14. *Kelly's Lincoln* (1897), *The City of Lincoln Directory* (1857), p. 84; *The Directory of the City of Lincoln* (1901–19), p. xxxvi. The Sibthorps were never mayors of the City of Lincoln during the nineteenth century.

15. D. Mills, *A Walk Round Canwick, The Lincolnshire Estate Village of the Sibthorps* (2002), p. 1.

16. *Kelly's Lincolnshire* (1885), p. 353 and *Kelly's Lincolnshire* (1937), p. 130.

17. D. Mills, 'The revolution in workplace and home' in D. Mills (ed.) *Twentieth-Century Lincolnshire* (History of Lincolnshire, XII, 1989), pp. 22–6.

18. Ibid., p. 23. See below, p. 114, for more detail on the sale of the Sibthorp estates.

19. Joan Mills, 'Notes on Canwick Mill', unpublished paper lent by Dr Dennis Mills.

20. Ibid.

21. Mills, 'Revolution', Table 2.3, p. 26.

22. See J. Saville, *Rural Depopulation in England and Wales, 1851–1951* (1957), p. 48 for the proportion of the Lincolnshire labour force employed in agriculture in a national context in 1931.

23. The figures quoted here were derived from *BPP, Census of England and Wales: County Tables: Population* for the years 1841, 1871, 1901 and 1931.

24. S. Bennett and N. Bennett, *An Historical Atlas of Lincolnshire* (1993), pp. 4–8.

25. J. Thirsk, *English Peasant Farming. The Agrarian History of Lincolnshire from Tudor to Recent Times* (1957), p. 321.

26. Ibid., pp. 310–17.

27. For a discussion on the specific effect of the depression on the income and finances of the Sibthorp family, see p. 114 below.

28. C. Brears, *A Short History of Lincolnshire* (1927), p. 187.

29. N. Wright, *Lincolnshire Towns and Industry, 1700–1914* (History of Lincolnshire, XI, 1982), p. 141.

30. Brears, *Short History*, p. 187.

31. Mills, 'Revolution', p. 19.

32. Lincolnshire Archives (hereafter LA), SIB 1/5, Canwick Shooting Book, 1883–1940. See the notes to the Appendix for more details on the books and the sampling employed.

33. Thompson, *English Landed Society*, p. 340.

34. Mills, 'Walk around Canwick', pp. 14–15.

35. Census Enumerators Books (hereafter CEB) 1881, TNA, RG11/3238/92/20.

36. See J. J. Hurwich, 'Lineage and Kin in the sixteenth-century aristocracy: some comparative evidence on England and Germany', in A. L. Beier, D. Cannadine and J. M. Rosenheim (ed.), *The First Modern Society. Essays in Honour of Lawrence Stone* (1989), pp. 33–65 for a discussion of the bilateral nature of landed kinship systems and relations as opposed to patrilineal inheritance.

37. BPP 1874 LXXII, *Return of Owners of Land, 1872–73*, part I, pp. 33–108, for Lincolnshire.

38. After this date, many of the Sutton visitors who had been guests at the shoot, such as Hugh and Henry, had died.

39. LA, 3SIB 1/27, Family correspondence and papers, 1839–71, letter from Constance Elizabeth Amcotts to her sister, Louisa Cracroft-Sibthorp, 24 Nov. 1858.

40. This is based on the tables in J. Bateman, *Great Landowners of Great Britain and Ireland* (1883), p. 506.

41. Lord Liverpool bought Hartsholme from the Shuttleworth Family at the end of the nineteenth century. Olney, *Rural Society*, p. 44.

42. 1901 Census, RG13/1059/71/10/58.

43. *Kelly's Directory of Lincolnshire* (1905), p. 128 and *Kelly's Lincolnshire* (1913), p. 135.

44. 1901 CEB, RG13/1059/71/9/52, *Kelly's* (1937), p. 130.

45. 1881 CEB, RG11/3238/131/7 and RG11/3237/40/1.

46. 1901 CEB, RG13/1059/69/5/35.

47. *Kelly's Lincolnshire* (1913), p. 581.

48. Ibid., p. 202. The main landowner was Coningsby and it seems strange that the two brothers would have different land agents. However, both are listed contemporaneously as land agents to the Sibthorps. Into the 1900s, Samuel Oglesby was listed as the 'senior estate agent' and it may be that these were part of a team of agents working on different aspects of estate management.

49. *Kelly's Lincolnshire* (1913), p. 662.

50. D. Mills and J. Mills, *The Dower House, Canwick: Some Historical Notes* (2003), p. 4.

51. *Kelly's Lincolnshire* (1896), p. x. In 1901 his daughter, Edith, was still resident at the Dower House. See 1901 Census, RG13/1059/70/8/47 and Mills and Mills, *Dower House*, p. 4.

52. *ODNB*, 'Shuttleworth, Joseph, 1819–83'; 'Clayton, Nathaniel, 1811–90'. For a description of the relationship of the Clayton and Cockburn families see Olney, *Rural Society*, p. 44.

53. *Kelly's Lincolnshire* (1913).

54. Kelly's directories between 1885 and 1937 list the patron of the living as the Mercer's Company.

55. *Kelly's Lincolnshire* (1913), p. 326.

56. Olney, *Rural Society*, p. 147.

57. *Ruddock's Directory of the City of Lincoln* (1913), p. xxxix.

58. *Kelly's Lincolnshire* (1905), p. 366.

59. *Kelly's Lincolnshire* (1885), p. 325.

60. Wright *Lincolnshire*, 156. *ODNB* gives Joseph Shuttleworth's wealth at death as £554,612.

61. See Olney, *Lincolnshire Politics*, esp. pp. 4, 182–231.

62. F. Hill, *Victorian Lincoln* (1974), p. 34.

63. Olney, *Lincolnshire politics*, p. 4.

64. For Lincolnshire 'new wealth' see Olney, *Rural Society*, pp. 41–5. The literature on the wider topic of the 'gentrification' of British entrepreneurs

is extensive and has been discussed at length elsewhere. See F. M. L. Thompson, *Gentrification and the enterprise culture: Britain, 1780–1980* (2001), pp. 1–23, for one of the more recent and incisive analyses of the literature.

65. Hill, *Victorian Lincoln*, p. 189.
66. Olney, *Rural Society*, p. 44. By the 1880s, Joseph's son, Alfred had taken up residence at Hartsholme Hall. See *Kelly's Lincolnshire* (1885).
67. Ibid., p. 182.
68. Hill, *Victorian Lincoln*, p. 73.
69. *Kelly's Lincolnshire* (1909), p. 247.
70. Ibid., p. 361.
71. *Kelly's Lincolnshire* (1885), p. 529.
72. Ibid.
73. *Kelly's Lincolnshire* (1896–1904), p. 7.
74. *Kelly's Lincolnshire* (1885), p. 267.
75. *Kelly's Directory of the City of Lincoln* (1894), p. 5.
76. Hill, *Victorian Lincoln*, p. 71.
77. *ODNB*, 'Shuttleworth, Joseph, 1819–83'.
78. *Kelly's Lincolnshire* (1896), p. 16.
79. Ibid.
80. *Kelly's Lincolnshire* (1913), p. 772.
81. 1881 Census, RG11/3243/65/9 and *Kelly's Lincolnshire* (1885), p. 539.
82. Hill, *Victorian Lincoln*, pp. 1–3.
83. Shuttleworth and Larken: Census 1881, RG11/3243/64/8 and RG11/3243/65/10 respectively. Mason: *Kelly's Lincoln* (1885), p. 5.
84. Mills, Mills and Trott, 'New light', pp. 25–37.
85. LA, 3SIB 1/30, Family correspondence and papers 1839–71, letter, Weston Cracroft-Amcotts to his sister, Louisa Cracroft-Sibthorp, 10 Mar. 1870.
86. *The Times*, 2 Sept. 1905, p. 4. Rimington-Wilson is one of the 'Big Shots': B. P. Martin, *The Great Shoots. Britain's Premier Sporting Estates* (1987), pp. 235–6; Obituary, *The Times*, 1 Apr. 1927, p. 16.
87. *The Times*, 1 Sept. 1883, p. 10.
88. Olney, *Rural Society*, pp. 13–14.
89. P. Smith and D. Mills, 'Lindum – a Lincolnshire House in Norway', *Lincolnshire Life* (Mar. 2001), pp. 22–3. This was Charles De Laet Sibthorp's house and it is not clear if the family still owned the house in the later nineteenth century. Given that Charles accrued huge debts on the estate, it is probably less rather than more likely that they did. See Mills, Mills and Trott, 'New light'.
90. The author must again thank Dr Dennis Mills for supplying him with copies of the guest books, and Penny Smith for transcribing them and permitting reference to be made to them in this article.
91. As stated before, this information was recorded in the shooting books.
92. Mills, Mills and Trott, 'New light', pp. 34–6. See above, p. 98, for details of Charles de Laet's debts.
93. See above, pp. 101–2. Mills, Mills and Trott, 'New light', pp. 34–6.
94. D. Mills and J. Mills, *A Potted History and Pedigree of the Sibthorps of Canwick Hall* (2002), p. 2.
95. LA, SIB 1/5. The exact identity of Mr Panton has not been found. The name was a fairly common one in Lincolnshire and there are several possible relations of Langham's in the county, including several farmers and shopkeepers with homes and businesses in and around the Boston area. However, it is most likely that Langham Panton was a close relation to Mr Robert Panton, a private resident of Lincoln, who lived in Bailgate East. *Kelly's Lincolnshire* (1919), p. 360.
96. *Burkes' Landed Gentry* (1937).
97. Mills and Mills, *Potted history*, p. 2.
98. N. Tranter, *Sport, Economy and Society in Britain, 1750–1914* (1998), p. 32.
99. This process of acculturation between landed and non-landed elites can be traced further back than the late nineteenth century. For other examples of this kind of urban-rural sociability and interaction in an earlier period, although in more industrialised areas and not necessarily based around shooting, see A. Vickery, *The Gentleman's Daughter: Women's Lives in Georgian England* (1998), K. J. Allison, *Hull Gent Seeks Country Residence, 1750–1850* (1981) and R. G. Wilson, *Gentleman Merchants: The Merchant Community in Leeds, 1700–1830* (1971).

Notes to Chapter 5: Wildfowling: its evolution as a sporting activity

1. Swan Upping – the ceremonial process of capturing and marking cygnets on their beaks, with the same mark as their parents to denote ownership. This custom is still undertaken by a number of medieval corporations including the Dyers and Vintners companies on part of the Thames.
2. P. Marson and G. Cullingham, 'The annual taking up and marking of Thames swans', *Windlesora* (1981), p. 72.
3. B. Vesey Fitzgerald, *British Game* (1946), p. 162.
4. In terms of plumage and body size taxonomists

now generally recognise 12 different races of Canada geese ranging from the cackling Brantac (*B. canadensis minima*), little larger than a Mallard, to the giant Canada (*B. canadensis maxima*). Most Canada geese in Britain are believed to be that of the slightly smaller nominate race (*B. canadensis canadensis*) although they are a racial mixture and some are closer in size to *maxima*, although whether this is the result of genetics or the abundance of food remains a matter of conjecture.

5. For a detailed contemporary account of the way wildfowl were captured in different parts of the world see H. A. Macpherson, *A History of Fowling* (1897).

6. For a review of the different ways in which ducks were netted, see M. Billett, *A History of English Country Sports* (1994), p. 117.

7. For wildfowling in the fens after drainage, including the use of decoys and the London trade in wildfowl, see H. C. Darby, *The Draining of the Fens* (2nd edn, 1956), pp. 153–62.

8. G. L. Atkinson-Willes (ed.), *Wildfowl in Great Britain* (1963), p. 16.

9. R. Payne-Gallwey, *The Book of Duck Decoys: their Construction, Management and History* (1886), preface.

10. J. Whittaker, *British Duck Decoys of Today* (1918), preface.

11. Vesey-Fitzgerald, *British Game*, p. 134.

12. Ibid., pp. 132–4.

13. J. Marchinton, *The History of Wildfowling* (1981), p. 138.

14. Atkinson-Willes (ed.), *Wildfowl in Great Britain*, p. 18.

15. 'Hang fire' was the delay between the flintlock striker igniting the powder in the flash pan on the side of the gun and the burning gunpowder travelling down into the barrel, setting off the main charge of powder.

16. For a detailed analysis of the different types of punt or swivel guns, see T. Walsingham and R. Payne-Gallwey, *Shooting: Moor and Marsh* (1886, repr. 1985), pp. 280–93.

17. Ibid., p. 276.

18. Marchington, *Wildfowling*, pp. 84–5.

19. Walsingham and Payne Gallwey, *Shooting: Moor and Marsh*, p. 162.

20. Ibid., p. 275.

21. Larger bore guns, such as the eight or four bore had substantially greater killing power, as they could fire more than twice the shot load of the normal 12 bore.

22. N. M. Sedgwick, 'Inland marsh shooting' in M. Sedgwick, P. Whitaker and J. Harrison, *The New Wildfowler in the 1970s* (1970), pp. 153–69.

23. R. Payne-Gallwey and Lord Walsingham, *Letters to Young Shooters* (2 vols, 1890), I, p. 72.

24. J. Wentworth Day, *Wild Wings and Some Footsteps* (1948), p. 127.

25. Sea-Pie, 'Last of the Professionals', in *The Shooting Times and Countryman*, 18 Aug. 1951, p. 501.

26. For a detailed analysis of catching plovers in specially constructed spring loaded nets which were manually operated, see A. James, *Memoirs of A Fen Tiger. The Story of Ernie James as told to Audrey James* (1986), pp. 88–90. Traditionally the plover catching season lasted from 1 September to 1 March. However, since 1947, plovers have been protected birds.

27. The Lapwing Act 1926 finally prohibited the collecting of their eggs during the spring laying season.

28. A wild goose chase originally denoted a type of horseracing invented in the sixteenth century where the lead horse went off in any direction and the succeeding horses had to follow at precise intervals, like geese following their leader in formation. Later the term evolved to mean 'a pursuit of anything as unlikely to be caught as a wild goose', any foolish, fruitless or hopeless quest. R. Hendrickson, *Encyclopedia of Word and Phrase Origins* (1997).

29. J. Wentworth Day, *Coastal Adventure* (1949), p. 123.

30. Hawker, who was an ardent and indefatigable shooting man, kept a record of every single day's shooting (mostly in Hampshire) from his sixteenth year until he died in 1853, 51 seasons in all. His diaries were edited (or rather mangled) for publication by R. Payne-Gallwey as *Diary of Col. Peter Hawker* (2 vols, 1893). For a discussion of the diaries see, Sedgwick *et al.*, *New Wildfowler*, pp. 319–21.

31. Marchington, *Wildfowling*, p. 81.

32. *ODNB*, 'Daniel, William Barker, 1754–1833'.

33. *Gentleman's Magazine*, first ser., 72 (1802), p. 621.

34. Walsingham and Payne-Gallwey, *Shooting: Moor and Marsh*, p. 314.

35. *Ibid.*, p. 72.

36. J. Wentworth Day, *King George V as a Sportsman* (1935), p. 25.

37. C. J. Cornish, 'A day with a Norfolk gunner', *Badminton Mag.* (1897), pp. 299–304.

38. J. Ruffer, *The Big Shots. Edwardian Shooting Parties* (1989 edn.), p. 45.

39. His co-author, Thomas the sixth Lord Walsingham, was widely acclaimed as the man most likely to rival Lord Ripon for the position of best shot of his time. His obsession with shooting brought the family financial ruin. Sadly most of the estate records and game books, amounting to fifteen tons, were destroyed in the Second World War when the roof of the old dairy in which they were being stored collapsed and rain saturated them. See B.P. Martin, *The Great Shoots, Britain's Premier Sporting Estates* (1987), p. 109.

40. For Millais, see above, pp. 22–3.

41. For a detailed account of his exploits see A. Chapman, *Retrospect. Reminiscences and Impressions of a Hunter-naturalist in Three Continents* (1928).

42. Wentworth Day, *Coastal Adventure*, p. 83.

43. Payne-Gallwey, *Moor and Marsh*, p. 200.

44. Wentworth Day *Coastal Adventure*, p. 84.

45. Marchinton, *Wildfowling*, p. 103.

46. *ODNB*, 'La Chapelle, Victor Octave Xavier Alfred de Morton de, Count de la Chapelle in the French nobility, 1863–1931, lawyer and wildfowler'.

47. Wentworth Day, *Coastal Adventure*, p. 231.

48. Daniel, *Rural Sports*.

49. Payne-Gallwey, *Moor and Marsh*, p. 162.

50. Vesey-Fitzgerald, *British Game*, p. 136.

51. Ibid., p. 136.

52. Ibid., p. 136.

53. Ibid., p. 136.

54. For a detailed review of the decline in goose number in the Wells area of Norfolk see letter from J.C.M. Nichols, author of *Birds of Marsh and Mere* (1926) and *Shooting by Moor, Field and Shore* (1929) in N. Sedgwick, *Wildfowling and Rough Shooting* (1950), p. 41.

55. A. Savory, *The Norfolk Fowler* (1953), p. 72.

56. Nichols in Sedgwick *et al.*, *New Wildfowler*, p. 41.

57. C. Willock, *The New ABC of Shooting* (1985), p. 231.

58. A.K.M. St Joseph, 'The Development of Upland Feeding by Branta Bernicla Bernicla in southeast England', in M. Smart (ed.), *Proc. First Tech. Meeting on Palaearctic Migratory Bird Management* (1979), pp. 1132–45.

59. The population of Brent geese has been declining since the 1920s. See RSPB data and website www.rspb.org.uk/birds/guide/b/brent-goose/index.asp.

60. The commonly accepted view that any member of the public has the right to shoot on the seaward side of sea walls was finally shown to be false by the case of *Beckett v. Lyons* (1967), Sedgwick *et. al.*, *New Wildfowler*, p. 31.

61. Sea-Pie, 'Last of the Professionals', p. 501.

62. There is material in the history of WAGBI in Sedgwick *et. al.*, *New Wildfowler*, pp. 21–6, and the Patrington Haven hut is illustrated in plate 21, opp. p. 160.

63. S. Duncan and G. Thorne, *The Complete Wildfowler* (1911); Sedgwick *et. al.*, *New Wildfowler*, p. 331.

64. 'Obituary, Mr James Wentworth Day', *The Times*, 6 Jan. 1983, p. 12.

65. Wentworth Day, *Wild Wings*.

66. Wentworth Day, writing in *The Field* in 1931 and later reprinted in his book *The Modern Fowler* (1934), p. 191 and in *King George as a Sportsman*, p. 154.

67. Ibid., pp. 25–7.

68. Buxton, *The King in his Country*, p. 52.

69. Ibid. p. 52.

70. For a detailed account of the early history of the development of Slimbridge see Scott's autobiography *The Eye of the Wind* (1961). Scott's contribution to wildfowl conservation in general, and the conservation of endangered species of ducks and geese in particular, gave him an outstanding international reputation in this area.

71. *Parliamentary Debates (Commons)*, fifth ser., 526, 9 Apr. 1954, cols 669–84.

72. *Ibid.*, col. 727.

73. For a detailed account of the provisions of the Act, see J.C. Gow, 'Wildfowling and the Law in England', and T.J.M. Watson, 'Wildfowling and the Law in Scotland', both in Sedgwick *et. al.*, *New Wildfowler*, pp. 17–40, 41–2.

74. The idea of the use of artificial decoys to attract ducks and geese within range on their feeding grounds was generally frowned upon by amateur wildfowlers, who considered this style of shooting unsporting. See Sedgwick, 'Inland Marsh Shooting' in Sedgwick *et. al.*, *New Wildfowler*, pp. 154–68.

75. *Parliamentary Debates (Commons)*, fifth ser., 526, 9 Apr. 1954, cols 686–90.

76. Atkinson-Willes (ed.), *Wildfowl in Great Britain*, p. xv.

77. *Parliamentary Debates (Commons)*, fifth ser., 748, 16 June 1967, col. 970.

78. J.A. Field, 'Punt-gunning' in Sedgwick *et al.*, *New Wildfowler*, p. 143.

79. *Parliamentary Debates (Commons)*, fifth ser., 748, 16 June 1967, col. 952.

80. *Ibid.* col. 953.
81. www.wildlife-landscaping.co.uk
82. *Parliamentary Debates (Commons)*, sixth ser., 10, 29 Oct. 1981, col. 1025.
83. See for example D. Tomlinson, 'Protect or Shoot', *Shooting Times and Country Magazine*, 2 July 1981.

84. *Wildlife and Countryside Act 1981.*
85. For a detailed account of the activities of her father-in-law, who was regarded as the last of the 'Fen Tigers', see James, *Memoirs of a Fen Tiger.*
86. Sedgwick, 'Inland Duck Shooting' in Sedgwick *et al., New Wildfowler*, pp. 153–68.
87. E. Bergie, *Fowler in the Wild* (1987), p. 7.

Notes to Chapter 6: 'A delightful sport with peculiar claims': the specificities of otter hunting, 1850–1939

1. Henry A. Bryden, *Nature and Sport in Britain* (1904), p. 250.
2. L. C. R. Cameron, *Minor Field Sports* (1921), p. 145.
3. George F. Underhill, *Hunting and Practical Hints for Hunting Men* (1897), p. 73.
4. L. C. R. Cameron, *Otters and Otter-Hunting* (1908), p. 35.
5. Bryden, *Nature and Sport*, p. 251.
6. The Carlisle Hunt Club was the first subscription pack. It had been set up in 1863. The Hawkstone OH became a Hunt Club in 1870.
7. The word peculiar has a number of meanings. It is defined in the Oxford English Dictionary as: 'Distinguished in nature, character, or attributes from others; unlike others, *sui generis*; special, remarkable; distinctive.' To an observer unfamiliar with a practice, peculiar attributes are unusual, eccentric or bizarre. An insider who likes a practice for its peculiarities on the other hand those same attributes are remarkable, unique, or special. Criticism from the former often leads to defensive responses from the latter. The term serves to identify differences and set apart. In this chapter each of these definitions are used.
8. Walter Cheesman and Mildred Cheesman, unpublished diaries of the Crowhurst Otter Hounds, 1904–06, East Sussex RO, AMS5788/3/1–3, 1904, p. 3.
9. 'Stonehenge' [J. H. Walsh], *British Rural Sports* (1856 edn), p. 169.
10. Cheesman and Cheesman, Crowhurst diaries, 1904, p. 3.
11. N. W. Apperley, *A Hunting Diary* (1926), p. 63. This diary records fox, hare, otter, marten-cat and foumart hunting in mid-Wales in the 1860s and 1870s.
12. Robert Colville, *Beagling and Otter-Hunting* (1940), p. 150.
13. Cheesman and Cheesman, Crowhurst diaries, 1904, p. 3.
14. 'Stonehenge', *British Rural Sports*, p. 169.

15. *The Field*, Mar. 1886, cited in James Lomax, *Diary of Otter Hunting, 1829–1871* (1892), p. 297.
16. 'MEHC', 'The decadence of otter hunting', *The Field*, 6 Oct. 1906, p. 585.
17. In G. Downing, *The Hounds of Spring. The History of the Eastern Counties Otter Hounds* (1988), p. 26, we are told that the honorary whip, Mr W. Nash, cycled 'about 5,000 miles' to reach the packs' 70 meets during the 1906 season.
18. W. H. Rogers, *Records of the Cheriton Otter Hounds* (1925), p. 146.
19. Geoffrey Pring, *Records of the Culmstock Otterhounds, c.1790–1957* (1958), p. 69.
20. S. W. Varndell, 'The decadence of otter hunting', *The Field*, 8 Nov. 1906, p. 744.
21. This is not to say that in certain circumstances hunt staff and hounds did not 'lie-out'. Otter hunts with large hunting territories continued this practice well after 1939.
22. 'MEHC', 'The decadence of otter hunting', p. 585.
23. Rogers, *Cheriton Otter Hounds*, p. 254.
24. 'MEHC', 'The decadence of otter hunting', p. 585.
25. Reverend G. C. Green, *Collections and Recollections of Natural History and Sport in the Life of a Country Vicar* (1886), p. 147.
26. 'Berserk', 'Otter hunting from London', *The Field*, 7 Aug. 1909, p. 253.
27. L. C. R. Cameron, *Rod, Pole and Perch. Angling and Otter-hunting Sketches* (1928), p. 102.
28. cited in Geoffrey R. Mott, *Records of the Dartmoor Otter Hounds, 1740–1940* (1970), p. 6.
29. Green, *Collections and Recollections*, p. 150.
30. Daphne Moore, *In Nimrod's Footsteps. Some Reflections of Hunting on a Shoe-string* (1974), p. 127.
31. J. Ivester Lloyd, *Come Hunting!* (1952), p. 227.
32. *Ibid.*, p. 221.
33. Aubyn Trevor-Battye, 'July: Otter hunting', in Oswald Crawfurd (ed.), *A Year of Sport and Natural History* (1895), pp. 158–63.
34. Arthur Heinemann, 'Otter hunting', in

F.G. Aflalo (ed.), *The Sports of the World* (1903), p.345.

35. Rawdon B. Lee, 'Otters and otter hunting', *The Field*, 31 Mar. 1906, p.486.

36. Douglas Macdonald Hastings, 'Hunting the otter', *Picture Post*, 22 July 1939, p.54.

37. D.J. Bell-Irving, *Tally-Ho. Fifty Years' Sporting Reminiscences* (1920), p.121.

38. Cameron, *Otters and otter-hunting*, pp.63–67.

39. L. Wardell, 'Otter-hunting', in F.E. Slaughter (ed.), *The Sportswoman's Library* (2 vols, 1898), II, pp.171–81.

40. Sir W. Beach Thomas, *Hunting England* (1936), p.46. Beach Thomas was equally doubtful about whether fox-hunting footpacks were really foxhunters: of the Lake District footpacks, he observed 'It is like another sport' (p.18).

41. Rawdon B. Lee, 'Otters and otter hunting', *The Field*, 1 Apr. 1899, p.444.

42. Respectively May 1908, Northern Counties Otter Hounds (Mr Arthur Jones, Master), Ellishaugh Bridge to Catcleugh Reservoir and Blakehopeburn, ending with a kill and October 1907, Carlisle Otter Hounds (Mr J.M. Graham, Master) on Eden below Carlisle. Drag hit off 8 a.m., otter put down 10 a.m., given up at 6.45 p.m. in the dark.

43. Apperley, *Hunting Diary*, p.67.

44. Plunger, 'Reminiscences of otter-hunting', *The Field*, 9 Aug. 1862, p.137.

45. Hastings, 'Hunting the otter', p.54.

46. Green, *Collections and Recollections*, p.144; Richard Clapham, *The Book of the Otter* (1922), p.109.

47. Rogers, *Cheriton Otter Hounds*, p.253.

48. Trevor-Battye, 'July: otter hunting', p.158.

49. Colville, *Beagling and Otter-Hunting*, p.149.

50. E.W.L. Davies, 'The otter and his ways', in Duke of Beaufort and Mowbray Morris (ed.), *Hunting* (1886), p.289.

51. Trevor-Battye, 'July: otter hunting', p.158.

52. Bryden, *Nature and Sport*, p.253.

53. Cameron, *Otters and Otter-Hunting*, p.12.

54. William Turnbull, *Recollections of an Otter Hunter* (1896), p.30.

55. Heinemann, 'Otter hunting', p.345.

56. Ibid., p.345.

57. Clapham, *Book of the Otter*, p.150.

58. Earl of Coventry and L.C.R. Cameron, *Otter hunting* (1938), p.53.

59. 'MEHC', 'Decadence of Otter Hunting', p.585.

60. Waddy Wadsworth, *Vive la Chasse. A Celebration of British Field Sports, Past and Present* (1989), p.159.

61. 'MEHC', 'Decadence of otter hunting', p.585.

62. Coventry and Cameron, *Otter Hunting*, p.53.

63. Green, *Collections and Recollections*, 'Chapter VIII, Otter-hunting in Devon – Uncertainty of the sport – Its charm – Good Days – The Erme, Avon, Plym, and Tavy', pp.143–4.

64. Cited in Downing, *Hounds of Spring*, p.33.

65. Ivester Lloyd, *Come Hunting!*, pp.222–3.

66. L.C.R. Cameron, *The Otter-hunters' Diary and Companion for 1910* (1910), p.11.

67. B.G.E. Webster, *The Culmstock Otter Hounds* (1953), p.6.

68. Geoffrey R. Mott, *Records of the Dartmoor Otter Hounds, 1740–1940* (1970), p.89.

69. Ibid., p.91.

70. Cited in Downing, *Hounds of Spring*, pp.30–3.

71. Ibid.

72. Cameron, *Otters and otter-hunting*, p.54.

73. Wadsworth, *Vive la Chasse*, p.128.

74. Cameron, *Otters and Otter Hunting*, p.118.

75. Cameron, *The Otter-hunters' Diary … 1910*, p.15.

76. The condition of the hunted water often affected the waiting process. A deep river with dense foliage on both banks and vegetation on the water, for instance, provided more cover for the quarry than a shallow stream with grassy verges and could therefore, in theory, take longer to 'gaze' an otter.

77. Admittedly, it is impossible to pinpoint exactly when, where, or by whom the stickle was first introduced as descriptions of otter hunting are rather exiguous prior to the 1830s. It could in fact have been a much older practice, which was not described until this period. Although not mentioned in earlier descriptions, it can be safely assumed that the otter hunters who initiated this practice regarded otter hunting as a group activity.

78. Cited in Downing, *Hounds of Spring*, p.17.

79. Cheesman and Cheesman, Crowhurst diaries, 1904, p.3.

80. As an aside, Lord Lilford was one of the eight founders of the British Ornithologists' Union, established in 1858. He went onto become its President from 1867 until his death in 1896. Aubyn Trevor-Battye, *Lord Lilford on Birds. Being a Collection of Informal and Unpublished Writings by the Late President of the British Ornithologists' Union, with contributed papers upon falconry and otter hunting, his favourite sports* (1903), p.110.

81. J.C. Bristow-Noble, 'Should otter be hunted?', *Madame*, 9 Sept. 1905, p.515.

82. M.A. Lulham, *The Wye Valley Otter Hounds, 1874–1935* (1935), p.34.

83. J. Lowerson, *Sport and the English Middle Classes, 1870–1914* (1993); D. Matless, *Landscape and Englishness* (1998).

84. Cameron, *Rod, Pole and Perch*, p. 95.

85. Ibid., p. 96; K. F. Barker, *The Young Entry. Fox-hunting, Beagling and Otter-hunting for Beginners* (1939), p. 114.

86. Moore, *In Nimrod's Footsteps*, p. 194.

Notes to Chapter 7: Science, sport and the otter, 1945–1978

1. This paper is derived from research funded by the Economic and Social Research Council on 'Cultures of Nature: the formation of environmental knowledges in England, 1945–70', award number R000238559.

2. On the latter issue see also David Matless, Paul Merchant and Charles Watkins, 'Animal Landscapes. Otters and Wildfowl in England, 1945–1970', *Trans. Institute of British Geographers* 30 (2005), pp. 191–205.

3. *Hereford Times* (hereafter *HT*, consulted in Hereford City Library), 21 Apr. 1945, p. 7.

4. *HT*, 11 Aug. 1945.

5. See for example *HT*, 24 May 1963.

6. Robert Colville, *Beagling and Otter Hunting* (1940), p. 182.

7. Ibid., p. 173.

8. Ena Adams *et al.*, *Deer, Hare and Otter Hunting* (1936).

9. Colville, *Beagling*, p. 178.

10. Adams *et al.*, *Deer, Hare and Otter Hunting*, p. 107.

11. Anthony Buxton, *Fisherman Naturalist* (1946), pp. 118–9.

12. 'Hickling Broad', BBC Radio Midland Home Service, 9 May 1947, 21.30–22.00, transcript in BBC Written Archives, Caversham Park, Reading.

13. Buxton, *Fisherman Naturalist*, pp. 119–20.

14. Colville, *Beagling*, p. 180.

15. Adams *et al.*, *Deer, Hare and Otter Hunting*, p. 109.

16. Colville, *Beagling*, p. 163.

17. Adams *et al.*, *Deer, Hare and Otter Hunting*, p. 116.

18. Thomas Davison, *Angler and Otter* (1950), p. 22.

19. Ibid., p. 23.

20. Alan Savory, *Norfolk Fowler* (1953), p. 118.

21. ibid, p. 116.

22. His books also include H. A. Gilbert and Arthur Brook, *Secrets of Bird Life* (1924); H. A. Gilbert and C. W. Walker, *Herefordshire Birds* (1941). Gilbert was a member of the International Wildfowl Committee, the Woolhope Club and a founder member of the Herefordshire Ornithological Club in 1951.

23. 'Protection for Otters', *HT*, 12 May 1950.

24. 'The Hooked Otter: Angler's Reply', *HT*, 19 May 1950.

25. Colville, *Beagling*, pp. 198–9.

26. M. C. C. Chapman, 'The 1949 Committee on Cruelty to Wild Animals', in Patrick Moore (ed.), *Against Hunting* (1965), p. 139.

27. Ibid., p. 140.

28. Quoted in Marie Stephens, *The Otter* (1957), p. 7.

29. TNA, FT1/39, Maurice to Diver, 7 July 1949.

30. Ibid., Moncrieff to Maurice, 4 July 1949.

31. Ibid., Diver to Maurice, 14 July 1949.

32. Ibid., cutting of letter to editor of *Manchester Guardian*, 5 Dec. 1950.

33. Ibid., J. C. Sharp to Editor of the *Cornish Post*, 28 July 1951.

34. Ibid., extract from *Hansard*, 30 July 1951.

35. Ibid., J. C. Grant to Diver, 7 Aug. 1951.

36. Ibid., Diver to Grant, 5 Nov. 1951.

37. Stephens, *Otter Report*, p. 74.

38. Ibid., p. 74.

39. Ibid., p. 8.

40. Richard Fitter, 'The Countryside', BBC Radio Midlands Home Service, 23 Aug. 1955, transcript in BBC Written Archives, p. 11.

41. Stephens, *Otter Report*, p. 19.

42. Ibid., p. 37.

43. Ibid., p. 19.

44. Ibid., p. 20.

45. Ibid., p. 25.

46. Ibid., p. 29.

47. Ibid., pp. 29–32.

48. Fitter, 'Countryside', pp. 11–12.

49. Stephens, *Otter Report*, p. 62.

50. Bertram Lloyd, *A Vile Sport: Facts about Otter-hunting* (1956), back cover.

51. Ibid., p. 1.

52. TNA, FT1/39, 'Note', 28 June 1955.

53. Ibid., Hume to Nicholson 13 Mar. 1958.

54. Ibid., Nicholson to Hume 17 Mar. 1958.

55. See for example Chris Philo and Chris Wilbert (eds), *Animal Spaces, Beastly Places* (2000); Michel Callon, 'Some elements of a sociology of translation: the domestication of the scallops and the fishermen of St Brieuc Bay', in John Law (ed.) *Power, Action and Belief. A New Sociology of Knowledge* (1986).

56. *ODNB*, 'Williamson, Henry William (1895–1977)'.

57. Henry Williamson, *Tarka the Otter: His Joyful*

Water-life and Death in the Country of the Two Rivers (1963), p. 7.

58. id., *The Linhay on the Downs* (1938), p. 187. It is likely that the reviewer in question was Frances Pitt.

59. These were not the only books about otters. In Phyllis Kelway's *The Otter Book* (1944, repr. 1945 and 1946), 'Juggles, the otter, is our heroine and how she grows from mischievous babyhood into a lovable young woman is charmingly told' (dustjacket text).

60. Gail Davies, 'Science, observation and entertainment: competing visions of postwar British natural history television, 1946–1967', *Ecumene* 7 (2000), pp. 432–60.

61. *ODNB*, 'Maxwell, Gavin (1914–1969)'.

62. E. G. Neal, *Topsy and Turvy: My Two Otters* (1963), p. 3.

63. Ibid., p. 6.

64. Gavin Maxwell, *Ring of Bright Water* (1963), p. 131.

65. Ibid., p. 104.

66. Philip Wayre, *The River People* (1977), pp. 41–2.

67. Maxwell, *Ring of Bright Water*, p. 128.

68. Neal, *Topsy and Turvy*, p. 40.

69. Gavin Maxwell, *The Rocks Remain* (1963), p. 142.

70. Neal, *Topsy and Turvy*, p. 62–6.

71. Maxwell, *The Rocks Remain*, p. 23.

72. Ibid., p. 90.

73. Philip Wayre, *The Wind in the Reeds* (1965). See also Wayre's *The River People* (1976).

74. Wayre, *The Wind in the Reeds*, p. 163.

75. Dr Charles Walker was committee member, 1954–59, vice-president, 1961–68 and President, 1969–70 of the Herefordshire Ornithological Club, Chairman of the Herefordshire and Radnorshire Nature Trust, 1963–70, committee member of the Woolhope Naturalists Field Club, 1945–46, 1948–49, 1953–58 and its 'Ornithology' Section Editor, 1945–70. His diaries for 1951–74 are held in the Herefordshire and Radnorshire Nature Trust archive. Walker also kept notebooks from 1968–70 and 1974–76 recording reports of local residents on otter populations and their habits, and the effects of hunting, also held in the HRNT archive. We are grateful to Dr Anthea Brian for giving us access to a recorded interview with Walker.

76. HRNT, Walker notebook, '1959–1964'.

77. TNA, FT1/39, 'Note for the File. Otters' by W. D. Park, 26 July 1967.

78. Ibid., 'Note', M. W. Holdgate to J. F. D. Frazer, 19 Sept. 1968.

79. Ibid., Bob Boote to C. J. Gibbs, 3 Aug. 1967.

80. Ibid., Fuller to J. D. Frazer, 4 Sept. 1968.

81. Ibid., Anon to Fuller, 5 Sept. 1968.

82. Ibid., 'Draft interim report on Otter Survey', Jan. 1969, p. 4.

83. Ibid., 'Draft interim report ' p. 1–2.

84. Ibid., 'Draft interim report, Appendix 1: Summaries of Areas'.

85. Ibid., 'Draft interim report', p. 2.

86. Ibid., 'Draft interim report', p. 4.

87. Ibid., 'Draft interim report', Appendix 1: Summaries of Areas'.

88. Ibid., 'Draft interim report', p. 4.

89. Ibid., 'Draft interim report', p. 5.

90. Ibid., 'The British Field Sports Society's Conclusions on the Otter Survey', 27 Feb. 1969.

91. Charles Coles (ed.), *The Complete Book of Game Conservation* (1971); Matless, Merchant and Watkins, 'Animal Landscapes'.

92. 'MP campaigns to save otters from extinction', *Guardian*, 14 May 1969 (clipping in TNA, FT1/39).

93. 'One MP could kill the Bill to save otters', *Morning Star*, 14 May 1969 (clipping in TNA, FT1/39).

94. TNA, FT1/39, 'Natural Environment Research Council. The Nature Conservancy. Protection of Otters Bill, Office Note', 19 June 1969.

95. Ibid., 'Parliamentary note'.

96. Ibid., W. D. Park, 'Otters and Hares', 27 July 1969.

97. 'Otter-Hunters' bid to counter blood sports criticisms', *HT*, 9 May 1969, p. 17 on which the following account is based.

98. 'Otter Hunting', *HT*, 30 May 1969, p. 12.

99. Ibid.

100. 'Otter hunting is condemned by local vet', *HT*, 27 June 1969, p. 1.

101. 'Herefordshire Nature Trust Notes: Badger and Otter', *HT*, 6 June 1969, p. 14.

102. 'Otter Hunting' *HT*, 18 July 1969, p. 14.

103. HRNT archive, Walker notebook on 'otters'.

104. H. Greenwood, *The history of the Hawkstone Otter Hounds* (1991).

105. HRNT, Walker notebook on 'otters', pp. 33–4.

106. Ibid., pp. 33–4.

107. P. R. F. Chanin and D. J. Jeffries, 'The decline of the otter *Lutra lutra* L. in Britain: an analysis of hunting records and discussion of causes', *Biological J. Linnean Society* 10 (1978), pp. 305–28.

108. R. Strachan and D. J. Jefferies *Otter Survey of England, 1991–94* (1996), p. 118.

109. Ibid., p. 120.

110. Ibid., p. 10.

Notes to Chapter 8: The development of salmon angling in the nineteenth century

1. W. Radcliffe, *Fishing from the Earliest Times* (1921), C. Voss-Bark, *A History of Fly-fishing* (1992).
2. Dame Juliana Berners (attrib.) *The Treatise of Fishing with an Angle* (1496), pr. in trans. in J. McDonald, *The Origins of Angling and a New Printing of* The treatise of fishing with an angle (1963), p. 40.
3. Ibid., p. 39.
4. T. Barker, *Barker's Delight: or, The Art of Angling* (1659), p. 25.
5. Col. R. Venables, *The Experienced Angler, or Angling Omproved, being a general discourse of angling; imparting many of the aptest wayes and choicest experiments for the taking of most sorts of fish in pond or river* (1662). R. Franck, *Northern Memoirs* (1651).
6. A. Herd, *The Fly: Two Thousand Years of Fly Fishing* (2003), pp. 108–10.
7. G. C. Bainbridge, *The Fly Fisher's Guide* (1816), p. 36.
8. Herd, *Fly*, p. 168.
9. Barker, *Barker's Delight*, p. 25.
10. Venables, *Experienced Angler*, p. 39.
11. Quoted in Herd, *Fly*, p. 114.
12. Richard and Charles Bowlker, *The Art of Angling* (1774 edn), first published in Worcester, 1747. See also S. Taylor, *Angling in all its Branches* (1800).
13. T. Williamson, *The Complete Angler's Vade-mecum* (1808).
14. W. Bilton, *The Angler in Ireland: or an Englishman's Ramble through Connaught and Munster during the Summer of 1833* (2 vols, 1834), I, p. 36.
15. Herd, *Fly*, p. 155.
16. T. Stoddart, *The Angler's Companion to the Rivers and Lochs of Scotland* (1853), p. 168.
17. Voss-Bark, *History of Fly fishing*, p. 70.
18. G. M. Kelson, *The Salmon Fly* (1895).
19. Ibid., p. 72.
20. Herd, *Fly*, p. 217.
21. Ibid., p. 229.
22. Sir H. Maxwell, *Salmon and Sea Trout* (1898), p. 33.
23. H. Cholmondeley-Pennell, *Fishing: Salmon and Trout* (1895), pp. 56–70; Herd, *Fly*, p. 252.
24. *Parliamentary Debates (Commons)*, third ser., 38, 18 June 1837, col. 1544, 'Petition from landowners on the River Suir'; ibid., 42, 9 May 1838, col. 1074, 'Salmon fisheries Ireland'. M. Silverwood, 'From fisher to poacher: public right and private property in the salmon fisheries of the river Nore in the nineteenth century', in M. Silverwood and P. Gulliver (eds), *Approaching the Past. Historical Anthropology Through Irish Case Studies* (1992), pp. 99–141.
25. P. Bartrip, 'Food for the body and food for the mind. The regulation of freshwater fisheries in the 1870s', *Victorian Stud.* 28 (1984–5), pp. 285–304.
26. Ffennell, Jardin and Rickards all have biographies in *ODNB*, where Jardine is described as 'a keen sportsman, hunting with the Stirling and Linlithgow foxhounds, shooting deer and birds and fishing the Annan, which flowed through the grounds of Jardine Hall.' *ODNB* makes no comment on Rickard's sporting interests and he lacks an obituary in *The Times*.
27. BPP, 1861, XXIII, *Royal Commission into the Salmon Fisheries, Minutes of Evidence*, p. 265; A. Grimble, *The Salmon Rivers of Scotland* (1913), p. 2; J. W. Kempster, *Our rivers* (1948), p. 116.
28. A. Netboy, *Salmon: The World's Most Harassed Fish* (1980), pp. 71–2.
29. D. Sutherland, *The Salmon Book* (1982), p. 16.
30. R. M. Macleod, 'Government and resource conservation: The Salmon Acts Administration, 1860–1886', *J. British Studies* 7 (1968), p. 115.
31. *RC Salmon Fisheries, Minutes of Evidence*, p. 420.
32. Sutherland, *Salmon Book*, p. 16.
33. *RC Salmon Fisheries, Minutes of Evidence*, p. 263.
34. Ibid., pp. 15 (Kings Garth, Cumberland); 496 (Wrey, Devon); 418 (Test, Hants).
35. D. Mills, *Ecology and Management of Atlantic Salmon* (1989).
36. B. W. Clapp, *The Environmental History of Britain Since the Industrial Revolution* (1994), pp. 72–80; Netboy, *Salmon*, pp. 61–105; T. Baines, *Yorkshire Past and Present* (two vols, 1871), 0, p. 217.
37. *RC Salmon Fisheries, Minutes of Evidence*, pp. 162–8.
38. Ibid., p. 388.
39. Baines, *Yorkshire*, pp. 211–68; *RC Salmon Fisheries, Minutes of Evidence*, p. 251.
40. Ibid., p. 224 (Lt. Col. C. J. Tottenham, Dee); p. 245 (E. Peplow, fisherman, Severn).
41. Ibid., p. 9.
42. Ibid., p. 60.
43. Ibid., p. 35.
44. Macleod, 'Government and resource conservation'.
45. Cumbria RO, Carlisle, DWM 419, Derwent Conservancy Board, Minute Book, 1880–1891; DWM 463, Derwent Conservancy Board, assorted papers, list of riparian owners; 1881 Census *passim*; John Bateman, *The Great Landowners of Great Britain and Ireland* (1883) end, repr. 1971).

46. Grimble, *Salmon Fisheries of Scotland*, p. 163.

47. BPP, 1872, XVI, *Eleventh Annual Report of the Inspectors of Salmon Fisheries, England and Wales, 1871*, p. 45.

48. TNA, MAF 41/847: Derwent Conservancy Board Licence Duties, 1891–1947; Cumbria RO, Carlisle, DWM 372–463: Minute Book of the Derwent Conservancy Board, 1880–1908: Cash Book of the Derwent Conservancy Board, 1888–93.

49. D. J. V. Jones, 'The Second Rebecca Riots; a study of poaching on the Upper Wye', *Llafur* 2 (1976), p. 43; BPP, 1881, XXIII, *Report by Inspector of Fisheries on Changes of Law Required to Remove Grievances in Radnorshire, as regards Salmon Acts*, p. 6.

50. J. M. Denwood, *Cumbrian Nights* (1932), p. 52.

51. BPP, 1873, XIII, *Report of the Select Committee on the Game Laws, Minutes of Evidence*, p. 22.

52. S. Mills, 'Salmon: demise of the landlord's fish', *New Scientist*, 11 Feb. 1982; M. Shoard, *This Land is Our Land. The Struggle for Britain's Countryside* (1987), p. 298; C. C. Tranch, *The Poacher and the Squire. A History of Poaching and Game Preservation in England* (1967), p. 220; Denwood, *Cumbian Nights*.

53. 'Foul hooking' is a term which relates to the hooking of a fish in any part of the body other than the mouth. The operation of a snatch involved throwing the hook end, sometimes with a weight, across the body of salmon and then retrieving line quickly to impale the hooks in the flesh of the fish. The salmon would then be dragged in by hand. Since they could be easily hidden in the pocket, snatches became much more popular than spears with poachers after 1861.

54. J. Mackenzie, *The Empire of Nature. Hunting, conservation and British imperialism* (1988), pp. 296–310; W. Beinart, 'Empire, hunting and ecological change in Southern and Central Africa', *Past and Present* 128 (1990), pp. 162–86.

55. Mackenzie, *Empire of Nature*, pp. 298–304.

56. R. Blake, *The Solway Firth* (1966), p. 147.

57. W. Scott, *Red Gauntlet* (1894).

58. Jones, 'Second Rebecca Riots', p. 44; *Report on Changes of Law Required to Remove Grievances in Radnorshire*, p. 6.

59. Netboy, *Salmon*, p. 83; T. T. Stoddart, *The Art of Angling, as Practised in Scotland* (1836), p. 89.

60. W. Scott, *Guy Mannering* (1892).

61. Stoddart, *Art of Angling*, p. 89.

62. Ibid., pp. 95–6.

63. W. Scrope, *Day and Nights of Salmon Fishing on the Tweed* (1843), p. 233.

64. T. T. Stoddart, The angler's companion to the rivers and lochs of Scotland (1853), quoted in Sutherland, *Salmon Book*, p. 99.

65. Ibid., p. 21.

66. Kelson, *Salmon Fly*; Cholmondeley-Pennell, *Fishing: salmon and trout*; F. Francis, *A Book on Angling* (1867).

67. Sutherland, *Salmon Book*, p. 21.

68. Keith Thomas, *Man and the Natural World. Changing Attitudes in England, 1500–1800* (1983), p. 243.

69. Herd, *Fly*, p. 247.

Notes to Chapter 9: Starting a Hare: exploring the history of coursing since the mid-nineteenth century

1. H. Cunningham, *Leisure in the Industrial Revolution, c.1780–c.1880* (1980), although one of the key texts in the history of leisure and sport, makes very little of field sports. In this, he is followed by other writers such as N. Tranter, *Sport, Economy and Society in Britain 1750–1914* (1998), and T. Collins and W. Vamplew, *Mud, Sweat and Beers* (2002), who only refer in passing to coursing and even then with only moderate accuracy. Other authors, for example, J. Burnett, *Riot, Revelry and Rout: Sport in Lowland Scotland before 1860* (2000) deliberately exclude field sports from consideration.

2. See D. Hart-Davies, *When the Countryside Went to Town* (1997).

3. *Bailey's Hunting Directory* (hereafter *BHD*) was first published in 1897 by Vinton and Co. in London and is now issued annually by J. A. Allen & Co. As explained in the 1966–67 edition, p. 322, details of packs of all types of hounds have been published for around a hundred years.

4. There are a number of individual studies of hunting with beagles, such as J. O. Paget, *The Art of Beagling* (1931), D. H. Appleton, *The Beagle Handbook* (1959) and J. C. J. Hobson, *Beagling* (1987). Some volumes of the *Victoria History of the Counties of England* (*VCH*) also contain articles on beagling and hunting with harriers, for example, *VCH Dorset*, II, p. 315; *VCH Hampshire*, II, pp. 336–43. The entries in *BHD* also identify the area in which the packs operated and articles describing meets can be found in local newspapers.

5. *The Coursing Calendar* (hereafter the *Calendar*) was first published in 1857 with a review of the

1856–57 coursing season and information about the 1857–58 season, while *The Greyhound Stud Book* (hereafter *Stud Book*) first appeared in 1882. The Secretary of the National Coursing Club is also Keeper of the *Stud Book*. Both *Calendar* and *Stud Book* are published by the National Coursing Club in Newmarket. Charles Blanning is the current Keeper.

6. For example, H. Cox and Hon. G. Lascelles, *Coursing and Falconry* (1892, repr. 1986), and H. A. Macpherson *et al*, *The Hare* (1896, repr. 1986).

7. L. Hall, *Fifty-Six Waterloo Cups* (1922) and H. Edwardes Clark, *The Waterloo Cup, 1922–1977* (1978).

8. C. Blanning and Sir M. Prescott, *The Waterloo Cup: The First 150 Years* (1987).

9. Out of 40 English counties, 38 are dealt with in the *VCH* series. Of these, 21 contain articles on coursing, of which eight are less than a page in length and only five exceed two pages.

10. A number of articles, for example in the Kent and Hampshire volumes, were written by Frank Bonnet who wrote coursing articles under the name 'East Sussex', while the Rev. Pierce A. Butler, who wrote as 'Purbeck Pilgrim' wrote about hare hunting with beagles and harriers in the Dorset volume.

11. The Northumberland County History Committee (eds), *A History of Northumberland* (15 vols, 1905–40) does not include a study of sports of any kind in its volumes.

12. Sir J. Paskin in *VCH Wiltshire*, IV, pp. 382–3; Rev. D. T. W. Price in *VCH Shropshire*, II, pp. 183–5.

13. See A. Croxton Smith (ed.), *Hounds and Dogs* (1948), pp. 196–264, and *Coursing News. The Coursing Supporters' Newsletter* 1 (NCC, Newmarket 2003) for details of the various types of hounds and their present activities in England.

14. See Stonehenge [J. H. Walsh], *The Dog in Health and Disease* (1887), pp. 309–10; A. Rollins, *All About the Greyhound* (1982), pp. 11–13; C. Blanning, 'The origins of the breed', in J. Barnes (ed.), *The Complete Book of Greyhounds* (1994), pp. 7–9.

15. A. Birley, *Garrison Life at Vindolanda* (2002), pp. 147–51. There are a number of writing tablets which have been recovered during the Vindolanda excavations in Northumberland which contain information about dogs and hunting equipment used by the garrison of the fort. I am grateful to Peter Atkinson, MP, for drawing my attention to this reference.

16. R. Almond, *Medieval Hunting* (2003), chs 2 and 3. Information in these two paragraphs is drawn from this study. See also C. M. Woolgar, *The Great Household in Late Medieval England* (1999) for further information about the place of hunting in the households of the aristocracy and landed elite.

17. The Laws of the Leash attributed to the Duke of Norfolk are printed in full with comments in D. Brown, 'Historical sketch of Coursing', in D. Brown (ed.), *Stud Book*, III, (1884), pp. xxv–lix.

18. See F. G. Emmison, *Tudor Food and Pastimes* (1964), pp. 84–7 and A. L. Rowse, *The Elizabethan Renaissance: The Life of the Society* (1971), pp. 184–6.

19. Brown, *Stud Book*, III, follows exactly this pattern.

20. W. Johnson, 'Coursing in Lincolnshire in the seventeenth century', in *Local Historian*, 41 (Lindsey Local History Society, 1944), pp. 14–17.

21. P. B. Munsche, *Gentlemen and Poachers. The English Game Laws, 1671–1831* (1981), p. 5.

22. Several writers have given information about the Swaffham Cub; the account given by Brown, *Stud Book*, III, pp. xxxv–vi has been used here.

23. Initially there was only one meeting each year at which a sixteen-dog course was run for a £50 cup, but subsequently the programme was enlarged.

24. Brown states that courses of four miles were common. A number of pictorial sources, *VCH Middlesex*, II, p. 263, *VCH Hertfordshire*, I, p. 369 and B. Vesey-Fitzgerald, *British Game* (1946), p. 177, all show that the coursers were mounted and pursued the greyhounds and hares in this manner. Brown, *Stud Book*, III, p. xxxv also makes the point that these early clubs used a hare finder rather than beaters to locate the hare for the hounds to course.

25. The ridden form of coursing continued alongside the modern form of coursing for some years. Gradually the ridden form died out although it may have persisted until the 1890s in the form used by the Cliffe and Hundred of Hoo Club. See Cox, *Coursing and Falconry*, pp. 182–9.

26. Thomas Goodlake, *The Courser's Manual or Stud Book* (1828). Goodlake produced a further volume, *Continuation of the Courser's Manual or Stud Book* in 1833; Brown, *Stud Book*, III, p. xl.

27. Thomas Thacker, *The Courser's Companion; or a Treatise on the Laws of the Leash* (1829).

28. *The Courser's Companion, Second Edition, revised and enlarged: to which is added The Breeder's Guide on Breeding in all it branches; in two volumes* (1834).

29. 1 and 2 William IV, ch. 32. See Munsche, *Gentlemen and Poachers*, Appendix, for a detailed analysis of the full changes introduced by this piece of legislation.

30. Although referred to by, for example, C. Richardson in 'Coursing the Hare' in H. A. Macpherson *et al.*, *The Hare* (1896, repr. 1986), pp. 111–35, little research has been carried out on this aspect of coursing. Information about the aspects of estate management referred to in this paragraph are taken from Durham University Library, Dept. of Special Collections, Baker Baker Papers, Correspondence of Mrs Isabella Baker Baker, 1880–91.

31. D. B. Plummer, *The Complete Lurcher: A Manual* (1979, 1982 impression), pp. 11–15.

32. Some writers have believed that young hares were born all the year round, that they were born one at a time, that the doe had a series of wombs in which foetuses of various ages could be carried and that some/all hares were hermaphrodites. For a summary of these and other fanciful beliefs, see G. Ewart Evans and D. Thomson, *The Leaping Hare* (1972), pp. 18–32.

33. T. Thorne and C. Blanning, *A Coursing Year* (1987), p. 6.

34. Information in this paragraph is taken from T. Thacker, *The Courser's Companion*, second edition.

35. T. Thacker, *The Courser's Annual Remembrancer and Stud Book* (1840–49) after which R. A. Welsh, *Thacker's Annual Remembrancer and Stud Book* (1850–56).

36. D. Brown, 'National Coursing Club Portraiture', in *The Greyhound Stud Book*, XI (1892), pp. xxiii–xlvi. Marjoribanks was the first President of the Club and Sefton the second; Brown, *Stud Book*, III, p. lv.

37. For full details of the Waterloo Cup and its history, see Hall, *Fifty-six Waterloo Cups*, Clark, *Waterloo Cup* and Blannings and Prescott, *Waterloo Cup.*

38. Brown, *Stud Book*, III, p. liv.

39. Brown, *Stud Book*, III, p. lv.

40. For the growth in participation in sport in the nineteenth century, see Tranter, *Sport, Economy and Society in Britain*, pp. 13–31.

41. For the growth of subscription packs and the growth in foxhunting, M. Billett, *A History of English Country Sports* (1994), 152–4, and R. Holt, *Sport and the British* (1989, 1992 edn), pp. 50–4.

42. A. Metcalfe, 'Organised sport in the mining communities of south Northumberland, 1800–99', in *Victorian Stud.* 25 (1982), pp. 469–95 and T. Beestall, 'Landlords and Tenants', in G. E. Mingay (ed.), *The Victorian Countryside* (2 vols, 1981), II, p. 437.

43. Stonehenge, in his *Manual of British Rural Sports* (see n. 44 below) itemises the costs of rearing and training greyhounds and concludes that 'huge kennels cost no inconsiderable sum'. However, between the third edition of the book in 1857 and the fifteenth of 1882, the calculated cost of rearing a greyhound puppy fell from £9 4s. to £9. Set against the costs of training a race horse, such sums were well within the means of many middle class coursing enthusiasts. Adult greyhounds were also bought and sold. For example, *The Field*, 8 Mar. 1890, p. 22, lists a sale of 85 greyhounds at prices from one and a half guineas to 51 guineas. The majority cost less than 20 guineas each. Other costs are drawn from an unpublished kennel book of the 1850s and 1860s in the possession of Mr Gerry Wood of Shildon, Co. Durham to whom I am most grateful for sight of this volume.

44. See 'Stonehenge' [J. H. Walsh], *The Greyhound* (first edn, 1853); *Manual of British Rural Sports* (first edn, 1853) and *The Dog in Health and Disease* (first edn, 1859). All three books went through numerous editions before Walsh died and they continued to be revised and published posthumously. In addition, Walsh edited the *Coursing Calendar and Review* which was subsequently continued by *The Field* until 1918.

45. Nationally, for example, *The Field* began publication in 1858 and carried regular reports of most coursing meetings conducted under the auspices of the National Coursing Club. At a regional level, reports of local and major coursing events were to be found in newspapers such as the *Newcastle Courant*. Local papers, such as the *Hexham Courant*, often had a more restricted readership and reported only those coursing events which took place in the area where the readers lived.

46. Although it is not possible to state with any accuracy the number of hares that land should carry in order to make coursing worthwhile, it is possible to estimate with some degree of reliability the area of land required to permit a full coursing meeting to be conducted. Examination of maps of grounds on which coursing has been conducted in recent times would suggest that an area of ground of 1,000 to 3,000 acres would be appropriate.

47. The Tarnities estate near Cockermouth in Cumberland is a case in point. From 1854 to 1873 it was the centre of excellent coursing, but in 1873 the estate was sold and the new owner withdrew permission to course. Consequently, coursing practically ceased in the Cockermouth area. *VCH Cumberland*, II, p. 470.

48. T. G. Leadbetter, *The Biggar Coursing Club* (privately printed, Biggar, 1922), pp. 42–5. I am grateful to Mr Julian Burchill for the opportunity to examine one of the surviving copies of the 40 that were printed.

49. 'Three True Unionists', *The Stud Book of the Bothal Club* (Morpeth 1887).

50. O. Stable and R. M. Stuttard, *A Review of Coursing* (1971, 1973 edn), p. 12, para. 42. Nomination is the right to name a greyhound to take part in a particular coursing contest. The right was given by clubs to their most experienced members in order that the best dogs would take part in contests.

51. Three directories have been used: Kelly's *Directory of Northumberland* (1873); T. F. Bulmer (ed.), *History, Topography and Directory of Northumberland* (1886) and Kelly's *Directory of Northumberland and Durham* (1910). The estate papers are in Northumberland RO, Sample of Matfen papers, ZSA 8, Bothal Estate Rentals, 1883–94.

52. I am continuing to conduct research into the problem of club membership at Bothal and elsewhere.

53. Rev. D. T. W. Price in *VCH Shropshire*, II, pp. 184–5.

54. In 1878 it is alleged that over 100,000 people saw a bitch, Coomassie, win the Waterloo Cup for the second time. This triumph followed the three victories of the little Irish dog, Master McGrath between 1868 and 1871 who was later presented to Queen Victoria. Coursers by 1880 had every right to feel proud of their sport and that it was going from strength to strength.

55. The most succinct and helpful account of 'Park coursing' is to be found in Blanning and Prescott, *Waterloo Cup*, pp. 17–23 on which this section of the paper is based.

56. The last park course closed in 1914, but the sport survives in Ireland.

57. The Ground Game (Hares and Rabbits) Act, 43 and 44 Victoria ch. 47. For an interesting discussion of the Act and the way in which it applied in one particular county, see J. H. Porter, 'Tenant Right: Devonshire and the 1880 Ground Game Act', in *AgHR* 34 (1986), pp. 188–97.

58. Brown, *Stud Book*, III, p. lvi. Cox and Lascelles, *Coursing and Falconry* and Macpherson *et al*, *The Hare* also contain a number of critical references to the Act.

59. W. H. Wakefield of Sedgwick quoted in the *Northern Farmer*, 5 Mar. 1870, p. 3.

60. *VCH Cumberland*, II, p. 470 gives details of the clubs that had disappeared in the county as a result of the Ground Game Act.

61. *The Coursing Calendar – Spring Season* (1921), p. 5.

62. Blanning and Prescott, *Waterloo Cup* (1987), pp. 34–49.

63. Essex, Norfolk and Shropshire saw the greatest revival in terms of numbers of clubs between 1921 and 1931.

64. *The Coursing Calendar – Spring Season* (1907), p. 5.

65. *The Coursing Calendar – Official Calendar for Season 1921–22* (1921), p. viii.

66. Information about Major Renwick is taken from Burke's *Peerage, Baronetage and Knightage* (73rd edn, 1939), p. 2065, Renwick of Newminster Abbey; *The Times*, 11 Sept. 1956, Obituary of Major G. A. Renwick; conversations with Mr Guy Renwick (grandson) on 17 and 21 May 2003 and a recorded interview with Mr Cecil Corbett (husband of the Major's housekeeper – deceased) of Otterburn in Sept. 2004. I am grateful to both Mr Renwick and Mr Corbett for the information supplied. The Renwick family may have purchased a landed estate (Newminster Abbey) and been given a baronetcy but their wealth came from shipping and, later, road haulage, in which the Major was heavily involved. Mr Corbett recollected that business friends of the Major as well as landed families, local farmers and other country folk attended Club meetings.

67. Information provided by the family indicates that when the Major purchased Holystone Grange, the estate was only about a thousand acres in size. Subsequent purchases trebled or quadrupled this figure. An estate saw mill was built in Holystone village and a purpose-built greyhound kennels constructed on the same site.

68. National Coursing Club, *Fixtures List, 2003–2004* (2003).

69. For a broad ranging analysis of the changes in land ownership, see D. Cannadine, *The Decline and Fall of the British Aristocracy* (1990), pp. 88–138.

70. Holt, *Sport and the British*, p. 186.

71. Unless otherwise stated, information for this section of the paper is drawn from H. Edwards Clarke, *The Greyhound* (sixth edn, 1978), pp. 51–

66; D. Bennett, *The Sporting Life Guide to Greyhound Racing and Betting* (new edn, 1992), pp. 9–66 and M. Tanner, *The Legend of Mick the Miller* (2003). Apparently, the first efforts involved dragging a dummy hare across a field in a straight line and permitting the greyhounds to chase it. The sport lacked much in the way of interest and attracted few supporters!

72. *The Times*, 9 Oct. 1926, p. 14, gives a very clear summary of the season and states that at one meeting the crowd exceeded 17,000. The article also refers to the popularity of the sport, mentioning that about 250 bookmakers attended the meetings and also that the sport drew large numbers of female spectators who found it exciting but without cruelty and bloodshed. The correspondent also remarked that up to 300 motor cars had been parked outside some meetings – thus suggesting the affluence of some of the spectators.

73. *The Times*, 13 Apr. 1927, p. 5 reported disputes between the Liverpool Greyhound Club Limited and also the Leeds Greyhound Racing Association Limited and the proprietors of the Manchester track, the Greyhound Racing Association Limited.

74. This continues to be the practice today. All greyhounds are entered in the Stud Book whether destined for coursing or racing.

75. This information was supplied to me personally by Sir Mark Prescott.

76. See S. Lynam, *Humanity Dick Martin, 'King of Connemara', 1754–1834* (1975, 1989 edn).

77. For a detailed account of these developments, see H. Kean, *Animal Rights* (1998) chs 2–5 and E. S. Turner, *All Heaven in a Rage* (1964).

78. Ibid., pp. 235–6. The League was founded in 1891 and remained active until 1919. Its activities were not solely related to animal welfare but encompassed a number of other, human, issues as well.

79. Kean, *Animal Rights*, pp. 184–5.

80. See *The Times*, 3 June 1921, p. 7, and 24 Feb. 1925, p. 9, for examples of the aftermath of this activity.

81. *The Times*, 11 Aug. 1924, p. 16. Foot (1880–1960) was MP for Bodmin between 1922–24 and 1929–35. A life-long Methodist and staunch opponent of field sports, Foot was the father of the Michael Foot, Labour leader 1980–83, an equally prominent anti-field sports campaigner.

82. *The Times*, 2 May 1967, p. 15, Eric Heffer on moving the second reading of the Live Hare Coursing (Abolition) Bill.

83. Turner, *All Heaven in a Rage*, pp. 283–4.

84. Ibid., p. 285.

85. National Archives, HO 144/22579, Committee for the suppression of the Waterloo Cup coursing, petition. I am grateful to Richard Hoyle for drawing my attention to this document and for obtaining a copy. The material will repay lengthier research but this is hampered by the loss of the Diocesan records through wartime enemy action. The petition demonstrates a strong commitment by numbers of clergy, Anglican and non-conformist, as well as many prominent Liverpudlians to this cause.

86. Turner, *All Heaven in a Rage*, p. 286.

87. *Picture Post*, 20 Mar. 1943, pp. 13–16.

88. Stable and Stuttard, *Review of Coursing*, pp. 88–9.

89. For a succinct account of the problems of the 1970s and the success of the revival, see Blanning and Prescott, *Waterloo Cup*, pp. 68–93.

90. Stable and Stuttard, *Review of Coursing*, pp. 17–20.

91. Ibid., p. 16.

92. See the Keeper's Introduction to *Stud Book*, 110 (1991), p. v.

93. The author is grateful to John Carter, the proprietor of the Sheffield Greyhound Stadium, for discussion and confirmation of these points – personal communication Sept. 2004.

94. Above, pp. 26–8.

95. *Report of the Committee on Cruelty to Wild Animals*, Cmnd. 8266 (1951).

96. *The Times*, 2 May 1967, p. 15.

97. Obituary, *The Times*, 28 May 1991, p. 27.

98. Stable and Stuttard, *Review of Coursing* made a number of important recommendations to alter the rules of coursing and the way meetings were organised. Almost all of these were put into effect and reduced the number of hare deaths to less than ten per cent of those coursed. R. Isaacson, *The Wild Hunt* (2001), p. 250.

Notes to Chapter 10: Foxhunting and the Yeomanry: county identity and military culture

1. The document is in the Shropshire Record Office, CP 177, Lydbury North Civil Parish Records. Nicholas Mansfield, *English Farmworkers and Local Patriotism, 1900–1930* (2001).

2. See Mansfield, *English Farmworkers*, ch. 4 and id., 'Volunteers and Recruiting' in Gerald Gliddon

(ed.), *Norfolk and Suffolk in the Great War* (1988). The military history of the Yeomanry is summarised in Army Museums Ogilby Trust, *Year of the Yeomanry* (1994). It is discussed academically in I. F. W. Beckett, *The Amateur Military Tradition, 1558–1945* (1992) and its social history is also covered in two articles in the *J. Society for Army Historical Research*; O. Teichman, 'The Yeomanry as an aid to the civil power', 19 (1940), pp. 75–91 and 127–143 and Philip Talbot, 'The English Yeomanry in the nineteenth century and the Great Boer War', 79 (2001), pp. 45–62. Of the dozens of regimental histories, the most useful social history has been J. D. Sainsbury, *The Hertfordshire Yeomanry. An Illustrated History, 1794–1920* (1994). The Marquess of Anglesey, *A History of the British Cavalry, 1816 to 1919* (4 vols, 1973–86) discusses the yeomanry in relation to regular cavalry.

3. Mansfield, *English Farmworkers*, pp. 43–6. See also the author's unpublished paper, 'Foxhunting, Yeomanry and the idea of county', given to the 1999 Oral History Society conference.

4. Beckett, *Amateur Military Tradition*, p. 75, and Sainsbury, *Hertfordshire Yeomanry*, pp. 26–7. John K. Dunlop, *The Development of the British Army, 1899–1914* (1938), p. 53, described them as 'what might be called in the language of today, a "White Guard"'. John Belchem, *'Orator' Hunt: Henry Hunt and Working-class Radicalism* (1985).

5. For a summary of the early Yeomanry see *Year of the Yeomanry*, p. 8 and J. E. Cookson, *The British Armed Nation, 1793–1815* (1997), pp. 27–8.

6. Beckett, *Amateur Military Tradition*, p. 103; Pamela Horn, *History of the French Invasion of Fishguard, 1797* (1980).

7. Beckett, *Amateur Military Tradition*, pp. 140–1 and Arthur Sleigh, *The Royal Militia and Yeomanry Cavalry Army List, 1850* (repr. 1991), pp. 31, 34, 40 and 48. Mansfield, *English Farmworkers*, p. 85.

8. ibid, p. 85.

9. E. P. Thompson, *The Making of the English Working Class* (1968), p. 752; Beckett, *Amateur Military Tradition*, pp. 103, 137; A. J. Peacock, *Bread or Blood. The Agrarian Riots in East Anglia, 1816* (1965) and Gwyn A. Williams, *The Merthyr Rising* (1978), pp. 153–4. For a balanced summary of the whole 'insurrection' issue, see Edward Royle, *Revolutionary Britannia, 1789–1848* (2001).

10. Beckett, *Amateur Military Tradition*, pp. 135, 138 and Mansfield, *English Farmworkers*, p. 85.

11. Anglesey, *British cavalry*, I, has the most realistic assessment of British regular cavalry, see pp. 37,

43, 50–3 and 59; also Michael Glover, *Wellington as a Military Commander* (1968), p. 225.

12. Cecil Woodham-Smith, *The Reason Why* (1968), p. 17, Anglesey, *British Cavalry*, I, pp. 215, 278 and 171. (Packs were taken to the Sikh Wars and on the disastrous Afghan campaign of 1839.) His point, p. 95, that there was no difference between light and heavy cavalry in the British service, probably also increased the trend to hunt. Mansfield, *Foxhunting*, p. 5, *League Against Cruel Sports Journal*, November 1929, Christoper Sykes, *Orde Wingate* (1959), pp. 43–4 and 91. Wingate, an artilleryman was unofficially discouraged from hunting by officers from more prestigious regiments.

13. Mansfield, *English Farmworkers*, p. 85.

14. Beckett, *Amateur Military Tradition*, p. 192.

15. Mansfield, *English Farmworkers*, p. 84 and Gerald French, *The Life of Field Marshal Sir J. French* (1931), pp. 23–4. (French's favourite author was Surtees).

16. Talbot, 'English Yeomanry' pp. 54, 56, Beckett, *Amateur Military Tradition*, p. 189 and Mansfield, *Foxhunting*, p. 10. For the incident at Lichfield, *The Times*, 17 June 1884, p. 9 and 20 June 1884, p. 10.

17. Beckett, *Amateur Military Tradition*, p. 134, Sainsbury, *Hertfordshire Yeomanry*, p. 79, Talbot, 'English Yeomanry', p. 55 and Mansfield, *Foxhunting*, p. 4. I am grateful to Richard Hoyle for details of foxhunting yeomen in Staffordshire, for which see relevant obituaries in *The Times*, 3 Feb. 1912, 26 Nov. 1913, 10 Apr. 1929, 19 Sept. 1932 and 22 Sept. 1937.

18. Dunlop, *Development*, pp. 106, 116 and 148. (Although much is made of the Boer War in Yeomanry regimental histories, only 'a very small proportion' – 13 out of 1,205 in the second wave of Imperial Yeomanry – actually came from county yeomanry regiments, despite being given superior terms to the Volunteers. Mansfield, *Farmworkers*, p. 86.)

19. For Haig's support of the arm blanche see Gerard J. De Groot, 'Ambition, duty and doctrine. Haig's rise to high command', p. 43, in Brian Bond and Nigel Cave (eds), *Haig – A Reappraisal Seventy Years On* (1999). Allenby's hunting is referred to in Brian Gardener, *Allenby* (1963). Haig's main sporting passion – probably due to having been beaten by Allenby to the mastership of the Staff College pack – was golf.

20. Mansfield, *English Farmworkers*, pp. 15 and 104–5.

21. David A. Clarke (comp.), *Great War Memories*.

Soldiers' Experiences, 1914–1918 (1987), p.31.

22. Mansfield, *English Farmworkers*, pp.104–5. Beckett points out that as early as 1794 Yeomanry were accused of not wanting to leave their farms, *Amateur Military Tradition*, p.75.

23. Mansfield, *English Farmworkers*, pp.105–6. Alan Sillitoe's uncle was another example of a working class recruit to the South Nottinghamshire Hussars, who was unlucky to be killed in an accident whilst carrying out his trade as a blacksmith. See *Raw Material* (1979), pp.43, 46. Decades before this author, he also made (p.107) the connection between foxhunting and the slaughter on the Western Front.

24. Mansfield, *English Farmworkers*, p.104; *Year of the Yeomanry*, pp.15, 51.

25. Sainsbury, *Hertfordshire Yeomanry*, p.206 and Mansfield, *English Farmworkers*, p.106.

26. Mansfield, *English Farmworkers*, p.185.

27. Beckett, *Amateur military tradition*, p.246, *Year of the Yeomanry*, p.9.

28. Mansfield, 'Foxhunting', p.9 and *Year of the Yeomanry*, p.34.

29. Alun Howkins, 'Mass Observation and Rural England, 1939–1945', *Rural Hist.*, 9 (1998), p.85 and Mansfield, 'Foxhunting', pp.9–10.

30. ibid, p.10.

31. ibid, pp.10–1, *Year of the Yeomanry*, p.6.

Notes to Chapter 11: The fortunes of English foxhunting in the twentieth century: the case of the Oakley Hunt

1. The best account of twentieth-century foxhunting remains R.Carr, *English Fox-hunting: A History* (1976) although his account of the twentieth century is merely an 'epilogue'. Jane Ridley's *Fox Hunting* (1990) is lightweight. The short essay by Carr, 'Country Sports', in G.E.Mingay, *The Victorian Countryside* (2 vols, 1981), II, pp.475–87 is suggestive. There is much useful material in a few pages of D.Cannadine, *The Decline and Fall of the British Aristocracy* (1990), pp.360–9 (although this is concerned with the state of hunting before 1939 and has nothing on the post-war situation). For the literature against foxhunting, see Carr, *English Fox-hunting*, pp.195–214. Amongst useful contemporary accounts of the state of hunting, see W.S.Dixon, *Fox-hunting in the Twentieth Century* (1925); Sir William Beach Thomas, *Hunting England. A Survey of the Sport and of its Chief Grounds* (1936), H.A.Higginson, *Foxhunting: theory and practice* (1948), Wilson Stephens, 'Hunting Today' and 'Hunting and the farmer', both in C.Willock (ed.), *The Farmer's Book of Field Sports* (1961), pp.224–48; M.Clayton, *The Chase. A Modern Guide to Foxhunting* (1987, rev. edn 1989).

2. John Masefield, 'Fox-hunting' in *Recent Prose* (1924), pp.159–60, 162. Admittedly this essay was an introduction to the American edition of Masefield's *Reynard the Fox*. In private correspondence Masefield was less sentimental about fox hunting but still held that it was '*the* passion of the English country people'. Constance Babington Smith, *John Masefield, A Life* (1978), pp.180–1.

3. Stephens, 'Hunting', p.230.

4. David C.Itzkowitz, *Peculiar Privilege: A Social*

History of English Foxhunting, 1753–1885 (1977); Robert Churchward, 'Fox-hunting', in P.Moore (ed.), *Against Hunting, A Symposium* (1965), p.46; L.P.Curtis, 'Stopping the Hunt, 1881–1882: an aspect of the Irish Land War', in C.H.E.Philpin (ed.), *Nationalism and Popular Protest in Ireland* (1987).

5. *The Country Gentlemen's Estate Book, 1921* (1921), pp.253–4; for similar comments, Cannadine, *Decline and Fall*, p.368; M.Huggins and J.Williams, *Sport and the English, 1918–39* (2006), pp.138–40.

6. Carr, *English Fox Hunting*, pp.243–4 for encroaching suburbia; Thomas, *Hunting England*, p.12. Thomas refers to the problem of wire on a number of occasions, pp.17, 21, 26–7, 32, 70 etc.

7. This tension resulted in a feud within the ranks of the Oakley: below p.268. In 1984 Captain Ronnie Wallace of the Heythrop was quoted as recommending that hunts should lease shooting rights. Clayton, *Golden Thread*, p.78.

8. Above, pp.36–8.

9. Higginson, *Foxhunting*, p.134; Clayton, *Chase*, pp.19–20, 26, 28. Churchward too described the amount of time spent in sweet-talking and arm-twisting farmers and landowners and the pressures placed on unsympathetic farmers: 'Fox-hunting', pp.30–1, 35, 46.

10. e.g. Captain M.H.Haynes, *Riding and Hunting* (sixth edn, 1928), pp.334–5.

11. See Higginson, *Foxhunting*, pp.208–10 on the tensions arising from 'strangers' hunting.

12. Clayton, *The Chase*, p.122. Beach Thomas was approving in 1936: *Hunting England*, p.13.

13. I owe this point to Dr Jeremy Burchardt.

14. C.C.McKenzie, 'The origin of the British Field

Sports Society', *International Journal of the History of Sport*, 13 (1996), pp. 177–91.

15. Above, pp. 15, 238; Clayton, *The Chase*, p. 138. What follows is largely drawn from Thomas, *Politics of Hunting* although his book was (regrettably) published at the height of the controversy over access to 'public' land.

16. Clayton, *The Golden Thread*, p. 65; M. Clayton, *Foxhunting in Paradise* (1993), pp. 167–8 (the Fernie lost 5,000 acres including 15 coverts and reduced its meets from three to two a week).

17. I hope to write further about this episode.

18. J. N. P. Watson, *The Book of Foxhunting* (1977), p. 191.

19. Introduction to Clayton, *The Chase*, p. viii.

20. Stephens, 'Hunting today', p. 231.

21. *Spectator*, 23 July 1977, p. 23.

22. Moore, *Against Hunting*, p. 23.

23. X213/271 (ts of P. Lawson Johnston, 'The Oakley hunt – fifty years of change and development'), p. 3. Miss Lawson Johnston made similar comments to J. N. P. Watson in 1981, *Country Life*, 31 Dec. 1981, p. 231. Caroline Blackwood, *In the Pink* (1987), ch. 13.

24. Thomas, *Politics of Hunting*, p. 62.

25. *Spectator*, 31 July 1982, pp. 15–16; 14 Aug. 1982, p. 17, 14 Feb. 1976, p. 6.

26. See here M. Clayton, *Foxhunting in Paradise* (1993).

27. Dorian Williams, *Pendley and a Pack of Hounds* (1959).

28. Carr, *English Fox Hunting*, p. 115.

29. The following is based on Ralph Greaves, *A Short History of the Oakley Hunt* (n.d., c.1950), a copy of which may be found in X213/207, together with J. Godber (ed.), *The Oakley Hunt* (Bedfordshire Rec. Ser. 44, 1965) and a typescript history of the hunt which precedes the X213 list in BLARS.

30. Greaves, *A Short History of the Oakley Hunt*, pp. 6–8.

31. X213 list, typescript history, p. 3.

32. BLARS, WG2992–5.

33. X213 list, typescript history, p. 5.

34. Dorian Williams quotes the adage 'Every hunt in the country has a few people who get twice as much fun out of hunting the Master as they do out of hunting the fox'. Williams, *Pendley*, p. 185.

35. X213/243.

36. Higginson, *Foxhunting*, pp. 134–5.

37. Ibid., pp. 137–8.

38. Churchward, 'Fox-hunting', p. 32. See also D. W. Brock. *Foxhunting. What it is, and how it is conducted* (rev. edn. 1973), pp. 5–7 and Pearl

Lawson Johnston's description of how hunts ran themselves between the wars: 'Beyond this fixed sum it was up to the masters to balance the books by making considerable personal contributions towards kennel wages, the cost of transport and fuel, and the provision of mounts for themselves, the Huntsmen and whippers in'. X213/271, p. 12.

39. Clayton, *The Chase*, pp. 26–7; *Golden Thread* pp. 17–18.

40. Cannadine, *Decline and Fall*, pp. 355–6.

41. Higginson, *Foxhunting*, pp. 208–9; Clayton, *The Chase*, p. 33.

42. Car followers are noted by William Beach Thomas, *Hunting England*, who refers to the practice of securing caps from them.

43. *The Times*, 6 Aug. 1959; *Bedford Record*, 6 Mar. 1979 (BLSL clippings collection).

44. *Country Life*, 31 Dec. 1981, p. 2312. There was also a fear that a site near Thurleigh would be developed for London's third airport: e.g. *Bedfordshire Times* (hereafter *BT*), 7 Mar. 1969.

45. *Ampthill News*, 27 Nov. 1973 (BLSL clipping file).

46. X213/271, p. 2.

47. X213/226; and see the collection of newspaper clippings in X213/225. Sanders was described as farming 1,800 acres at Snelson in 1963 (*BT*, 22 Feb. 1963) and 2,000 acres in the *Daily Mail* of 13 Apr. 1965: reporting a settlement on 6 Jan. 1967, the *Bedfordshire Times* said that 3,000 acres had been closed to the hunt. Part of the antagonism may have been that in the mid-1950s he had sought, and been passed over, for the mastership. So much appears from X213/265.

48. No hunt accounts show real costs as so much was received by gifts from well-wishers in the local farming community including meat for the hounds (for which see the comments in Williams, *Pendley*, pp. 113–14).

49. See G. Fergusson, *The Green Collars. The Tarporley Hunt Club and Cheshire Hunting History* (1993), pp. 275–6 for an acrimonious correspondence of 1906 between a hunt and a subscriber who they thought was paying too small a subscription and which makes plain the relationship between number of days in the field and subscription.

50. X213/244.

51. For Robert Arkwright, *The Field*, 7 May 1887, p. 624, 8 Dec. 1888, p. 821; For Esme Arkwright, *The Times*, 12 Nov. 1934, p. 20. In 1907 Arkwright gave his recreations as hunting and salmon fishing in Norway and Scotland. *Berkshire, Buckinghamshire and Bedfordshire in the Twentieth Century* (1907).

52. X213/267–8, 58, 59.

53. *BT*, 15 Feb. 1957 (in BLSL clippings collection).

54. In some lists Kidd is named as F. B. Kidd but tracing his career through *The Times* makes it clear that there was only one man. The key references are 19 Dec. 1899, p. 7 (graduation results, Cambridge); 13 Jan. 1913, p. 13 (resigns West Kent), 21 Feb. 1919, p. 5 (report that he has taken the Oakley); 28 Oct. 1919, p. 6; 20 Mar. 1924, p. 7 (resigns N. Cotswold); 24 Jan. 1953, p. 8 (retires from North Warwickshire); 25 Mar. 1966, p. 14 (funeral report). His parentage comes from a notice to his late Father's creditors, *The Times*, 14 Feb. 1918, p. 13; for his father's probate, 5 Feb. 1918, p. 9.

55. For Farrar see the notice of his death in *The Times*, 6 Aug. 1915, p. 9; his widow's obituary, *The Times*, 1 Jan. 1923, p. 13. When the youngest daughter was married in 1935, Esme Arkwright's widow, Lord and Lady Luke and Lord and Lady Melchett, were noted as guests; ibid., 30 Apr. 1935, p. 19.

56. *The Times* obituary of the second Lord Luke suggests that there may have been an in-joke here, for the ox, on which the the family fortune was based, was St Luke's symbol in art.

57. For Lord Luke died in 1996 aged 90: see the obituaries in *The Times*, 28 May 1996, *Daily Telegraph*, 28 May 1996 and *BT* (the latter rather a poor thing, which makes no mention of his association with the Oakley), 30 May 1996, all kindly supplied by BLSL. The Bovril company was sold, after his retirement, in 1971.

58. X213/261.

59. For these arrangements see *Foxhunting in Bedfordshire, Cambridgeshire and Hertfordshire* (?1967), p. 19. *Baily's* records J. G. Harris as master, 1962–66.

60. X213/270.

61. X213/262.

62. X213/264.

63. X213/265, 266.

64. For the circumstances of Harris' resignation, see X213/266 and for Stockdale, *BT*, 14 Jan. 1966.

65. *BT*, 26 Feb. 1960; 8 Feb. 1963; 6 Mar. 1964; 18 Mar. 1968.

66. For the establishment of supporters' clubs in other hunts about the same time, Williams, *Pendley*, pp. 178–9.

67. X213/271, p. 8.

68. *BT*, 26 Feb. 1960; 14 Feb. 1964; 4 Feb. 1966.

69. Churchward, 'Foxhunting', p. 27.

70. *BT*, 7 Jan. 1982 (BLSL clippings file). His reason for being in England was that he wished to secure an English education for his children.

71. X213/271 p. 14.

72. *BT*, 19 Mar. 1971; *Ampthill News*, 27 Nov. 1973 (both BLSL clippings file); *County Life*, 31 Dec. 1981, p. 231.

73. *BT* 16 Dec. 1982, *Luton Times*, 22 Dec. 1982 for the banning resolution (both in the BLSL clippings file).

74. *BT* 7, 14 Feb. 1964. Barter and Sheppard had adjacent letters in March 1969. For Vera Sheppard, see her memoir, *My Head Against the Wall. A Decade in the Fight Against Blood Sports* (1979). See also the letters in *BT*, 7, 14 Jan. 1966.

75. They had arrived by 1972: *The Times*, 14 Sept. 1972, p. 3.

76. *BT*, 8 Feb. 1963. The intention to hold a fair had been reported on 4 Oct. 1963.

77. *BT*, 6 Mar. 1964.

78. For the fair, see advert 3 July and report 10 July 1964 both in *BT*, for the formation of the society *BT*, 20 Mar. 1964.

79. *BT*, 5 Feb., 12 Feb. 1965.

80. *BT*, 31 Jan. 1964.

81. *BT*, 1 Jan. 8 Jan. 1960.

82. *BT*, 12 Feb. 1960.

83. Sheppard, *My head against the wall*, pp. 22–3.

84. *Ampthill News*, 27 Nov. 1973 (BLSL clippings file).

85. *BT*, 7 Jan. 1982 (BLSL clippings file).

86. *BT*, 23 Mar. 1962.

87. *BT*, 6 Apr. 1962.

88. Above, Table 11.3 and pp. 276–7.

89. Williams, *Pendley*, p. 176.

90. Ibid., chs 9–10.

91. Ibid., p. 114.

92. Stephens, 'Hunting Today', p. 225.

List of contributors

Daniel Allen has recently completed a Ph.D at the University of Nottingham on the cultural and historical geographies of otter hunting in Britain from 1830 to 1939. His wider interests include the history and ideas of the anti blood-sports movement.

Edward Bujak received his Doctorate from the University of East Anglia in 1998 and since 2001 has been the Assistant Professor of British Studies and History at the Centre for British Studies at Harlaxton College in Lincolnshire. His book, *England's Rural Realms: Landownership and the Agricultural Revolution*, is due to be published in 2007.

Richard Hoyle is Professor of Rural History at the University of Reading and the author of numerous books and articles, mostly on early modern issues where his books include *The Pilgrimage of Grace and the Politics of the 1530s* (2001). He also serves as editor of *Agricultural History Review*. He was a British Academy Research Fellow in 2004–6.

John Martin is a Principal Lecturer in Economic and Social History at De Montfort University, Leicester. His research has focused on the transformation of the rural sector in the twentieth sector. His publications include *The development of modern agriculture: British farming since 1931* (2000) and his one of the co-editors, with Brian Short and Charles Watkins, of *British Farming in the Second World War* (2006).

Nick Mansfield has been Director of the People's History Museum in Manchester since 1989 and is the author of *English Farmworkers and Local Patriotism, 1900–1930* (2001).

David Matless is Professor of Cultural Geography at the University of Nottingham. He is the author of *Landscape and Englishness* (1998) and editor of *Geographies of British Modernity* (2003).

Paul Merchant was a Research Fellow in the School of Geography, University of Nottingham on the ESRC-funded project 'Environmental Knowledges in England, 1945–1970'.

Dr Harvey Osborne is currently a researcher with the Suffolk College, Ipswich. His doctoral research at the University of Lancaster examined nineteenth-century initiatives to protect and conserve salmon populations in England and Wales and related social conflicts. Current research activity focuses on themes such as rural crime and protest, poor law reform, field sports and conservation.

Ian Roberts is an Honorary Fellow of the History Department at Durham. His research interests are on aspects of the history of the Anglo-Scottish borders since the mid-eighteenth century including field sports. He is currently exploring the Anglo-Irish cattle trade in the North East in the twentieth century.

Mark Rothery is currently a Teaching Fellow at the Department of History, University of Exeter. His PhD, completed in 2004, focused on the social and cultural history of the English landed gentry in the late nineteenth and early twentieth centuries. Between 2004–5 he was the Economic History Society's Postan Postdoctoral Research fellow at the Institute of Historical Research., London.

Charles Watkins is Professor of Rural Geography and Head of the School of Geography at the University of Nottingham. His recent books are *Ligurian Landscapes* (2004) and, with Ben Cowell, an edition of the *Letters of Uvedale Price* (Walpole Society 2006).

Index